THE NAZI CONSCIENCE

Claudia Koonz

THE NAZI
CONSCIENCE

The Belknap Press of
Harvard University Press
Cambridge, Massachusetts
London, England

First Harvard University Press paperback edition, 2005

Library of Congress Cataloging-in-Publication Data

Koonz, Claudia.
    The Nazi conscience / Claudia Koonz.
        p.   cm.
    Includes bibliographical references and index.
    ISBN 0-674-01172-4 (cloth: alk. paper)
    ISBN 0-674-01842-7 (pbk.)
    1. National socialism—Psychological aspects.
    2. Germany—Historiography.   3. Political culture—Germany.
    4. Holocaust, Jewish (1939–1945)   I. Title.

    DD256.5.K6185 2003
    943.083′01′9—dc21   2003051964

Contents

For Jan

Prologue

"The Nazi conscience" is not an oxymoron. Although it may be repugnant to conceive of mass murderers acting in accordance with an ethos that they believed vindicated their crimes, the historical record of the Third Reich suggests that indeed this was often the case. The popularizers of antisemitism and the planners of genocide followed a coherent set of severe ethical maxims derived from broad philosophical concepts. As modern secularists, they denied the existence of either a divinely inspired moral law or an innate ethical imperative. Because they believed that concepts of virtue and vice had evolved according to the needs of particular ethnic communities, they denied the existence of universal moral values and instead promoted moral maxims they saw as appropriate to their Aryan community. Unlike the early twentieth-century moral philosophers who saw cultural relativism as an argument for tolerance, Nazi theorists drew the opposite conclusion. Assuming that cultural diversity breeds antagonism, they asserted the superiority of their own communitarian values above all others. *extension of nationalism*

Conscience, as we usually think of it, is an inner voice that admonishes "Thou shalt" and "Thou shalt not." Across cultures, an ethic of reciprocity commands that we treat others as we wish to be treated. Besides instructing us in virtue, the conscience fulfills a second, and often overlooked, function. It tells us to whom we shall and shall not do what. It structures our identity by separating those who deserve our concern from alien "others" beyond the pale of our community. Our moral identity prompts us to ask, "Am I the kind of person who would do that to this person?"[1] The texts of Western moral philosophy and theology are littered with less-than-fully-human "others." In the Hebrew Bible, outsiders are treated harshly. With barely a thought, classical Greek philosophy excludes barbarians, slaves, and women from fully human status. Christian charity extends primarily to Christians. Many of the major treatises of the European Enlightenment treat Africans, American Indians, and women as creatures without reason, bereft of fully human status. In 1933 Carl Schmitt, a distinguished political theorist and avid Hitler supporter, paraphrased a slogan used often in Nazi circles when he denounced the idea of universal human rights, saying: Not every being with a human face is human.[2] *fundamental, basic assumption*

This belief expressed the bedrock of Nazi morality. Although it might seem that a human catastrophe on the scale of the Holocaust was caused by an evil that defies our understanding, what is frightening about the racist public culture within which the Final Solution was conceived is not its extremism but its ordinariness—not its savage hatreds but its lofty ideals. The men, and a few women, who popularized Nazi racism expounded at great length about what they called "the idea" *(die Idee)* of National Socialism. What outsiders saw as ideology, Nazis experienced as truth. Seen from a Judeo-Christian vantage point, the amalgam of biological theories and racist passions that characterized the Nazi belief system does not qualify as a moral, or even coherent, ideology. Compared with, for example, Adam Smith's liberalism or Karl Marx's communism, *die Idee* of Nazism lacks formal elegance and a humane social vision. Nonetheless, Nazism fulfilled the functions we associate with ideology. It supplied answers to life's imponderables, provided meaning in the face of contingency, and explained the way the world works. It also defined good and evil, condemning self-interest as immoral and enshrining altruism as virtuous. Binding ethnic comrades *(Volksgenossen)* to their ancestors and descendents, Nazi ideals embedded the individual within the collective well-being of the nation.

Hitler, always an astute reader of his audiences' desires, heard Germans' hunger for a government they could trust and a national purpose they could believe in. From his earliest days as a political orator, he addressed that longing. In phrases his opponents ridiculed as empty and followers heard as inspirational, Hitler promised to rescue old-fashioned values of honor and dignity from the materialism, degeneracy, and cosmopolitanism of modern life. His supporters' lists of grievances were long, and their anxieties ran deep. Bolsheviks threatened revolution; emancipated women abandoned their family responsibilities; capitalists amassed immense fortunes; and foreign states robbed Germany of its rightful status as a European power. Hitler transformed his followers' anger at cultural and political disorder into moral outrage. In place of the Weimar Republic, which he ridiculed as weak and feminine, Hitler promised the dawn of a resolute masculine order. Where once religion had provided a steady moral purpose, Nazi culture offered an absolutist secular faith.

Unlike liberal regimes, in which the moral calculus turns on the concept of universal human rights, the Third Reich extolled the well-being of

threats

the ethnic German community as the benchmark for moral reasoning. Nazi morality explicitly promoted racist and sexist assumptions at a time when ideals of equality had begun to make themselves felt throughout the Western world. German racial theorists, eager to be seen as modern and progressive, dignified age-old prejudices with the claims of science. They appealed not so much to malevolence as to ideas of health, hygiene, and progress in their campaign to elicit compliance with policies that might otherwise have been seen as cruel and violent. Mobilizing citizens in a modern and enlightened nation, Nazi rule relied not only on repression but also on an appeal to communal ideals of civic improvement. In a vibrant public culture founded on self-denial and collective revival, ethnic Germans were exhorted to expunge citizens deemed alien and to ally themselves only with people sanctioned as racially valuable. The road to Auschwitz was paved with righteousness.

The emerging solidarity did not so much render victims' sufferings invisible as make them marginal to the larger purpose of an ethnic renaissance. That the collaborators in mass murder acted according to an internal logic does not, of course, suggest that their moral principles were any more praiseworthy than their actions. Nor does it imply that their pretensions to morality constrained their criminality. Indeed, ethnic righteousness may well have facilitated the clear consciences of those who robbed, tormented, and murdered their helpless victims. In this book, I examine the incursion of a secular, ethnic faith into an area of human life traditionally assigned to religion: the formation of conscience. Although we often take for granted the existence of a universal ethic based on the sanctity of all human life, the history of Nazi Germany reveals how pretensions to ethnic virtue created the conditions within which evil metasticized.

An Ethnic Conscience

I view myself as the most independent of men . . . obligated to no one, subordinate to no one, indebted to no one—instead answerable only to my own conscience. And this conscience has but one single commander—our *Volk!*

—*Adolf Hitler, October 8, 1935*

"Conscience" is a capacious term, encompassing elements of identity, awareness, and idealism as well as an ethical standard. It evolved from the Latin *con* (with) and *scientia* (knowledge). In medieval vernaculars, "consciousness" (in German, *Bewußtsein*) was used interchangeably with "conscience" *(Gewissen).* With the emergence of modern German and English in the sixteenth century, "conscience" began to part company with "consciousness." When Martin Luther defied papal authority in 1517, he famously declared, "Here I stand. I cannot and will not recant." Against accusations of heresy, he explained, "I have rescued my conscience because I could declare that I have acted as I saw fit."[1] From the late Renaissance, "conscience" *(Gewissen)* was seen as an irrefutable guide to virtuous behavior. While Christians understood conscience as the voice of God, secularists looked to reason as its source.[2]

Over the centuries, the conscience came to be understood as private and constant. For the Enlightenment philosopher Immanuel Kant, it was one of two poles that held his life in order. "Two things fill the mind with ever new and increasing admiration and awe . . . the starry heavens above and the moral law within."[3] In 1962 the text of Vatican II declared, "Their conscience is people's most secret core, and their sanctuary. There they are alone with God whose voice echoes in their depths."[4] Modern human rights doctrine assumes the existence of a universal moral code. Article one of the 1948 Declaration of Human Rights states explicitly, "All human beings are born free and equal in dignity and rights. They are endowed with reason and conscience and should act towards one another in a spirit of brotherhood." Across many cultures, the declaration implies, people who issue or obey orders to torture, loot, or murder violate the dictates of conscience.[5] Thus, "conscience" refers to an ethically attuned part of the human character that heeds the Hippocratic command: "First, do no harm."

But, although every major culture honors the injunction to treat others as you hope they will treat you, the ideal often collapses in practice because the meaning of "others" is not always clear. In *Civilization and Its Discontents* (1929), Sigmund Freud expressed his doubts about the Golden Rule. Because a feeling of moral obligation increases with our affection for an individual, loving one's neighbor presupposes a bond, a shared sense of belonging. "If," he wrote, the Golden Rule, "commanded 'Love thy neighbor as thy neighbor loves thee,' I should not take exception to it." But loving a stranger, Freud suspected, ran counter to human experience. "If he is a stranger to me . . . it will be hard for me to love him."[6] The universe of moral obligation, far from being universal, is bounded by community.

Like the vague German word *Weltanschauung* (attitude or worldview), "conscience" guides individual choice by providing structures of meaning within which identity is formed.[7] Like "reason" (and "science"), "conscience" is fluid, formed not only by timeless mandates but also by particular cultural milieus. Knowledge about the identity of those "to whom we do what" provides the mental architecture within which moral thinking occurs. In traditional societies, religious leaders tell the faithful who deserves moral consideration. But in modern societies experts create assumptions about which people belong within the community of shared moral obligation.[8] Similarly, in Nazi Germany, experts provided the knowledge, the *scientia,* about which humans deserved moral consideration—according to conscience *(con scientia).*

The recollections of a former Hitler Youth member, Alfons Heck, illustrate how such knowledge formed moral thinking. In 1940, when Alfons watched the Gestapo take away his best friend, Heinz, and all Jews in his village, he did not say to himself, "How terrible they are arresting Jews." Having absorbed knowledge about the "Jewish menace," he said, "What a misfortune Heinz is Jewish." As an adult he recalled, "I accepted deportation as just."[9] In wartime Berlin, Hitler's chief architect and director of armaments production, Albert Speer, would pass large groups of forlorn people standing at the local railway station. He chose not to think about the terrible fate that awaited them. Years later, he recalled, "I had a sense of somber goings-on. But I was rooted in the principles of the regime to an extent that I find hard to understand today."[10] Although Jews had been fellow citizens before 1933, by the time Germany invaded Poland in 1939 they no longer belonged to Germans' universe of moral obligation. This transformation did not just happen. The expulsion of Jews from Germans' universe of moral obligation was carefully engineered. In this book, I explore the process that made Jews strangers in their own country.

The term "Nazi conscience" describes a secular ethos that extended reciprocity only to members of the Aryan community, as defined by what racial scientists believed to be the most advanced biological knowledge of the day. Guided by that knowledge as well as the virulent racism expressed in *Mein Kampf,* the Nazi state removed entire categories of people from most Germans' moral map. But this expulsion, so radical in retrospect, was not as unprecedented as it might seem today. Of the assumptions that defined the Nazi conscience, three had counterparts elsewhere. Only the fourth was without close historical precedent at the time.

The first assumption of the Nazi conscience was that the life of a *Volk* is like that of an organism, marked by stages of birth, growth, expansion, decline, and death. Although earlier writers, like Johann Wolfgang von Goethe, had expressed similar philosophical views, the organic metaphor became widespread in social science and political rhetoric later in the nineteenth century. Writing at roughly the same time as Charles Darwin, Herbert Spencer described the evolution of "barbarous tribes" into advanced civilizations as the triumph of a superior sociological organism.[11] Early in the twentieth century, pessimists predicted that the West, like a "mature" organism, had to struggle for its very existence against degeneration and ultimate extinction.[12] This struggle required individual sacrifice and collective effort. In the early 1930s, with unemployment rates hovering above 30 percent, politicians in Europe and North America reactivated the rhetoric of the Great War by inveighing against class conflict, materialism, and profiteering while beseeching citizens to give their all for collective survival. Inspired by the 1931 papal encyclical *Quadragesimo Anno,* Catholic leaders called for burden-sharing between rich and poor. In his first inaugural address, Franklin D. Roosevelt asked Americans to be prepared to sacrifice for economic recovery as if the nation were engaged in a foreign war. In the Third Reich, a Nazi mantra exhorted ethnic Germans to "put collective need ahead of individual greed." The alternative was death of the community.

The second assumption in the Nazi conscience was that every community develops the values appropriate to its nature and to the environment within which it evolved. Values are relative, contingent upon time and place. But whereas some social scientists of the day, like the anthropologist Franz Boas, placed cultural relativism in the service of tolerance, Nazi theorists invoked relativism to vindicate their own superiority. In interwar Europe, Hitler was not alone in celebrating ethnic identity and excoriating the universalism of the "alien" Enlightenment.[13] The European political landscape was populated with antisemites like General Julius Gömbös, prime minister of Hungary in the mid-1930s; the French fascist Charles Maurras; Leon Degrelle, chief of the Belgian Rexist movement; and Jósef Pilsudski, president of Poland. Like Benito Mussolini, these populist leaders saw ethnic revival—not tolerance—as the prerequisite for national health. Joseph Goebbels captured the mood in his booklet *The Little ABC's of National Socialism,* a catechism for Nazi speakers published in the early 1930s. In response to the question: "What is the first Commandment of every National Socialist?" loyal Nazis answered, "Love Germany above all else and your ethnic comrade *[Volksgenosse]* as your self!"[14]

The third element of the Nazi conscience justified outright aggression against "undesirable" populations living in conquered lands whenever it served the victors' long-term advantage. Western expansion, from the Crusades through colonialism, has been described by its proponents as not only materially profitable but also morally beneficial. Because of Europeans' putative superiority (exhibited by, among other attributes, their white skin, manly courage, self-discipline, and idealism), it could be morally acceptable—especially in wartime—to extinguish "lower" civilizations that stood in the way of "progress." This understanding informed the logic of L. Frank Baum, a journalist in South Dakota, speaking of Native Americans:

> The nobility of the Redskin is extinguished, and what few are left are a pack of whining curs who lick the hand that smites them . . . The Whites, by law of conquest, by justice of civilization, are masters of the American continent and the best safety of the frontier settlements will be secured by the total annihilation of the few remaining Indians. Why not annihilation? Their glory has fled, their spirit broken, their manhood effaced; better that they should die than live like the miserable wretches that they are.[15]

Generations of readers have revered the author of this editorial for his Wizard of Oz books. Baum was not seen as a moral monster but as a man of good will who expressed an understanding of race shared by millions of white Europeans and North Americans faced with the alleged problem of nonwhite populations who inconveniently occupied white men's desired *Lebensraum* (living space).

The fourth assumption underlying the Nazi conscience upheld the right of a government to annul the legal protections of assimilated citizens on the basis of what the government defined as their ethnicity. Although state-sponsored ethnic cleansing directed at assimilated minorities gathered force at the close of the twentieth century, there were few precedents in 1933. Following many political revolutions or religious wars of the past, members of defeated factions or sects had suffered banishment because of their suspected allegiance to heretical beliefs or defeated factions; but Jews in Nazi Germany had participated in no uprisings. Pogroms in Europe and the Turkish extermination of the Armenians had been directed against culturally separate communities, but not, as in Germany, against citizens assimilated into the dominant culture. When an economy is depressed, nativism mobilizes prejudice against the foreign-born, and in times of war it had sometimes happened that people were seized by panic about "enemy aliens" living in their midst. But in the 1930s, a time of economic recovery, Germany was at peace. The "unwanted outsiders" resided not in a distant "heart of darkness" or in enemy trenches but within mainstream society. Where Social Darwinists had metaphorically depicted nation-states as organisms struggling against one another, Nazi theorists used the language of parasitology to describe a danger *within* the ethnic organism.

When responding to critics, Nazi racial experts muted the distinctiveness of their aims by noting analogues elsewhere.[16] The extrusion of resident aliens and citizens with Jewish ancestry from Germany resembled, they said, the 1922–23 population exchange that followed war between Turkey and Greece.[17] The second and much more commonly mentioned parallel was with the United States. While rabid antisemites praised the lynch mobs that kept African Americans "in their place," more sober but equally determined racial policymakers expressed the hope that one day Nazi racial codes would be as widely accepted as U.S. immigration quotas, antimiscegenation laws, involuntary sterilization programs in twenty-eight states, and segregation in the Jim Crow South.[18]

What set Nazi policy apart from other ethnic exclusions, however, was its victimization of fellow citizens who bore no physical or cultural markers of their difference. Germans who were alleged to have Jewish ancestors, as well as Aryan citizens alleged to have damaged genes or homosexual inclinations, shared a heritage, language, and culture with their tormentors. But while the prospect of readmission to mainstream society was held out to so-called defective Aryans who reformed their ways, Jews (and later gypsies) were banished from the moral community. Coded as dangerous beings to whom no obligation applied, they became "problems" to be solved with ruthless efficiency.

Transforming ordinary citizens who happened to have Jewish ancestors into alien beings was no small task. In the nineteenth century, despite the protests of antisemites, Jewish Germans had been admitted to universities without quotas and had participated in cultural life, elite social circles, the professions, business, politics, and the sciences (although some venues, such as the upper officer corps and the diplomatic service, remained virtually closed). During World War I Jewish Germans fought and died for their fatherland in the same proportions as Christian Germans. Of 38 German Nobel Laureates named between 1905 and 1937, 14 had Jewish ancestors. More Jewish young people married Christians than married Jews, and until 1933 the term "mixed marriage" referred to Protestant-Catholic and African- or Asian-German unions, not to Jewish-Christian couples.[19]

A comparison of antisemitic acts and attitudes toward Jews in the popular press of Germany and four European nations (France, Great Britain, Italy, and Romania) from 1899 through 1939 demonstrates that Germans, before 1933, were among the least antisemitic people.[20] Perhaps the best evidence of the relative openness of German society to Jews was the fact that no census had gathered data on ethnicity.[21] Until Nazi rule, only the 500,000 Germans who registered as members of a Jewish religious community could be statistically identified. The remaining 200,000 or 300,000 citizens with Jewish ancestors who did not affiliate with a congregation were statistically invisible in a population of about 65 million.

In January 1933 all Germans belonged to the same nation. Over the next six years, the Nazi state expelled citizens it defined as Jews from the *Volk*. In the context of Nazi Germany, *Volk* is almost always translated as "race" because of the clear intent behind Nazi policy and Hitler's own obsession with racial purity and pollution.[22] But to understand how support for Hitler's racial aims was created, it is essential to distinguish between *Rasse* and *Volk*, which were not interchangeable in Nazi language. Although the adjective *völkish* translates accurately as "ethnic," the English cognate "folk" connotes merely "traditional," "rural," or "quaint." An alternative translation, "people," has lost its once-powerful appeal to ethnic solidarity.

The popularizers of Nazi doctrine used the immense appeal of ethnic revival to generate compliance with racial persecution. The expansive term *Volk* held out an egalitarian and ecumenical promise to members of a so-called community of fate, whereas "race" rested on empirical foundations so dubious that not even Nazi zealots could define it. When Nazi writers demeaned Jews, they called them "racial comrades" *(Rassengenossen),* and when they celebrated Aryans they wrote of "ethnic comrades" *(Volksgenossen).* Hitler could (and often did) rhapsodize for hours about the ethnic body politic *(Volkskörper),* the ethnic community *(Volksgemeinschaft),* the ethnic soul *(Volksseele),* or simply *das Volk.* But neither Hitler nor his deputies spoke of a racial state *(Rassenstaat).* When they used the word "race," as in racial pride *(Rasssenstoltz),* racial politics *(Rasssenpolitik),* or racial protection *(Rasssenschutz),* a despised "other" lurked in the shadows. The Nazi state was founded on ethnicity and race—on self-love and other-hate.

From 1928 to mid-1932, when electoral support for Nazi candidates leapt from 2.6 percent to 37.4 percent, antisemitism played little role in attracting voters to Nazism. Masses of Germans, disillusioned with a foundering democracy and terrified of communism in a time of economic catastrophe, were drawn to the Nazis' promise of a radically new order under Hitler's control. Archival research as well as memoirs and oral histories make it abundantly clear that Germans' attitudes toward "the Jewish question" began to depart from Western European and North American norms only after the Nazi takeover. Germans did not become Nazis because they were antisemites; they became antisemites because they were Nazis.[23]

Beginning in 1933, sophisticated persuasive techniques prepared German civilians and soldiers, in large ways and small, to collaborate with a regime that in wartime engineered the extermination of Jews, Gypsies, POWs, homosexuals, and all categories of people deemed "unwanted." As the historian Raul Hilberg emphasized, the Final Solution depended not on the extremism of Hitler and a few top leaders but on the creation of a loose consensus, a "latent structure" that was "not so much a product of laws and commands as it was a matter of spirit, of shared comprehension, of consonance and synchronization."[24] Because perpetrators grasped the ultimate aims of racial extermination, they improvised and often exceeded their orders. Describing the millions of ordinary soldiers who arrived at the front primed to murder racial enemies, the historian Omer Bartov commented, "The creation of this consensus among the troops was probably the single most significant achievement of the Nazi regime's educational efforts."[25]

Historians during the 1990s sought the origin of this consensus in two very different contexts. Some, like Daniel J. Goldhagen, identified in German culture a hatred of Jews so profound and ancient that genocide scarcely required explanation. Others, like Christopher R. Browning, acknowledged that the creation of a gulf between Christians and Jews constituted "a major accomplishment for the regime" but looked to the force of peer bonding and battlefield conditions as the most important factors in explaining men's readiness to commit face-to-face mass murder.[26] For different reasons, both approaches virtually ignore the period I explore, 1933–1939, a time many Germans later recalled as "the normal years" of the Third Reich. Seen against the enormity of Nazi savagery, it is easy to imagine that German collaborators in persecution shared the seething paranoia of Adolf Hitler and his closest comrades. Extreme outcomes, it would seem, must result from extreme beliefs. But careful investigations of public opinion in Nazi Germany reveal that, while most Germans shared the "polite" or "cultured" antisemitism common in Western Europe and North America, they disapproved of diehard Nazis' coarse racist diatribes and pogrom-style tactics.

Self-interest explained the behavior of rapacious Nazi bosses. Grudges motivated many people to make denunciations to the Gestapo. Fanatical racism, fueled by a lust for violence, incited pogrom-style attacks on Jews and their property. What surprised Jewish Germans during this period was not the cruelty of kleptocrats, fanatics, and malcontents, but the behavior of friends, neighbors, and colleagues who were not gripped by devotion to Nazism. Most Germans fell into this category. Jews sadly noted their mundane lapses: the silence of a store clerk who refused to answer an inquiry, the politely worded requests to drop their memberships in leisure and civic associations, or the embarrassed silence that greeted them as they walked into a favorite cafe.[27] When well-meaning non-Jews tried to console their Jewish friends by suggesting they would be happier in Palestine, their Jewish friends despaired.[28] Professionals were incredulous when they overheard talk about "the Jew," perhaps spiked with adjectives like industrial, wily, mobile, or uncreative. Jewish academics were disillusioned when esteemed colleagues exalted simple-minded and primitive concepts of the *Volk* as the "elemental" ideals of the "authentic" Germanic soul.[29] At every level, ties between Jews and their surroundings loosened and ultimately broke. "The end was isolation."[30] What was it that transformed ordinary Germans, who had not, before 1933, been more prejudiced than their counterparts elsewhere, into indifferent bystanders to—and collaborators with—persecution?

Germans who, in 1933, were ordinary Western Europeans had become, in 1939, anything but. Ascertaining motive, whether in a courtroom or history book, can never be more than a speculative venture. Historians can, however, describe the public culture within which individuals weighed options and made choices. Nazi society has often been described in terms of two attributes. As Hannah Arendt put it in the 1950s, an "iron band of terror" held Germans in its grip, and propaganda indoctrinated them so totally that "plurality disappears into One Man of gigantic proportions."[31] Archival research in the 1990s cast doubt on the omnipotence of terror and propaganda. Because the dreaded Gestapo had actually been understaffed and inefficient, ordinary citizens without Jewish ancestors or close ties with Marxism had considerable leeway to circumvent Nazi measures of which they disapproved.[32] Memoirs by Jews who emigrated from Nazi Germany bear out this conclusion in their descriptions of the few loyal friends who offered comfort and aid—usually without suffering harsh reprisals. Even soldiers at the front could avoid obeying orders that disturbed them. Not mindless obedience but selective compliance characterized Germans' collaboration with evil.

If terror in Nazi Germany was less draconian than previously assumed, then the next likely suspect, as Arendt suggested, was the ideology drummed into Germans' minds by Joseph Goebbels's legendary Ministry of Popular Enlightenment and Propaganda. Although Goebbels was notorious for his racism, before 1939 his ministry devoted relatively little attention to popularizing racial hate. Propaganda denounced the Versailles Treaty, the Stalinist menace, and critics of Nazism, but warnings about racial danger barely figured in prewar mass-market productions. For example, only two comedies and one historical drama among approximately 2,000 films approved by Goebbels and his staff from 1933 through 1939 featured overt antisemitism. Newsreels ignored both race and Jews. Although Hitler made disparaging remarks about Jews, he did not invest his immense political capital in popularizing the measures that would achieve the racial cleansing at the heart of his program. His reticence may have resulted not only from concern about foreign criticism but from his attentiveness to mainstream opinion in Germany.[33] Even passionate antisemites in the party realized that rage against Jews (*Judenkoller*) could be counterproductive and understood that moderates had to be convinced by other means. Comparing subtle persuasion to a gas, Goebbels wrote,

"The best propaganda is that which, as it were, works invisibly, penetrates the whole of life without the public having any knowledge of the propagandistic initiative."[34] To be credible, racial reeducation had to emanate from apparently objective sources. Not propaganda but knowledge had the power to change attitudes.

While passionate antisemitism created solidarity among hardcore Nazis, a more sober form of racial thinking held the potential for mobilizing broad segments of the population. I use the term "ethnic fundamentalism" to describe the deeply anti-liberal collectivism that was the hallmark of public culture in the Third Reich. The term bears an affinity with both religious fundamentalism and ethnic nationalism.[35] Like the former, ethnic fundamentalism claims to defend an ancient spiritual heritage against the corrosive values of industrialized, urban society. Like the latter, ethnic fundamentalism summons its followers to seek vengeance for past wrongs and to forge a glorious future cleansed of ethnic aliens. Its leaders, often endowed with a charismatic aura, mobilize followers to participate in a moral universe that is accessible only to those who share a language, religion, culture, or homeland. The double standard inherent in such arrogance spawned a degree of hypocrisy that astonished outsiders. For insiders, arrogance (called ethnic pride) formed the matrix for disseminating the central elements of Nazi ideology—the cult of the Führer and his *Volk*, phobic racism, and the conquest of *Lebensraum*.

Much has been written about Nazi propaganda as the myth that masked a harsh reality. I am less interested in exposing the myth/reality gap than in exploring the process by which racial beliefs came to shape the outlook of the ordinary Germans on whose cooperation Nazi policies depended. Although the Third Reich had characteristics of totalitarian regimes, it also bore the marks of a collapsed democracy. Germans were accustomed to participating in a lively public culture. Nazi takeover did not mean the destruction of that culture so much as its re-formation. A deadly uniformity did not descend on Germany when Hitler became chancellor. To be sure, critics were silenced, but for the vast majority of Germans who approved of Hitler's rule, a panoply of outlets for a revived civic spirit opened up. Within three contexts, I analyze the popularization of a concept of ethnic virtue that, in its many variations, inexorably expelled Germans stigmatized as alien from their fellow citizens' universe of moral obligation.

The first context, explored in Chapters 2, 4, and 10, centers on Hitler's role as a preacher of communitarian morality among members of the *Volk*. Hitler presented himself as the embodiment of virtue in a dual narrative that he reiterated throughout his political career. In this parable, he paired his own autobiography with the melodrama of the *Volk* itself, re-telling the tale of humble but proud origins; courage in the face of assaults by the cruel, the craven, and the powerful; and, teetering on the cliff of ca-tastrophe, rebirth. A veritable Goliath in David's clothing, Hitler depicted himself as a paragon of virtue and heralded his rule as the restorer of a stern moral order.[36] Hitler's success in presenting himself as the very model of piety who said barely a word about race, however, carried the risk that hardcore followers would fear he had betrayed the radical racist core of their Nazi faith. Relying on the general public to support the popu-lar aims he mouthed so often, Hitler perfected the technique of commu-nicating his ultimate aims in coded messages that primed insiders to await the day when they could act on their hatred. He alone decided when that day had arrived.

With Hitler and Goebbels keeping a discrete distance from racial policy, it fell to midlevel party men to imbue public culture with not only ethnic pride but racial contempt. Despite Hitler's notorious scorn for "eggheads," the campaign to popularize racial thinking depended on highly educated specialists to dignify antisemitism with the aura of objectivity. In Chap-ters 3, 5, and 6, I examine the public relations campaigns of youthful party functionaries, ideologues, and physicians, and new converts to Na-zism from an older generation. In the language of marketing, they "rebranded" Jews as pariahs—Jews who, before 1933, had been friends, neighbors, and colleagues. Distinguished Germans with no prior record of support for Nazism, among them the philosopher Martin Heidegger, the theologian Gerhard Kittel, and the political theorist Carl Schmitt, made a crucial contribution to a version of antisemitism that was both respect-able and ruthless. After Hitler seized power in 1933, the Nazi Party Office of Racial Politics, directed by a 29-year-old physician, Walter Gross, in-fused public culture with a vision of ethnic pride subtly laced with racial fears. The skill of Nazi proselytizers in adjusting their message to suit the tastes of particular audiences was illustrated by the Nazi conquest of the teaching profession.

At the third site in the production of Nazi morality, discussed in Chap-ters 7, 8, and 9, I examine the creation of a working consensus about ra-cial aims and strategies within the inner circles of the men charged with formulating and administering racial policies. Before seizing power, Hitler and his comrades had apparently not done much programmatic thinking about "the Jewish question." Back in 1919 Hitler had written a letter in which he contrasted what he called emotional (violent) and rational (bureaucratic) tactics. In the 1930s, the men who conceived and administered terror against Jews formed inter-agency networks and created a milieu within which differences could be worked out. Accompanying harsh administrative persecution, a series of government-sponsored think tanks disseminated the latest racist research that represented Jews not as a biological danger but as a moral contagion. In the face of such "knowledge" of Jewish malfeasance, the Golden Rule became, in effect, "Do unto others as you imagine they have done unto you." Whether because of Hitler's chronic indecision or his political genius, two sharply contrasting approaches to solving the Jewish problem developed among "emotional" Stormtroopers (*Sturmabteilung,* SA) and "rational" SS *(Schutzstaffel)* men. In the contest between these two forces, a powerful—yet flexible—consensus allowed considerable latitude for individuals to radicalize its content according to the opportunities available.

The Final Solution took shape not on the distant eastern front nor as a series of fiats issued after the invasion of the Soviet Union in June 1941. Rather, powerful cadres within the government, party, and SS formed a genocidal consensus within Germany during six years of administrative networking, theoretical disputes, and factional infighting prior to Germany's invasion of Poland in 1939. No single agency or theory guided its implementation. Racial experts disagreed about racial science; Hitler procrastinated; Interior and Justice Ministry functionaries vacillated. Stormtrooper thugs clashed with SS racial detectives. Cognitive dissonance dogged supposedly objective terms like German blood, *Volk* and *Rasse,* Nordic race, and Aryan and non-Aryan. And yet the direction of policy was never in doubt. The emergent consensus was so powerful that anomalies only solidified it. At a time when no foreign danger threatened and the national economy was robust, the political advertisers of racial fear and ethnic pride created what contemporaries called a "gulf" or "pit" between a righteous ethnic majority and the less than 1 percent of their fellow citizens decreed as unwanted. The etiology of this consensus evolved not as a clear evil but rather as the shadow side of virtue.

The mobilization of a cadre of citizens prepared by ethical ideals to persecute fellow citizens who had done no wrong reveals the potential for a dedicated minority to win what Nazis called the "battle for public opinion." It cannot be emphasized too often that, during the years before World War II, as racial culture spread throughout the Third Reich and hardcore Nazis demanded the "destruction of Jewry," no concrete plans for physical extermination existed. Committed Nazis, however, used the prewar period to popularize a shared vision of a *Volk* so righteous and an enemy so vile that only the timing and techniques of an ultimate war to the death remained in doubt.

In a short story by Jorge Luis Borges, a former concentration camp commandant and convicted Nazi war criminal reflects on his life just before he is to be hanged. Although he fully accepts the justice of his sentence, he does not regret his crimes because, in his words, "Essentially, Nazism is an act of morality, a purging of corrupted humanity, to dress him anew."[37] Scholars have analyzed the broad outlines and subtle nuances of Nazi ideology without taking Hitler's promise of a new moral order seriously. In this book, I examine the comprehensive ethical revolution that formed the backdrop and paradigm for the Nazi race war and prepared Germans to tolerate racial crime well before the advent of genocidal murder battalions and extermination camps.

The Politics of Virtue

The highest purpose of an ethnic state *[Volksstaat]* is concern for the preservation of those original racial elements that bestow culture and create the beauty and dignity of a higher human nature.

—Adolf Hitler, Mein Kampf, *Chapter 2*

Although it may strain credulity to conceive of Adolf Hitler as a prophet of virtue, therein lay the secret of his immense popularity. Modern readers are likely to dismiss Hitler's interminable speeches as vapid, overwrought, and deceitful. But his followers, bitterly disillusioned by the bankrupt promises of liberal democracy, heard them as inspirational. Early in his career, Hitler displayed an unusual ability to intuit his audiences' deepest spiritual as well as political longings. Responding to Germans' sense of national impotence and their desire for political leadership they could trust, Hitler made himself into a political preacher of virtue. As a campaigner in the 1920s and as *Volk* chancellor after January 1933, he cultivated a lofty, nonpartisan image by extolling the ethical superiority of the "Aryan" *Volk* and presenting himself as the very model of the virtues he praised: the epitome of selfless devotion, humble origins, and abstemious tastes.

Hitler discovered his genius for persuasion on the streetcorners of Munich in the midst of revolutionary turmoil in 1919. There, as he recalled in *Mein Kampf,* he came to realize that "all great, world-shaking events have been brought about, not by written matter, but by the spoken word."[1] Because "the mass of people as such is lazy," he observed, they would not read anything that contradicted their views, but they would linger to hear a good speech even if they resisted its message at first. "In these [early] years I often faced an assemblage of people who believed the opposite of what I wanted to say, and wanted the opposite of what I believed. Then it was the work of two hours to lift two or three thousand people out of a previous conviction, and finally to lead them across to our convictions and our philosophy of life."[2] Unlike a writer, a speaker "can always see in the faces of his listeners" what rouses them. Audiences provide the attentive listener-orator with the ideas that will incite them. "The speaker will always let himself be borne by the great masses in such a way that instinctively the very words come to his lips that he needs to speak to the hearts of his audience. If he errs . . . he has the living correction before him."[3] Appropriating the formula of successful salesmen, he would begin by acquainting himself with his audience and studying their reactions to several topics. When he had identified their desires, he would explain confidently why only his Nazi movement could fulfill them. Listeners would say to themselves, "Of course, that's just what I have always believed."[4] After a particularly successful speech, Hitler would boast, "I had before me a surging mass full of the holiest indignation and boundless wrath."[5]

No matter how much his approach changed from one audience to another, Hitler created the impression of constancy by repeating adjectives like "unflinching," "decisive," "relentless," and "absolute." Against his enemies' malevolence, Hitler pledged to restore faith in the *Volk*. While other politicians tore at Germany's unity, Hitler promised wholeness. More quickly than his rivals, Hitler seized on the most advanced communications media to enhance his appeal. Before the invention of electric amplification, politicians (Hitler included) became hoarse after speaking for 15 minutes to a hundred or so people; with amplification, Hitler could address tens of thousands. Years later Hitler recalled, "Without the loud speaker we would never have conquered Germany."[6] Contemporaries often likened Hitler to an actor because of the way he would study his gestures in photographs and perfect his signature poses in front of a mirror. Like a movie star on the silent screen, Hitler would gesticulate wildly and exaggerate his facial expressions. But, unlike an actor, he wrote his own scripts.

Hitler's style, with its whiplash verbal violence, florid metaphors, and convoluted syntax, provided the elements of what the historian Ian Kershaw called the "Hitler myth." But Hitler's charisma depended on his message as well as his theatrical skills. Opponents of Nazism heard only hatred as Hitler ranted against the Treaty of Versailles, Communists, rival politicians, and democracy. But they overlooked the pattern of Hitler's speeches in which he counterposed every outburst of fury with the exalted rhetoric of a higher purpose. To modern readers, these paeans to moral purity and pious tributes to selflessness seem as hypocritical as they are banal. But for Germans who remembered the war fever of 1914 or had grown up listening to their elders' reminiscences, Hitler's blend of idealism and hatred struck a resonant chord.

At three decisive turning points, Hitler's career hung in the balance. In each case, brutal Nazi militias, acting on Hitler's wishes, committed flagrant crimes that might have undone him. The first turning point occurred when Hitler stood trial for his role in the Beer Hall Putsch in 1923. The next two outbreaks of violence occurred in the early months after Hitler became chancellor in 1933, when Nazi vigilantes terrorized first the Communists and then the Jews. In each case, Hitler demonstrated his consummate skill at preserving his image as the upholder of rectitude.

As a fledgling politician in 1919, Hitler deployed a menu of hatreds that

1. "Germany." Situated between the profiles above and "Deutschland" below, the coffin predicted the stark fate that awaited a *Volk* threatened by Jewry. Hitler, as an artist, avoided painting the human form, but the initials "A.H." suggest his input was decisive in the production of this 1920 poster and postcard.

disease

attracted a miniscule band of fanatically loyal followers. In flamboyant phrases, he juxtaposed the "rebirth of Germans' moral and spiritual powers" and the elimination of the Jewish "racial tuberculosis."[7] His earliest speeches seethed with repellent images of rapacious capitalists, craven diplomats, corrupt politicians, and bloodthirsty Bolsheviks—all of whom, no matter what their surface manifestations, emerged from a single source, "world Jewry."[8] Addressing bitter veterans and disillusioned citizens, he swore "with relentless determination to strike evil at its roots, and, with cold determination, to annihilate it utterly."[9] A friend who asked him how he would solve "the Jewish problem" vividly recalled Hitler's answer.

> His eyes no longer saw me but instead bore past me and off into empty space . . . "Once I really am in power, my first and foremost task will be the annihilation of the Jews . . . I will have gallows built in rows—at the Marienplatz in Munich for example—as many as traffic allows. Then the Jews will be hanged indiscriminately, and they will remain hanging until they stink . . . for as long as the principles of hygiene permit . . . Other cities will follow suit in this fashion, until all Germany has been completely cleansed of Jews."[10]

A police reporter captured the mutual empowerment of orator and audience in a crescendo of hate. After opening a typical speech in 1920 with a lackluster discussion of international justice, Hitler switched gears to speak of Germans' wartime hatred of Great Britain, and listeners began to shout, "Hurrah! That's Right!" When he asked who directed the failed German war effort, the crowd roared, "The Jews." Connecting "Jewry" to "international capital" evoked more "stormy applause." "Our *Volk* must be immunized with the feeling of hatred against everything foreign . . . We must be first and foremost Germans . . . We must exterminate [*ausmerzen*] the poison if we want to recover. One day the day will come when the sun will break through! [Interrupted by enthusiastic, extended applause.]"[11]

Responding to the rabid antisemites in his movement, Hitler would fulminate about "Jewry" as an omnipresent moral danger and swear to "keep alive the flame of idealism . . . that will inflame all German hearts so powerfully that it will burn out the epidemic of egotism, the Jewish-Mamon spirit." Germans must not rest until "our oppressors lie on the ground before us . . . smashed [*zerschmettert*]."[12] Screaming about "filthy Jews" and "the image *[Gestalt]* of paid traitors and Jewish villains *[Kanaillen],*" he would work himself into a rage.

In his notes for a speech entitled "Politics and Race" in the late spring of 1923, Hitler answered the question "Why must we destroy the Jew?" with a pledge to protect German "morality, customs, sense of justice, religion, etc."[13] The situation in Germany was bleak. France and Britain demanded overdue reparations payments, while French soldiers occupied the industrial Ruhr River basin. Hyperinflation drove the reichsmark, which had traded at 4 to the dollar in 1914 and 17 to the dollar in 1919, to over 4 trillion marks to the dollar. Communist and rightwing militias brawled in the streets. This combined diplomatic, economic, and political crisis had all but destroyed public confidence in the Weimar Republic.

With a membership of 55,000, in early 1923 the Nazi Party was largely unknown outside Bavaria. As the situation in Germany deteriorated, the toughs in Hitler's militia, the SA (Stormtroopers) called for revolution. On the night of November 8–9 Hitler gave the order and, together with General Erich Ludendorff and two Bavarian politicians, marched with a brigade of 2,000 brown-shirted SA men into Munich, where they planned to arrest key officials, seize communications, and replace the constitution. At the Odeonsplatz in central Munich, police blocked the street. For less than a minute, shots rang out. Fourteen Nazis and four policemen were killed. The putsch collapsed. Hitler, Ludendorff, and the other conspirators were charged with high treason.

The trial began the following February. As an Austrian citizen who had already violated his parole restrictions, Hitler faced possible deportation or life in prison. His political future depended on his ability to elicit his judges' sympathy. By the end of his second speech, Hitler's "ear" for his audience's desires guided him to mute racial hate and extoll the *Volk*. This formula defined his public persona from that point forward. Making his selfless devotion to the *Volk* the centerpiece of his courtroom defense, Hitler told the story of his tiny band of idealists who had dared to sally forth against evil. In long tirades and snappy rejoinders, he converted his botched attempt to overthrow the government into a virtue. "In such a critical moment a *Volk* cannot be saved by quiet reflection *[ruhige Überlegung]* . . . only fanaticism, hot, reckless, and utterly brutal fanaticism offers the means to rescue a *Volk* from enslavement."[14]

Hitler's rhetoric worked its magic from the first day of the trial. The conservative but by no means pro-Nazi judges openly admired this audacious

2. Hitler's exaggerated gestures resembled the body language of silent film actors. His authorization of these six postcards suggests that Hitler intended the photographs to have the aura of devotional objects. Hitler's statue-like poses convey the traits attached to his Führer myth: piety, devotion, and steadfastness.

traitor. "Why, he's a colossal fellow, this man Hitler," one remarked to another.[15] Over the next six weeks, Hitler, the uncouth agitator, remade himself into an innocent patriot who had been betrayed by a democracy too weak to defend Germanic honor. As part of his show of humility, Hitler called himself a drummer, but in his towering pretensions to high virtue he resembled a trumpeter.[16]

Hitler transformed his public self from a raging antisemite into a resolute tribune of the *Volk* who captivated audiences with his vision of "cleanliness everywhere, cleanliness of our government, cleanliness in public life, and also this cleanliness in our culture . . . that will restore our [national] soul to us." Although he made unmistakable references to Jews (in, for example, his promise to cure "German lungs" of "racial tuberculosis"), he avoided the diatribes of his earlier speeches.[17] Sharpening the question-and-answer format that later became his stock-in-trade, he caricatured his critics' allegations and countered them with assurances of his own personal virtue. While his co-conspirators insisted on their innocence, Hitler accepted his responsibility for violating a constitution he despised. Against the law of the land, he defended his "moral right before God and the world to represent the nation. That is a moral issue, and not a question of a majority."[18]

With passion verging on hysteria, Hitler cast German history as a melodrama of national sacrifice, virtue, and suffering. From the Wild West novels by Karl May, which he read and reread throughout his life, and the Wagnerian heroes he adored, Hitler crafted a national morality play. Its main characters—a victimized Volk, an "alien" villain, and a lone hero—replayed the themes of wartime propaganda that had stirred him as a soldier. Deleting "Jewry" from his oratory, Hitler excoriated the Versailles Treaty and Bolshevism while castigating liberals as too cowardly to defend the Volk.[19] On trial for his political life, he transformed himself from a sectarian agitator into a moral revivalist who called for an ethnic rebirth that would dissolve the boundaries of class, religion, and ideology. As he recalled later, he learned how to "speak to locksmiths and university professors at the same time . . . in a form . . . that really lashes them into a wild storm of applause."[20]

The judges allowed him ample time to expound on "two philosophies," weak-willed liberalism versus ethnic honor.[21] What, Hitler thundered, could "morality" mean when liberals allowed the Versailles Treaty, imposed by vindictive enemies, to become "the supreme law of the land"? He ranted against the treaty as "a law which advocated immorality in 414 articles." To violate its provisions was an act of patriotism.[22] Hitler did not deny his militias' treasonous intent but rather enveloped their crimes in rhetorical clouds of "honor, liberty and fatherland." Under the democratic Weimar Republic, Hitler reiterated, "law and morality are no longer synonymous." Because the constitution weakened the nation, democracy—not foreign powers—betrayed the Volk. Ruled by spineless liberals and socialists, the state had deteriorated into a materialistic institution, an "organization of people who apparently have only one goal: to guarantee each other's daily bread."[23]

Flamboyant rhetoric and convoluted syntax conveyed a sense of urgency, a "decisive battle for existence or non-existence." Again and again, Hitler depicted a harsh "struggle of two great philosophies . . . between the new ethnic [völkische] movement . . . and pacifist-Marxist values." On one side stood the pure-hearted Nazis and on the other cowardly liberals and socialists who "have soiled everything that was great, noble, sacred."[24] In the witness box, Hitler invoked the high moments in German history, which had been, like Bismarck's breach of the Prussian constitution in the 1860s, treason that succeeded.[25] Instead of "accepting blow after blow with the meekness of sheep," Hitler quoted military theorist Carl von Clausewitz's *On War*, written at the time of the Napoleonic Wars, to the effect that any nation which voluntarily submits to humiliation is doomed. Hitler added, "It is better to perish with honor."

In his defense, Hitler transformed a fiasco into a publicity coup that spread his name throughout Germany and Europe. After defending treason as patriotic for over six weeks in the witness box, Hitler in his closing speech appealed to a morality that stood above the written law. To his judges he said, "Even if you pronounce us guilty a thousand times over . . . the goddess of the eternal tribunal of history one day will, with a smile, rip up the Prosecutor's opinion and the verdict of the court. She will acquit us."[26] Hitler's strategic blunder of November 9, 1923, became a public relations triumph.

On April 1, 1924, the judges announced they would not deport Hitler because he had fought in the Bavarian army and, they added, because he "felt so German."[27] Compared with the sentences handed down to Marxists found guilty of high treason, which ranged from fifteen years to life, Hitler's five-year sentence barely counted as a rebuke. Although sometimes he depicted himself as a martyr who suffered "under lock and key," most of the time he reminisced fondly about his life in a Bavarian detention center as being a university experience financed by the state.[28]

Reading about their Führer's trial speeches, some Nazis worried that their movement had lost its antisemitic edge. Hitler reassured them that his earlier ideas about "the Jewish question" had been "too mild! . . . only the toughest battle tactics" would suffice to solve "a question that is for our *Volk* and all peoples a question of life and death."[29] During the summer, his comrade Rudolph Hess transcribed Hitler's daily ruminations with the intention of compiling them as a book, *Four and a Half Years of Struggle against Lies, Stupidity, and Cowardice*—subsequently shortened by his Nazi publisher to *Mein Kampf (My Struggle)*. With Hess as his sole listener, Hitler's racist venom returned in force. He raged about "a parasite in the body of other races that eternally searches for nourishment *[Nahrboden]* for his own race . . . He is and remains a typical parasite, a freeloader, that spreads like a dangerous bacillus . . . Wherever it erupts, the host *Volk* perishes sooner or later."[30] He railed against "ethical and moral poisoning" in the form of "deserters, pimps, and rabble" and "supercilious arrogant know-it-alls." Phobias obsessed him. "If you cut even cautiously into such an abscess, you found—like a maggot in a rotting body, often dazzled by the sudden light—a kike." As he paced back and forth dictating his magnum opus to Hess, this autodidact fashioned a Manichean universe in which he pledged to win "the positive struggle for the soul of our *Volk*" and "exterminate its international poisoners."[31]

Upon his release from prison a scant ten months later, the party press hailed the event as "a Christmas present to the *Volk*," and Hitler set out to rebuild his fragmented movement.[32] His February 1925 speech to 3,000 followers in the Bürgerbräu beer hall was a triumph of reconciliation. After roiling up the crowd with hatred for the Treaty of Versailles, he called for unity among all ethnic Germans and summoned his warring deputies to renew their allegiance to him, accompanied by ecstatic cheers from the crowd.[33] The new course was set. As he reached out to better-educated audiences, he held his virulent hatreds in check. Of course, when he used phrases like "one single enemy," his comrades understood the meaning. Acutely aware that the authorities could prohibit him from speaking in public or deport him, Hitler had ample reason for caution. In place of lengthy fulminations against Jewry, he would enliven his speeches with racist wisecracks and side comments.[34] He invoked medical metaphors, warning, for example, about "Jewry that wants to create a world of slaves" and "infection of our national ethnic body *[Volkskörper]* by blood poisoning."[35] He would link "Jewish" to despised values like urbanism, materialism, and greed. For comic relief, he joked about "upstart Jewish composers, scribblers, painters who drown our *Volk* in their pathetic trash *[Dreck]*."[36] In a typical three-hour speech, Hitler would mention Jews in passing, as in a slur against the "Jewish press" for promoting decadent "Jimmy [probably a reference to Jim Crow] culture."[37] He would blame moral degeneration on sexual intercourse between Jews and non-Jews, which he called "racial treason" *(Rassenschande)* or "bastardization."[38] Whatever his example, Hitler cast the honest but trusting Aryans as vulnerable to Jewish deceit.[39]

During the late 1920s, Nazi organizers campaigned vigorously to expand their following beyond the less than 6 percent who voted for Nazi candidates. During these years, Hitler perfected his new persona. Rather than proclaiming his racism at every opportunity, Hitler learned to express his racist fury only when it suited his overall strategy. In early 1928, for example, the Catholic Center Party in Bavaria chastised Hitler for his antisemitism and ridiculed him as a "political priest." Hitler turned the tables on his Catholic opponents in two lengthy rebuttals, in February and August. Each speech lasted between two and three hours, and together the transcripts take up 47 closely printed pages. Hearing "much laughter" in response to anticlerical and antisemitic humor, he lambasted his Catholic rivals for their hypocrisy and quoted from their antisemitic posters printed just a few years before. After expounding on the need for unity among all Christians and "Germany for the Germans," near the conclusion of his February speech he raged against Jewish "swindlers," cowards, and the "Jewish hunger for profits and greed for power." Concluding his August speech, Hitler pledged to "battle against poisoning by Jewish blood and culture." Denouncing Marxists who denied racial danger, he warned, "They will come to understand it when their children toil under the Jewish overseer's whip."[40] Having vented his hatred, Hitler closed both speeches with a summons to self-sacrifice. "As you have in the past, give your love to ethnic Germany, this unhappy *Volk* . . . Send your gratitude to those who have offered their lives" for the Nazi movement. Stormy shouts of *Heil!* and extended applause accompanied his exit. Other than in exceptional circumstances such as these, however, Hitler held his antisemitic fury in check.

Rather than concerning himself with the particular demands of the Nazi Party program, Hitler made himself into the leader audiences could trust. Dedicated followers transformed his phrases into brilliant posters with dramatic slogans such as, "Decline or Future?" "In the Name of National Unity!" "Freedom and Bread!" and "Germany's Fateful Hour." To cheering audiences he exhorted, "If you want to be happy as individuals, then take care that your *Volk* is alive and free." With "faith and persistence," he reiterated, rebirth was at hand.[41]

Eschewing vicious antisemitism, Hitler preached the virtues of ethnic fundamentalism: he celebrated German uniqueness; invoked organic symbols that depicted a living *Volk* beset by impurities from within; denounced perfidious foreign enemies; and appealed to the righteousness of a martyred *Volk*. Hitler reduced complex issues to quaint homilies, as when he represented an imperialistic *Volk* as a good father who wants to ensure his son's future, or denounced greedy "social snobs" who "cared nothing about a *Volk* that was healthy in body and soul." To poor peasants, he would say, "Forget your own sorrows, and work for your *Volk*."[42] From speech to speech, the villain shifted, but two stock characters starred in every melodrama: the *Volk* as an imperiled maiden and Hitler as her savior.

Between March 1925 and January 30, 1933, when he became chancellor, Hitler called out to Germans to abandon divisive rival parties and form "a Unity, a unified Will, with which the *Volk* will fight for its existence on Earth."[43] Where he had once fulminated against Jewry as a moral danger before his trial, in the late 1920s Hitler glorified the virtuous *Volk*. One of his longtime followers described the transformation of his Führer after a rally in 1928:

> Hitler has changed over the last years. His speeches are, as always, full of emotion and fire, spiced with his sarcastic wit. He makes quick side jabs. But he is much more moderate than before . . . No smear campaign. Not a single word against the Jews. No pitched attacks. But for all that, Hitler's speeches have a more powerful effect than ever . . . I would characterize his two-hour speech not so much as a campaign speech or a propaganda talk, but rather as philosophical reflections on the national economy and politics.[44]

A young Jewish woman who attended a Hitler rally out of curiosity was similarly surprised. The "heiling," she recalled, was so loud she "thought the roof would fall in," but, in her opinion, Hitler said little of substance. He "put up sham accusations, only to refute them, used slogans by the hour, and said nothing else than praise of himself . . . Nothing even against the Jews."[45]

Exalted by his followers and dismissed as vapid by his opponents, Hitler balanced three themes in his speeches during the early 1930s: outrage against the Versailles victors, verbal abuse of his rivals, and extended ruminations about honor, struggle, glory, and morality. As his most rabid metaphors fell into disuse, he articulated an idealism that fused public virtue and ethnic purity. Thanks to the research of Theodore Abel, we have a vivid portrait of early Nazi joiners to whom these themes appealed. In 1935, when Abel advertised a mock essay contest for the best essay by an "old fighter" (*alte Kämpfer:* a Nazi from the earliest days of the movement) on "Why I became a National Socialist," nearly 600 authors submitted entries. In their essays, old fighters cast the decision to join the Nazi Party (or, as they called it, "our Freedom Movement") in moral terms. While spewing contempt for what they saw as the decadence of Weimar democracy and modernist culture, they fervently described their longing for a principled man of action.[46] One woman recalled being thunderstruck by the appearance of an "idealism for which we have waited so passionately for all these years whether or not we realized it. Yes, our *Volk* needs knowledge about the meaning of its existence: of knowing what it means to belong to a particular *Volk!*"[47] After he heard Hitler speak in 1926, one old fighter recalled, "The German soul spoke to German manhood through him. From then on I could never swerve in my allegiance to Hitler. It was his unlimited faith in his *Volk* and his desire to liberate them."[48]

Although antisemitism was not censored from subsequent editions of *Mein Kampf,* it became easier with each passing year for Hitler's more moderate supporters to attribute the book's vulgar racism to a bygone phase of Hitler's life. Yet the racist planks of the 25-Point Nazi Party Program were clear to anyone who cared to read them: only individuals with "German blood" would be citizens *(Volksgenossen)*; no Jew could be a civil servant or work in the media; "non-Germans" who had immigrated after 1914 would be expelled from Germany; and department stores (believed by Nazis to be Jewish-owned) would be confiscated and turned over to small shopkeepers. The methods were unclear, but the long-term goal was explicit: "The Party combats the Jewish materialist spirit domestically and abroad."[49] Leaving coarse antisemitism to his deputies, Hitler's politics of virtue elevated him above the party machine he controlled.

Over the years, Hitler elaborated on the biography he had created in

3. "Greeted by an endless human ocean in the Berlin Lustgarten park" (top). "More than 100,000 Saxons on the South Meadow in Chemnitz" (bottom). When Hitler staged his dramatic electoral campaign by airplane in 1932, Heinrich Hoffmann's booklet, *Hitler Over Germany,* allowed those who were not in the crowd to share the jubilation vicariously.

Mein Kampf by transforming his palpable failures into a myth of humble origins, terrible obstacles, and iron will. Speaking in the third person, he would open his speeches with a set-piece party narrative in which he reminisced about "an unknown man and German soldier who entered political life, led only by the commands of conscience."[50] In pathos-laden tones, he would remark, "I know why my enemies hate me" and then proceed to paint a self-portrait of a fearless crusader for justice. While Nazi militias viciously attacked their rivals and hounded Jewish public figures in the 1932 election campaign, Hitler presented himself as a youthful and fearless alternative to the 83-year-old President Hindenburg. His publicity team brilliantly engraved an image of a daring Hitler on the public mind by transporting the candidate on a spectacular speaking tour via airplane. In an era when air travel was considered dangerous, Hitler literally descended from the clouds to address audiences of between 120,000 and 300,000 at major cities. An inexpensive booklet of "art" photos of his airborne speaking tour, printed in an edition of 500,000, enabled Germans who did not actually join the throngs to experience the vicarious thrill of this publicity stunt. Hitler lost the run-off election, but he had implanted his image securely in the public mind.

In January 1933 Hitler used the Nazi Party plurality to negotiate his way into the chancellorship via a series of back-door political deals. In retrospect, his position may seem to have been invulnerable. But at the time, his hold on power appeared tenuous indeed. Between the national elections in July and November 1932, support for Nazi candidates had begun to ebb for the first time. Hindenburg (who personally disliked Hitler) could have dismissed him.[51] Of eleven cabinet ministers in the Hitler government, only three (including Hitler) were Nazis. The 196 Nazi Reichstag delegates were outnumbered by 388 non-Nazi delegates. Yet, grasping the potential of modern media, Hitler engineered the appearance of a mandate.

Within hours of his appointment as chancellor, two announcers, speaking to an estimated 20 million listeners, described the torchlight parade in Berlin and hailed the hardworking new Führer. Speaking in the breathless cadences of sportscasters, they reported, "Cheers continue to well up. Adolf Hitler stands at the window. His face is serious. He was torn away from his work. There is no trace of a victory mood in his face. He was interrupted. And yet his eyes shine over the awakening Germany, over this sea of people from all walks of life . . . workers of the mind and fist . . . I hope that our listeners receive just an idea, an inkling, of this great specta-

4. "Finally! Enough! Elect Hitler." In this 1932 poster, the commercial graphic designer and longtime Nazi Mjölnir (pseudonym for Hans Schweitzer) conveyed the Nazi promise to replace a moribund democracy with a powerful masculine will.

cle."[52] Two days later, Hitler pledged to restore "family . . . honor and loyalty, *Volk* and *Vaterland*, culture and economy" and recover the "eternal foundation of our morality and our faith." He declared "merciless war against spiritual, political and cultural nihilism." On February 10 Hitler spoke for two hours, not about politics but about moral rebirth: "To do justice to God and our own conscience, we have turned once more to the German *Volk*." He concluded to thunderous cheers, "We are not fighting for ourselves, but for Germany!"[53]

Meanwhile, Nazi militias broke the law with impunity. A headline in a daily newspaper reported, "Four die in party clashes." British Ambassador Sir Horace Rumbold warned the Foreign Office in London about the Nazis' "irresponsibility and a frivolous disregard for all decent feeling which is without precedent."[54] An American diplomat described the mood: "In the streets of Stuttgart the spectacle of Fascist bravoes [sic], clad in the military uniforms of the National Socialist Army and going about in groups of four or five, with arrogant and swaggering attitude."[55] A Jewish Berliner, Rudolf Steiner, described how "the atmosphere in the streets changed totally—instead of people strolling harmlessly, now the SA, Stormtroopers, paraded in brown shirts." The police stood aside as militias "made spaces Jew-free."[56] Nazi crimes were highly visible, but, as in 1924, Hitler framed them as the courageous acts of zealous patriots.

Attired in a white shirt, tie, and black suit with a discreet swastika lapel pin, Chancellor Hitler fulminated about hostile foreign powers, the Bolshevik menace, cultural decline, and spineless liberals. Exuding ethnic fundamentalism, he said barely a word about Jewry.[57] Many observers approvingly commented that Hitler had mellowed. Rumbold, like other seasoned diplomats, was taken in. "It is interesting to note that Hitler has expunged from his litany all the anti-Semitic passages."[58] In a nationally broadcast speech at the Sports Stadium in Berlin, Hitler refrained from traducing "racial enemies" and for well over an hour celebrated the "pillars of our national character *[Volkstum]*." Again and again, Hitler rehearsed the melodrama of a martyred *Volk* at the mercy of petty political hacks—the corrupt "party bosses" who had "exterminated the . . . glorious empire of our past." Assailing the "political parties of decay" that had "distracted and battered . . . destroyed, shredded up and dissolved an unsuspecting *Volk*," Hitler deployed his question-and-answer format and lied with aplomb.[59]

On trial in 1924, he had boasted that he was immune to the desire for "personal power, material considerations *[materiellen Unterlagen]*, or per-

5. "Our last Hope. Hitler." In a time of economic depression and political stagnation, Mjölnir depicted ordinary voters as members of a despairing and feminized crowd. Having cast their ballots for other parties in the past, in 1932 they looked to Hitler as the leader who would bring change.

sonal vengeance."[60] In 1933 he repeated his performance. Had he grabbed power? No. Accepting the chancellorship "has been the most difficult decision of my life." Was it true, as critics alleged, that he was greedy? Not at all. He worked "neither for salary nor for wages. I have done it for your sake!"[61] So few were his material needs that he lived from his author's royalties from *Mein Kampf.* "I do not want a Swiss villa or a bank account." To those who doubted his word, he pledged, "We will not lie and we will not cheat." Was it true, as critics alleged, that he had no concrete proposals to address the economic crisis? Yes. Until "a thorough moral purging of the German *Volkskörper* is complete," he would not concern himself with the economy."[62] What did "health" mean? Hitler rambled on about his aesthetic vision of a pure ethnic culture. The humble footsoldier of the putsch trial now mounted the podium as the Führer of his *Volk.*

Reaching out to non-Nazis, Hitler even embraced two popular causes he despised, pacifism and Christianity. Answering those who maligned him as a warmonger, Hitler retorted, "I have been described as a man who makes bloodthirsty, inflammatory speeches . . . Gentlemen, I have never made an inflammatory speech . . . No one wishes for peace and quiet more than the German *Volk.*"[63] He praised Christianity as the "foundation of our entire moral health *[Basis unserer gesamten Moral]*" and the family as "the germ cell of our ethnic and political body *[Volks- und Staatskörpers].*" He called for recovery from "the terrible need of our political, moral and economic existence."[64] In a time of collapse, he insisted, "this sovereign nation has no other desire than to gladly invest the power and weight of its political, ethical, and economic values not only toward healing the wounds inflicted on the human race . . . but in cooperation."[65] The cadences of Hitler's February 10 speech at the Sports Palace reminded Rumbold of a "revival meeting." French Ambassador André François-Poncet ascribed the mass acclaim to "a moral power" *(La force morale).*[66] That Hitler could have been seen as a moral authority seems preposterous, especially at a time when Nazi militias beat up, tortured, and murdered so-called enemies with impunity. Amidst the widespread fear of chaos Hitler's rhetoric worked its magic.

On the night of February 27–28, 1933, a terrorist attack set the Reichstag ablaze. Headlines called it the first stage of a Communist revolution. Acting on Hitler's "advice" and with cabinet approval, President Hindenburg suspended civil rights. Nazi newspapers called for "hard hammer blows" against "the criminal Communist hand" that caused the fire. Hitler condemned the "dastardly attack" and praised the "self-sacrificing fire-

6. "I have preached in Germany for thirteen years. Countless millions know our program." To Germans who found Hitler's bombast repellent, images like these, published in Heinrich Hoffmann's booklet, *The Hitler No One Knows*, projected a reassuring image of reasonableness.

men" who saved the Reichstag from total destruction. Using the emergency powers vested in him by President Hindenburg, Hitler authorized Hermann Göring (cabinet minister without portfolio and acting Prussian interior minister) to deputize 10,000 heavily armed SA troops as police auxiliaries. Göring ordered them to shoot "enemies" at the slightest provocation.[67] Behind them stood nearly a million fellow Stormtroopers, joined by other veterans' organizations, spoiling for a fight. When prisoners' lawyers demanded their release, Hitler declared that traitors had no rights.[68] Speaking on radio, Hitler whipped up fears of Bolshevism. The 1917 revolution in St. Petersburg had taken place only 2,000 miles from Berlin, and Lenin's Communist Party had a miniscule following compared with the nearly 6 million (or 17 percent) of the German electorate that had supported the Communist Party in November 1932. With images of the Reichstag blaze on the front page of every major newspaper, Nazi rule became the lesser of two evil extremes. Hitler was well on the way to fulfilling a promise he had made a few weeks earlier: "In ten years there will be no more Marxists in Germany."[69]

Observers' confusion about the scale of the repression testifies to the chaos. The American historian Sidney B. Fay reported that 4,000 "enemies" had been jailed in early March.[70] By early April, 20,000 were held in protective custody, according to an estimate by *The New York Times*. Interior Minister Frick reported 100,000. Rumbold thought that between 30 and 40 people had been murdered, but other sources reported nearly 200.[71] Local Stormtrooper units attacked Jews and Communists with "cattle prods, revolvers, riding whips, cattle chains, steel bundles *[Stahlruten]*, shoulder straps, and leather belts"—"weapons of the spirit," in the words of one disgusted bystander.[72] At Dachau near Munich and Oranienburg near Berlin the government built large concentration camps to house prisoners, and smaller camps proliferated so quickly not even the chief of the Gestapo could keep track.[73]

The violence blended hooliganism with hardened sadism. Teenagers and young Brownshirts outdid themselves in the mental and physical torment of their victims. A French traveler in Germany described the experiences of a Socialist he had met, who "talk[ed] slowly, as if in a dream": "They made me mount a platform, like a trained dog. The prisoners formed the public. They made me say in a loud voice, 'I am the biggest Jewish pig in the city.' Then for a very long time they made me walk on all fours under the table. A young SA leader . . . with a riding crop entered the room and shouted, 'Well, here's the bastard I've been wanting to beat with my own hands for a very long time!'"[74] Anyone who read Hermann Göring's proclamation in early March understood that the constitution no longer protected anyone. "My Fellow Germans! . . . I don't have to conform to any kind of justice. I am concerned only to exterminate and destroy *[zu vernichten und auszurotten]*."[75] Rumors circulated. Resolute foreign journalists verified reports at considerable risk to themselves.

In the March 5, 1933, Reichstag elections, Germans had an opportunity to register their reactions to the new regime. Would fear of Bolshevism outweigh disgust at the Nazis' rampant violence? With unlimited funds, control of the national broadcasting network, and their left-wing critics in jail, the campaign was far from fair. Hitler appealed to the *Volk* via national radio. "Once again you can hold your heads high and proud . . . You are no longer enslaved!" Nazi organizations celebrated at thousands of local "freedom bonfires." Goebbels noted in his diary, "All Germany is like a glowing torch. This has indeed become . . . a 'Day of National Awakening!'" Overwhelmed by "indescribable enthusiasm," Goebbels anticipated a landslide.[76]

But when the electoral returns came in, the mood at campaign headquarters was subdued. German voters, who turned out at a record 89 percent, did not in fact produce a "great triumph." Despite the intimidation and censorship, less than half (43.9 percent) of the voters chose Nazi candidates. A correspondent for *The Spectator* called the results "morally, a Government defeat [because] 56 percent of the voters of Germany dared to express their hostility."[77] Hitler himself was stunned.[78] Nevertheless, headlines on March 6 proclaimed, "With Adolf Hitler into the Third Reich! Our extraordinary victory. A Great Triumph! The *Volk* Demands It!"[79] Counting the Nationalists (who had agreed to support Hitler), slightly over half of all voters, or 51.8 percent, voted for Nazi rule. A reporter for *The New York Times* commented, "It is hard to overlook the fact that a campaign marked by flagrant repression . . . by unremitting efforts to frighten the neutral voting masses into support of the Nazi regime, resulted in a bare 51 percent majority for the anti-democratic coalition."[80] To obtain dictatorial power, Hitler needed an amendment to the Weimar constitution, which required the support of two thirds of the Reichstag.[81]

Hitler addressed the nation as if from a pulpit, exacerbating listeners' fears of chaos (caused by Nazi militias as well as the Reichstag fire) and exalting ethnic faith. "I can't free myself from believing in my *Volk*, I can't escape from the conviction that this nation will once again arise; I can't distance myself from the love of this, my *Volk,* and I hold on, firm as a rock, to the conviction that some time the hour will come when the millions who hate us today will stand behind us and will with us welcome what has been created together, struggled for under difficulty, attained at such a cost: the new German Reich [empire] of greatness and honor and strength and glory and justice. Amen."[82]

With the Communist Party outlawed, Nazi leaders negotiated with Catholic, Liberal, and Nationalist parties. When the vote was taken, only 91 Reichstag delegates, all of them Socialists, voted against granting Hitler dictatorial powers for four years. At an open-air commemoration in Potsdam on March 24, Hitler stood reverently beside Hindenburg and promised, "In order to follow God and our own conscience, we turn yet again to the German *Volk*."[83] With bowed head he asked, "May divine providence bless us with enough courage and enough determination to perceive within ourselves this holy German space."[84] With thousands of Communists and hundreds of left-wing opponents of Nazism in jail or in exile, Hitler made a public show of calling for curbs on militia violence. But the old fighters had no intention of settling down. With nearly 1,500,000 Nazi Party members (over half of them newcomers) divided into 33 regions *(Gäue)* and 827 party districts, central authority was stretched thin. Powerful local leaders acted autonomously. A resident who lived near the SA barracks on Friedrichstraße in Berlin reported: "For several days during the week after elections the neighbors and passers by heard the screams and moans of people inside." When the police broke in, they found 70 Communists, several dead, the others badly beaten.[85] Such violence was excused as an unfortunate side-effect of a campaign to protect the *Volk*.

During these months, Hitler made some of the most effective radio speeches of his career. From being merely a chancellor, Hitler promoted himself as *Volkskanzler,* or people's chancellor. He glorified the shabby political deal by which he had been appointed as an "upheaval" and then called it an "outpouring" *(Aufhebung, Wiedererhebung,* or *Erhebung)* of ethnic spirit. By March the Nazi takeover had become a "national revolution." The discursive shift from "upheaval" to "revolution" excused acts that would be criminal in normal times as being only the byproduct of a disciplined revolution.[86]

The words of an English reporter reveal how effectively the conceptual shift functioned. When viewed as part of a normal political change, Nazi terror was horrifying. "But once one realizes that what has taken place in Germany during the last few weeks falls nothing short of a national revolution, one is bound to admit that normal standards of political and parliamentary life are for the time being not appropriate measures of judgment." Imagine, he added, what would happen in Britain if Communists tried to burn the Houses of Parliament![87] With the Nazi takeover cast as a "revolution," Stormtroopers' crimes became collateral damage on the path toward a stable future. Nazi thugs continued their reign of terror with impunity.

Hitler's rhetoric of virtue ascended to new heights. As at his putsch trial, he invoked the memory of the two million patriots killed in the Great War and pledged that he would win the battle Weimar politicians had lost by purifying the ethnic community or, as he began to call it, the *Volkskörper* (ethnic body politic). Rescuing the *Volk* from a democratic system mired in decay was "the most difficult [task] faced by any German statesman since the beginning of history." Speaking in the voice of prophecy, Hitler announced that "the great age has now dawned for which we have hoped for 14 years. Germany has now awakened."[88] At this point, acclaim from respected Germans who had no prior association with Nazism clinched Hitler's upstanding image. The Protestant theologian Otto Dibelius, who had not previously supported Hitler (and who later joined the resistance), opened his March 21 sermon in Berlin with the text that had been read in the Reichstag on the first day of the Great War: "If God be for us, who can be against us." He rejoiced that at last all Germans lived under "One Reich, one *Volk*, one God."[89] From other pastors, priests, university rectors, and conservative politicians came similar expressions of gratitude. Crimes against alleged terrorists met with widespread acclaim.

Outrages against Jews, however, evoked very different responses from the very Germans who cheered criminal repression of Marxism. Against the former, Hitler ranted in lurid detail; about the latter he said virtually nothing. Especially in the aftermath of the Reichstag fire, most Germans found the threat of a Communist revolution credible, but only hardcore racists took "Jewry" seriously enough to excuse brutality against defenseless civilians. But the core of Hitler's party support rested on the SA's militancy. After years of operating illegally, Stormtroopers lusted for more, not less, violence.[90] Although it was clear from *Mein Kampf* that Hitler saw Marxism as a manifestation of subversive Jewish power, he forcefully condemned antisemitic violence. "Harassment of individuals, the obstruction of cars, and disruptions to business are to be put to an absolute stop . . . Never let yourselves be distracted for one second from our watchword, which is the destruction of Marxism."[91] Where Nazi popularity was low, militias were relatively restrained, but in Nazi strongholds, antisemitic violence increased.[92] Stormtroopers, often joined by an antisemitic association of white-collar workers, pillaged Jewish-owned businesses and harassed individuals who "looked Jewish."[93]

In the eastern German state of Silesia, where Nazism was popular, local toughs "arrested" a livestock dealer in the capital, Breslau, cropped his hair, branded him with a swastika, and rubbed his wounds with salt.[94] Stormtroopers distributed flyers with a message ostensibly signed by Göring: "Any Jewish girl or woman who is on the streets after dark may be assaulted by any Stormtrooper without fear of punishment. I assume responsibility."[95] Nazi thugs treated Jewish prisoners with special cruelty. The historian Fritz Stern, who was seven at the time, recalls the fate of one of his father's patients, the radical Socialist Ernst Eckstein, who was tortured to death in a Nazi jail after his house had been bombed.[96] Stormtroopers invaded Wertheim's Department Store and marched into the local courthouse. Shouting "Out with the Jews!" they insulted bystanders, broke into offices, courtrooms, and judges' chambers, and drove out Jewish judges and lawyers. For over a week, they barricaded the courthouse, demanding "curbs on the influence of the Jewish justice system." When the local police chief asked the national police for help, he was told to avoid clashes with the SA, and a week later he was replaced by a staunch Nazi Party member. Even though the Silesian Jewish community filed a complaint with the League of Nations, attacks continued.[97] Similar scenarios were repeated in Nazi strongholds throughout Germany.

Dorothy Thompson reported that the March pogroms sent thousands of Jews abroad.[98] Arturo Toscanini protested Nazi crimes by canceling his contract to conduct at the Bayreuth Wagner Festival. Albert Einstein convened a "moral tribunal" against Nazi atrocities. When the police ransacked the home of the Jewish theologian Martin Buber, international Christian and Jewish organizations objected. Protesters against Nazi antisemitism in England, France, Greece, the Netherlands, Poland, and Romania called for a boycott of German products. The American Jewish Congress and the Organization of Jewish War Veterans sponsored a protest rally at Madison Square Garden on March 27 and threatened to boycott German manufactured goods.[99]

Whereas violence against Communists met with acclaim in Germany and abroad, racist terror backfired. New damage control strategies were in order. Against a credible danger, severe measures seemed warranted; where a threat seemed fraudulent, people around the world objected. The international news media condoned the repression of leftists but despised violence against Jews.[100] "Germany's isolation is extraordinary," Goebbels exclaimed. At Hitler's urging, Vice Chancellor von Papen wrote an open letter reassuring the American Chamber of Commerce that Jews were safe in Germany. The financier Hjalmar Schacht met with Jewish leaders in New York. Göring apologized to the major Jewish organization in Germany, telling them that Communists had suffered more than Jews from Nazi violence.[101] Government delegations met with American business organizations and circulated reassurances to the press.[102] Hitler remained a cipher in public. Even an experienced observer of Germany in the U.S. Embassy believed that "there is much reason to believe that the Chancellor, Mr. Hitler, does not approve of the indiscriminate and general action which has been taken against Jews . . . He is believed to be very moderate in his views in this respect."[103] A *New York Times* reporter predicted that "Hitler will abandon his anti-Semitic stand."[104]

As always, Nazi leaders responded to public opinion in Germany as well as abroad. Already in 1933, networks were being established to monitor what Nazis called "mood and attitude" *(Stimmung und Haltung)*. It soon became clear that most Germans deplored lawless attacks on Jews. Avoiding race and speaking in the most general terms, Hitler pledged, "The *Volk* shall now for all eternity act as custodian of our faith and our culture, our honor and our freedom!"[105] While Stormtroopers beat up Jews and defaced Jewish property, Hitler spoke for hours about "the rich blossoming and flourishing," the "new life," the "renaissance," "the moral purge of the ethnic body politic," "honor and dignity," and the "unity of spirit and will."[106] Although news of antisemitic attacks was censored, pogroms took place in full public view. In theory, Hitler might have defended antisemitic terror, as he had championed the repression of suspected Bolsheviks after the Reichstag fire. But at this crucial point he did not invest his immense popularity in defending pogroms.

Within days of the Reichstag's vote to give Hitler dictatorial powers for four years, plans for a national boycott against Jews were announced in the press. Although it seems clear that Hitler drafted the April 1 boycott announcement, he did not sign it. On the eve of the boycott, Hitler underscored his distance from the action by leaving Berlin. Goebbels mounted a national publicity campaign that depicted the action as self-defense against "a clique of Jewish men of letters, professors, and profiteers" who maligned Nazi rule in the foreign press.[107] Like Nazis' vindication of anti-Communist terror, propaganda described the boycott as protective. "As a basic principle, it should be stressed that the boycott is a defensive measure which was forced on us." On March 28 Goebbels noted in his diary, "The boycott organization is complete. We only need to press the button. Then it starts."[108] As on the eve of the March elections, he exuded confidence. Addressing Germans on the radio, he commanded all shoppers to "defend" themselves against "troublemakers and profiteers of this treasonous smear campaign."[109] Headlines screamed, "The World-wide Jewish Campaign against Germany!" and "Foreign Jewry Calls for Murder!" Automobiles displayed signs, "Jewry Declares War against Germany!" and "The Jews Are Our Misfortune!" Posters told German women shoppers to avoid Jewish businesses. "For 14 years you, German women, have marched shoulder to shoulder with the brown front against the Jews . . . The battle is hard and relentless. Personal considerations must be extinguished . . . Do not spend a single penny in a Jewish business! Not only today, but forever, the Jew must be expelled from the *Volk* and state!"[110] On April 1 pairs of SA men were to station themselves in front of all "Jewish" businesses to prevent potential customers and clients from entering.[111]

The Jewish literary scholar Viktor Klemperer wrote in his diary on March 30: "Mood as before a pogrom in the depths of the Middle Ages or in deepest Czarist Russia. We are hostages."[112] Rabbi Leo Baeck observed that a thousand years of Jewish history in Germany had come to an end.[113] Neither of them, however, considered leaving. No one knew what to expect. "The scene here is capable of changing with such kaleidoscopic rapidity . . . that one must constantly bear in mind the evil possibilities which are latent in the situation," wrote George A. Gordon, the interim chargé d'affaires in the U.S. Embassy.[114]

Even before it began, the boycott revealed disarray among the Nazi faithful and apathy among non-Nazis.[115] What made a business "Jewish"—its stockholders, its name, or its owners? Why, zealots asked, were foreign-owned "Jewish" businesses, like the 82 Woolworth stores in Germany or Hollywood movies, exempted? Even some Nazis disapproved of the boycott because it was so obviously counterproductive.[116] In large cities like Cologne, which had a passionately antisemetic *Gauleiter* (regional leader), a determined cadre of Stormtroopers smashed store windows and posted signs, "Germans Defend Yourselves! Don't Buy From Jews!"[117] But where Nazism was weak, Stormtroopers left their posts, drank a few beers, and marched through the streets singing antisemitic songs. An American who walked through Berlin, for example, called the boycott "a tame affair," adding, "I still feel that the majority of the people on the street were inclined to treat the matter as more or less of a joke (if they were not personally involved!) and that they will continue to buy at their favorite stores regardless of the boycott."[118] Ordinary Germans were divided between, as one witness recalled ominously, those who "shook their heads" in disgust and those who "cursed the Jews."[119]

After disappointing results, Goebbels proclaimed victory. "The Reich government is pleased to announce that the counter-boycott against the agitation of Germany's enemies has been a success."[120] But to a British journalist he admitted, "The weapon of a defensive boycott if used too often can only become blunt. The influence of German Jews must be limited through other incremental measures."[121] The national boycott was never repeated. Having authorized it, Hitler said nothing about Jewish policy in public until he announced the Nuremberg Racial Laws in September 1935.[122] A *Business Week* reporter concluded, "The best informed authorities in Berlin expect a steady decline of jingoist action against the Jews." A conservative British journalist concurred: "Herr Hitler has not inaccurately been called the most moderate member of his own party."[123]

Adapting to domestic and foreign disapproval, Nazi leaders experimented with what contemporaries called a "cold pogrom." Quotas, preferential status for non-Jews, and restrictive membership clauses in occupational and social organizations institutionalized "respectable" antisemitism. At first, the measures seemed confused. "The harsh and ridiculous are being indiscriminately mingled in Germany to-day," wrote a British reporter. Among many absurdities, he noted that "Jewish medical students (in so far as any Jews are permitted still to study medicine) are not to be allowed to dissect non-Jewish corpses."[124] In Cologne and Berlin, municipal officials terminated Jewish physicians' right to reimbursement from the national medical insurance program *(Krankenkasse)*. In Thuringia and Cologne, service and construction contracts with Jewish firms were canceled. Some Christian parents withdrew their children from classes taught by Jewish teachers.[125] A Nazi criminal refused to be tried by a Jewish judge.[126] Conductors Bruno Walter and Otto Klemperer were not allowed to complete their concert seasons.[127] Fritz Stern noted acidly that Richard Strauss, the celebrated composer of "A Heroic Life" *(Ein Heldenleben)*, quickly stepped to the podium to replace a banished Jewish conductor.[128]

Scattershot local measures were supplemented by the national April Laws, which imposed quotas on Jewish lawyers, ended medical reimbursements for Jewish physicians, and dismissed state employees (including educators) who had Jewish ancestors. By expelling outspoken Marxists from the civil service at the same time, the antisemitic laws were presented as part of a wider "housecleaning." Laws "against overcrowding in the schools" established a *numerus clausus* for Jewish children and expelled teachers. At a time when up to a third of new graduates in the professions could not find jobs, the prospect of "clearing out" Jewish competition had an obvious appeal for non-Jews. Regional occupational associations sent letters to "esteemed colleagues" whom they believed to be Jewish, requesting them to fill out ancestry questionnaires, return their official seals, resign their membership numbers, and submit their military service records together with identification photos.[129]

The April Laws drew opposition from unexpected quarters. President Hindenburg told Hitler that the expulsion of "my old Front soldiers" with Jewish ancestors was "utter anathema to me . . . If they were worthy of being called up to fight and bleed for Germany, they ought also to be seen as worthy of remaining in their professions to serve the Fatherland."[130] In his carefully worded response, Hitler assured the president that he would exempt all frontline veterans and their children. This unexpected gesture of conciliation reassured many. Since the possibility of appeal remained, ethnic cleansing had the gloss of due process.[131] Even though vicious antisemitic outbursts continued, the existence of new laws, many softened by exception clauses, held out the hope that vulgar antisemitism could be contained.

Reactions to the cold pogrom were mixed. On May 4 George S. Messersmith described Jews' "moral suffering such as I have not seen anywhere and under any conditions heretofore."[132] Others were more sanguine. "Though thousands of Jewish professional men throughout Germany will find themselves faced with starvation, the numbers condemned to that fate are less than at first seemed probable."[133] To many, the April Laws merely formalized the kinds of exclusions common elsewhere. In the United States, for example, Hollywood actors changed their names to obscure their "racial" backgrounds, and Supreme Court Justice James McReynolds refused to speak to his fellow justices who were Jewish.[134] Rumbold, whose personal efforts aided many Jews in Germany, explained the April Laws to the Foreign Office. "Nobody could deny that the legal profession, the medical profession, and the teaching profession [in Germany] were swamped by Jews, that all the bank directorships were in their hands, that the press . . . was in their clutches, that entry into the theaters, the broadcasting corporation, not to mention the cinema, or such purely Jewish institutions as the Stock Exchange, was debarred to the blue-eyed Teutonic stock."[135] Journalists uncritically borrowed two of Hitler's favorite terms, "moral cleansing" and "purging," in their dispatches.[136] A U.S.

diplomat reported that "office-holding Jews and Gentiles of varying shades of Communistic, Socialistic and Republican belief have been dismissed with impartial thoroughness." He spoke of "German racial culture" and added "cleaning out" to his vocabulary.[137] The ease with which foreigners accepted the cold pogrom suggests something of their own assumptions about Jews.

After April 1933, daily life seemed more orderly for most Jewish citizens.[138] Ignoring the jeers of loudmouth SA men, non-Jewish shoppers and merchants continued to patronize the businesses that offered the best quality and price, regardless of the ethnicity of storeowners. Patients who could pay for their own medical treatment consulted their Jewish family doctors as they always had. Jewish war veterans, called "Hindenburg exceptions," remained at their posts. Of 4,585 Jewish lawyers in Germany, two thirds kept their positions because they had fought at the front.[139] Truancy laws meant that only Jewish children who resided near Jewish schools (of which there were very few) were expelled from public schools. A fateful pattern was established: after devastating physical violence against Jews, the regime curbed unsanctioned racial attacks and in their place enacted antisemitic laws. Many victims and bystanders failed to appreciate the threat of these bureaucratic strategies that in the long run proved far more lethal than sporadic attacks.

An eyewitness who later left Germany recalled his countrymen's reactions. "The people did not seem very enthusiastic, but nobody did anything about it."[140] Some of the best evidence for Germans' general indifference toward Nazi antisemitism appears in Gestapo reports that complain about peasants who refused to switch to Aryan dealers because they saw no reason to place ideology above profit, especially in hard times.[141] The virulently antisemitic tabloid *Der Stürmer (The Stormtrooper)* printed hundreds of indignant letters from readers describing shoppers who forced their way past SA guards and denigrating wives of local Nazi leaders and civil servants who continued to "shop Jewish."

While most Germans did not endorse radical anti-Jewish measures, militant Nazis felt empowered to persecute Jews at will. Despite orders for restraint, they smashed windows at night and scrawled graffiti near Jewish homes. Hitler Youth members taunted Jews in the street with "Yid" or "Jewish Pig" *(Judensau).*[142] Roving gangs of Nazi hoodlums assaulted Jews and their property. Nazi leaders, like other successful revolutionaries, confronted a dilemma: the violence that fed their most loyal followers repelled the newcomers on whom political stability rested.

As the chief of a powerful state, with a sophisticated media network, Hitler deployed the politics of virtue to detach his persona from party radicals and reach out directly to the *Volk*. To achieve the broad consensus on which his continued power would rest, Hitler in effect de-Nazified his public image by refining the myth of his personal virtue and summoning his *Volk* to celebrate ethnic revival.

Allies in the Academy

We see the goal of philosophy in servitude . . . The Führer has awakened this will in the whole nation and has fused it into *one single* will.
No one can be absent on the day when he displays his will! Hail Hitler!

—*Martin Heidegger,* Bekenntnis der Professoren, *1933*

Three months after Hitler was named chancellor, Karl Jaspers greeted his
friend Martin Heidegger, who came to visit him in Heidelberg. In his
memoirs, Jaspers recalled, "I went to Heidegger's room to welcome him.
'It's just like 1914 . . .' I began, intending to continue: 'again this deceptive
mass intoxication,' but when I saw Heidegger radiantly agreeing with my
first words, the rest stuck in my throat . . . Face to face with Heidegger,
himself gripped by that intoxication, I failed. I did not tell him that he
was on the wrong road." Jaspers continued, "I no longer trusted his transformed nature at all. I felt a threat to myself in view of the violence in
which Heidegger now participated."[1]

Heidegger was not alone in being "gripped by that intoxication." The
American theologian Reinhold Niebuhr, who witnessed the tumult firsthand, wrote, "It is difficult for an outside observer who has not breathed
the atmosphere in Germany to imagine the intensity of feeling which
has accompanied recent events here."[2] A modern democracy had been
taken over by a party that only five years before had been a disreputable
fringe movement that had attracted less than six percent of all voters. The
achievement seemed scarcely credible.

Disbelief translated into the conviction that the Hitler phenomenon
would die out quickly. British Ambassador Horace Rumbold had predicted
that the educated elites would never yield. "The entire intelligentsia of
the country, its scientists, writers, artists, the Bar, the Church, the universities are, with very few exceptions, ranged against this [Nazi] minority."[3]
In late March, Rumbold still believed they would hold out. "It was comparatively easy to convert the unemployed and the youth of both sexes,
the peasants and small shopkeepers. It will be a much more difficult task
to persuade the intelligentsia."[4] Rumbold could understand that 850,000
citizens, in a nation of 65,000,000, had joined the Nazi Party. And given
the chaotic political situation, it was not surprising that 17,300,000 Ger-

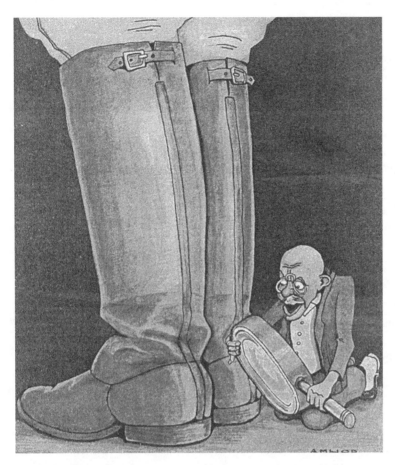

7. "The Nit Picker." Although many academics (among them Heidegger, Schmitt, and Kittel) welcomed Nazi rule, Nazi humorists continued to ridicule pusillanimous professors whose concern for petty details blinded them to the achievements of a militantly masculine regime.

mans would vote for Nazi candidates. But seasoned observers could not imagine how intellectuals would be attracted to a politician who regularly made them the butt of his wisecracks—ridiculing them as "eggheads" and "despondent weaklings" plagued with self-doubt. Why would tenured professors in German universities welcome the dictatorship of a man who had dropped out of school before finishing his secondary education, who at age 44 had never held a steady job except for four years in the military, and who had never been elected to public office? At least part of the answer to these questions may be found in the generational appeal of a resoundingly militarist movement. Paradoxically, the sudden embrace of Nazism by three distinguished academics who had not served in the Great War illustrates the immense appeal of a stridently masculine political movement among the very intellectuals Rumbold believed would hold out against Nazism.

The biographical trajectories of the philosopher Martin Heidegger, the political theorist Carl Schmitt, and the theologian Gerhard Kittel illuminate the sources of Hitler's popularity among highly educated Germans who had not supported the Nazis before January 1933. Having "converted" to Nazism, these three academics openly endorsed not only Hitler's dictatorship but his antisemitism as well.[5] It is impossible to ascertain the mix of idealism, self-delusion, and opportunism that prompted each man to embrace Nazi rule. But being public intellectuals, Heidegger, Schmitt, and Kittel left a paper trail that documents their early responses to the regime. Before 1933, these men had worked closely with Jewish colleagues and students; and, whatever prejudices they harbored, racism did not mark their scholarship. Within months of Hitler's takeover, however, they called for the expulsion of ethnic outsiders from the body politic. As widely admired professors with no prior record of supporting Nazism, Heidegger, Schmitt, and Kittel enjoyed higher credibility than did sycophants like Alfred Rosenberg and Joseph Goebbels.[6] Unlike most of the old fighters, who spewed coarse racism, these newcomers supplied the rudiments of Hitler's "rational" antisemitism which, before 1933, had been lacking.

The reactions of these three quite different men illustrate the ecumenical attractiveness of a charismatic force so plastic that listeners could fashion their own myths of the Führer. To Heidegger, Hitler was authenticity personified, to Schmitt he was a decisive leader, and to Kittel, a Christian soldier. The differences in their views of Hitler reminds us that the muddled doctrine denigrated as vapid by Hitler's opponents contributed to the resilience of the "Hitler myth." Three very different ideas of what constituted Nazism converged on one point—the desire for moral rejuvenation of the *Volk*—even as Nazi paramilitaries destroyed the civil society of the Weimar Republic.

Heidegger, Schmitt, and Kittel were born within a year of one another (and of Hitler) in 1888–1889. During the first world war, their generation had experienced the euphoria of national unity and heard the summons to sacrifice for national survival.[7] Seventeen million men served in the military. Two million died, and four million were severely disabled.[8] While their comrades served at the front, Heidegger, Schmitt, and Kittel dedicated their immense talents to their academic careers, becoming respected Herr Doktor Professor at a relatively young age. They did not share the experiences of peers who returned from the trenches, as Erich Maria Remarque put it in *All Quiet on the Western Front,* "weary, broken, burnt out, rootless and without hope."[9] But they encountered these men in their classes, and they mourned friends who had died in battle. Like most of their academic colleagues, they felt alienated from Weimar democracy and the modernist culture of the 1920s.[10] Perhaps because they had not served in the trenches, the three professors looked on the German soldier with special awe. They admired the war hero and best-selling author Ernst Jünger (Heidegger and Schmitt counted him among their close friends) and despised Remarque's pacifism.[11] Their academic prose bristled with bellicose metaphors and praise of strength, valor, sacrifice, and honor.

After remaining aloof from political engagement in the Weimar Republic, Heidegger, Schmitt, and Kittel joined the throngs cheering the Nazi takeover in 1933. Although they were not among the 300 professors who signed a petition endorsing Hitler's rule in March, within two months all three had become Nazi Party members.[12] They fell into a category that old fighters disparaged as "late bloomers" or "March victims" because they succumbed to Nazism only after the real battle was over.[13] Nazi Party membership brought enhanced opportunities (such as funding for racial studies and job openings created by the purge of ethnically or politically "unwanted" individuals), but Heidegger, Schmitt, and Kittel, with their secure university professorships, did not need these advantages.[14] Over the next several years, each of the three was disappointed in one or another aspect of Nazism, but none criticized Nazi policy or allowed his party membership to lapse. After 1945 all three disavowed the intensity of their faith in Nazism, but they never publicly regretted their support for Hitler or their embrace of a doctrine that was not only authoritarian and nationalist but genocidal.

As a boy growing up in a southwestern German village, Martin Heidegger's evident aptitude had won his teachers' attention. Financial aid from the Catholic Church enabled him to attend the rigorous Konradihaus boarding school on Lake Constance. In 1909, at age twenty, Heidegger entered the theological seminary in nearby Freiburg im Breisgau. Because of health problems, and possibly religious doubts, he withdrew from the seminary and prepared for an academic career. Dependent on the Church for financial support and yet beginning to question it as an institution, Heidegger pursued his studies. This was a tempestuous period, during which he became secretly engaged to be married, wrote poetry and literary criticism, and considered becoming a mathematician.[15] Although he did not interrupt his scholarly career, his poems suggest he experienced an emotional crisis.[16]

After the war, Heidegger would talk about having volunteered for military service in 1914. However, a university personnel officer looking for Heidegger's pension records during the 1920s failed to verify his claim, and later research revealed that after being conscripted in 1914 Heidegger was deemed unfit for military service because of a weak heart and neurasthenia. Besides being scorned as "shirkers," such men were assigned to war-related jobs that kept them far from the troops so that their "mobilization psychosis" would not infect others.[17] Heidegger's contribution to the war effort consisted of working for the censorship division of the local post office and serving briefly in a meteorological unit during the final months of the war.[18]

Although students and professors in Freiburg formed an association to support the war effort, Heidegger seems scarcely to have noticed the war fever of the time, although upon learning of a close friend's death in battle, he dedicated his next monograph to his memory.[19] As a man of short stature (about five feet, four inches) and apparently plagued by poor health, Heidegger stood at the sidelines.[20] A former student recalled, "It seems to me that he was—to use the common slogan—not a 'soldierly type,'" whose failure to serve at the front "no doubt contributed to elevate the experience of the front-line soldier to the status of a heroic myth."[21]

The war years were eventful for Heidegger in personal terms. After breaking his secret engagement, Heidegger married Elfride Petri, a student at Freiburg who came from an affluent Protestant Prussian family. Soon after they were married, he renounced the Catholic Church but not his Catholic faith.[22] Thanks to the endorsement of his mentor, Edmund Husserl, the young philosopher secured a post at Marburg University. Perhaps falling in with the mood of his veteran-students, Heidegger railed against the stultifying atmosphere of the hierarchical university structure. In the tradition of Nietzsche, Schopenhauer, and Kierkegaard, he lashed out against its strictures; but unlike them, he remained within its protective walls. In his lectures on Plato as well as in passages of his 1927 masterpiece, *Being and Time,* Heidegger described his hopes for a revived university that could break free of complacency and incite a "spiritual renewal of life in its entirety." Renouncing the nihilism of many cultural critics, Heidegger searched for an authentic ground, a confrontation with mortality and conscience.[23] Heidegger defined himself during these years as a "Christian *theologian*" (emphasis in the original) rather than a philosopher.

From all reports, Heidegger was a charismatic and unconventional professor. When Jaspers first met him in 1920, he was struck by his "urgent and terse manner of speaking." A graduate student recalled, "Heidegger cultivated an entirely different style with his students . . . We went on excursions together, hikes and ski trips." In his lectures he would pause to solicit students' reactions.[24] He cast the student-teacher relationship as a battle or struggle between a wise elder and his questioning student. Though intensely masculine and competitive in academic settings, Heidegger's intimate letters from the 1920s brimmed with the overwrought and sentimental language of his student poetry.[25] rugged + strong

When discussing philosophy, Heidegger dramatized his prose with terms like "struggle" (*Kampf* or *kämpferisch*), "crisis," "upheaval," "following" (*Folgen*), and "leadership" (*Führertum*).[26] He rendered his own life as a series of duels against Catholic dogma, philosophical convention, rugged ski trails and mountain paths, and academic hierarchy. As a young man, Heidegger had described evil as night, darkness, a yawning void. The "nothingness" terrified him, and yet it also lured him because, he believed, existence (*Dasein*) itself was born in night and nothingness. The daylight of culture transfigures the dark and enables individuals to rise to the good. As a philosopher, Heidegger pledged to "break free of the idols that everyone has and to which they habitually sneak away."

The youthful iconoclast subjected the academic world as well as conventional philosophy to withering criticism. Several years later, one of Heidegger's students observed that the "power of the fascination that emanated from him was partly based on his impenetrable nature . . . only half of him was an academic. The other, and probably greater, half was a militant and a preacher who knew how to interest people by antagonizing them."[27] In his lectures, Heidegger expressed the hope that a "trinity of priests, soldiers, and statesmen" would save the nation. His sense of impending crisis did not take on partisan shadings in the lecture hall, but it appears that after 1931 he began to admire Hitler. A guest at one of Heidegger's weekend outings with his students recalled his wife's favorable remarks about Nazism and added that Heidegger "doesn't understand much about politics, and that is probably why his detestation of all mediocre compromises leads him to expect great things of the party that promises to do something decisive . . . to oppose communism."[28] In 1929 the philosopher exhibited overt racial prejudice—as far as records reveal, for the first time—in a letter to the Ministry of Education complaining about "the growing Judaization *[Verjudung]*" of university life.[29]

Within weeks of Hitler's appointment as chancellor, Heidegger joined a committee formed by Ernst Krieck, the ardently anti-intellectual Nazi educational theorist. Shortly afterward, Heidegger spoke out forcefully against the "homelessness of blind relativism" and called for "German scholarship that was informed by its ethical responsibility for truth." To Jaspers he wrote, "One must involve oneself . . . A philosopher's duty is to act as a participant in history."[30] In April Heidegger was nominated for the post of rector of Freiburg University, an honor for which he campaigned with the approval of local Nazi leaders. In part because colleagues with Jewish ancestry and leftists did not attend the election meeting, the vote for Heidegger was overwhelming.[31] Heidegger set out to use the rectorship as a steppingstone to further participation on a national level.[32]

One of Heidegger's first public lectures as rector was a eulogy for the Nazi martyr Leo Schlageter, whom Hitler also admired. Like Heidegger, Schlageter had been raised in the Black Forest and had studied at the Konradihaus. On the tenth anniversary of Schlageter's execution, Heidegger memorialized the youthful martyr's "hardness and clarity" and imagined how the rugged local landscape had sustained him as he faced death "alone and abandoned by his *Volk*." In sermon-like cadences, Heidegger asked the audience to allow his memory to "stream through them."[33]

On the day after his Schlageter eulogy, the new rector delivered his inaugural address. Those in attendance received not only invitations but instructions explaining when to shout the Nazi greeting, "Sieg Heil!" and the text of the Nazi marching anthem, the "Horst Wessel Lied"—much as worshippers might receive guides to a Sunday service. The professors filed in, resplendent in their academic robes. Decidedly untraditional was the large complement of brown-shirted Nazis. Heidegger, dressed in an open-collar shirt and hiking knickers, issued a resounding "call to arms, an intellectual summons" and ordered an enthusiastic "stepping-into-line with the times." Heidegger's joy at the demise of what he saw as Weimar's superficial democracy was reflected in the word "essence" *(Wesen),* which punctuated his speech—as in "the essence of truth," the "primordial essence of science," a "will to essence," and a "kind of knowing that has forgotten its own essence." His syntax was as fuzzy as his emotions were clear. In martial cadences, Heidegger called for "spiritual legislation" to

8. Martin Heidegger's restyled moustache and black shirt may suggest his admiration for Hitler and perhaps also nostalgia for the Catholic faith of his youth.

"tear down barriers between departments and smash the stagnation and falseness of superficial professional training."[34] His speech was redolent with forceful language—"overthrow," "danger," "relentless clarity," "discipline," "last-ditch stand," and "force." Old assumptions would be "shattered." Students and faculty would form a "battle community" *(Kampfgemeinschaft)* that fused labor, power, and knowledge.[35]

Heidegger celebrated the "blood-bound strength, the power that most deeply arouses and most profoundly shakes the existence of the *Volk*." His audience could not have misunderstood the racial innuendo when he contrasted the "primordially attuned" spirit *(Geist)* with the "empty cleverness," "noncommittal play of wit," and "the boundless drift of rational dissection." His only direct quotation came not from philosophy but from Carl von Clausewitz's *On War*. Calling for a sweeping curricular reform, Heidegger proposed that work camps and military service should have equal academic weight with the traditional arts and sciences. The young applauded wildly. The professors barely clapped.

Jaspers, sitting in the front row, was among the unenthusiastic. After a festive reception, the two friends conversed about national and intellectual life. Later Jaspers, aghast at his friend's enthusiasm, asked, "How can

9. Heinrich Hoffmann enhanced the image of Hitler as a creative genius through his artistic rendering of Hitler's hands. This photograph was included in one of the mass-market booklets designed to afford Germans a close-up glimpse of their new Führer. At the dawn of celebrity journalism, Hoffmann demonstrated a flair for innovative public relations strategies.

so uneducated a man as Hitler rule Germany?" "Education is quite irrelevant," Heidegger responded. "Just look at his wonderful hands." The remark might seem entirely out of character for a distinguished philosopher, except for the fact that Hitler's personal photographer, Heinrich Hoffmann, had endowed Hitler's hands with iconic status in mass-market publications. His comment suggests that Heidegger, the lofty thinker, had imbibed the popular culture of the day. Then Jaspers asked Heidegger how he could put up with the Nazis' antisemitism. Wasn't *The Protocols of the Elders of Zion* sheer nonsense? Evasively, Heidegger spoke about a "dangerous international conspiracy." Jaspers concluded sadly, "Heidegger himself appeared to have undergone a complete transformation."[36]

Over the summer, Heidegger worked on university reform with a national commission in Berlin and lectured in support of Nazism at major universities. At a public lecture in Heidelberg, Heidegger joined Carl Schmitt and the Nazi Party's racial expert, Walter Gross, in a summons to "struggle."[37] In October Heidegger led his non-Jewish male graduate students (most in Nazi uniforms) on a five-day knowledge retreat *(Wissenschaftslager)* at his mountain cabin. Heidegger signed his letters "Heil Hitler!" He asked his Jewish students to find other mentors and cut off their financial aid. When his own mentor, Husserl, who was Jewish, died in 1937, Heidegger did not attend the funeral or send a condolence card to his widow.

In autumn of 1933, Heidegger and eight internationally respected German academics contributed brief statements to an elegant booklet justifying Hitler's leadership. In a pugnacious question-and-answer format, Heidegger took on critics. Was Nazism a "return to barbarism . . . the dawn of lawlessness . . . a smashing up of tradition? NO!" Nazism stood for order. Did Hitler act from dishonest motives? Again, "NO." "It was not ambition, not avarice for glory, or blind stubbornness and striving, but only the pure will to be responsible to ourselves . . . that commanded our Führer to leave the 'League of Nations.'" Against the worn-out democracies, Heidegger praised the "manly self-reliance" of the new regime and looked forward to the "eruption of a refined youth that has turned back to its roots." Their commitment to the state "will make this nation hard against itself."[38]

Heidegger, who in the 1920s had defined himself as a Christian theologian in search of authenticity, saw in Hitler the embodiment of the ethnic regeneration for which he had longed. Karl Löwith, who had studied with Heidegger in the 1920s, compared this longing for authenticity to Carl

Schmitt's admiration for a decisive leader.[39] In August 1933 Heidegger suggested to Schmitt that the two collaborate. "The gathering of the spiritual forces, which should bring about what is to come, is becoming more urgent everyday."[40] Little appears to have come of the proposal, but Heidegger's invitation suggests an affinity between the two. Like Heidegger, Schmitt embraced conflict in his theoretical works, praising Thomas Hobbes's affirmation of struggle as the very essence of society. In supporting the Third Reich, Schmitt condemned diversity because a monolithic *Volk* could more successfully compete against rivals than a factionalized state. Widely acclaimed as being among the two or three most original political theorists of the twentieth century, Schmitt's public enthusiasm for Nazism and his obdurate refusal to recant after 1945 have vexed admirers and detractors alike.

Schmitt, like Heidegger, had grown up in a provincial Catholic home; but unlike Heidegger, who was raised in a predominantly Catholic region, Schmitt lived in heavily Protestant Westfalia. As a law student, his concern about the moral condition of contemporary society found an unusual outlet in biting satires of pompous intellectuals, published in an antisemitic Bavarian periodical. Collaborating with a friend who was Jewish, Schmitt lampooned modern culture, with its "Jewish" parvenus and other stereotypes, in the kind of "polite" antisemitism common throughout Western Europe.[41] In contrast to the turgid academic prose fashionable at the time, Schmitt developed a staccato and lucid style that in later years he dubbed "dada before its time" *(dada avant la lettre).*

When war broke out in 1914, Schmitt, who at age 27 had a secure civil service job and a major academic examination to prepare for, did not enlist. After passing his exams and finishing his third monograph, he volunteered in February 1915, and during basic training secured a desk job with the army's legal division in Munich. Later, Schmitt would reminisce about a fall from a horse while serving in an elite equestrian regiment; but his account has not been documented. Some have wondered how he so quickly attained junior officer status and how a rather short man from northwestern Germany could have served in the honor guard of a Bavarian regiment in the first place.[42]

While (in his words) "the European world tore itself apart" and was laid waste by "the material and metaphysical ravages of war," Schmitt plunged into the bohemian subculture of Schwabing in Munich and mingled with avant garde authors, expressionist painters, and dada artists. He corresponded with Eugenio Pacelli (later Pius XII) and the pacifist Henri

Barbusse, attended lectures by the social theorist Max Weber, and wrote literary criticism. He also cultivated his acquaintance with the Serbian-German poet Theodor Däubler, who was known for his uncouth manner, immense bulk, and slovenly dress. In *Northern Lights,* his hyperbolic 1,200-page poem, Däubler's verbal cascades evoked not only Dante, Goethe, Nietzsche, ancient Persian lore, and Biblical imagery but also Wagnerian opera and avant-garde painting. Schmitt distilled Däubler's nearly impenetrable verse into a terse 66-page essay that explicated its poetic battles between knights and dragons, sun and moon, forces of light and darkness.[43] Uncovering the essential messages beneath Däubler's teeming prose, Schmitt perceived a terrible striving for unity. Referring to the ancient Persian myths in Däubler's saga, Schmitt wrote words that could have applied to Germany in 1916. Instead of striving for unity, "the *Volk* pushes itself on, instinctively wanting to submit and letting itself be whipped."[44]

Schmitt blended aesthetics and ethics with his loathing for modernity, which to him meant crass materialism.[45] Never, he resolved, would he settle into bourgeois life—a hollow world of "traffic, technology, organization . . . [in which] people are interested in everything, but enthusiastic about nothing."[46] Without religion to teach people to differentiate between good and evil, secular culture left them adrift among warring forces. "In place of the distinction between good and evil there appeared a sublime contrast between utility and destruction."[47] Schmitt (who later described himself as a *katechon*, Greek for "a force that holds the anti-Christ at bay") searched for transcendent virtue. During his Schwabing years, he fell in love with and married Pawla Dorotić, a Viennese woman who claimed noble Serbian descent and shocked even Schwabing artists with her emancipated ways. The young husband took the unusual step of adding her surname to his own, publishing under the name Carl Schmitt-Dorotić.

When the war ended and Communist revolution broke out in Munich, Schmitt abandoned bohemian Schwabing and divorced his wife. In 1924 he remarried and broke with the Church.[48] Thanks to his colleague and friend the economist Moritz Julius Bonn, he obtained a teaching position in Munich, where he became known for the taut logic and lucid style of his lectures and writings. With his Schwabing phase behind him, the young professor epitomized the well-dressed, stiff but cordial German professor. Although he had mocked Jewish culture as a youth, nothing suggests that Schmitt evaluated individuals in terms of their ethnic back-

brute

lack of record of anti semitism but was anti-semitic

ground. In 1928, for example, he dedicated one of his most important books, *Constitutional Principles*, to the memory of Fritz Eisler, a Jewish friend from his student days who had died in battle in 1914.

In lucid monographs, Schmitt shrewdly diagnosed the shortcomings of parliamentary democracy. He denounced as hypocritical the claim that elected leaders stood above conflict. The purported neutrality of the state served only to mask the endemic struggle for power among enemy interest groups.[49] For Schmitt, the very idea of universal rights embodied in the League of Nations was anathema because it produced a cacophony of contending values and claims. Similarly, in domestic politics, pluralism produced so many opinions that, in a crisis, when only decisive action could save the day, disputatious politicians wasted precious time in fruitless debate. As he watched the paralysis of Weimar politics during the world economic crisis, he accused politicians of being so contentious that they would rather allow their nation to collapse than cut off debate.

Human history, Schmitt insisted, originated with Cain and Abel, not Adam and Eve.[50] Unlike conventional political theorists, who thought in terms of static political forms, Schmitt located the "political" in the give-and-take of concrete power struggles. Just as aesthetics distinguishes between beauty and ugliness and ethics divides good from bad, "the specific political distinction to which political actions and motives can be reduced is that between friend and enemy."[51] In an often-quoted phrase written after 1945, he declared, "Tell me who your enemy is, and I will tell you who you are."[52] According to the political theorist Leo Strauss, Schmitt's writings in the 1920s already showed signs of a love of conflict that would become more obvious during the Third Reich.[53]

In 1932 Schmitt had an opportunity to apply his theory of absolutism to a political crisis that developed as the result of a reactionary coup d'état in Prussia. The forceful arguments in Schmitt's legal brief defending the coup attracted Hermann Göring's attention.[54] Upon learning that Hitler had become chancellor, Schmitt noted merely, "Irritated and yet somehow relieved."[55] Several colleagues in the Prussian government swore allegiance to Hitler and urged Schmitt to do the same. On May 1 Schmitt wrote, "I became a P.M. [party member] 298,860. Since the end of April 1933 I have been active with the Cologne group. There was a long line. I had myself registered like many others."[56]

Within days of Schmitt's joining the Nazi Party, on the night of May 10, Nazi students at all German universities burned books by Jewish authors. Schmitt cheered them on in an article for a regional National Socialist

women?
what was their belief

newspaper. He rejoiced that the "un-German spirit" and "anti-filth" of a decadent age had been burned out and urged the gov to annul the citizenship of German exiles (whose books were bur cause they aided the "enemy." "Writing in German does not make Jewish authors German any more than counterfeit German money makes the forger German."[57] In a style reminiscent of his youthful satires, Schmitt sneered that anyone who appreciated Jewish authors was unmanly. "Our educated grandmothers and aunts would read, with tears in their bourgeois eyes, verses by Heinrich Heine that they mistook for German." Schmitt had only one criticism of the book burners: they had consigned too few authors to the flames. Instead of burning only "un-German" writers' books, they should have included writings by non-Jewish authors who had been influenced by Jewish ideas in the sciences and professions (in which, he alleged, Jewish influence was both strong and pernicious). As a savvy newcomer to Nazi politics, Schmitt may have intuited that outspoken racism was a way to demonstrate the depth of his commitment to the movement, or he simply may have felt free to express prejudice when it was no longer taboo. Whatever his motives, a distinguished professor's endorsement of book burning contributed to Hitler's bid for respectability.

Schmitt's next contribution was a cogently written pamphlet for general readers, *State, Volk, and Movement: The Threefold Division of Political Unity,* in which he justified Hitler's dictatorship in theoretical terms. First, he defined politics itself as the battle between ethnic friend and foe.[58] Schmitt succinctly branded political liberalism and "asphalt culture" (code for Jewish influence) as a weakness that only the "ruthless will" of a decisive Führer could eliminate.[59] Second, he asked what Nazi society would look like. Its two constituent qualities were "homogeneity" and "authenticity." In place of squabbling politicians, German power would impose a single ethnic *(völkish)* will. Avoiding the term "Jew" and using "non-Aryan" sparingly, Schmitt celebrated the "essential sameness" and "homogeneity" *(Artgleichheit* and *Gleichartigkeit)* which unified ethnic Germans in the new community *(Volksgemeinschaft).*[60] The imperative that all citizens be *gleich* (which means both "same" and "equal") vindicated the expulsion of Germans with Jewish ancestors from public institutions. The demand for homogeneity, he wrote, evoked a "deeper" meaning than administrative "Nazification" *(Gleichschaltung).* He welcomed "the purification of public life of all non-Aryan, essentially foreign elements so that . . . coming generations of Germans will be pure . . . No alien type can interfere with this great and profound, but also inner—I would almost say intimate—process of growth . . . Our most important task is to learn how to distinguish friend from enemy . . . [We must] cleanse public life of non-Aryan, foreign elements."[61] With democracy crushed, Schmitt called for an ethnically pure nation.

In opposition to the universalist moral beliefs of both his Catholic upbringing and his neo-Kantian training, Schmitt worked out a theory of justice bound to the *Volk*, not to legal codes. Every ethnic community develops the legal values appropriate to its "blood and soil" *(Blut und Boden)*. In Schmitt's view, authenticity, defined as allegiance to one's *Volk*, accounted for more than abstract universals as the basis of morality and the law. Schmitt expected the political leadership to enforce moral behavior among its ethnically homogeneous subjects.[62] Although he rarely mentioned Hitler by name, Schmitt left no doubt about the identity of the forceful leader whom he expected to cleanse society (not just the state) of corrosive elements. Despite Schmitt's embrace of struggle, he welcomed the end of conflict in German political life. After years of corrosive political wrangling, ethnic Germans once again lived within an overarching trinity, which he described variously as "heart, brain, and feelings" and "understanding, soul, and intellect." Schmitt (who had written a monograph entitled *Political Theology*) envisioned a political sphere so vast and so absolute that it resembled medieval Catholicism.

The pentimento of Schmitt's (and Heidegger's) formal philosophy reveals traces of religious devotion—expressed as a dream of ethnic wholeness that could stave off corrosive modernity. Gerhard Kittel developed an antisemitic theology that complemented Schmitt's political theory and Heidegger's philosophy. Kittel had grown up in an academic family. Although his monographs were forgotten soon after his death in 1948, his authoritative ten-volume *Theological Dictionary of the New Testament* remained a key research tool for decades. Like Heidegger and Schmitt, Kittel as a student had been drawn to philosophical polarities. Although other Protestant theologians, like Emanuel Hirsch and Paul Althans, also embraced Nazism, only Kittel placed his erudition so squarely in the service of antisemitism.

Kittel grew up in Leipzig and, following in his distinguished father's footsteps, studied Protestant theology. Having completed his Ph.D. and post-doctoral studies on Jewish society at the time of Christ, Kittel was 26 when war broke out in 1914. While lecturing at the University of Kiel, he served as a Navy chaplain and wrote a commentary on "Jesus as Pastor" in which he praised Jesus for rejecting a rabbinical life of textual exegesis and instead becoming a minister *(Seelsorger)* among his *Volk*. In 1917 Kittel accepted a position at the University of Leipzig, where his father had just been appointed rector.[63] Like Heidegger and Schmitt, he did not see active duty at the front.

In his research, Kittel explored the similarities between Jewish texts and Christian parables, miracles, moral commandments, and folk sayings.[64] His enthusiasm for the Hebrew Bible reflected his father's liberalism but, like many academics in his generation, Kittel felt alienated from the Weimar Republic. As a student and young professor, he belonged to the reactionary German Christian Student Movement and edited a monograph series that reconciled Christianity with ethnic *(völkish)* traditions.[65] Like Schmitt and Heidegger, Kittel grappled with philosophical oppositions—in his case, the tension between piety (which he associated with faith) and learning (which he linked to reason).[66] During the 1920s Kittel wrote several monographs dedicated to reconciling Christianity and Judaism and compiled his theological lexicon. Despite poor health, he attended international conferences in Stockholm, London, and Vienna.

More than other Biblical scholars at the time, Kittel encouraged Jewish-Christian collaboration and took the unusual step of studying at two rabbinical institutes because, as he said, "All Christian culture and all Christian ethics have their roots in the moral consciousness of Old Testament piety."[67] In his dissertation he had thanked a mentor who was a Jewish scholar, and he dedicated a book in 1926 to a recently deceased Jewish colleague. Criticizing his colleagues' antisemitism, he urged "the members of our theological guild . . . to accept Rabbinic scholarship as integral to our studies—and not treat them, as we do now, like rare and often awkward *[umbequem]* birds."[68] Let us, he wrote, "work hand in hand" together. Although his alleged philosemitism angered some Christians, Kittel insisted that Jesus not only belonged to the Jewish "*Volk*, nationality and religion" but that his ethics, the heart of his teachings, grew directly out of Jewish culture.[69] Judaic theology provided, in Kittel's metaphor, the very "fountain from which Our Lord drank."

Liberals welcomed Kittel's open-mindedness in a generally conservative field.[70] As a Christian theologian, he took the superiority of Christianity over Judaism for granted, but he dismissed as pointless the sterile debates about the relative merits of either tradition.[71] In 1929 Kittel defined the relationship between Christian and Jew along four axes, three of which were positive ("heritage, Old Testament origins, and inner roots"). The fourth, "fundamental opposition," did not engage him until 1933, after which time he forgot the first three.[72]

In June 1933, within weeks of joining the Nazi Party, Kittel reversed his views of the "Jewish Question" at the fiftieth anniversary of the Christian association he had joined as a university student. Confessing to a "certain unease" when the topic of antisemitism came up, Kittel described how educated elites would observe random signs of Jewry's pernicious influence. But, because they lacked an analytic framework within which to grasp the meaning of what they saw, they would only make trivial jokes. The time had come for these sophisticates to heed the blunt antisemitism of *Volk* wisdom.[73] In his disjointed preamble, Kittel acknowledged that hostility to Jews might seem immoral. Christ, after all, not only commanded "humane" treatment of all people but preached the gospel of brotherly love. Kittel spoke out boldly to quiet the antisemite's "guilty conscience."

Like the well-trained theologian he was, Kittel categorized and numbered his opinions. He identified three varieties of antisemitism: the "harmless," the "vulgar," and the "unsentimental." The "harmless antisemitism" of a bygone liberal era—espoused by effete intellectuals, artists, and liberals in snobbish cultural circles—was actually not at all trivial because these "degenerate" literati had caused the "Jewish problem" in the first place by welcoming Jews into their midst. They would tell "insider" jokes about "circumcision and other rituals," but their casual antisemitic banter did not dissuade them from marrying Jews or, as he put it, allowing a "large dose of Jewish blood" to mingle with ethnic German blood. Kittel disparaged the second type, vulgar antisemites, because their emotional but ignorant hatred produced only empty bombast.

The third approach, founded on "ice-cold reason" and erudition, offered the only hope of averting the Jewish peril. Kittel ridiculed empathy with Jews as the "sickness of sentimentality" and claimed that expulsion had been inspired by reason, knowledge, and love. "God's commandment to love does not mean he wants us to be sentimental." The time had come for a stern and masculine order. Kittel approvingly paraphrased a remark by the Nazi ideologue Gottfried Feder that "only those who have totally mastered the Jewish question are entitled to make public pronouncements."[74] After over a decade of toiling in academe, Kittel placed his Hebrew erudition at the service of the new ethnic state.

Kittel listed four approaches to the Jewish question: "utter extermination" (*Ausrottung*), Zionism, assimilation, and historically grounded segregation. He rejected the first. "Extermination by force cannot be seriously

10. "Ah Choo! My nose is full!" In German slang, to say one's nose is full meant "I've had enough!" Readers of *Nettles (Die Brennessel),* the sophisticated Nazi humor magazine, would have recognized the former British Foreign Secretary Austen Chamberlain. By falsely implying that England expelled wealthy Jewish citizens (identified by their upper-class attire), this cartoon rationalized the Nazi drive to expel Jews from Germany.

considered."[75] If the Spanish Inquisition and tsarist pogroms had failed to exterminate Jews, Germany in the twentieth century certainly would not succeed. Zionism also would fail because Palestine was so small and already inhabited by Muslims. Besides, he added, the desert environment would require hard physical labor, which Jews found distasteful. The third solution, assimilation, constituted the very worst option because Christians could not defend themselves against Jews whom they could not recognize, and Jews, who could never really be at home, would feel permanently alienated from their own heritage as well as from their adopted culture.[76]

Kittel advocated a fourth option, relegating Jews to what he called permanent "foreign status" (*Fremdlingschaft*), whereby Jews who were citizens in 1933 would live in Germany as permanent aliens. Dismissing a geographical ghetto as unworkable, he proposed de facto cultural and economic expulsion.[77] The "outcasts" would live in the dominant society but be treated in every respect as inferiors. In Kittel's terms, citizens with Jewish ancestors (no matter what their religion) would have to act like obsequious "guests" who carefully avoided offending their "hosts" and clearly identified themselves as Jews to avoid deceiving non-Jews. To illustrate his position, he used the case of a hypothetical Italian conductor at the Bayreuth Festival who returned to Italy at the end of the opera season. But Jews, because they had no home to go home to, remained and "infected" their hosts. Without using the word "parasite," the metaphor beneath his unctuous tone was obvious. But in case readers missed the subtext, he promised if a "guest" in Germany did not behave properly, then "we will mercilessly show him to the door."[78]

Presenting himself as a fearless tribune of a truth so stark that few dared to express it openly, Kittel used his knowledge of contemporary Jewish intellectual culture to discredit Judaism. He cited works by Jewish theologians Martin Buber, Hans Joachim Schoeps, and Joseph Carlebach as evidence of the purported inner emptiness of both liberal and orthodox Judaism in a secular age. Pirating the self-criticism of Jewish intellectuals like Franz Werfel and Alfred Döblin, Kittel disparaged both orthodox and reformed Judaism—the former as sterile and the latter as inauthentic. Turning the responsibility for their plight back on Jews, Kittel claimed that two thousand years of religious separatism had created an irrevocably nomadic Jewish "race" that threatened Christians and offered no solace to Jews. "Although at first glance it might appear un-Christian," Kittel insisted on the ultimate morality of his solution. Using a question-and-answer format, he asked: Was it immoral to expel people who had done no wrong? No, because anti-Jewish laws applied to collectives, and individual Jews should not take punishment personally. Recognizing the pain Christians with Jewish ancestors would experience when they lost rights that their great-grandfathers had enjoyed, Kittel acknowledged that victims might perceive sudden ostracism as unjust. But he reiterated that on balance and in the long term, Christians and Jews would be better off.

As a theologian who openly acknowledged the anguish that stigmatized people would suffer, Kittel calmed the consciences of Christians who worried about the most central ethical issue. For centuries, Christian missionaries had called on Jews to accept Christ as their Savior. To faithful converts and children of converts, he now emphasized: *"With total and unmistakable clarity, the Church must make it clear that baptism does not affect Jewish identity . . . A converted Jew does not become a German but rather a Jew-Christian."*[79] To rationalize this betrayal, Kittel used two analogies, one sexist and one racist. Quoting Saint Paul, Kittel compared Jewish and German Christians to males and females who were equal in Christ's sight despite their differing roles and status. His second parallel came from missionaries in China, India, and the United States who never expected their converts to integrate into European society. Like former slaves in the American South, Jew Christians *(Judenchristen)* would develop their own ethnically appropriate denominations. "A full Jew Christian is in every respect as completely authentic as I am, but he cannot, for particular reasons, function in German parishes."[80] One day, he explained, every "ethically principled Christian" would understand the benefit of these measures, and the "finest among the Jews" would also concur. Insisting, *"Of course, it is not correct to say such demands are anti-Christian,"* he assured readers that it was "not heartless to impose these restrictions" as long as Jew Christians behaved with "love, wisdom, and tact."[81]

A swift and thorough cleansing, Kittel reasoned, would inflict less pain than piecemeal separation. Unlike moderates who wanted to banish Jews only from certain occupations such as the media and civil service, Kittel insisted that Jews be driven out of every conceivable public pursuit because Jews would use any connection to the *Volk* as a foothold from which to expand their influence. Kittel made it clear that he expected Jews to follow the example of the Italian conductor and exit when their "guest status" expired. By leaving the timing of their departure to Jewish Christians, Kittel displaced responsibility for expulsion from Nazi persecutors to their victims. But Kittel also admonished ethnic German Christians, "We must

11. "Escape. There goes our last hope, Sigi!" Whereas some caricatures implied that the Nazi government expelled Jews, others, like this one, suggested that the Jews themselves wanted to leave. In the caption, *Ausflucht* means both an "escape" and an "excuse or alibi."

not become soft. We must not allow the continuation of conditions that have proven a failure for the German and the Jewish peoples," even though Jews would suffer "relentless hardships and extreme consequences." He admitted that "an unusually large number of Jews will find themselves in severe need and must physically starve *[aushungern]* . . . Fine, noble, and educated human beings will break down mentally and collapse because their profession has been destroyed and their source of income has vanished."[82] Kittel assured Christians with troubled consciences that affluent international Jewish welfare agencies would surely come to the rescue. Unlike Heidegger and Schmitt, who seemed oblivious to the personal pain caused by persecution, Kittel confronted it directly with ethical arguments that rationalized Jews' short-term pain in the interests of Christians' long-term benefit. For him, the continued "pollution" of ethnic German blood constituted so obvious a danger that moral hardness was the order of the day.[83]

The first printing of *The Jewish Question* sold out quickly, and a storm of criticism broke over Kittel.[84] The racism of just one scholar of Kittel's stature, in moderates' view, outweighed dozens of tirades by vulgar anti-semites like Streicher and Rosenberg. With a degree of restraint that defies imagination, Martin Buber rebuked Kittel for "defaming Judaism and Jews." Despite Buber's excessively courteous tone, Kittel responded that comparing Jewish and Christian traditions was like "comparing fish and birds." The Hebrew Bible itself validated the concept of "guest status" for outsiders.[85] How, he asked indignantly, could Buber fail to appreciate how deeply he respected Buber's Biblical translations? With each round of criticism, Kittel became more self-righteous. When *The Jewish Question* went into a second edition, he included Buber's letter and his own vehement rebuttal. Kittel only altered one line of his original text. Besides ruling out "extermination" on pragmatic grounds, he added "on Christian grounds."[86]

The personal and political trajectories of Heidegger, Schmitt, and Kittel reflected the values of a generation of middle-class German men. Like so many of their peers, these *Doktor Professoren* welcomed ethnic solidarity in a time of political confusion, economic dislocation, and cultural pluralism. In their lecture halls and scholarship they had expressed a vague longing for a harmonious community *(Gemeinschaft)*. After watching politics from the sidelines, these three powerful thinkers cast their lot with a former front-fighter who represented stridently masculine values and ethnic authenticity. It is a mark of the success of Hitler's public persona that Heidegger, Schmitt, and Kittel not only fell in with the mood of ethnic solidarity in 1933 but elaborated their own very different visions of what might be accomplished. Succumbing to the atmosphere of battle—against Communism, cultural decadence, and Jews—they embraced a virile ethos.[87]

In early 1933 the Nazi revolution galvanized the energies of these three public intellectuals as no other civic concern had. Having apparently distanced themselves from the war fever of 1914, they enthusiastically enlisted in the second nationwide mobilization of their generation. To explain their commitment, they celebrated the heroic values that elevated the community over the individual, instinct over reason, authenticity over rationality, and hardness over empathy. Against the Enlightenment faith in universal humanity, they embraced a biologized hierarchy of human value that placed Aryan over Jew and Slav, genetically healthy over "congenitally damaged," and male over female. In Hitler they perceived the rebirth of a heroism that they had scarcely acknowledged before.

Schmitt, Heidegger, and Kittel rendered a vital service to Hitler and his band of political upstarts. In 1933 Nazi leaders had not yet found an effective formula for popularizing their radical antisemitism among non-Nazis. Violence often provoked sympathy for the victims, boycotts inconvenienced and angered consumers, and the vile slogans of the Nazi press offended educated elites. Heidegger, Schmitt, and Kittel supplied a restrained alternative to the old fighters' rage against Jews, or *Judenkoller*, that neither Hitler nor his deputies could have provided. Throughout 1933 Hitler preached veritable sermons to over 20 million radio listeners in which he glorified the ethnic revival but said barely a word about Jews. At this critical juncture, while Hitler himself was silent on the subject, Heidegger, Schmitt, and Kittel stepped in to translate the Nazis' crude slogans and repellent images into intellectually respectable justifications not only for dictatorship but also for antisemitism.[88]

The ready complicity of well-educated members of the middle class saddened those colleagues and friends who were expelled from circles they had trusted. A contemporary, Joseph Levy, commented bitterly that he and his Jewish friends had not been surprised that most Germans' welcomed Nazism, "but we would have expected more courage, more integrity, from the intellectuals . . . What became of their neighborly love, their humanity?"[89] To their well-educated peers—precisely the people most likely to have Jewish friends and colleagues—Heidegger, Schmitt, and Kittel provided the moral basis for the scores of antisemitic restrictions that followed the April boycott. They advanced the values of the Nazi conscience in their praise of a communitarian ethnic utopia. Each, in his own way, contributed to the redefinition of courage as the capacity to harm the vulnerable without shirking, in the name of the *Volk*.

The Conquest of Political Culture

Our party is not an organization, but on the contrary, the embodiment of burning faith in our *Volk*.

—*Adolf Hitler, November 21, 1922*

In the slang of the 1930s, brown meant Nazi as surely as red denoted Socialist. A Frenchman cycling through Germany in the early 1930s wrote of the "brown plague." The American journalist William Shirer described 30,000 people listening to Hitler as "a brown mass." In the words of his biographer, Joseph Goebbels cast a "brown spell" over the nation. Hitler addressed his militias as "my brown SA Men," "my brown army, my brown bulwark, my brown wall." A female Nazi proudly defined herself as one of Hitler's "little brown mice." A hostile German journalist depicted the "brown beetles" that swarmed everywhere in Berlin high society.[1] By the summer of 1933 opponents spoke of the brown steamroller that had flattened public life. In a letter to a friend, the German novelist Hans Carossa sardonically described the monochromatic landscape left in its path. "There's a lot going on here in Germany: we are being laundered, purified, scrubbed, disinfected, separated, nordicized, toughened up, and, I caught myself almost adding, alienated."[2] Another observer described "the great standardizing and stamping-in machine of the state [that] . . . manufactured ready-made citizens of those who formerly held the outrageous belief that they had a right to their own lives."[3]

The lively cultural diversity that epitomized the Weimar era vanished in 1933. While victims and critics of the Third Reich decried the barren political landscape, throngs of old fighters and new converts viewed the Nazi takeover as a thrilling experience. What anti-Nazis called a steamroller, Nazis called a bandwagon. Commercial culture supplied the artifacts for the new craze. Swastika logos adorned banners, lapel pins, watch-chains, boots, charms, plaques, and bookends. Cigarette manufacturers (probably unaware that Hitler despised smoking) introduced new brands with names like Kommando, Alarm, New Front, Drummer, and Comradeship. The latter brand featured a slogan, "Smoke K.Z. everywhere, all the time." Since "K.Z." stood for both the brand *(Kameradschaft Zigaretten)* and "concentration camp" *(Konzentrationslager)*, the message carried a special *frisson.* Premium coupons for marketing cigarettes bore photographs of Hitler and his comrades, and collectors swapped them like baseball cards.[4] Innovative craftsmen converted unsold Communist insignias into swastikas and sold them in tobacco shops.[5] In store windows, passers-by could gaze at portraits of the Führer surrounded by flowers in altar-like compositions. Newspaper kiosks stocked postcards and wallet-sized photographs of Hitler. Cheap editions of *Mein Kampf* sold out as soon as they arrived at bookstores.[6]

In celebration of the new era, towns and cities declared Hitler an honorary citizen. Streets named for Friedrich Ebert, the first president of the Weimar Republic, were renamed for Hermann Göring. The beloved folk song "The Lorelei" was banned because its text was a poem written by Heinrich Heine, who had been born to Jewish parents. Citizens of Frankfurt deemed the marker of his grave an eyesore and had it removed.[7] An alpine village changed its name to Hitler Heights *(Hitlershöhe)*. On April 20, 1933 (his birthday), Hitler beseeched his supporters to stop renaming public places in his honor. A few weeks later Goebbels, who complained in his diary that Nazi kitsch trivialized Nazism's great cause, banned the unauthorized use of Hitler's image.[8] This call for restraint was only one sign of a more comprehensive attempt to bring the disorderly exuberance of the "revolution" under control.

Like other successful revolutionaries, Nazi leaders faced a post-victory dilemma. The radicalism that animated doctrinaire Nazis alienated the ordinary citizens on whose support long-term stability depended. During the previous three years, the Nazi Party had scored stunning electoral victories by downplaying sectarian issues like race and appealing to ethnic fundamentalism. Emotionally powerful but programmatically vague slogans such as "Freedom and Bread!" and "Order at Home and Expansion Abroad" appealed to all Germans.[9] But the passion that fueled the movement flowed from fanatics who had little patience with platitudes. For them, Nazi victory was a green light for violence against Jews and settling old scores with political enemies. While Hitler continued to project an image of moral seriousness, local Nazi bosses became petty tyrants and Nazi thugs terrorized Jews.

Millions of moderates who had voted for Nazi candidates and welcomed the brutal repression of Communists objected to violence against Jews. Without credible evidence that Jews as a group constituted a danger to the German *Volk,* boycotts and sporadic pogroms ran the risk of alienating large segments of the non-Nazi population. Thus, while stalwarts clamored for radical action against Jews, newcomers demanded curbs against lawlessness. Confronted by what appeared to be irreconcilably opposed expectations, Nazi leaders exploited a source of power not possessed by earlier revolutionaries: a thoroughly literate citizenry and a technologically advanced media network.

Technological breakthroughs and innovative marketing strategies allowed Hitler to reach out beyond the Nazi Party and address voters directly. Citizens came to believe that they could intuit the "real Hitler"—the one that suited their own outlook—from their experience of a film or broadcast. As Nazi militias made war on the last vestiges of freedom, Hitler cast their crimes as protection against moral danger at home and enemies abroad. Labor unions, formerly split into dozens of rival associations, were drawn into a single Nazi-operated German Labor Front (DAF) under Robert Ley, to which, in 1934, 23 million employees and managers belonged. Women, who had won suffrage and equal rights in 1919, were relegated to a separate "feminine" sphere. Over 100 nationwide charitable, educational, recreational, and occupational women's associations and auxiliaries placed themselves under the command of the chief of women's activities, Gertrud Scholtz-Klink. Artists, writers, filmmakers, and intellectuals known for their disinclination to organize were pulled into eight guilds under the Ministry of Popular Enlightenment and Propaganda created by Goebbels.[10] Even begging was centralized, as posters admonished citizens to "Say no" to panhandlers and donate instead to the national charity, the Winter Relief.[11] Book burnings and censorship standardized print culture. Dissenting news media were driven out of business, and self-censorship became the norm. The denominational rivalries that had fractured Protestantism since the Reformation were dissolved under the leadership of a single Reich bishop, Ludwig Müller. Over and over, Hitler described repression as ethnic salvation from fragmentation and decline.

On July 14, 1933, a revolutionary package of decrees stabilized Nazi rule. Because laws were conventionally identified by their date of passing, this barrage of legislation carried a symbolic torque as Germany's historic response to the French Revolution. The new laws intruded into public and private life. A stiff-armed salute and a sharp "Heil Hitler" replaced the traditional "Good Day."[12] All non-Nazi political parties and organizations were outlawed, and the red-black-gold tricolor of democracy was supplanted by the red-black-white of imperial Germany. The federal constitution, which had preserved ancient regional identities and states' rights, yielded to centralized rule in Berlin. New measures allowed the state to revoke the citizenship of exiles who left Nazi Germany and of naturalized Germans (identified as "Jews from the East" in the law) who had immigrated to Germany after 1918. Hitler courted Catholics' support by signing the Concordat with the Vatican. The drive for a healthy body politic was launched by legislation that empowered public health officials to sterilize all citizens deemed "genetically unfit."

For all the political upheaval, many Germans and foreigners commented on the continuity between Weimar and Nazi Germany. During the entire period from 1933 to the end of the war, elections took place, city councils convened, and Reichstag delegates debated. After the Nazi revolution, civil servants who had no Jewish ancestors or strong ties to Marxist parties went to work at the same offices as before. The 1872 legal code and Weimar constitution were contravened but never officially revoked.[13] After Stormtroopers ousted Communist Party organizers from their headquarters, the renamed "Horst Wessel" houses did not look much different from the former "Karl Liebknecht" houses that had been named for a slain Communist leader.[14] Film directors avoided overt ideology and drew on popular themes from the 1920s, such as longing for leadership and fear of dark forces.[15] Icons of American culture remained popular. Germans read Hemingway, Thomas Wolfe, and William Faulkner; they sipped Coca Cola, danced to swing music, and flocked to Hollywood features like *Gone with the Wind*. On the surface, the Nazi dictatorship seemed to function within the framework of the public culture it destroyed.[16]

The word adapted by the Nazis to describe this unique process, *Gleichschaltung*, has no equivalent in other languages. "Nazification," "coordination," "integration," and "bringing into line" all come close, but none carries the mechanical overtones of *Gleichschaltung*. *Gleich* means both "equal" and "the same." *Schalten* means "to shift."[17] The conversion of A/C to D/C electrical current is a *Gleichschaltung*. The removal of anyone who "stained" or "soiled" the nation was "switching them off"—an *Ausschaltung*.[18] People judged "undesirable" because of inherited disabilities, non-German ethnicity, or Marxist allegiance were "switched off"—banished from mainstream society. "Biologically depraved" behavior, which could include anything from paranoia to vagabondism to homosexuality, also resulted in *Ausschaltung*. A German citizen, reporting anonymously for a London paper, captured both the mechanical and biological overtones of *Gleichschaltung* when he explained, "It means that the same stream will flow through the ethnic body politic *[Volkskörper]*."[19]

One of the keenest contemporary observers of the transformation of everyday life was Victor Klemperer, who was dismissed in 1935 from his position as professor of romance languages at the University of Dresden because of his Jewish ancestry. In his Nazi-imposed isolation, Klemperer obsessively gathered samples of Nazi discourse from speeches, films, radio programs, and newspapers, becoming in effect the first literary critic of the Nazi canon. Unlike most contemporary anti-Nazis, whose attention was drawn to the extremes of police terror and cheering throngs, Klemperer studied the quiet *Gleichschaltung* of everyday speech. "The mechanization of the individual," he wrote, "first manifested itself in 'Gleichschaltung' . . . You observe, you hear the switch flipped that sets everything in motion, not only institutions and offices, but individuals, too." Nazi phrases, like "Hitler weather" for a sunny day, glided smoothly into everyday conversation.[20] The Nazis, Klemperer wrote, "changed the values, the frequency of words, [and] made into common property words that had previously been used by individuals or tiny troupes. They confiscated words for the party, saturated words and phrases and sentence forms with their poison. They made the language serve their terrible system. They conquered words and made them into their strongest advertising tools *[Werbemittel]*, at once the most public and the most secret."[21] *Gleichschaltung* occurred so stealthily that most people hardly noticed.

Institutional *Gleichschaltung* occurred openly—and quickly. All civic organizations, clubs, athletic teams, civil service administrations, and occupational associations faced a stark choice: *Gleichschaltung* or dissolution. The former meant that officers had to belong to the Nazi Party or an affiliate, agendas required Nazi approval, and non-Aryans had to be expelled. Noncompliance meant being "switched off."[22] Even a minor display of independence might provide a pretext for the state to switch off an organization and confiscate its assets.[23] U.S. Chargé d'affairs George A. Gordon observed succinctly, "Whenever *Gleichschaltung* can not be obtained openly, the Nazis have resorted to other means of extending their influence."[24] Because the other means to which Gordon referred included physical assault, extortion, and blackmail, Nazis found it difficult to ascertain whether newcomers genuinely embraced party ideals or merely had been intimidated.

Because Hitler aimed to transform ethnic Germans' entire outlook, the difference mattered. In 1934 he explained to an American journalist how he kept in touch with "the man in the street," despite his busy schedule. He described his frequent lunchtime talks with a broad cross-section of followers who lined up for hours to have the privilege of spending a few minutes with him. He also referred to the specialists who briefed him on public opinion.[25] The habit of scrutinizing public response had begun in the 1920s when Hitler's chief of staff, Rudolf Hess, solicited information about morale from local leaders. After 1933 more sophisticated techniques were developed. Propaganda Ministry officials monitored attendance at films, plays, exhibits, and rallies, examined library circulation, and reported on book sales. In his frequent staff briefings, Goebbels routinely discussed audience reactions.[26] Heinrich Himmler created the security service (*Sicherheitsdienst,* or SD), which had a special surveillance section that by 1939 employed 3,000 staff members to analyze public opinion reports submitted by over 50,000 trusted Nazis.[27] The Gestapo censored mail, encouraged citizens to spy on neighbors, and gathered grassroots intelligence for "mood reports" *(Stimmungsberichte)* about illegal conduct and unwanted opinions. The national network of municipal governments *(Gemeindetag)* regularly solicited reactions to Nazi policies from its local chapters. As a check on their own sources, German police agents often obtained copies of the mimeographed monthly reports on public opinion gathered by clandestine observers within Germany and compiled by two groups of exiled German socialists, one known by its acronym Sopade and the other by its name New Beginnings.[28]

Thus, the most powerful dictatorship in Western Europe was directed by men who scrutinized their subjects' opinions as carefully as politicians in a democracy worried about their approval ratings.[29] What they learned in the summer of 1934 distressed them. Enthusiasm for Nazi rule was waning. Like the "Spirit of 1914" that dimmed once Europeans grasped the reality of war, the effervescent uprising of 1933 dissipated after the excitement of takeover subsided.[30] But, mobilized by propaganda drives, Germans had soldiered on after 1914, and after the excitement of the Nazi revolution paled, supporters of Nazi rule stayed the course.

Civil servants, professionals, educators, and labor organizers (as long as they were not identified as Jews or outspoken Communists) joined Nazi organizations under pressure. Humorists laughed at these "beefsteak Nazis"—brown on the outside, red on the inside. People joked that the Nazi Party initials (NSDAP) stood for "So you're looking for a little office, too? *[Na, suchst Du auch 'ne Pöstchen?]*" A Sopade reporter noted "accommodation and subordination stay on the surface, but deep down the bureaucrats work along in their old style, and they threaten gradually to make the new leaders dependent on their technical knowledge, experience and organizational influence."[31] Like a dairyman in a Hessian village who delivered milk privately to avoid ostracism, tradespeople circumvented Nazi Party pressure.[32] An opponent of Nazism, Rudolf Steiner, wrote that "National Socialism is victorious as an organization. Perhaps materially it is established as well—but not politically and intellectually." What, he mused, had changed in the so-called Third Reich? "People have transformed themselves . . . they put on masks. No one knows what the individual thinks [or] . . . what he feels, whether he hopes for the fall of this regime . . . because even the loudest spokesmen for the Nazis do not prove with their cheers that they believe in the ideology *[die Idee]* . . . What do the masses think? You can hardly guess . . . The masses, as well as individuals who are not Nazis, are silent and wait."[33] In his diary a German writer described the ease with which people "shifted themselves into gear" without being asked—self-Nazification *(Selbstgleichschaltung),* in the slang of the day.[34] On the way home from the theater, he noticed a colleague who was "anything but a Nazi" wearing a discreet swastika lapel pin. Why? asked the diarist. "Well! Why not? I'm no risk-taker."[35] A Socialist morale monitor concurred. "Wherever [the Nazi leaders] look, everything is brown, but nowhere can they be sure if this brown is genuine or just camouflage."[36] Ambassador François-Poncet reported that the recruitment of so many uncommitted Nazis made the state vulnerable to "intrigues, complaints, acts of insubordination, and resentments." One saw, he wrote, the "odd swastika emblem" everywhere, but added hopefully "the power *[la force]*" of Hitler's victory contained within it "a certain weakness."[37]

Despite a general feeling of let-down, however, Hitler's personal popularity remained strong. While politicians in the Weimar Republic had argued vehemently about pragmatic questions like taxes and social welfare policies, Hitler ignored controversial domestic issues and pledged to rescue moral clarity from the ravages of democracy. Besides advocating one or another economic or diplomatic initiative, Hitler would speak for hours about "*Volk* and fatherland . . . the eternal foundation of our morality and our faith" and "the preservation of our *Volk.*" He repeated the narrative of the innocent *Volk* and called for "a thorough moral purging." Although it is easy to dismiss Hitler's message as banal, its appeal lay precisely in the ordinariness of his homilies about the meaning of life, communal moral responsibility, and ethnic glory. Prince Heinrich August (son of deposed Kaiser Wilhelm II) thanked Divine Providence for sending Hitler.[38] An American living in Germany reported, "In a small town I was told with full belief . . . that Hitler was sent by heaven. I naturally thought, well, what can one expect of these small-town folks, but when one week later I heard the same words uttered in a handsome drawing room at a five o'clock tea, I was more than surprised."[39] A Jewish citizen wrote that the content of a Hitler speech mattered less than the "great joy and good

12. "The Last Portrait of the Führer before the Presidential Election." In 1932 Hitler posed for this and dozens of other studio portraits, which provided Hoffmann with a reservoir of images in subsequent years.

mood" it inspired.[40] A Sopade report from 1934 described immense posters that enlivened public spaces with Hitler's official portraits.[41]

A series of ingenious public relations campaigns enhanced Hitler's oratorical talents. As visitors to Germany unfailingly noted, Hitler's portrait was everywhere—in offices, schools, and businesses, on stamps and posters, and (on special occasions) projected onto giant screens. In a variety of formal postures, these portraits featured a sober Führer with his gaze fixed on a distant point. But a second side of Hitler enhanced the Führer myth. During the decade when celebrity journalism was in its infancy, his publicity team revealed to the public a leader who in private life was an ordinary guy. One of the first ventures to reveal Hitler's daily life was a series of photograph albums produced in collaboration with a cigarette manufacturer. The first of these oversized, handsomely bound volumes, which first appeared in 1934, were meant for display in domestic settings, like family or travel albums. And like stamp collectors' albums, they contained blank spaces and subtitles for the missing images that could be acquired by purchasing the sponsor's brand of candy or cigarettes. Heinrich Hoffmann, Hitler's personal photographer who accompanied him everywhere, captured the "inner" Hitler for display in the intimacy of the parlor—a pensive Führer, solitary and careworn, who seemed truly happy only when surrounded by adoring crowds. *Adolf Hitler: Pictures from the Life of the Führer,* with a first edition of 700,000, included snapshots of Hitler from the 1920s as well as recent photos of the chancellor taking time out from the burdens of his office to chat with admirers.[42]

Unlike the photographs that flooded Italian space with informal images of Mussolini as the personification of machismo, Hitler's private life conveyed an aura of ordinariness.[43] Hitler, the embodiment of the virtues he preached, appeared in rumpled suits and often gazed at the reader with a shy smile. Mass-produced photo books, such as *Hitler: An Escape from Daily Routine* and *The Adolf Hitler No One Knows,* allowed followers to glimpse a private life that was carefully constructed for public consumption. In these informal snapshots, Hitler emerged as a regular guy who took pleasure in his followers' adoration, loved his dog, enjoyed the outdoors, and appreciated fast cars.[44] Occasionally, one caught a glimpse of the Führer alone with his thoughts, perhaps reading a newspaper (never shown with the glasses he actually needed to read) or gazing into the distance, framed by the Bavarian Alps. A 150-page photo album glorifying ethnic revival, *Germany Awake! Background, Battle, and Victory,* went through four editions of 100,000 in 1933–34.[45] Essays by leading Nazis in

13. "Relaxation. Far from the noise and disorder of the cities, here the Führer re-covers from the stress of struggle. In the broad meadow near his little house, he reads opponents' newspapers. How he laughs at the tales of his champagne cel-lar, Jewish mistresses, luxurious villa, and French funding." In fact, Hitler enjoyed a sumptuous lifestyle but hid from public view his luxury automobiles, private art collection, and lavishly furnished homes. Photographs like these, published in mass-market booklets, familiarized followers with a private self that had been carefully constructed for public viewing.

these albums familiarized readers with the "great ideas" of the day. Inter-spersed among theoretical discourses were photographs and paintings of Stormtroopers, portraits of Nazi leaders, reproductions of great German art, and scenes of an avuncular Hitler surrounded by devoted young peo-ple. One caption expressed the message implicit in all the informal snap-shots: "Even the Führer can be happy!" Before the advent of color photog-raphy, reproductions of hand-colored photographs added a modern flair. In the concluding photograph of this album, Hitler stands alone with a fawn: Hitler, the animal lover. The Propaganda Ministry manufactured this ersatz intimate life to replace the facts of his early life Hitler had so thoroughly expunged from view.

During late 1933 and 1934, bookstores were stocked not only with *Mein Kampf* but with low-priced pamphlets and booklets of Hitler's speeches, histories of the Nazi Party, and biographies of the Führer. In these popular publications, the *Volk* was everywhere, but race *(Rasse)* was hardly to be seen. In 1934 a cigarette album, *The City of Work and Peace: One Year in the Rule of Adolf Hitler,* featured photographs of immense public works projects that promised to improve the nation's infrastructure and enhance communal life.[46] Hitler's "great cultural lectures" at the Nuremberg Rally in September 1933 were published by a regular commercial press as *Leadership and Loyalty.* In the very popular *Peace and Security* he reiterated his opposition to militarism. A 54-page booklet, *Hitler's Speeches for Equal Justice and Peace,* reassured those who were worried that Hitler wanted another war.[47] Pocket-sized books such as *The Speeches of Hitler as Chancellor* and *Young Germany Wants Work and Peace* predicted economic recovery.[48] Avoiding dogmatic language, these cheaply printed booklets, bound in red-and-white-striped cloth, taught that racial struggle determines history, that great men make history, and that Germans had the right to territorial expansion.[49] Walter Gross, director of the Office of Racial Politics, produced a pamphlet of bland quotations from *Mein Kampf*—from which racism was deleted—that was marketed as ideal for corporate giving. In these mass-market publications, Hitler's carefully crafted persona came to stand for ethnic revival, individual sacrifice, and the cleansing of cultural life. During these years Hitler virtually never mentioned three controversial themes that shaped his covert political agenda: crude antisemitism, contempt for Christianity, and preparation for a war of conquest.

Over the course of 1933, a softer image of Nazism displaced old fighters' raucous fanaticism. Like other revolutionaries who successfully seize power, Hitler publicly rebuked radicals in a drive to recruit new followers. Nazi theater registered the new direction quickly as it shifted from didacticism to generic entertainment. In the late 1920s amateurs had created the Nazi Fighting Stage *(Kampfbühne),* which produced confrontational plays designed to "indoctrinate through fun and entertainment."[50] Although most of the scripts have been lost, the titles convey their flavor: *Poison Gas; Rothschild Wins the Battle of Waterloo; Leo Schlageter; All Men are Brothers;* and *The Wanderer* (based on Goebbels's 1926 novel, *Michael*).[51] Traveling theater troupes spread these "fighting conversations" through-

seines ärmsten Sohnes bekennen und in einem grandiosen, gemeinsamen Opferwerk ihm die Gewißheit geben, daß er nicht vergessen wurde, sondern daß eine ganze Nation aufstand, um ihm zu helfen.

Das großartige Winterhilfswerk des deutschen Volkes, das Dr. Goebbels organisiert, legt Zeugnis ab von der tiefen Verbundenheit des ganzen Volkes.

Es ist das größte freiwillige Hilfswerk, das die Welt jemals gesehen hat.

Der vornehmste Grundsatz des Nationalsozialismus, daß Gemeinnutz

Winterhilfswerk des deutschen Volkes

vor Eigennutz gehe, erfährt mit diesem Hilfswerk seine schönste Erfüllung.

Keiner in Deutschland soll in diesem Winter das Wichtigste entbehren: die Hoffnung, daß auch er im kommenden Sommer zur Arbeit zurückkehren kann.

Bis dahin bestätigt ihm das ganze Volk, daß es fest entschlossen ist, ihm über den Winter hinwegzuhelfen.

Am 13. September 1933 verkündet im großen Festsaal des Propagandaministeriums Dr. Goebbels im Beisein des Führers das Programm des Winterhilfswerks.

out Germany. In 1933, as these semiautonomous ventures were regularized, dogmatic skits gave way to "living customs, songs, games, and dances that convey the simple truths of natural ethnic wisdom."[52] Hundreds of openair stages were designed for pseudo-medieval plays, called *Thingspiels,* that restored a "heroic spiritual force" to ethnic theater. Writing in 1933, a popular actress rejoiced that the Nazi takeover had rescued morality from "totally and essentially alien" Jewish rationalism. "Now reason stops leading us . . . a heroic Germanic passion commands. And it's high time, too!"[53] Outdoor extravaganzas enthralled millions during the annual Nazi Party rallies, the 1936 Olympics, and national holidays like May 1, Thanksgiving Day, and Heroes' Memorial Day *(Heldengedenktag).*

Reporters for the clandestine Sopade and New Beginnings networks in 1934 sadly acknowledged Germans' attraction to Nazi ideology, *die Idee.* To their dismay, they watched workers listen intently to a Hitler speech or toast May Day, which for the first time under Nazi rule was declared a paid holiday. They described the power of ethnic revival to unify Germans across class lines.[54] Even people who complained about corrupt local bosses admired Hitler. Although some inveterate anti-fascists optimistically insisted that "old loyalties" still operated behind the scenes, they admitted the *Volk* belonged to Hitler. Mass support for Nazism, however, came at a price. While ethnic uplift attracted newcomers, old fighters lusted for action—some for an offensive against big business and others for decisive measures against "Jewry." Bitter old fighters, accustomed to free-booting autonomy, found victory disconcerting.

Structural problems exacerbated tensions caused by the sheer numbers of people applying for party membership. In addition, victory generated more expectations than the party could fulfill. Some old fighters longed to settle scores with their political opponents; others took out their wrath against Jews. As compensation for years of sacrifice, many longtime Nazis anticipated receiving the desk jobs that opened up after 10 percent of all civil service positions were purged on political or racial grounds. When

14. This page from the trading-card album *The State of Work and Peace* featured Germans from all social backgrounds and ages contributing to the Winter Charity Drive—not by merely donating money but also by cooking, organizing collection drives, making Christmas decorations, and volunteering in soup kitchens. The colored photographs in this mass-produced album were included in a popular brand of cigarette packages. Much like stamp albums, these political albums had marked spaces for each image, but unlike stamp albums they included texts that familiarized collectors with Nazi leaders, programs, and goals.

15. "The Brown House [national Nazi Party headquarters] in Munich is the desti-nation of SA men from all districts of Germany. How their eyes light up when the Führer is among them!" This photograph, published in Hoffmann's *Youth Sur-rounding Hitler,* contributed to Hitler's personal campaign to solidify SA loyalty to him and to undercut SA General Ernst Röhm's popularity.

old fighters managed to obtain positions, they often became swaggering "brown bosses" with a reputation for corruption. Because so few long-time Nazis who benefited from patronage possessed the requisite skills to fill their posts properly, the reputation of the party suffered.[55] With fewer than 300 full-time administrators, the party headquarters in Munich was so overwhelmed by paperwork that its staff barely evaluated applicants' qualifications. The closing of the Nazi Party membership rolls in June 1933 was a tacit acknowledgment of internal disorder.[56] Although a steady stream of individuals were invited to join the Nazi Party, the general rolls did not officially reopen until 1937.

The explosion of membership in 1933 left many old fighters out in the cold and feeling betrayed. For over a decade Stormtooper brigades had provided the militaristic élan that had driven the movement. Suddenly, their ranks expanded out of all proportion to the command structure. Led by Captain Ernst Röhm, the Stormtroopers grew from about 71,000 in 1931 to 400,000 in late 1932, and, with the absorption of the Steel Helmet *(Stahlhelm)* veterans' organization, tripled its membership in 1933. Many Stormtroopers had not even bothered to join the Nazi Party, and most had not been schooled in Nazi doctrine.[57] Culturally and politically marginal, Stormtroopers scorned the comforts of bourgeois life and lusted for armed struggle against Bolsheviks, capitalists, and Jews. Hitler's swift victory caught them off guard.

These old fighters, many of them war veterans, viewed new arrivals to the Nazi cause suspiciously. As one put it, "The old SA-Man, faithful and courageous *(brav)* feels pushed aside by the influx of millions of young fighters." Amid increasing disaffection, many looked nostalgically at the bygone "time of struggle" with its political intrigue and street battles. Behind the rosy façade of *Gleichschaltung,* morale sank. Stormtroopers were

16. "Even peeling potatoes can be an SA service." This trading card suggested the "new look" of Hitler's private army after the Nazi takeover.

accustomed to being outlaws; as local Nazi Party honchos, many believed they stood above the law and looked down contemptuously on police and government officials.[58] Nazi stalwarts resented obeying the senior civil servants whom they had once considered their enemies. "It is ridiculous," complained local chief Wilhelm Kube, "that we, the actual victors of the National Socialist revolution, should have to follow the directives of bureaucrats!"[59] Thousands of disgruntled militiamen found an outlet for their aggression in antisemitic hooliganism and brutal assaults against individual Jews. Many supported Captain Ernst Röhm's call for a "second revolution" against big capitalists. During the year before Hitler ordered a purge of the SA in June 1934, he campaigned in person to curtail SA units' autonomy.

In 1933, Hitler could have outlawed the entire SA on the grounds that after political victory the militia had outlived its usefulness. But it was not Hitler's style to abolish party institutions, and besides a private army suited his purpose. Instead, he invested a great deal of energy in convincing Stormtroopers to desist from unsanctioned violence and become ideological soldiers. To assure himself of SA men's loyalty, Hitler solidified his popularity among broad masses of Stormtroopers in personal appearances throughout Germany. "We have taken power. No one can resist us. And now we must train [erziehen] the German Volk for this state—a tremendous challenge in the coming decade." Praising their loyalty in the past, he outlined a new mission for the future. "What we have achieved in three months is a miracle . . . and what lies ahead will not be less. Our struggle continues . . . We must carry on the struggle for the hearts and minds [das Innere] of Germany . . . We are entering a difficult era. Every aspect of life will be nothing but struggle. You have grown up in battle, do not hope for a quick peace."[60] By emphasizing the theme of struggle, Hitler masculinized the tedious missionary work of a new era.

Success, as Hitler put it in a speech to a devoted audience, depended on their ability to achieve the "inner conversion" of nominal Nazis who had joined Nazi associations out of careerism.[61] Instead of dismissing competent civil servants (including teachers) on suspicion of political unreliability, he ordered Nazi functionaries to win them over totally.[62] Any fool, Hitler said, could seize power. The test of greatness was holding on to it.[63] Describing the July 14, 1933, laws as the apex of institutional *Gleichschaltung*, Hitler played the sage: "More revolutions have succeeded in their first assault than have been successfully absorbed and brought to a standstill. Revolution is not a permanent condition . . . the stream of revolution once released must be guided into the secure bed of evolution. Here the education of the *Volk* is most important . . . The ideas in our program do not commit us to behaving like fools and destroying everything . . . The Party has now become the State, all power belongs to the Reich authority."[64] The time had come, he said, to slow down the "speeding locomotive" of revolution. In October 1933 he asked militiamen "to extend a hand to former adversaries who demonstrate their loyalty" to Nazi rule.[65] Militiamen were charged to "fill the entire *Volk* with a single ideal"— which, in practice meant making converts of their old enemies.[66]

With Hitler rhapsodizing about new challenges, Goebbels remade the identity of the SA man on the screen. The fates of three feature films to promote Nazism early in 1933 reflected the sharp reversal of SA men's functions. The content of the first two films and revisions of the third suggested the dawn of a new era. *SA-Mann Brandt* and *Hitlerjunge Quex* (Hitler Youth Quex) were filmed early in 1933, before Goebbels consolidated his control over the film industry. *Brandt* was a low-budget celebration of a slain Stormtrooper. *Quex* was based on a novel about a young Nazi martyr that had sold nearly 200,000 copies in the previous two years. In these didactic films, a youthful hero breaks his ties with his working-class family, casts his lot with a gang of courageous Nazi toughs, and dies at the hands of wild Communist ruffians. Their heroic deaths assured both heroes a place in the Nazi pantheon. The film censorship board approved *Brandt* on June 14, 1933, and *Quex* on September 19, 1933.

The third film glorified Stormtrooper Horst Wessel, who had been murdered in 1930 in the manner of *Brandt* and *Quex*. This film was rejected in late September 1933 even though the Nazi elite had already been invited to attend its festive opening on October 9. After major re-editing, *Wessel* opened as *Hans Westmar: One Among Many* on December 13, 1933. Aside from the initials H.W. in the protagonist's name, little remained of the original. Skillful editing converted the biography of the low-life thug-turned-martyr Wessel into a narrative about a virtuous youth who bore a striking resemblance to Hitler's fictive autobiography. Having grown up in a middle-class milieu, Hans Westmar does not alienate his family, and—far from picking fights with Communists—he preaches class reconciliation. Virtue in the Third Reich did not require reckless heroism as much as restraint. Hans explains, "We simply cannot talk in terms of class anymore. We are workers, too, but we happen to work with our heads. Our place is next to our brothers who work with their hands." The climax comes when undisciplined Communists brutally murder him.

The printed program distributed at the grand opening of the film underscored the newly-minted memory of the Nazis' victory as a narrative of reconciliation. "To completely win over the workers, he himself [Hans] must become one of them . . . He casts all temptation for the privileged life to the wind . . . The Red killers shoot him dead, but over his grave workers and students come together."[67] In an interview a few months later, Hitler depicted himself as the great peacemaker who had unified the alienated Marxist "mass man" and the greedy bourgeois capitalist. Like Hans Westmar, he pledged to reconcile the "comrade with the red worker's cap" and the "citizen with the bowler hat."[68] Westmar-Hitler symbolized ethnic awakening (Erhebung). Interclass harmony—the theme of Goebbels's favorite films, Fritz Lang's Metropolis and Sergei Eisenstein's The Battleship Potemkin—replaced political battle as the foundation of militia members' identity.[69] Antisemitism faded from official view along with brutal Stormtroopers.

During the winter and early spring of 1933–34, Hitler traveled almost constantly to address local chiefs and militia officers. When he was in Berlin, he hosted gatherings of regional leaders at his chancery. Whether addressing small gatherings or mass rallies of Stormtroopers, he created the illusion of intimacy that made listeners feel like members of his select inner circle. During these privileged encounters, Hitler would exhort "the obedient sons of National Socialism" to stop unsanctioned violence. Submit to my authority, he repeated; accept your new calling as proselytizers. Addressing Stormtroopers on the verge of rebellion, Hitler invoked the Biblical imagery of John 14:20: "Just as I am yours, so you are mine!" He paid homage to this "ancient, Iron Guard of the Revolution—as faithful and disciplined as the soldiers of the German Volk!"[70]

In his obsessive retelling of his own humble beginnings and his reliving of party history in speech after speech, Hitler remade the public memory of the "old days" in the image of Hans Westmar.[71] In descriptions of the Stormtroopers written before 1933, Nazi fighters risked death in combat with Communists. They roughed up Jews and disrupted placid petty-bourgeois life. Young men defied their parents; older men ignored wives and girlfriends. Through it all, they kept the rebellious spirit of the front soldier alive. But from the summer of 1933, Hitler praised a new kind of honor. In place of fighting and martyrdom, Hitler reminisced about disciplined, idealistic, and dedicated men who endured privation for the sake of a loftier goal. In every speech to the party faithful in his first year as chancellor, Hitler presented himself as the role model. "Fifteen years ago,

I began my struggle for Germany with a handful of people . . . Fifteen years of struggling for a *Volk* . . . I have come today because my heart has led me here to you to tell you how infinitely happy the German *Volk* is and how happy I am."[72]

Morality, in the official memory of the "Time of Struggle" *(Kampfzeit)* was embodied in patriotism, ethnic idealism, and self-sacrifice—the traits needed to stabilize Nazi rule. Hitler explained to a British journalist in early 1934: "Everyone knew that it was possible to raze buildings using shellfire, but these methods would never convince an opponent, they would serve only to embitter him. The only way to make a successful revolution lies in gaining a hold on one's opponent by persuasion."[73]

Nazi ruffians required intellectual retrofitting in order to debate with critics and inspire confidence among non-Nazis. In June 1933 Hitler announced the foundation of a special Institute *(Pflegestätte)* for the Cultivation of the National Socialist Spirit in the village of Bernau near Berlin.[74] Under the auspices of Nazi organizations, leadership training centers proliferated throughout the country. At these workshops in party dogma, from the podium, Hitler instructed Stormtroopers in how to parry hostile criticism. Step by step, he rehearsed the evils of "liberalism, Marxism, and *Reaktion*."[75] He asked old fighters to think of themselves as guardians of ethnic altruism. At the Roll Call of Old Fighters on March 19, 1934, he told his audience that "the victory of a *Weltanschauung* unleashes a revolution which changes the very core and character of a *Volk*." Becoming a serious National Socialist required extensive study. "The German revolution will be concluded only when the entire German *Volk* has been totally created anew, reorganized and reconstructed."[76]

Spreading the communal spirit also meant intensive community organizing—which included many tasks that in the 1920s had been labeled *Kleinarbeit* (little work). Instead of enjoying the perquisites of their new offices, old fighters were encouraged to organize neighborhoods, which entailed door-to-door canvassing, fundraising, and publicizing rallies—tasks that Nazi women had performed before 1933.[77] Men found it difficult to substitute such chores for the defiant subculture that was now banned. In his 1934 New Year's greeting, Goebbels enhanced routine chores with a masculine élan. "National Socialism means struggle *[Kampf]*, tough, tireless struggle for the spiritual and physical elevation of the German *Volk*." Headlines like "Fighter without A Sword" and "Unknown Nazi Orator" reinforced the message.[78] One unsung ideological crusader related how bravely he and other old fighters had defied hecklers

17. W.H.W. was the acronym for Winterhilfswerk, the state-sponsored Nazi Winter Charity. "I'm bringing you coal from the Winter Charity," declares the SA man. "My oh my," exclaims the mother, "just look at that. Until now we had only read about this in the newspapers." After the curtailment of SA autonomy that followed the Nazi takeover, the model SA man was charged to end political fighting and to place himself at the service of his *Volk*.

by holding their rage in check to remain within "legal" limits ordered by Hitler.[79]

Walter Thießler, one of Goebbels's most able staff members, understood the need for new "apostles of our ideal" when he assigned brown fighters to their new posts as "propaganda sentinels" *(Propagandawarter)*.[80] These fledgling persuaders received monthly fact sheets entitled "Will and Path"

(Wille und Weg) that were to be collected in loose-leaf notebooks to use as reference material for political lectures.[81] Although some disgruntled militiamen mocked this "occupational therapy" *(Beschäftigungstherapie)*, the constant activity diverted anarchic impulses and integrated rebellious old fighters within a command structure. Instructions, written in curt battle language, advised sentinels in the smallest details: for example, how to select and decorate meeting spaces, organize indoctrination film evenings, and publicize charity drives.[82] Of course, doctrine was important, the author noted, but the "creation of a harmonious atmosphere" was key. "People will not attend just to keep up appearances. No! They look forward to learning . . . and enjoying the comradely spirit in support of the *Volk* community." Decorating tips advised against cluttering windows with posters and suggested fonts for signage. Huge transparent banners with bold slogans could add color to drab towns. Sound trucks pulling oversized billboards were most effective at twilight. No detail was too petty to overlook.

In addition to organizing their own party functions, propaganda sentinels attended labor meetings, office conferences, and civic organizations, ranging from chess clubs to sports teams. Between March and May 1934, for example, Nazi leaders in the small West German city of Wiesbaden organized 263 meetings, 600 educational evenings, and nearly 400 rallies.[83] Throughout Germany, Nazi women sponsored poetry readings, workshops on childhood education, sewing circles, and reading groups. Ambassador Dodd grudgingly admired the tactic. "The method of educating the people through the medium of associations and societies is undoubtedly very effective as most adult Germans belong to at least several such organizations."[84]   use of existing structures

Clandestine Sopade reports, as well as regional Nazi Party activity surveys, brought mixed reviews. The old fighters' reliance on gut instinct sometimes galled well-educated audiences' sensibilities, but other audiences warmed to their blunt language and folksy manner.[85] Berlin Reichsbank employees, who attended the required evening lectures held in indoor tennis courts, "were shocked at the extremely low level of the lectures." One participant commented, "These methods increasingly work against the speakers."[86] Teachers in Munich complained about the obligatory meetings at which Nazi stalwarts reminisced about their front experiences, described recent rallies, and denounced academic scholarship.[87] But other audiences in Munich rallied to a proselytizer's call, "Race Is Life!" Debunking biological research as "deadly boring" *(toter Stoff)*, he waxed eloquent about "racial emotions." Instead of studying genes, he told people to trust their "healthy ethnic instincts." Comparing a perfect Aryan physique to a beautiful automobile, he declared, "You know quality when you see it. They both take your breath away."[88]

As Nazi organizers had realized during the 1920s, disappointment provided an opportunity to improve party strategies. After a few public relations fiascos early in 1933, inept racial trainers were not allowed to speak in neighborhoods where "critical intellectuals" could embarrass them. To remedy Nazi dilettantes' confusion about key concepts such as "Nordic race," "Aryan," and "alien blood," racial education was added to speaker-training courses.[89] Indoctrinators learned to sidestep controversial issues such as antisemitism, preparation for war, forced sterilization, and Nazi leaders' hostility to organized religion. Despite scattered complaints, these face-to-face encounters had the potential to create mutual trust by linking Nazi activists to established civic networks. Gradually, ties of benevolence and shared community projects appear to have ameliorated hostilities between old fighters and newcomer Nazis.

In the Nazi press, the emphasis on civic virtue was reflected in scores of mawkish essays. Typical of the genre was an article by a Nazi official that hailed "the moral demands of National Socialism" as a revolution.[90] Unlike the "barricade battles" against democracy, he wrote, old fighters in the new era inspired honor. Rudolf Hess, writing in the Nazis' theoretical journal, described Nazi ideals in moral, not political, terms: "Never place self-interest ahead of Party interests."[91] Authors purged accounts of bloody confrontations from their memoirs, recalling instead their "battles" to expand membership and "struggles" to boost turnout at local meetings. Back in the 1920s, one writer commented, recruiting just one new comrade had been more difficult than signing up 1,000 in 1933. Only because "iron discipline and unshakable faith in the values [die Idee] of Adolf Hitler unified many thousands in Will and Thought" had Nazism triumphed. Now "ideological conquest called for a nonviolent spiritual revolution."[92] A Reichstag delegate and Labor Front official praised "the unbelievable results" achieved when "we begin the task of sinking our Weltanschauung deep in the collective German Volk."[93]

Alongside the propaganda sentinel stood the radio sentinel (Funkwart) who received instructions that read like military commands for the conquest of public opinion: "target" critical intersections for loudspeakers; "coordinate" programs with shopping times; and above all, "gather intelligence" about public opinion.[94] District Nazi bosses produced their own

Ein Antlitz -   *vom Kampf geformt*

18. "A Visage Formed by Struggle." This series epitomized the use of Hitler's portrait to market his charisma. Although racial theorists insisted on the immutable biological origins of human behavior, popular writers suggested that life experiences shaped an individual's physiogamy.

weekly broadcasts, often replete with signature music. Goebbels's eager acolytes cast their mission in world-historical terms. After modernization had fragmented communal life and driven peasants into alienated urban *Gesellschaft* (society), a radio campaign could recreate the lost *Gemeinschaft* (community). Radio expert Eugen Hadamowsky told his Stormtroopers of the Spirit *(Geist):* "Today, for the first time in history, we have in radio a medium which enables us to mold nations of many millions by daily and hourly influence. Old and young, workers and farmers, soldiers and officials, men and women listen in front of their radios . . . Loudspeakers call across the athletic fields, the courtyards, the streets and squares of the big cities, the factories and the barracks. A whole nation listens." Modernity, he continued, bred cynicism and anomie, but it also offered the means to re-create community on an entirely new scale. The modern man "longs to be one of a crowd of people who think, feel, and react in the same way. The listener feels he is a part of this great entity that is not torn between countless differences of opinion, but revolves . . . around a central concern."[95] Government subsidies and do-it-yourself kits made the radios, or "people's receivers" *(Volksempfänger),* affordable even

→ feeling of nationalism

19. "The *Volk* listens to its Führer." Before a major Hitler speech, sirens sounded simultaneously throughout the Reich. Germans gathered to listen to the Führer's voice via radios at home or loudspeakers in factories, offices, and public spaces.

for the poorest Germans. On Hitler's birthday, primetime broadcasting integrated traditional fare and special celebrations.

- 16:20 Orchestra concert
- 17:00 *The Struggle for the Nation*
- 17:30 Classical Operettas
- 18:20 Nation-wide Hitler Youth Oath to Hitler
- 18:30 Mozart String Quartet
- 19:00 *Horst Wessel,* radio drama
- 21:00 Philharmonic concert[96]

key term

Overnight, *Gleichschaltung* turned the airwaves brown.

By 1934 Germany had the largest number of radios per capita in the world. Clandestine morale monitors were dismayed to see how people stood motionless in awed silence to hear Hitler's voice on loudspeakers in factories, schools, and squares.[97] "Talkie" newsreels and documentary films drew viewers into a space of intimacy with their leaders. Germans purchased 350,000,000 cinema tickets each year, and every metropolitan area boasted at least one movie theater with over a thousand seats. Giant-screen television viewing studios were designed, as one visionary told Hitler, to "plant your picture, my Führer, deep and ineradicably in every German heart."[98] Goebbels's staff masterminded a national radio oath-taking ceremony. On April 8, 1933, 600,000 Stormtroopers stood at attention throughout Germany at the same time. That evening Goebbels imagined them standing "like trees, a vast forest of heroism, a hard manly union."[99] A year later the drama was repeated when 750,000 party leaders, 180,000 Hitler Youth, 1,800 student leaders, and 18,500 Labor Front members stood at attention in front of their radios and simultaneously pledged allegiance to Hitler.

Gradually, the novelty of a voice coming from a box wore off, and many listeners requested the return of radio broadcasts of the Weimar era. As Hadamowsky ruefully noted, dissatisfied listeners simply turn off their sets. "Without listeners, radio loses its power." After several months of heavy-handed ideological radio programming, Goebbels recalibrated national radio from indoctrination to entertainment. "Political announcements *[Kundgebungen]* on the radio . . . have become so ubiquitous that programs constantly change, creating the danger that listeners' interest disappears. Listeners can turn off the radio." Even the primetime *National Hour* was curtailed.[100] Popular music, consumer tips, drama, serialized novels, newscasts, and advice for housewives, youth, and farmers re-

20. "The New Obelisk in Carolingian Square, Munich." A 1932 cartoon in the Munich humor magazine *Simplicissimus* mocked Hitler's monumentomania by proposing several possible monuments to Hitler as a well-known soldier, as Salome, and as a mechanical drummer. Satirical portrayals of Hitler as effeminate appeared not to bother him earlier in his career, but his celebrity status as Führer made it important to curtail this kind of irreverence.

turned to their former prominence.[101] In the hope of achieving popular acclaim from the broadest possible audience, Nazi media produced a lively vernacular culture and scaled back overtly ideological productions.

In early 1934 Nazi leaders spoke less about winning new followers and more about disciplining recalcitrant Nazis. Hitler ranted about "insane fools, little worms, carpers, little pygmies"; Goebbels lashed out against "killjoys, fault-finders, saboteurs, agitators"; and Göring assailed "interest cliques" and "unproductive critics."[102] Listeners may have wondered who these creatures were. Soon they found out. On the night of June 27–28, 1934 Hitler ordered a special unit of SS men to murder SA-Captain Ernst Röhm and 40 of his closest comrades. Before the purge ended, between 80 and 100 people had been killed, including not only Röhm and 40 other Stormtroopers but also political opponents, civil servants, hostile journalists, erstwhile comrades, and retired military officers. Approximately one thousand people were arrested and held without charge for a few weeks, and in some cases for several months, while their offices were ransacked, presumably for incriminating documents that Hitler wanted destroyed.[103] These frantic searches, combined with his payments to blackmailers at the time, suggest that Hitler worried about the disclosure of facts about his background that he wanted to bury. Perhaps he worried about rumors that he had a Jewish grandfather, or maybe he wanted to thwart gossip about his sexual proclivities. A Führer who in speech after speech flaunted his spotless moral character could ill afford personal scandal or Röhm's threat of a "second revolution" against capitalists and the military.[104] But the fact that the upholder of morality ordered a mass murder demanded a justification that would seem credible in the eyes of ordinary Germans as well as Nazis. Using the formula of his 1924 trial speeches, Hitler stage-managed the aftermath. In much the same way that a political fiasco became a courageous putsch, the purge of June 1934 became known as "The Night of the Long Knives." Success depended on Hitler's ability to strip an obvious crime of its political meaning and reframe it as a moral act.

Immediately after the murders, Hitler withdrew from public view. A press release described his "grave conflicts of conscience" (without further explanation) and supplied lurid details about the "sexual deviants" murdered in their beds at dawn. Goebbels reassured Germans that, as he put it, the "plague boils, hotbeds of corruption, symptoms of degeneracy . . . are being cauterized." On July 13 Hitler emerged from seclusion and delivered an hour-long radio speech to the Reichstag. Assuming personal responsibility for the purge, as he had for the 1923 putsch, Hitler claimed to have rescued the *Volk* from a threat so dire that only drastic action could have stopped it. "The National Socialist state will wage a 100 years war, if necessary, to stamp out and destroy . . . every last trace of this phenomenon which poisons and makes dupes of the *Volk* . . . the little colony of

21. Ernst Ludwig Kirchner's "Self-Portrait as Soldier" (1915) epitomized what National Socialist critics called degenerate art. Instead of glorifying military valor, Kirchner showed himself smoking a cigarette. His amputated hand symbolically impeded him from painting. Unlike Hitler's favorite artists who honored womanhood in neoclassical nude paintings, Kirchner, his critics alleged, demeaned womanhood with this image of a prostitute.

drones . . . deserters and mutineers."[105] In conclusion, he pledged to "protect the morality of the *Volk.*"

After the Röhm purge, Hitler ordered a crackdown against corruption, luxurious banquets, limousines, and drunkenness.[106] In *Der Stürmer* he told Stormtroopers to cease "storming" *(stürmen)* in the streets and instead to develop a "stormy inner being."[107] Addressing them in person, he said,

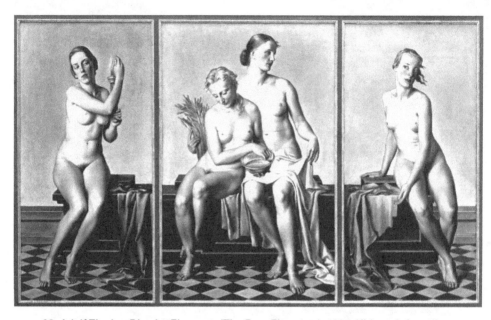

22. Adolf Ziegler, *Die vier Elemente* (The Four Elements), 1937. Hitler reinforced conventional tastes and values not only in his lengthy discourses on aesthetic purity but by personally collecting National Socialist Realist art and sponsoring huge exhibitions. Like so many of his choices, Ziegler's triptych, which adorned the living room of Hitler's Munich residence, echoed Italian Renaissance art forms.

"I am determined to . . . wage the battle for the soul and the unity of the *Volk* . . . You will stand beside me as you have in the fifteen years which lie behind us. And just as we succeeded in conquering 90 percent of the German *Volk* for National Socialism, we will and must be able to win over the last 10 percent . . . This will be the crowning glory of our victory."[108] The battle of the streets became a campaign to win hearts and minds.

Two respected jurists set the intellectual seal on impunity for state-sanctioned murder. Minister of Justice Hans Gürtner, who was not a Nazi Party member, justified the murders because he feared that otherwise citizens might distrust their government. Carl Schmitt explained that because Hitler's will was the supreme law of the land, "the true Führer is always also judge. The status of judge flows from the status of Führer . . . The Führer's deed was, in truth, the genuine exercise of justice. It is not subordinate to justice, but rather it is itself supreme justice."[109] Hitler's self-defense made explicit the basis of Nazi jurisprudence: crimes committed in the name of protecting the *Volk* from moral danger were legal. Declaring his exclusive right to identify that danger and excise it, Hitler justified the curtailment of freedoms as protection against disorder. In just over a year, he had mobilized ethnic populism to replace a constitutional democracy with a regime that could murder in the name of morality—and make its justification credible in the eyes of most Germans.

Writing during the closing months of World War II, the philosopher Alexandre Koyre alerted readers to the vulnerability of democracies to subversion by ruthless insiders who have no scruples about deceiving their subject-citizens. Koyre observed that, although lying was as old

23. Hitler gazing sternly into the eyes of a Stormtrooper. This image from a large-format (12″ × 22″) photograph book honoring the Stormtroopers conveyed the impression that a special bond connected the Führer with his most faithful followers—even as the Stormtroopers lost status relative to Heinrich Himmler's SS.

as civilization itself, "modern man—*genus totalitarian*—bathes in the lie, breathes the lie, is in thrall to the lie." Koyre mentioned gangsters, religious fraternities, lobbyists, and sects as well as political cliques. Although hardcore members may be disillusioned when they hear their leaders' public disavowal of their true aims, gradually they come to appreciate the need for leaders' discretion in a mass society.[110] The "truth remains constantly concealed, unuttered"—and yet intuited, an open secret. Hitler refrained from revealing the depths of his antisemitism in public, confident that the party faithful would grasp the true meaning behind his public silence. He and his deputies forged what Koyre called an "open conspiracy," in which the leadership expresses the deepest purpose of the organization as a "cryptogram" designed to mollify outsiders while accurately communicating its message to insiders.

Addressing the general public, Hitler discussed economics and diplomacy in considerable detail. On only three occasions between April 1933 and the invasion of Poland in September 1939, did Hitler directly vent his phobic racial hatred.[111] Addressing the Reichstag at the 1935 Nuremberg Rally, he delivered a preamble to the laws that destroyed Jewish citizens' legal status in Germany. Against the background of the Spanish Civil War and Mussolini's visit to the Nuremberg Rally in September 1937, Hitler railed against the Jewish-Bolshevik "contagion" and called on the leaders of "civilized" Western European nations to follow his lead in combating the "Jewish-Bolshevist, international league of criminals." Then, on the occasion of the sixth anniversary of his chancellorship, Hitler delivered a radio address in which he predicted that, in the event of world war, Jewry would be "exterminated." Compared with the range of topics he covered in dozens of two- and three-hour speeches, racial policy hardly figured in his pronouncements.

Nevertheless, Hitler found ways of sending "cryptograms" to hardcore Nazis to reassure them that despite his public restraint he had not abandoned the racial core of his beliefs. When denouncing an already unpopular idea, Hitler would casually describe it as Jewish. At the 1934 Nuremberg Rally, for example, he told women Nazis at the 1934 Nuremberg Rally that "the catchword 'women's emancipation' . . . [was] merely a phrase invented by the Jewish intellect."[112] Another of his rhetorical strategies was to project his hatred of Jews onto his victims who, he alleged, planned to "wage a battle for life and death" until the "final struggle" against the Third Reich. In the process, Hitler injected the concept of lethal racial warfare into public culture.

24. "Long Live Germany!" In this painting, Hitler, attired in his SA brown shirt, took up the banner of Nazism to lead throngs of disciplined SA men. The oak leaves of the frame suggested ancient Germanic origins, crowned by the swastika and eagle. Where one might expect to see a peace dove in flight against the rays of the rising sun, an eagle soared.

Mein Kampf itself became a third kind of cryptogram. During the years when Hitler barely mentioned racial policy in public, virulently anti-semitic quotations from *Mein Kampf* adorned Nazi Party publications. Hitler's words would appear as frontmatter or in decorated boxes adorning articles on racial issues. Perhaps the high point in the canonization of *Mein Kampf* came on April 20, 1936, Hitler's forty-seventh birthday, when the Reich League of German Government Officials gave their Chief a copy of *Mein Kampf* that had been transcribed by hand in medieval script on leather parchment.[113] Bound in iron and weighing 75 pounds, this 965-page tome sent a clear signal that whatever Hitler said in public, civil servants understood that the racist promises in *Mein Kampf* remained as central in 1936 as they had been in 1924.

Needless to say, no one doubted Hitler's antisemitism. But a skillfully managed public relations campaign allowed moderate Germans to rationalize their support for Nazi rule. They could become "yes but" Nazis—welcome ethnic fundamentalism and economic recovery while dismissing Nazi crimes as incidental. The marketing strategy that allowed this kind of doublethink was established by the end of 1934 and remained in place until the collapse of Nazi rule. No matter what the crime—whether the "legal" theft of Jewish property, imprisonment in a concentration camp, or murder—it was committed in public. Hitler declared his intentions openly in *Mein Kampf*. But Hitler's benign public image and careful news management minimized their impact. Media reporting on concentration camps and mass arrests described Nazi terror as protective. Allegations about victims' guilt were framed in moral, not political, terms, and protesting voices were discredited as foreign-influenced. By preserving his public distance from the unpopular aspects of his rule, Hitler—flanked by a team of political advertisers—communicated in cryptograms to the Nazi faithful while reassuring mass audiences that his intentions were benign.

Ethnic Revival and Racist Anxiety

We have achieved great success in our drive to implant concern for the biological life of the nation into the conscience of the *Volk*.

—*Walter Gross, lecture at the Convention of the Office of Racial Politics, June 1935*

In late June 1933 Interior Minister Wilhelm Frick convened a blue-ribbon committee on demographic and racial policy. Included on the guest list were individuals who seemed to have little in common: a leader of Nazi women, the Interior Ministry's expert on racial affairs, an art historian, the chief judge in the Nazi Party court, and the mayor of Darmstadt, together with internationally respected eugenicists, Nazi Party ideologues, and medical reformers. Some guests belonged to the Nazi Party, but most did not.[1] As they gathered, committee members may have anticipated that Frick would propose new antisemitic measures. But in his 45-minute welcome he spoke only obliquely about the dangers of "racial mixing and racial degeneration" and of "people from alien backgrounds" *(Fremdstämmigen)*. Jews were not the objects of the new racial policy—imperfect Aryans were.

Frick explained an ambitious program to evaluate "our ethnic body politic *[Volkskörper]* according to its genetic value" as only one dimension of a comprehensive moral revolution that would revive communal values. Warning against complacency, Frick announced that it would be an unfortunate misunderstanding to imagine that the new regime had ended its mission when it rescued the *Volk* from political disintegration. Not at all, Frick cautioned. With the Nazi hold on power complete, the "positive work" of ethical renewal would begin. In the urgent rhetoric of social Darwinism, Frick warned that Germans were fighting for their survival. But the threats he described did not lurk outside German borders; they lay within the *Volk* itself. Because of the materialism and lamentable moral decline of the Weimar era, three deleterious trends had to be thwarted: birth control that reduced the *Volk* by encouraging a "two-child family system," extravagant social welfare programs that wasted money on so-called hopeless clients, and "sexual freedom [that promoted] the mannish woman *[Mannweib]*."[2] In passing, he worried about Jewish emigrants from the East and the dangers of "racial mixing," but this was not the imminent threat. In Frick's mind, the danger of "ethnic death" stemmed from moral failure, which he identified as a pervasive egocentrism that allowed those who were "fit" (from an evolutionary point of view) to limit family size while encouraging the "unfit" to thrive. Only an entirely new civic ethos could rescue the *Volk* from the ravages of urbanization, mechanization, and moral degeneracy.

Frick described an ambitious program to "eradicate" *(ausmerzen)* the bad and "select" *(auslesen)* the beneficial. Pro-natalist incentives, genetic counseling, and improved health care were flanked by stricter laws against birth control and abortion, rigorous premarital medical examinations, and an involuntary sterilization program. A week later, Frick praised ethnic morality to a nationwide radio audience. In earlier times, Nature had allowed the weakest to perish before reaching maturity. Modern medicine, by "artificially" enabling weaklings to survive, had damaged the long-term health of the *Volk*. Criticizing the "outmoded" command to "love thy neighbor," Frick advocated state-sponsored eugenic intervention that fulfilled "Nature's wishes."[3] No matter how powerful the state's coercive methods were, ethnic recovery ultimately depended on individual willingness to comply.

Over the next decade, philosophers and medical ethicists in Nazi Germany pondered the merits of health care rationing, genetic counseling, involuntary sterilization, and euthanasia—issues referred to vaguely in the Nazi Party program but otherwise ignored in the party press. Once, during a party rally in 1929, Hitler had discussed the ethics of sterilization in a comment that if, of one million newborns, 10,000 of the least desirable died, it would result in a net gain for the *Volk*.[4] While saying nothing more in public, Hitler revealed his preoccupation with moral issues in a closed cabinet meeting a few weeks after Frick's June 1933 speech, when he justified sterilization as "morally incontestable" because it was a lesser evil than the "hereditarily ill people [who] reproduced themselves in considerable quantity while in contrast millions of healthy children remain unborn."[5] His apparent unwillingness to publicly endorse specific ethnic improvement projects suggests that Hitler anticipated opposition.[6]

State-directed sterilization contravened two deeply rooted principles: one was the secular precept enshrined in John Locke's *Second Treatise* that "every man has a property in his own person," and the other was the prohibition against any interference in reproduction, which Pope Pius XI forcefully restated in his 1930 *Casti Connubbi*. The framers of the Nazi sterilization program looked to other precedents, such as a 1927 U.S. Supreme Court ruling, written by Justice Oliver Wendell Holmes, to justify sterilization. In the wake of world war, when "the best of a generation of young men risked their lives for the nation," Holmes wrote, "it would be strange if it could not call upon those who already sap the strength of the state for these lesser sacrifices . . . in order to prevent our being swamped with incompetence . . . Three generations of imbeciles are enough."[7] The Nazi sterilization program developed within a broad context of eugenic programs in 28 American states as well as several European nations.[8]

What distinguished Nazi "ethnic improvement" schemes was not the logic that underwrote them but their magnitude. Between 1907 and 1945 in the United States (the closest parallel), 45,127 people were sterilized. But in Germany, the internationally respected eugenicist Friedrich Lenz calculated that 1 million feeble-minded Germans (in a population of 65 million) should be sterilized, while Agricultural Minister Walter Darré put the total at ten times that many.[9] Frick prepared his radio audience for a rate of one in five.[10] For eugenics programs on this scale to function effectively, couples would have to willingly submit their family health records for scrutiny and obey rulings by genetic health courts. Physicians and social workers would have to coerce resistant clients to forego not only childbearing but also marriage because under Nazi law infertility precluded marriage. Teachers, social workers, and medical personnel would have to report "suspicious" cases to municipal officials. Panels of legal, medical, and social welfare experts were convened to investigate cases, and appeal procedures were worked out.[11] To achieve the requisite level of assent, fundamental values would have to be transformed. In *Mein Kampf*, Hitler acknowledged how difficult it would be to change attitudes about such personal issues. "The ethnic state must perform the most gigantic educational task. And some day this will seem to be a greater deed than the most victorious wars."[12]

The responsibility for carrying out this "great deed" of ethical transformation fell to Walter Gross, a 29-year-old physician who had been appointed three months earlier to create the National Socialist Office for Enlightenment on Population Policy and Racial Welfare. Even though the sterilization law itself was temporarily kept secret so as not to offend the Vatican, Gross delivered a nationally broadcast radio speech concerning racial policy on July 14, 1933, the day the cabinet approved sterilization legislation. This marked the first public appearance of the man who was charged to create a consensus in support of the racial programs at the core of Nazi ideology. For the next twelve years, Gross infused public culture with knowledge about the supposedly superior *Volk* and the undesirable "others," by which he meant Jews, the "genetically damaged," African Germans, gypsies, homosexuals, and "asocial" elements (sex criminals, hoboes, and others).

Like many midlevel functionaries in the Nazi hierarchy, Gross was well educated, younger than the old guard, and a longtime party member. More sober than Hitler's closest comrades, Gross and other young "old fighters" who had joined the party before 1933 were ideally suited to popularize ethnic improvement, especially among Germans who remained apathetic or hostile to Nazi rule. Too young to have fought in the war, this generation had absorbed wartime patriotism as adolescents. Educated in universities during the 1920s, they were careerists who radiated know-how and efficiency. Hitler's architect, Albert Speer, epitomized this cadre, which also included Nazi Women's Bureau Director Gertrud Scholtz-Klink, film director Leni Riefenstahl, SS jurist Werner Best, SS Internal Security Chief Reinhard Heydrich, jurist and governor of occupied Poland Hans Frank, chief of the Lublin ghetto Odilo Globonik, Auschwitz commandant Rudolf Höss, and Adolf Eichmann, director of Jewish evacuation during World War II.[13]

From 1933 to 1945 Gross oversaw an ambitious public relations drive to heighten ethnic consciousness among the general public and to prepare hardcore Nazis for increasingly radical measures. Besides being influential advocates of racial purification, Gross and his staff wielded considerable influence behind the scenes of racial policymaking.[14] The historian of science Robert Proctor notes that "it would have been difficult for anyone living in Germany at this time not to have been touched by the activities of the office."[15] And yet Gross has all but disappeared from historical view. Several factors explain this oversight. As a team player, he remained in the shadow of flamboyant and more senior leaders like Alfred Rosenberg, Julius Streicher, and Joseph Goebbels. As a midlevel functionary, he did not exercise the power of notorious desk murderers like Eichmann or concentration camp commandants like Höss.[16] Heinrich Himmler's drive for power kept Gross, who did not join the SS, outside his inner circle.[17] Rudolf Hess's flight to Britain in May 1941 meant that Gross lost a key sponsor. Most important, by burning his files in April 1945 and then committing suicide, Gross removed evidence that would have incriminated the more than 3,000 members of his national network of racial educators.

Without oral histories and research in regional archives, the history of Gross's operations would have vanished.[18]

Walter Gross grew up in the milieu of the educated middle class. In 1919, when he was 15, his parents relocated from eastern Germany because of territorial losses mandated by the Treaty of Versailles. From his first days as a medical student, Gross gravitated to the most reactionary and antisemitic circles at the University of Göttingen, one of the most conservative universities in Germany.[19] At age 21, this serious young man joined the Nazi Party. Two years later, in 1927, Gross and his friends founded the Göttingen chapter of the National Socialist Student League. One of Gross's closest comrades was Achim Gercke, a rabid antisemite who was compiling an index-card database of 500,000 Jewish Germans' racial and genetic backgrounds with the aim of tracing their subversive power. As medical students, the young Nazis were influenced by a trio of internationally respected eugenicist professors, Eugen Fischer, Fritz Bauer, and Friedrich Lenz, as well as the medical ethicist Martin Staemmler, who advocated the elimination of "unfit" elements from the ethnic community. In Gross's first article, published in 1927, he cast racial improvement as primarily a moral imperative and cited Nietzsche as his authority.[20]

In 1929 Gross accepted a medical residency in Braunschweig, married Elfriede Fehsenfeld, whom he had met as a teenager, joined the Stormtroopers, and became more active in the National Socialist League of Physicians. Because of his political activities, he soon moved to Munich, where he served on the Nazi Party Committee for Ethnic Health *(Volksgesundheit)*.[21] Gross demonstrated his talents as a recruiter by organizing weekend conferences for physicians that blended political ideology, tourism, medicine, and collegiality.[22] From his earliest public lectures, he revealed a talent for adjusting his tone to audiences' backgrounds. When speaking to non-Nazis, Gross exuded ethnic fundamentalism; to Nazi comrades he vented his antisemitism.

As a self-styled racial philosopher, Gross described the crisis atmosphere of 1930 as an "upheaval of all values." Although cosmopolitan liberals had appropriated Nietzsche's moral philosophy because of its iconoclastic secularism, Gross reclaimed Nietzsche's ethics for conservatives. In the hyperbolic style that became his hallmark, Gross described the impact of the great philosopher: "Like a brilliant flash of lightning, Nietzsche slashed through the barren gray of a liberal era."[23] Nevertheless, Gross had no patience with the defiant ethos of lawless Stormtroopers. A transformation in values could not be coerced; it could only be inspired by the vision of a strong *Volk* bound so tightly together by "social conventions of blood and race" that all civil strife would end. A new ethnic "voice of conscience" *(Gewissensbissen)* would guide individuals to place the benefit of the *Volk* above their own self-interest.[24]

Writing for the hardcore Nazi readers of Alfred Rosenberg's virulently antisemitic periodical *World Struggle against Jewry,* Gross expressed in pedantic prose the depths of his racism. "I have arrived at the sober conclusion that the Jewish nature is different from ours and that, in particular respects, it directly opposes ours." Using historical examples, he connected racial degeneration to international Jewry and blamed Jews for causing the world war, Germany's defeat, and Weimar democracy, which "extinguished German character." Gross reiterated bogus statistics that demonstrated Jews' domination of medicine, the media, and banking. This "deadly enemy," camouflaged as assimilated Jewry, covertly poisoned the *Volk* by substituting its "vengeful God" for the "heroic Germanic God."[25] From its thinly disguised hostility to Christianity to its use of fraudulent evidence, Gross's article was merely a pretentious restatement of the crude racism of many Nazi tracts.

Gross distinguished himself, however, by his ability to bury his racism when addressing the unconvinced. An ideological chameleon, he could exude pious ethnic pride to a civic association and spew rabid racism to committed Nazi physicians. With his medical degree, academic demeanor, energy, and passionate oratory, Gross was the ideal racial publicist. Moreover, party chiefs could trust him because his membership number 2,815 (based on the date of joining) placed him high among the roughly 27,000 Nazis who joined the party in the mid-1920s.[26] A summons from Berlin came quickly. Deputy Leader of the Nazi Party Rudolf Hess appointed Gross to found the new National Socialist Office for Enlightenment on Population Policy and Racial Welfare. Although many self-appointed experts proposed such a bureau,[27] Hess selected Gross, perhaps because he sensed that the dynamic, youthful Gross would be able to stand up to critics.[28] "Our enemies' scorn," Hess wrote, struck directly at the very "heart" of the Nazi *Weltanschauung.* Gross's task was to win respect for Nazi programs among all Germans, to serve as a clearinghouse for racial proposals and to provide crash courses in racial principles for committed Nazis. Hess charged Gross with "training the entire nation to ethnic values without compromising with liberals." Yet over the next several years Hess's and Gross's complaints about their critics' "hate" and "scorn" suggested their frustration.[29]

Prof. Adolf Bartels

Dr. Walter Groß

Prof. Dr. med. Martin Staemmler

Prof. Dr. Schultze-Naumburg

25. Four pioneering racial scientists. In this illustration for Charlotte Koehn-Behrens' booklet *What Is Race?* the youthful Walter Gross takes his place alongside three academic researchers who had achieved recognition before 1933: Adolf Bartels, Martin Staemmler, and Paul Schultze-Naumburg.

When the journalist Charlotte Köhn-Behrens asked Gross in 1933 about his responsibilities, he answered, "Not research—that is the scientist's concern; not legislation—because that's done by the Interior Ministry; but [my task is] exclusively the schooling *[Erziehung]* of the *Volk* in biological attitudes and feelings."[30] The German verb *erziehen* suggests "to raise," "to train," and "to educate." The noun *Erziehung* suggests education in values as well as knowledge. "Moral education" is a close approximation. Talking to physicians, Gross described his task as "something totally new, unique, and unprecedented . . . [including] everything that influences people . . . that seizes them emotionally and streams over them."[31] Hess's choice of "enlightenment" *(Aufklärung)* instead of "propaganda" in the name of Gross's program was significant because in German, as in English, "enlightenment" evokes the eighteenth-century Age of Reason, with its overtones of revealed natural law. "Propaganda" fluctuates according to short-term policy needs. In Nazi usage, the latter incited immediate action, while "enlightenment" conveyed the idea that new attitudes come about through knowledge.[32] "Propaganda" carried a stigma of inconstancy, whereas "enlightenment" revealed the truth. Gross asked rhetorically, "What does the German *Volk* understand about racial welfare? Until today, nothing at all . . . People think of themselves as individuals and don't even realize they [are] merely single links in a great chain of life."[33] Gross imagined himself the creator of a vast new sector of national life that drew together public and private spheres as well as science and politics.

When Gross delivered a 20-minute radio speech on July 14, 1933—the day on which the sterilization law was approved—he took Nietzsche's call for a "transvaluation of values" as his text. "The [Nazi] Revolution that has just begun not only creates new political forms, but also new human beings and a new understanding of history. New values and judgments change our views of not only the future but of the past. This transvaluation of values marks our times and justifies it as a genuine spiritual revolution."[34] In the first ten minutes of his speech, Gross waxed lyrical about "the voice of the Blood streaming through history" and "the longing of the Blood for its own state and justice—liberated from the alien spirit that has trapped it for so long." Cautioning against "false humanity" and "exaggerated pity," Gross explained racial policy as a moral crusade for purity against the corrosive egotism of liberal philosophy. Then he outlined the three-pronged battle against "careless breeding" against falling birthrates among the so-called fit, against "unbridled childbearing" among the putatively unfit, and against racial mixing. For the first time in history, a nation suffering racial decline (that is, Germany) was about to be reborn because biologists had discovered the secret to eternal ethnic life, and racially aware political leaders were determined to apply that knowledge.[35] Without mentioning the word "Jew," Gross disparaged "unrestrained and spiritually homeless peoples" and quoted Hitler's opinion that "racial blending" was the "original sin" of humankind. Astute listeners must have sensed the menace behind his comment: "The rose that does not bloom will be pulled up and tossed in the fire, and the gardener will chop down the tree that bears no fruit."[36]

The headlines in the Nazi news media captured the theme of Gross's radio address: "The eternal voice of the blood in the stream of German history."[37] His speeches in the summer of 1933 were remarkable as much for their silence about National Socialism as for their explicit moral injunctions. Rather than speaking about race, Gross used one of Hitler's favorite terms, the *Volkskörper*. As a young party man with no academic credentials, he must have been pleased to share the podium in July with Carl Schmitt and Martin Heidegger at the University of Heidelberg.[38] Speaking to physicians a few weeks later, Gross announced an "enlightenment campaign" that would rally "warm hearts" and arouse "the passionate hu-

Gesetz zum Schutze der Erbgesundheit des deutschen Volkes
vom 18. Oktober 1935.

26. This statue commemorates "The Law to Protect the Genetic Health of the German *Volk*" of October 18, 1935, which required genetic screening of all couples planning to marry. Enacted within weeks of the antisemitic Nuremberg Race Laws, the measure suggested that members of the *Volk* must subject themselves to racial scrutiny. This slide appeared among 72 slides with accompanying text that instructed Hitler Youth about how to live a "Healthy Life." In addition to quotations by leading Nazis and photographs of the misbegotten, artistic renderings of racial purity accompanied explanations of racial policy.

man desire for the salvation of our *Volk* from humiliation and their thousand-year-old historical tragedy."[39] Describing "a great new age for the physician," Gross called for "a revolutionary professional ethic that mandates medical care for the *Volk* and not the individual."[40]

After only a few months in his new position, Gross was honored with an invitation to speak at the September 1933 Nazi Party Rally in Nuremberg. On the eve of the rally, Hitler read the speakers' texts. Although he ordered Goebbels to delete coarse antisemitism, Gross's sermon on ethnic morality passed muster. Speaking on national radio, Gross lamented the financial and cultural expense of maintaining "unworthy" beings at state expense. He railed against the liberal "experiment" that had nearly extinguished a healthy *Volk*. "They used to say . . . that every race in the world is a work of God. We, too, believe in precisely that idea, and therefore we demand a clean separation between blood and blood, so that mixed breeds will not confuse God's works and thus will not degenerate into hideous deformities."[41] Hitler and his comrades were self-taught bigots who mingled romantic Nordic racism with crude antisemitism. Arcane jargon about genotypes, phenotypes, skull measurements, and Mendelian inheritance laws meant nothing to them. But these long-time Nazis admired Gross, a young man of science who avoided technical issues and spoke in grandiose metaphysical terms. After the Nuremberg Rally, Goebbels commented approvingly, "Dr. Gross spoke very well about racial questions."[42] A few years later Goebbels found him "very reasonable" and easy to work with.[43] This positive reaction contrasted with Goebbels's response to a leading eugenicist: "He gave a bloody stupid talk about genetic care and families. If these gentlemen would only refrain from jabbering so much rubbish!"[44] Gross's sentimental outbursts and biological metaphors achieved the correct tone.

In the late spring of 1934, Hess rewarded his protégé Gross by charging him to create the National Socialist Office of Racial Politics (ORP) to promote ethnic thinking in every aspect of public life. A list of ORP subdivisions indicates its scope: education, propaganda, foreign relations, counseling, applied demography, public relations, science, and activities for women and girls. Over the next eleven years, Gross both collaborated with and competed against some of the most influential men in the Nazi hierarchy: Achim Gercke and Bernhard Lösener, both experts on Jews, in the Interior Ministry; Gerhard Wagner, head of the Nazi Physicians' League; Minister of Education Bernard Rust; and chief Nazi ideologue Alfred Rosenberg.[45] In the chaotic Nazi state, Gross was assigned the respon-

27. "Only genetically healthy offspring guarantee the continuation of the *Volk*." The man protected the mother with a shield inscribed, "The Law for the Prevention of Genetically Damaged Offspring, July 7, 1933." The caption, "We do not stand alone!" reassured readers by surrounding the couple with the flags of other modern nations (including the United States, Japan, England, Switzerland, and Finland among them) that had passed eugenic legislation.

sibility of transforming the fanatic racism of Hitler and his comrades into a coherent policy that would inspire confidence among both lay and professional audiences. Hess instructed Gross in 1934: "In addition to imposing a single orthodoxy on racial policy and guiding the education of and propaganda for specialists . . . [you will] resolve disputes related to empirical demographic and racial political questions."[46] At a leadership training course, Hess underscored the centrality of Gross's mission when he commented that a scientist who does not partake of the ethnic will is as racially worthless as the staunch National Socialist who is ignorant of racial principles.[47]

With over two dozen employees in its Berlin headquarters and affiliates in the 32 Nazi districts, the ORP had a high public profile and well-developed bureaucratic connections. At the grassroots, the ORP operated through regional and district offices. At the national level, it trained and certified racial political educators and medical school professors. Gross collaborated wlith other national Nazi associations like the Labor Front and the National Socialist Women's League to develop racial education projects.[48] By the late 1930s about 3,600 ORP representatives in Austria and Germany consulted on racial questions, directed racial training institutes, and coordinated research findings.

Gross faced in two directions throughout his career. When writing for mass-distribution periodicals and speaking with non-Nazis, Gross exuded ethnic fundamentalism—glorification of the *Volk,* punctuated by terse warnings about racial danger. Instructing Nazi Party organizations, Gross said less about the *Volk* and lashed out against the "Jewish menace." Like advertisers of the day, Gross adjusted his message and delivery style according to particular media and audiences. Addressing ordinary citizens, Gross assumed a folksy manner, often responding to critics with outbursts like, "That's simply false and crazy! *[Das ist törricht und falsch!]*" and "That's rubbish! *[Das ist Quatsch!].*" In question-and-answer formats he would paraphrase critics, gently rebuking the unconvinced (whom he addressed in the familiar *Du*). "Just talk this over with us for a while," he would tell them, "and you will come to appreciate the greatness of our cause." On occasion he would declare, "Only a crazy fool . . . could be so confused."[49] Ever the visionary, Gross was given to effusive proclamations, such as: "Anyone who cannot think in terms of grand epochs, who does not sense the breath of eternal life in himself and does not also have the ordinary person's healthy, earthy smell can only wreak havoc in this endeavor."[50]

Female audiences seemed to evoke his most passionate outbursts. Against enemies who accused Nazi "barbarians" of turning women into "breeding cattle," Gross praised the egalitarian new order in which a person's racial qualities, not their material wealth, determined status. Again using the familiar *Du,* Gross told women, "What you are, what I am and what I can become in my entire life—all that has been predetermined by our genetic inheritance."[51] He delivered a virtual sermon to women on the theme "You are nothing. Your *Volk* is everything" and told them how fortunate they were to be "little drops in the mighty bloodstream of the *Volk*."[52] Gazing out at audiences through his rimless glasses, Gross epitomized the earnest crusader for a "body and soul reformation" of the *Volk*.

Years later, a staff member recalled that his former chief had often seemed disappointed by the paucity of talented young researchers. The surfeit of recently graduated physicians assured a steady stream of applicants who sensed the possibility for funding in racial political projects, which Hess often described as applied biology.[53] But Gross worried that many applicants were motivated by opportunism and not belief. Over the years his optimism about imposing a coherent racial policy on party and state agencies also faded. From his first days in office, intense rivalries within established Nazi Party institutions inhibited Gross's efforts to standardize racial dogma. Sensing the centrality of race to the new regime, the Nazi Teachers League, the army, the Foreign Office, the SS, the Justice Ministry, and the Labor Front each established their own offices for racial affairs. In July 1933 Goebbels announced he would initiate a separate "propaganda campaign" in collaboration with Nazi physicians to popularize an "absolutely objective, sober, and clear-cut" approach to racial issues, but soon gave up the idea.[54] Interior Minister Frick undercut Gross's authority by establishing his own Panel of Experts on Racial Research. SS leader Heinrich Himmler kept Gross's office at a distance and monitored all potential "friction" between his race experts and Gross's programs.

Gercke, Gross's comrade from the university, despaired at "the uncontrolled proliferation of so-called 'racial offices' that threaten to endanger the success of racial thinking." Too many rival operations by unauthorized persons had, in Gercke's view, given racial improvement a bad name. Citizens resented these self-important racial "commissars" and laughed at extravagant claims advanced by "Racial Offices of Just about Anywhere."[55] Gross competed with the National Socialist Physicians' League (30,000 members) and 620 public health associations within the Public Health Office of the Interior Ministry. At the district level, Gross's liaison officers depended on local leaders' good will.

In these settings, Gross's low-profile networking style, unusual among rancorous Nazi chiefs, served him well. Operating quietly in the interstices of the Nazi Party and the civil service, Gross expanded his influence laterally. His rewards did not elevate him to high office, but they did situate him within a network of peers. In the late 1930s, he was one of only six physicians among 500 Reichstag delegates and was promoted to the rank of *Hauptamtsleiter* (director of a major office), which placed him just beneath the top tier of Nazi functionaries. At crucial junctures, Gross was brought in as a consultant on racial policies. In these settings, he consistently advocated radical long-term aims and restrained—that is, bureaucratic—means. Unlike many seasoned old fighters, Gross understood that the tactics which had won supporters for Nazism before 1933 would be counterproductive in the Third Reich. In the "time of struggle" raucous Nazis had used intimidation to delegitimize liberal institutions.[56] But after January 1933, Gross cautioned that strong-arm tactics were counterproductive because they engendered hypocrisy and resentment among potential converts to racial thinking.[57]

Describing his vision as an ethnic "reformation" or "revolution," Gross often compared his task to smelting iron and forging steel. Over the course of the next several years, he directed his far-flung network of racial-political persuaders to create a *Volk* for which ordinary Germans would willingly sacrifice.

The Office of Racial Politics, in its first year of existence, published 14 booklets in editions of up to 500,000 that were designed for racial education workshops, leadership training courses, and curricular supplements in schools. Gross's 32-page selection of passages from the 700 pages of *Mein Kampf* presented a Hitler devoid of bigotry—a sage towering above ordinary politicians. On the cover, a visionary Führer, dressed in civilian clothes, gazed into the distance. In his introduction, Gross described Hitler as the personification of innocence, a Christ-like savior, a "genius [who is] recognized as unquestionably the most important world historical figure of our day" because he had discovered the "great Truth" of the universe, the "eternal genetic inequality of all men." Hitler's racial paradigm opened up a new understanding of the healthy ethnic body politic, Mother Nature's laws, the rise of Western science, art, and technology, the power of self-sacrifice, and the heroic Germanic past. Gross used the adjective "Jewish" sparingly, mainly to describe character traits like arrogance and impertinence. Aside from one quotation in which Hitler compared ethnically mixed marriages *(Rassenschande)* to "unions between ape and human," the topic of race barely appeared. Starting in 1935, the ORP produced educational films, slideshows, and oversized posters about eugenics for national distribution.

Because the newly appointed racial experts at every level of the bureaucracy needed racial education, Gross commissioned his friend Gercke to compile an annotated bibliography to guide fledgling public lecturers.

Like Gross, Gercke exuded appeals for Germans to experience, for example, "hot love for our own kind." Striking a theme familiar among eugenicists, Gercke announced, "Our *Volk* is sick, wretchedly sick," and insisted that only a moral transformation could heal it.[58] After years of welfare that kept too many defective people alive, the time had come to take stock. "Racial ideas . . . are the therapeutic doctrine of our era," he wrote, "and the racial question" was "the very axis on which the National Socialist worldview *[Ideenwelt]* turns." Only 32 of the 233 "scientific and philosophical" works in his biography focused on race and the "Jewish question." Gercke, like Gross, seethed with antipathy toward Jews, yet he simulated impartiality by including some titles that "did not reflect Nazi views."

In 1933 Gross launched a mass-market illustrated magazine, *Neues Volk (New Volk),* in a format resembling the slick appearance of *Life* and *Look* magazines in the United States, as well as mass-market German women's magazines. The breezy middlebrow tone of *Neues Volk,* together with its popular science features on race, reached out to readers who dismissed *Der Stürmer* as trash and distrusted overtly Nazi media as unreliable. As the circulation grew from 75,000 in 1933 to over 300,000 in the late 1930s, the periodical could be found in physicians' waiting rooms, schools, and public libraries as well as private homes.[59] Gross pledged that *Neues Volk* would "acquaint readers with ancient truths so we can restore our *Volk*. In simple, comprehensible form, readers will learn how our blood needs to be healed and what we must do to create a new, strong generation worthy of future generations."[60] Except for occasional quotations by Hitler (which were usually printed as epigraphs within boxes), few authors mentioned Hitler or referred to Nazi racial dogma. Contributors were identified by their academic degrees and occupations, not by their Nazi Party titles. In photographs, ORP staff usually wore civilian clothes.

Lavishly illustrated articles reported on such diverse topics as one day in a National Youth Service Corps camp, a character sketch of "Mussolini, the Father of His *Volk*," travel tips, and reproductions of canonical Germanic art. Quaint peasants, courageous SA men, healthy skiers, radiant mothers, and robust children filled the pages. Advertisements for tourism, personal hygiene, and sports suggested that the target readership was health-conscious, progressive, and patriotic. But insidious racial messages found their way into hereditary charts, cartoons ridiculing conspicuous consumers and childless couples, and exposés of Jewish influence in high

Inmitten dieser Schar befinden sich drei Idioten, alle drei erblich belastet, die bereits 11, 16 und 29 Jahre in Anstaltsverwahrung sind. Sie haben dem Staat bisher Kosten von 12100, 17600 und 31900 RM verursacht und haben noch ein langes ziel- und zweckloses Leben, keinem zu Nutze, vor sich

Links oben und rechts: Schaubilder, die überall auf den Betrachter tiefe Wirkung ausüben

28. "Sterilization: Not Punishment—but Liberation. What Parent would wish to place such a terrifying burden on their children? Who would choose to be guilty of this?" Nazi racial precepts reversed conventional morality based on the sanctity of human life by vindicating, in the interests of the *Volk*, the state-directed prevention of births deemed unwanted. Although the individuals in this photograph were stigmatized by the absence of gender markers and shaved heads, the accompanying article admonished readers to respect their sterilized fellow Aryans.

places. Bioethicists explained why sterilization harmonized Christian morality and assured readers that the Golden Rule applied only to your "racial comrades."[61]

Amid the diverse topics covered in the magazine, a single leitmotif predominated: ethnically aware Germans could make their lives more meaningful by participating in collective projects that benefited the *Volk*.[62] The visual layout of *Neues Volk* juxtaposed the aesthetically "desirable" with the "repugnant." After six issues entirely devoted to ethnic pride, in December 1933 a warning about "racial undesirables" appeared. Reich Police Chief Kurt Daleuge described the techniques he had found effective in tracking down "The Criminal Jew." Mug shots identified "Jewish-looking" criminals as "pickpocket, confidence man, drug dealer [the only female face], fence, and passport counterfeiter."[63] Photographs of healthy Aryans and treasures of Germanic art in the rest of the issue imparted a moral valence to a putative racial contrast. For the most part, the magazine focused on "positive" images. But within this benign context, a small number of repellent photographs captioned with scare headlines injected powerful doses of anxiety about so-called misfits.

Among scores of articles about physically fit and racially ideal Aryans, occasional "informational" photographic essays would interrupt the upbeat mood. "France and the Black Danger," for example, featured photographs of French women mingling with soldiers from Senegal. Anthropologists' photographs of Native Americans and African Americans that illustrated "The Value of Race" exoticized racial difference.[64] Articles on the bioethics of sterilization paired photographs of mentally incapacitated children with their healthy counterparts under captions like "Do we want this? Or this?"[65] Readers of *Neues Volk* were invited to submit photographs of ideal Germans. Sample genetic family trees included a few photos of "defective" forbearers, suggesting that "genetic damage" could lurk in even the healthiest families.[66] Demographic charts, illustrated with drawings of selfish urban dwellers and generous Aryan peasants, warned that open farmland was vanishing and Jews were extinguishing the traditional peasantry. A photographic essay positioned "Snobs, Gents, Dance Crazed Youth, and Barflies" (English in the original) against photographs of German amateur runners and Hitler Youth members. A snapshot of the African-American singer Josephine Baker in Paris and her admirers was printed opposite the photo of a German boys' choir.[67] "Tastelessness or Racial Oblivion?" asked the caption for photographs of mixed-race friendships.[68] A sad, "genetically sick" face gazes at readers,

29. "The genetically ill damage the community. The healthy preserve the *Volk.*" An illustrated SS training manual incorporated photographs that originally appeared in *Neues Volk* and also reproduced the graphic convention that juxtaposed so-called undesirables on the left with ideal types on the right.

and on the opposite page two cheerful skaters skim across a frozen pond.[69] The *Neues Volk* tantalized readers with descriptions of supposedly dangerous and degenerate "outsiders" while praising the virtuous, vigorous, and healthy.

In 1936, after the Nuremberg Laws destroyed Jews' civil rights and Nazi bosses accelerated the expropriation of Jewish-owned property, *Neues Volk* implicitly urged readers not to take pity on the suffering of Jewish friends and colleagues. A series of unflattering photographs featured Jewish refugees in Paris enjoying material prosperity and cultural decadence—an image that reinforced Gerhard Kittel's suggestion that impoverished refugees would be cared for by "world Jewry" and Carl Schmitt's proposal to cancel the passports of exiled Germans.[70] A collection of photographs showing allegedly Jewish people in public recreation facilities bore the headline: "Jewish Persecution in Germany?" and asked readers to see for themselves "how many signs of Jewish life we still see around us."[71] Recounting her life in Nazi Germany, a young Jewish woman recalled the impression left by *Neues Volk:* "Under this suggestive title, [the magazine] was occupied exclusively with the publication of pictures and articles about the damage done by racial mixing. The photographs depicted the most horrible types of mixtures of white and black races. The articles, by contrast, directed attention only to the Jews, who were seen to present at least as great a danger as the Negroes."[72]

A summary of Gross's public appearances in 1935 conveys the scope of his dual efforts to popularize ethnic fundamentalism among general readers and to forge consistent racial doctrine among policymakers. Early in the year Gross delivered his first lectures at the University of Berlin. In February he explained "positive population policy" to 140 Protestant ministers from all over Germany.[73] A few weeks later he addressed 20,000 youth in the Nordic Society.[74] At an annual teachers' convention Gross urged that "racially superior" students be placed in accelerated courses so they would graduate more quickly.[75] Speaking in the Interior Ministry to the second blue-ribbon committee on racial improvement, Gross encouraged delegates to proceed with the secret sterilization of children born to African-French fathers and German mothers.[76] To diplomats at a Foreign Office reception, Gross lectured on "German demographic policy and its impact abroad," and a few days later he convened the annual ORP convention.[77] In June he opened a weeklong ORP workshop by announcing that the "national conscience" had been filled with National Socialist concepts.[78] In Cologne he spoke to the Nazi Women's League about

30. "Jews Persecuted in Germany?" Of course not, this collage retorted. In addition to implying that Jews in Germany had the leisure and means to go to the beach, smoke in a bar, and have a drink in a public garden, the newspaper clippings reported that Jewish physicians, despite laws to curtail their practices, had not been driven from their profession.

"Blood and Race."[79] In August Gross participated in the International Congress for Population Research in Berlin and organized a racial politics workshop at the Nuremberg Rally.[80] His national radio talk, "Holy Is the Blood," was translated for foreign distribution. Addressing physicians in Thuringia, he explained why racial values could not be coerced but had to be inspired.[81] In November Gross directed a short course in which physicians explored both physical and emotional dimensions of racial health.[82]

Whether or not they considered themselves Nazis, Germans encountered Gross's ideas in many settings. The ORP collaborated with a racial studies institute in planning a Museum of Race in Frankfurt.[83] It sponsored traveling exhibits designed to arouse ethnic pride and racial *Angst* through photographic panels of so-called defectives and ideal Aryans. Captions asked, "How was it in the past? How should the future look?"[84] A

1937 exhibit, "The German Face in the Mirror of Centuries," illustrated the changeless facial structure of a superior *Volk*. Each year the ORP produced an illustrated calendar with images of "racially ideal" Germans, which sold between 150,000 and a half million copies.

The ORP also trained a veritable corps of ethnic educators. On a campus near Berlin, more than 1,400 speakers took intensive eight-day ORP courses in racial science in the 1930s. Described by an instructor as "a challenging education" *(harte Schulung),* these courses blended missionary zeal and military discipline in preparing participants to speak knowledgeably about racial matters in their home districts.[85] Over a thousand SS men each year studied at the school. Recent medical school graduates studied racial science there before taking up positions in district offices. In three typical months, from April to June 1938, Gross's office organized 1,160 meetings, each of which drew about a hundred Nazi organizers.[86] Later that year, Gross estimated that his office had organized 64,000 public assemblies and educated over 4,000 Nazi Party leaders (a third of them women) in racial policy.[87] Pamphlets like "Racial Politics in Wartime," "Can You Think Racially?" "Peasantry between Yesterday and Tomorrow," "German Racial Care," "Race and Religion," and "Racial Thinking and the Colonial Question" popularized knowledge about ethnic health and racial damage. In every publication readers were deluged with supposedly objective demonstrations of Germanic superiority—and warned that the Jewish danger was so extreme it could undermine even a courageous *Volk*.

Gross's talent for injecting racial fears into inspirational ethnic fundamentalism may explain why he was often selected to explain racial policy to non-Germans.[88] Between 1934 and 1937 he participated in major world congresses of demographic and eugenic scholars in Zurich, London, Berlin, and Paris. At the 1938 International Anthropological Society convention in Copenhagen, he vehemently defended biological racism against the anthropologist Franz Boas, who believed in the universal humanity of all peoples.[89] When explaining Nazi racial policy to foreign critics, Gross would praise the antimiscegenation laws, Jim Crow practices, and involuntary sterilization programs in the United States.[90]

In 1935 U.S. Ambassador William Dodd uncritically described a talk by Gross, whom he called the director of the "Racio-Political Buro": "Racial knowledge and race hygiene is not so much a scientific study or a study for a specialist as it is a spiritual question in which the principal point at issue is: 'for or against Germany,' said Dr. Gross. The disappearance of past peoples and cultures had been due far more to a decadence of their living substance than to political or economic reasons. National Socialism had been the first to recognize this fact in law and it was important that a feeling for these laws be instilled in the hearts and minds of the entire population."[91] A few months later, Gross conveyed similar sentiments to 700 Germans living in London. When foreign students gathered at the University of Berlin in 1936, Gross boasted that erstwhile critics of Nazi ethnic improvement programs had changed their opinion so decisively that now they envied Germany. "And so in these days we once more unfurl our banner that supports Life against the Dark Forces of Death. We shall serve the future by the profession of faith: sacred is the blood that the Almighty has given to us."[92]

In 1936 Gross founded a monthly newsletter for German-speaking readers abroad, the *Rassenpolitische Auslands-Korrespondenz (RAK)*.[93] Within a year its circulation reached 25,000, and Gross began an English-language edition, the *Racio-Political Foreign Correspondence (RFC)*. On its masthead, Gross was called the chief of the Bureau for Human Betterment and Eugenics, a name that harmonized with the international eugenics discourse of the day.[94] News in the *RFC* featured topics such as eugenic law in other nations, medical ethics, Italian racial policy, French-colonial racism, the Japanese soul, and the international fight against Communism, as well as summaries of talks by Hitler, Interior Minister Frick, Gross, and other racial researchers. In an English-language anthology, *Germany Speaks,* published for foreign distribution, Gross praised the comprehensive Nazi racial project. In "Blood and Race," a pamphlet published in Milwaukee, Wisconsin, Gross praised racial policy as God's will. "If we attempt to preserve the differences and particular virtues of other races—given to them by Heaven—then we are serving the Creator and His laws, for we are thus carrying out a more religious work than those contentious academic circles who place ideas above real pulsating life."[95] When addressing the unconvinced, Gross diluted his racism and spoke in the "polite" Judeo-phobic idiom common in Europe at the time.

Besides intuiting his audiences' responses, Gross had an ear for his superiors' concerns. During the 1930s, when Hitler claimed to be a pacifist, Gross deplored war because it kills off the most valuable stock.[96] When Goering announced his four-year economic plan in 1936, Gross explained its relevance to ethnic improvement. As Hitler and Mussolini worked out an *entente,* Gross collaborated with the Italo-German Academy of Racial Studies in Rome.[97] In the aftermath of the November 1938 "Crystal Night" pogrom, ORP liaisons distributed press releases documenting the so-called Jewish danger to local news media.[98] Always *au courant*, the dynamic Gross made ethnic health relevant to every passing trend and palatable to a broad spectrum of public opinion.

In the first months of Nazi rule, Gross had hailed radio as a miracle medium. Like Goebbels and his staff, however, Gross reconsidered when he realized that listeners who were bored by lectures about "chromosome counts or Mendel's Laws" would simply turn off their sets.[99] Visual media, by contrast, offered the prospect of captive audiences. Over the next decade, Gross's office produced several series of slide lectures in editions of 1,000 that circulated throughout the national school system and local party organizations. Like other Nazi indoctrinators, Gross appreciated the potential of films to enthrall captive audiences in a darkened room. Because a film "encompasses the body and the soul simultaneously," he wrote, it was the ideal medium to reinforce racist instincts.[100] Moving images of allegedly defective and racially undesirable people on a large screen jolted viewers. After viewing an ORP film, probably *The Victim of the Past*, Goebbels shuddered, "It made my flesh crawl. Horrible stuff." *Victim* opens with a quotation from Gross's 1933 party rally speech. Photographs of the supposedly "unworthy" life illustrated his words. "Here the spirit of a liberal-pacifist age has left its most horrifying fruits. We have all been shocked that the state and society have spent great sums of money motivated by sympathy and charity to maintain criminals and mentally deranged people. They have defended the feeble-minded and idiotic . . . Meanwhile, the son of a good German family hardly has money for a crust of bread. We build palaces for the feeble-minded."[101] Hitler was so impressed by *The Victim of the Past* that he ordered Gross to produce more films like it.

In the mid-1930s other ORP documentaries went into production: *Sins against Blood and Race; The Sins of the Fathers; The Inheritance; What You Inherit; All Life Is Battle; Off the Beaten Track; Palaces for the Mentally Ill;* and *Genetically Sick.*[102] Images of severely disabled people were enhanced by graphic designs that mimicked "degenerate" aesthetic styles. As in *Neues Volk,* the misbegotten were juxtaposed with the athletic. Male experts wore white lab coats and spoke in resonant movietone voices that contrasted with the chaos of asylum life. Five hundred copies of major ORP films were distributed to regional offices for screenings by 20,000 local Nazi associations; in 1934 alone, these associations sponsored 110,000 film programs. At a leadership training retreat in 1935, SS instructors praised ORP films.[103] Short ORP documentaries were regularly shown between the coming attractions and the newsreels at feature films. Altogether, an estimated 20 million people viewed at least one ORP film per year. These varied productions bore Gross's characteristic blend of sentimental ethnic glorification and somber prophecy. Because Gross feared that "empty speeches and pure scholarship" bored audiences, he exhorted his staff to appeal to warm hearts rather than cold reason.

Gross constantly called for vigilance in "eliminating destructive spirits." It disturbed him that so many physicians and natural scientists had in the 1920s so willingly accepted Jewish peers into their circles, and he feared that they secretly maintained ties with them after 1933. Show Jews no mercy, he admonished.[104] In front of women's volunteer organizations, Gross glorified the *Volk* in flowery allegories, but his tone changed when he spoke to the committed Nazis in the Women's League *(Frauenschaft)*. As ethnically conscious consumers, he told them, women must drive Jews out of business by shopping Aryan, even if that meant that they "would have to pay a few pennies more or walk a few extra steps."[105] At times, Gross confessed his frustration at Nazi leaders whose muddled notions about race provided "enemies" with fodder for criticism.[106] Although Gross looked favorably on alternative medicine, when the situation mandated he would cast his lot with mainstream physicians and discredit extremists as cranks.[107] He castigated the Nordic racial movement as misguided because scientists proved that a single "Nordic race" did not exist.

For about 5,000 racial experts, the ORP published the *Information Service (Informationsdienst)*, a biweekly newsletter that exhorted readers to continue their relentless "nonviolent" war against "Jewish blood" and "defective genes."[108] In regular contributions to the Nazi medical journal *Goal and Path (Ziel und Weg)*, which had a circulation of 40,000, Gross prepared his colleagues for aggressive antisemitic measures. Under his direction, the ORP trained physicians and staff to perform sterilizations.[109] At dozens of the medical bioethics seminars on race that were required for medical licensing, Gross explained Nazi race policies.[110] When he joined Nazi leaders at training encampments at the Vogelsang Castle, he lectured to as many as 800 medical students about "liberating" the ethnic community from its "undesirable" elements.[111] Gross regularly offered courses for physicians at the luxurious Alt-Rehse conference center and lectured at the Military Academy on "The Fundamentals of National Socialist Racial Policies."[112]

Gross and his staff wielded considerable influence as consultants to virtually every branch of the civil service. The ORP published a guide that helped Nazi teachers to identify and provide "special education" for disabled students, thereby placing them under surveillance.[113] He and his staff contributed expert opinions on definitions of "Jewishness," the status of unwed mothers, African-Germans' mental traits, gypsies' racial identity, and the racial value of Jewish-German *Mischlinge* (Germans with Jewish and Christian ancestors). No matter what the policy issue, Gross's office presented the case for an unsentimental racial policy.

Operating at the margins of the upper echelons in the Nazi Party and charged with popularizing racial values among ordinary Germans, Gross's facility for matching his approach to particular constituents made him a good barometer of opinion. When speaking to general audiences, Gross appealed to ethnic pride; among Nazis, he mobilized racial hatred. In publications for insiders, he occasionally expressed anger at his less-than-zealous peers, concern about the conundrums that plagued his racist philosophy, and frustration at the failure of biologists to produce physiological evidence of race. Concerning each of the three initiatives that he touted with such bravado to the general public—natalism, sterilization, and antisemitism—Gross confessed, in Nazi medical venues, his growing disillusionment. In the case of natalism, birth rates increased in 1934–35 and then dipped below predictions, despite the world's most generous incentives for childbearing. It must have irked Gross, the father of four children, that fertility rates among high-ranking Nazis remained below replacement levels.

Gross also encountered setbacks in the involuntary sterilization program because of stiff opposition from the Catholic Church.[114] At the beginning, when extreme cases were proposed for sterilization, many non-Catholics and even a few Catholics seemed to accept the necessity of the policy.[115] By 1935, however, as more and more doubtful cases were screened for so-called genetic damage, hostility mounted. The archives of the Ministries of Education and Interior, as well as SS Security Service surveys and clandestine Sopade reports, corroborate a growing fear of sterilization.[116] A woman ORP liaison officer explained, "Despite an occasional success, the collaboration with social workers in the regional Office for Youth Welfare remains unsatisfying mainly because of philosophical principles."[117] One sign that the Nazis themselves were disappointed in the program is the fact that sterilization statistics, so widely publicized in 1934, were kept secret after 1935.

The third initiative, antisemitism, also left much to be desired, according to articles in ORP newsletters. Too many ordinary citizens, it seemed, treated "racial outsiders" kindly.[118] Over the next few years ORP staff members appeared to realize that public opinion may have been less vital than they thought. A determined cadre of convinced racial experts, backed by the judicial and police systems, could administer racial programs without the general public's realizing their extent. The key to success lay not in a massive public education campaign but in orderly procedures and a cadre of dedicated administrators.

As a passionate "true believer," Gross in the mid-1930s agonized about how to assess the sincerity of newcomer Nazis. How could anyone know if an individual's motives for collaborating were genuine or opportunistic? People would shout "Heil Hitler!" at meetings, hang swastikas in their windows, and donate to Nazi Party charities. And yet, he fretted, these same people might use birth control, maintain ties with Jews, laugh about racial policy, and tell "dirty jokes" about serious subjects like sexuality. Such people could even join the Nazi Party! But to be a Nazi, in his view, meant more than approving Hitler's success in reviving the economy and violating the hated Treaty of Versailles. It required conversion to the belief that struggle shaped human destiny and that racial hierarchy determined human value.

Like other old fighters, Gross disliked the rules and procedures that deadened the spirit of Nazism. But to trusted peers, Gross admitted his despair at the disorder endemic in Nazi rule.[119] Too often, "bureaucratic myopia" caused crucial racial issues to be "stuffed in one or another drawer" and forgotten. Faithful Nazis would dutifully purchase racial education materials, Gross wrote, but the "deluge" overwhelmed them.[120] In the Nazi periodical *Der Angriff,* Gross criticized experiments with artificial insemination as "degenerate" and "Jewish" because they tore away "the delicate veil of respect for the original secrets of Nature."[121] In the late 1930s, Gross criticized the Propaganda Ministry for approving films that not only failed to convey Nazi racial beliefs but embodied the individualistic morality of a liberal era he despised.[122] Gross brooded over internal ideological schisms and internecine turf wars that impinged on his efficiency. His own dissatisfaction did not, however, motivate Gross to reconsider his racist faith; on the contrary, every frustration deepened his anger at the victims.

In 1933 he had imagined that well-funded empirical research would produce conceptual clarity. As a synthesizer of scientific data and a popularizer of racial thinking, Gross (and probably his sponsor, Hess) believed the ORP would act as the arbiter of racial orthodoxy. But after three years of research, Gross confessed that "the origin of pathological hereditary qualities is not at all as transparent and intelligible as the constant announcement of new discoveries suggests."[123] Having lectured for two decades about the objective evidence of racial character, it irked him that individual racial evaluations still had to be based on "Jewish" appearance and family name. Having denounced both liberalism and Marxism for their crass materialism, he appears to have suspected that his racial paradigm might actually be materialist, too. If genes, for example, determined character, then what was the point of educating people to think racially? If gypsies gave up their nomadic life style and settled down, were they still racially dangerous? Did Hitler's views fit with those of non-Germans like Darwin and Galton, the progenitors of evolutionary racial biology?[124] For all Gross's pretensions to certainty, "race" served only as the master metaphor by which he interpreted his world.[125] At some point he must have sensed that evidence of Jews' otherness lay not in biology but in a history of putative Jewish malice.

Gross, who in 1933 had ebulliently embraced the challenge of his new office, was plagued by the contradictory requirements of politics and science. In the former, effective leadership depended on clarity, whereas in the latter, doubt was the prerequisite of further research. He cast his lot with politics. "The Nazi Party became great by affirming . . . fundamental facts. It can preserve its unity only if it limits its teaching to the most general and fundamental facts of ethnic existence."[126] Scientists might quibble, but political leadership must guarantee that "the ideal remains pure and unchanging, otherwise every initiative will implode."[127] For Gross, the antidote for disappointment appears to have been constant activity as a lecturer, editor, author, administrator, and consultant on racial policy.

Gross's demeanor fit the popular stereotype of an academic. Looking at him, party zealots and non-Nazis alike saw an earnest idealist who spoke with conviction about the Nazi mission to rescue the *Volk* from racial danger. In nontechnical language and dramatic metaphors, he announced the latest breakthroughs in a science that most audiences only vaguely understood. Using charts, itemizing his major points, formulating his ideas in a logical format, and appropriating Biblical, sometimes apocalyptic, language, Gross explained the ethical principles according to which anyone deemed "undesirable" had to be expunged from moral consideration. As he often told lay audiences, he set no store by legislation but wanted "decent folks with a new feeling for justice and injustice, [and] a love of truth" to grasp the new spirit of a racial era.[128] In much the same terms as Gerhard Kittel, Gross vindicated the ostracism of Christian Jews because it served the long-term collective benefit of a homogenous *Volk*. Before concrete plans for physical annihilation had been drafted, Gross and his colleagues in the ORP established the ethical foundations for extermination by presenting the *Volk* as an endangered organism. Konrad Lorenz, a Nazi Party member who later received a Nobel prize for his research on animal behavior, in an article for Gross's Nazi Office of Racial Politics compared the *Volkskörper* with "defective" members to a healthy individual who had malignant tumors. "Fortunately," he added, "the elimination of such elements is easier for the public health physician and less dangerous for the supra-individual organism than such an operation by a surgeon would be for the individual organism."[129] The *Volk* itself had become the body to be purified, and "unwanted" people had become mere malignancies.

Gross's memos, articles, and lectures from the 1930s provide a rare glimpse into the process by which a genocidal consensus evolved among proponents of a relentless bureaucratic war against Jews in Germany. Operating at a midmanagement level, he kept an eye on his superiors' expectations and monitored grassroots opinion. Like an astute marketing specialist, Gross calibrated his approach to suit his audience. Facing Germans who found the crude racism of old fighter Nazis repellent, Gross praised the righteousness of the *Volk*. But among insiders, Gross urged ruthless action, even as he came to doubt the empirical basis of his proposals. His cognitive disarray, far from motivating him to reconsider, deepened his commitment to purify the *Volk* and expunge the racial dangers that were so real in his imagination. Gross's lethal intent, so evident in retrospect, was cast as part of a tough-minded approach to high-minded plans for ethnic improvement.

The Swastika in the Heart of the Youth

When an opponent says "I will not come over to your side," I calmly say, "Your child belongs to us already . . . You will pass on. Your descendants, however, now stand in the new camp. In a short time they will know nothing but this new community."

—Adolf Hitler, November 6, 1933

In the spring of 1933 Hitler and Goebbels exuded confidence about their mastery of the persuasive techniques that would convert every ethnic German into a devoted Nazi. Having led their band of fanatical followers from the margins to the mainstream of political power between 1929 and 1933, they thought it reasonable to assume that the momentum would continue and soon every member of the *Volk* would be converted. Barely a year after their takeover, however, Nazi leaders' ebullient predictions vanished. Hitler consoled himself with the thought that even if many German adults withheld their total loyalty, the future belonged to Nazism because his regime would indoctrinate Germany's youth. A year later, in a speech featured in the film *Triumph of the Will,* he pledged that soon young people would not even be able to imagine the bygone "infection of our poisonous party system . . . They will not even understand the language of that alien age." Youth, he said, "has been consigned to us and has become ours body and soul. They live in this proud Germany of the swastika and will never again let it be ripped from their hearts."[1]

Success in shaping the "body and soul" of future Nazis depended on teachers' commitment to Nazi principles—chief among them a view of human nature centered on race and struggle, a belief in absolute Aryan superiority, and a communitarian ethos anchored in *Volk* and Führer. Ethnic identity was enhanced by a long list of antipathies: contempt for Jewry and all "lesser" races, scorn for universal humanism, and hostility to Christianity. With the swastika in their hearts, Nazi youth were taught to love fellow Aryans and expel outsiders from their moral community. Interior Minister Wilhelm Frick put Nazi aims bluntly in 1933: "The primary obligation of the school is to raise youth for service to the *Volk* and state in the spirit of National Socialism." Progressive educators, he claimed, had baffled students with too many "supposedly objective" choices and left

"Geist von unserem Geist!" JUGEND UM HITLER

31. "Spirit of our Spirit." Images of Hitler and his young followers in Hoffmann's celebrity booklets reinforced Hitler's claim that the future belonged to National Socialism.

them defenseless against the ravages of a decadent culture. Schools must end individualism and competition among ethnic comrades so that the *Volk* could fight as a unit against racial danger.[2] Frick invited his audience to share his dream of restoring the "genetic health" *(Erbgesundheit)* of the National Socialist German *Vaterland* and asked teachers to minimize book-learning and to mold students' character by teaching Truth.

A conversation recorded by Verena Hellwig, a teacher who subsequently emigrated from Germany with her Jewish husband, illustrates the depth of Nazi teachers' commitment. In 1933, when Hellwig expressed sadness that diverse opinions would disappear, a fellow teacher responded, "According to Hitler, there is only one belief, and anyone who does not relinquish all other ideas and accept this is not a genuine National Socialist and becomes an enemy who must be opposed ruthlessly and without sentimental qualms." When Hellwig spoke about human dignity, he admonished her, "What is at stake is not the fate of an individual. What's at stake is the fate of an entire Nation."[3] The first stage, the institutional *Gleichschaltung* (Nazification) of teachers' associations and the expulsion of unwanted people and ideas, took about three years to complete but on the whole proceeded smoothly. The next step—what teachers, like RPO staffers, called "inner" *Gleichschaltung*—proved more difficult.

In early 1933, regional, religious, and subject-oriented teachers' associations fused into a single National Socialist (NS) Teachers League. From the point of view of Nazi teachers, the transition began auspiciously with a great leap in membership. Between late 1932 and early 1933 the league had grown from 5,000 to 11,000. By late 1933 league membership soared to 220,000; only 80,000 teachers refrained from joining. League Chief Hans Schemm exulted, "How splendid it is to watch these pledges of allegiance to Nazism flood in."[4] Slightly less than a third (or 84,000) of all members took the additional step of joining the Nazi Party in 1933.[5] This proportion was roughly comparable to the percentages of civil servants and physicians who belonged to the party, and significantly higher than the less than 10 percent of the general adult population who joined in the 1930s.[6] But teachers who did not join the Nazi Party in 1933 appear not to have been tempted to do so afterward, and most of those who joined in later years were recent graduates of Nazi pedagogical institutes. Before Hitler's takeover, the major teachers' associations had staved off Nazi influence, and their members probably did not welcome *Gleichschaltung.*[7]

Despite the deluge of applications for membership that delighted

32. "Youth Serves the Führer! Every ten-year-old belongs in the Hitler Youth." A poster popularizing membership in the Hitler Youth, which became mandatory in 1939.

Schemm, teachers' support for Nazi rule was not as sudden as it appeared. Much of the flood resulted from covert Nazis, who before 1933 had not dared to violate the constitutional ban on political activities among teachers, joining up.[8] Other newcomers joined the NS Teachers League for reasons unrelated to their endorsement of Nazi values. With over 70,000 unemployed teachers seeking positions, concern for job security suggested the advisability of membership.[9] Whatever their motives, by 1937, 97 percent of all teachers belonged to the Nazi Teachers League.[10] No doubt many members genuinely welcomed Schemm's promise of "One *Volk*. One School. One Teachers League."[11] Many anticipated that a single, nationwide organization would exert more leverage and reduce inefficient competition among rival teachers' associations. Small-town elementary and trade school teachers warmed to the egalitarian promise of the new regime and anticipated that their status and pay would catch up with the more prestigious urban, university-track schools.

Concurrently with a major membership drive, the party began to purge teachers' ranks of so-called undesirables, which meant Jews and outspoken leftists. While relatively few classroom teachers lost their jobs in 1933, between 15 and 20 percent of about 3,000 school supervisors were expelled and replaced by Nazis, and 60 percent of all professors in teacher education colleges were dismissed. Women supervisors were disproportionately affected since, according to Nazi principles, only a masculine will could provide leadership.[12] At the university level, of 7,979 professors, 1,145 (about 15 percent) lost their jobs, mainly because of their Jewish ancestry or Jewish spouses.[13] Although Jewish war veterans (the "Hindenburg exceptions") temporarily remained at their posts, they were gradually forced out after Hindenburg died in 1934. The very few colleagues who objected were met with silence.[14]

Unwanted ideas suffered the same fate as unwanted teachers. Within weeks of Hitler's appointment as chancellor, libraries had been "cleansed" not only of books by Jewish authors but books that described Jews or other so-called alien ethnic groups in a favorable light. On May 10, 1933, Nazi university students throughout the nation threw tons of banned books into bonfires and justified this intellectual vandalism as an act of moral purification. No more Karl Marx, with his Jewish materialism; no more Thomas Mann, with his decadent individualism; and no more Sigmund Freud, with his "ego-cultivation" or *Ich-Sucht*. Instead, a "we-psychology" or "us-age" would obliterate an "egotistical era" or *Ich-Zeit*. Not freedom but service compelled members of the *Volk* to sacrifice their own self-interest in the name of collective health. Ernst Krieck, appointed to a chair in pedagogy at Frankfurt University, rejoiced at the demise of a "world that had become gay [schwül] and stale [stickig]" and declared war against everything "pouring out of big city cultural warehouses, which exuded rot and disintegration."[15] With unwanted people and ideas removed from view, it was difficult to ascertain whether teachers' support was superficial or profound.

Nazi teachers, who themselves had participated in subversive activities during the Weimar Republic, understood that expulsions and mandatory curricula could not control what teachers actually taught in their classrooms. Acquiescing on the surface to the demands of what Krieck termed the "total education state" did not guarantee that teachers would relinquish individualism and embrace the Volk. When Rust asked rhetorically, "What's to become of you teachers?" his answer suggested the kind of radical transformation he aimed at. "You must become something different than what you were."[16] Only the thoroughly converted would fulfill Krieck's command to "standardize the inner education of all members of the nation to produce uniformity of bearing, attitude, identity, and tasks."[17] Instead of thoughtful citizens, Nazi teachers promoted what they called "action-oriented" Germans (Tatmenschen).[18] In place of tolerance and diversity, a supposedly objective racial scale of human value bifurcated the world into "desirable" us and "dangerous" them.

Immediately after the Nazi takeover, dedicated Nazi teachers campaigned hard to win over their colleagues. Like Walter Gross, they spoke of transforming superficial Gleichschaltung into a "deep" racial outlook and, like him, they alternated between ethnic uplift and racial hate to accomplish that goal. Spearheading the campaign for "inner" Gleichschaltung were NS Teachers League President Schemm and Education Minister Rust. Schemm had founded the league in 1929 to "create in children's hearts a living spiritual monument, a Cathedral of German knowledge so solid that it will be harder than granite and steel."[19] War hero, chemistry teacher, regional leader, Bavarian minister of culture, and now chief of the NS Teachers League, Schemm was a charismatic speaker who radiated Aryan good looks and believed in the force of personality. "A joyful, racially valuable teacher with impeccable character who approaches students with love can open up the door to the students' spirit far better than a rigid pedagogue who adheres to formal teaching methods." Although his demeanor was informal, he made his views clear. "From now on, it is not up to you to decide the truth of anything, but to determine whether it conforms to the meaning of the National Socialist Revolution."[20]

Rust, who lacked Schemm's penchant for florid rhetoric, was a decorated soldier who suffered from the after-effects of a severe wound to the head. An outspoken old fighter, Rust had lost his position as senior teacher in 1930 probably because he had flagrantly violated the ban against political activity. Stephen Roberts, an Australian historian who interviewed Rust in 1935, described him as "a sallow little man with habitually clenched teeth. Forever spoiling for a fight, he is never happy unless knocking down obstacles. Subtlety means nothing to him; he prefers to use his head as a battering ram."[21] This "little man" became the reich minister of science, education, and *Volk* culture and reformed Nazi schools on the model of a Stormtrooper encampment. He based promotions on dedication to Nazism and charismatic teaching, not on academic achievement. Without flourish or philosophy, Rust bluntly ordered teachers to "raise and educate the ethnically aware German person."[22]

The ministry mandated that "no student shall graduate unless he has perceived that the future of a *Volk* depends on race and inheritance and understood the obligation this places on him."[23] Because textbook production would take three or four years, Schemm and Rust encouraged crash courses to re-educate teachers using mimeographed hand-outs and cheaply produced books. Poems promoting ethnic solidarity could be distributed easily. Thus children memorized:

> Keep your Blood pure,
> it is not yours alone,
> it comes from far away,
> it flows into the distance
> laden with thousands of ancestors
> and it holds the entire future!
> It is your eternal life.[24]

Regional NS Teachers Leagues and the Labor Front published interim materials.[25] "Teaching newsletters" distributed by Alfred Rosenberg's office provided guidelines for ideological training.[26] Classroom charts dramatized the supposedly objective contrast between so-called useful and useless Germans.

Fortified with supplementary materials, Nazi teachers called meetings to communicate the latest racial science research and explain the Nazi

33. "Blood is holy and sacrosanct." This photograph was embellished by a poem that expanded on one of Walter Gross's favorite metaphors: the ethnic blood stream is like a mighty river. "Keep your blood pure. It does not only belong to you. It comes from far away. It flows far into the future. It has come from thousands of ancestors and the future flows within it. Keep the cloak of your immortality pure."

Halte Dein Blut rein.
Es ist nicht nur Dein.
Es kommt weit her.
Es fließt weit hin.
Es ist von tausend Ahnen schwer
und alle Zukunft strömt darin.
Halte rein das Kleid
Deiner Unsterblichkeit.

(Will Vesper)

Party program. In Munich, for example, at a series of evening meetings, SA proselytizers expounded on various topics, ranging from memories of trench warfare and descriptions of Nazi rallies to denunciations of "sterile" scholarship and disquisitions on physical education for racial fitness.[27] The local Nazi Teachers League in Breslau published over a hundred booklets that sold for a few cents apiece with titles such as *Our Blood Laws; The National Revolution of 1933;* and *5,000 years of the Swastika.*[28]

Starting in the mid-1930s, more substantial materials appeared. The

Office of Racial Politics (ORP) brought out a series of pamphlets for students with titles like *Can You Think Racially?*[29] Pedagogical manuals explained *Racial Education as the Basis of All Education.*[30] A 1936 publication, *The Jew and the German,* described "the Jew's physical qualities," which included his "almond-shaped eyes, with heavy upper lids that droop over the eyeball" and an awkward, lumbering gait that the author found "creepy." Instead of speaking like a "normal" person, "the Jew" muttered in a special "intonation that made his voice both melodic and guttural." A vignette contrasted the Jewish and the Aryan soul: gazing on a tranquil mountain scene, an Aryan felt spiritually uplifted, whereas a Jew calculated the value of the timber. From this putative contrast, the author concluded that "the Jew is hostile to the state in which he lives."[31]

When old fighters hectored their colleagues with rhetoric from the days before Nazi victory ("the time of struggle"), many seasoned teachers were offended by their overt incitements to ethnic hatred and racism. Some teachers lamented the loss of local autonomy and resented nationally mandated lesson plans, textbooks, and curricula.[32] Catholics defied orders to remove crucifixes from classrooms.[33] While many female teachers welcomed the restoration of separate instruction for girls and boys, they deplored the replacement of female by male supervisory personnel in girls' schools.[34] Many secondary teachers (especially at the university preparatory schools) found the anti-intellectualism of old fighters, and of Hitler himself, offensive. The clandestine Sopade surveys of public opinion reported in late 1934 that their diehard Nazi colleagues seemed confused. "No one knows, not even the leaders, what National Socialism actually is . . . The initial spirit and internal order are gone."[35] A year later the ideologue Alfred Rosenberg became a laughingstock among teachers, and contempt for Rust and Schemm ran "incredibly deep"; many teachers privately denigrated them as "idiots" and "honcho windbags."[36]

Open criticism subsided in 1933, but mistrust among educators persisted. Despite Rust's stern exhortations, not all teachers submitted to standardization. Memoirs by Jewish students make it clear that while most Nazi teachers treated them cruelly, many other teachers did not comply with racist regulations.[37] Surprise visits from national ideological inspection teams damaged morale.[38] Spies (often disguised as teaching assistants but actually old fighters or Hitler Youth members) infiltrated secondary and primary schools. Non-Nazis called them "appendixes" because, although they were useless, they could cause great harm. At schools and universities, secret faculty committees (nicknamed "murder commissions") kept colleagues under surveillance. Not the least of non-Nazi teachers' concerns was the possibility of denunciation by a member of the Hitler Youth or a Nazi supervisor. Rector Martin Heidegger in Freiburg, for example, denounced an internationally respected scientist on the basis of antiwar comments that the latter had made two decades earlier.[39] In 1935 Schemm initiated a major investigation of "a secret list" of teachers who had been denounced as "traitors" by their colleagues. His death in a plane crash halted the plan.[40]

Paradoxically, as overt opposition to Nazism diminished, "polarities and conflicts" began to divide Nazis themselves.[41] Improvised evening lectures not infrequently revealed disagreements (or confusion) about racial issues among old fighters.[42] While some fulminated about Jews as a biological danger, others warned against the cultural depravity of Jewry. Some instructors even voiced their own unorthodox views, as when a lecturer in Berlin insisted that blue eye color alone determined racial identity and implored young people to "listen to the voice of the blood when you marry."[43] Hostility festered between proponents of local autonomy and other Nazis who supported stronger coordination to eliminate ideological disarray.[44] Faultlines divided old fighters and careerist newcomers. In the upper echelons the Ministries of Interior and Education competed against one another, and both quarreled with the NS Teachers League.[45] Women teachers, under their pugnacious leader, Dr. Auguste Reber-Gruber, demanded better treatment from their male colleagues.[46] For all his military bluster, Rust had little aptitude for holding his own against ministers or adjudicating the turf wars that fragmented the educational establishment.[47]

Although educators had joined the NS Teachers League en masse in 1932–33, teachers were conspicuous for their lack of interest when the Nazi Party reopened its rolls to new members in 1937. As the economy began to recover at the end of the decade, the surplus of teachers in the early 1930s gave way to severe shortages. Although statistics do not reveal the cause of the scarcity, it must have been exacerbated by unhappy teachers who left the profession. Young, "freshly-baked" products of Nazi teacher-training programs joined faculties, but pedagogical colleges graduated fewer students each year. The historian Michael Kater called teachers "one of the most disillusioned sub-groups" in Germany after the mid-1930s.[48]

The interim pamphlets on Nazi doctrine gradually fell into disuse, perhaps because non-Nazis failed to see the pedagogical value of memorizing the "great" dates in Nazi Party history, racial typology, and the verses of

Nazi marching songs. But unlike the blatantly partisan course material that sowed discord, ethnic fundamentalism held out the promise of building a broad consensus in support of Nazi rule. Teachers who did not wholly embrace the new order discovered that, as long as they did not openly criticize Hitler or Nazi policy, they could balance compliance and dissent. For all the rhetoric about absolute beliefs, no iron-clad dogma was imposed on teachers. As one former pupil in Nazi schools put it, "People floated along in a confused jumble of Christian and National Socialist attitudes."[49]

Whether or not they realized it, zealous Nazi teachers intuitively followed Hitler's model when they minimized divisive Nazi dogma about world Jewry and celebrated the *Volk*. This superficially milder version of Nazi ideology was both more palatable and more insidious. Alongside explicitly racist materials, less strident schoolbooks represented Hitler as a benign and nonsectarian Führer of a proud *Volk*. Instead of citing his ravings about "pestilence" and "bacilli" from the early 1920s, Nazi educators emphasized Hitler's selfless devotion to his *Volk*. Primers opened with "Heil Hitler!" Swastikas adorned banners, coloring books, classroom decorations, and toy tanks. A typical reading lesson described schoolchildren's excitement as they prepared for a visit by the chancellor. Eighth graders, for example, practiced penmanship by writing significant Nazi terms: H as in Hitler, Hess, Himmler, Hierl; and K as in *Kriegerpilot* (fighter pilot), *Kamerad* (comrade), and Kiel (a naval base). *My First Book* included illustrations of children helping their mothers decorate their homes with roses and swastikas.[50]

Hitler, the celebrity, was accessible to all students in the many photo booklets featuring his biography along with shots of the Führer surrounded by flocks of adoring youth. In booklets for younger children, photos presented an avuncular Hitler, whereas in booklets for older children an unsmiling Führer admonished: "In the dedication of one's own life to the community lies the crowning glory of all sacrifice."[51] Guidelines instructed teachers to "strengthen racial consciousness" and "promote enthusiasm for contemporary German achievements, such as transportation and machines."[52] Because these ecumenical subjects were less obviously identified with Nazism, teachers who might have balked at adulation of the "martyrs" of the Beer Hall Putsch found a generic ethnic uplift acceptable.

The moderate tone of the new pedagogical materials marked a shift in Nazi persuasive strategy from confrontation to stealth. In 1937, when the

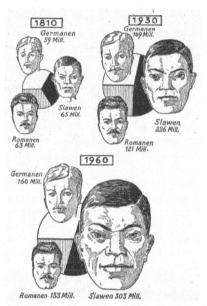

34. Illustrated statistics lent an aura of objectivity to ethnic panic. These charts demonstrate that: (1) Slavs reproduce faster than Germans, (2) a two-child system threatens the birthrate among ethnic Germans, and (3) disabled offspring cost taxpayers more than healthy children.

educational administration stabilized and new textbooks began to appear, the incendiary tone of the earlier teacher-training lectures and interim pamphlets vanished. Supposedly objective information demeaning Jews was inserted within an overarching framework that was written in the sober language of science. New lesson plans integrated quotations by Hit-

Mein Führer! (Das Kind spricht):

    Ich kenne dich wohl und habe dich lieb
                        wie Vater und Mutter.
    Ich will dir immer gehorsam sein
                        wie Vater und Mutter.
    Und bin ich erst groß, dann helfe ich dir
                        wie Vater und Mutter,
    und freuen sollst du dich an mir
                        wie Vater und Mutter!

35. An illustration for a school play in which the child declares, "My Führer! I know you well and love you like my father and mother. I will always obey you, like my father and mother. And when I grow up, I will help you like father and mother. And you should be proud of me, like my father and mother."

ler and Nazi intellectuals among words of classical authors like Friedrich Schiller and Goethe; ethnic adjectives spiced descriptions of historical figures. A traditional puppet show, for example, the Kaspar Theater, underwent reconfiguration that deleted "racially alien" characters, Christian myths (such as angels and the Devil), and jokes about life in the Third Reich—in other words, virtually every conventional source of the show's humor. Popular classics by foreign authors were edited to emphasize ethnic pride. Robinson Crusoe's relationship to Friday took on master-slave qualities, for example, and the Christianity so salient in Johanna Spyri's *Heidi* vanished. Adaptations of ancient Norse sagas linking honor to sacrifice and vengeance gradually displaced Christian morality tales. Teachers' guidebooks suggested that collective morality could be introduced in classrooms with themes like this: "The idea of loyalty was very important to the Germanic *Volk,* as it is for us today. Every single member of the large group of followers should show as much honor and readiness for sacrifice and loyalty as those living close to the Führer. If they left the Führer, they would be helpless."[53] Karl May's novels about the American Wild West (despite being read enthusiastically by Hitler and other Nazi chiefs) fell from official favor, presumably because they glorified the American West instead of the German East. Subtle messages pervaded the new lesson plans. In Latin classes, for example, practice essays justified Mussolini's claims to Ethiopia; geography lessons referred to eastern Europe as German *Lebensraum* (living space); and in biology classes, students memorized the traits of many non-Germanic races, with "the Jewish race" consistently found wanting.[54]

When addressing general audiences, devoted Nazis muted their poisonous racism and instead foregrounded ethnic fundamentalism. They spoke about their "longing for inner freedom, for the joy in work itself and not merely as a means of growing rich. National Socialism is nothing more than the greatest celebration of life." They claimed they wanted to take nothing away from students but to add "profound moral attitude *[Haltung]*" to every subject taught.[55] Rather than dwelling on biology and race, they emphasized the spiritual qualities of the *Volk.* An inclusive call for Germanic renewal had the potential to amelioriate non-Nazi teachers' disenchantment with the day-to-day bureaucracy and enable them to overlook the fanaticism of some fellow teachers.

In scholarly publications for teachers as well as in schoolbooks, "the Jewish Question" was integrated as one of many biological topics. Its very lack of salience made it more effective than blatant racial hate. Even the notorious *Nazi Primer,* a Hitler Youth textbook translated in 1938 by exiled Germans to discredit Nazism, devoted only three of its 256 pages to Jews.[56] Jewish exclusion was presented as a byproduct, not the major aim, of ethnic fundamentalism. Generic conservative themes like *Volk, Vaterland,* and *Führer* excluded Jews as surely as class outings deprived Jewish children of a shared educational experience.[57] Memoirs of childhood in the Third Reich are filled with slogans and poems dedicated not so much to the Nazi Party as to the *Volk.* Homilies exhorted students to shun greed and embrace self-sacrifice. Rhetoric like that of Walter Gross encouraged youths to think of themselves as humble links in a self-perpetuating, transgenerational ethnic community. The living, by inference, owed a greater obligation to their dead ancestors and to future generations than to their "racially alien" neighbors and friends. De-Nazified ethnic education could be more effective than overt ideological training.

Students collected money for party and state charities under the slogan "Collective need before individual greed" *(Gemeinnutz geht vor Eigennutz)*. Posters reminded them, "You are nothing. Your *Volk* is everything!" Schoolroom banners imparted advice such as "Divisiveness destroys; agreement builds" *(Zwietracht zerstört; Eintracht vermehrt)*. Team members repeated, "One for all and all for one" *(Ein für alle; alle für einen)*. Hitler's photo bore the caption, "My will is your faith!" A primer opened with this command: "The Führer says, 'Learn to sacrifice for your fatherland! We are all mortal. But Germany must live on.'"[58] Alfons Heck, a German who had been six in 1933, recalled, "To me the Fatherland was a somewhat mystical and yet real concept . . . infinitely dear and threatened by unrelenting enemies."[59] A girl with three Jewish grandparents wavered between pride in feeling special and a desire to be like her classmates in the Nazi Girls' League (Bund Deutscher Mädel, or BDM). Years later, writing in the third person, she reflected on the source of the attraction. "Above all, it probably was the admonition for self-sacrifice, which had touched her deepest instincts."[60] Three decades after the end of Nazi rule, Melita Maschmann remembered her BDM leader's words, "You must believe in Germany as firmly, clearly and truly as you believe in the sun, the moon and the starlight. You must believe in Germany as if Germany were yourself; and as you believe your soul strives towards eternity. You must believe in Germany or your life is but death."[61] Another former BDM member recalled how deeply she had been moved by "the ardent, fanatic voice calling out from the flaming bonfire on that summer solstice night, 'We pledge to stay pure and to consecrate ourselves to the Flag, Führer, and Fatherland!'"[62]

While ideological tracts from the pre-1933 days (including Goebbels's *The ABC's of National Socialism*) fell into disuse, the new textbooks that began to appear in 1936 inculcated communitarian moral principles in traditional formats such as fables and legends. Behind the quaint stories a searing message was clear. The cuckoo often represented the Jew because, as one avid reader of *Der Stürmer* put it, "His curved beak reminds us of the Jew's nose. His feet are small, that's why he can't run. Wanting her offspring to sing like thrushes, a mother cuckoo laid an egg in a thrush's nest and watched the mother thrush raise her baby. But, genetic make-up predestined the baby bird to chirp only 'cuckoo.'"[63] A children's book written by a bioethicist conveyed ethnic moral values in a story about storks. On the day before the annual migration, the mother stork sobs while the father, backed by neighbor storks, insists that their little stork, who has trouble flying, must remain behind. "Isn't that cruel?" a peasant boy who witnessed the abandonment asks his father. "Not at all, son. Why should we allow the sick to endanger the healthy? . . . Excess offspring serve no purpose. Without this awareness, our *Volk* could not continue to grow."[64] In math exercises, students calculated the relative costs to the taxpayer of "healthy" and "unhealthy" children and the amount of money squandered on cigarettes.[65] Cost-effective health care, such assignments implied, was moral because it allowed welfare agencies to invest in the "more valuable" ethnic comrades.

The only story in this collection that mentioned Jews told of young Ruben Schmus who was "born in the Jewish alley of Bialystock and speaks a mixture of Polish, German and Hebrew, known as Yiddish." The father deals in stolen goods, and, "because he's open-minded, he does not ask how they were obtained." To improve his sons' opportunities, he sends Ruben and his brothers to Berlin and other Western European capitals. They prosper and, having connections, even aspire to become university professors. "Too bad for them that January 30, 1933, abruptly terminated the whole travesty *[dem ganzen Spuk]*. That's how Jewry 'works,' devoid of conscience and full of cunning; [Jewry] is the grave digger of Germany."[66] The author of this tale assumed that children would recognize January 30, 1933, the day Hitler became chancellor, as the dawn of a new era, much as children recognize July 4, 1776, in the United States or July 14, 1789, in France. The lessons were clear: a racial community must cast off its weakest members; all "unfit" individuals sap the strength of the *Volk;* and ethnic outsiders exist beyond the horizon of moral obligation. In effect, these principles authorized the strong to attack the vulnerable.

Nazi educators appropriated the Golden Rule to mean, as Schemm put it, love your ethnic comrades so deeply that you would willingly die for them.[67] In a handbook for Nazi teachers, Immanuel Kant's categorical imperative—"Act only on that maxim which you would wish to become a universal law"—was described as "the only conceivable basis for collective life" because it praised "a spirit of mutual assistance" and condemned egotism.[68] A slogan summed up Nazi morality: "Treat your comrade as you would like him to treat you." From there it was only a short step to the assumption that noncomrades were not human. A Nazi lecturer implicitly exempted Jews when he told pupils, "Treat your fellow humans the way you wish they would treat you."

Gender separation in classrooms and in the Hitler Youth enhanced ethnic compartmentalization. After the emancipated 1920s, ethnic educators pledged to restore the "honor and esteem" of an "almost lost generation" by "releasing what makes a female female."[69] Girls were told to "practice the great motherly art of service and sacrifice" and to stay pure and clean until marriage.[70] One female teacher praised the "barbaric" Germanic men who defended their territory but added that women's maternal qualities had preserved the "body, soul, and wisdom" of the *Volk*.[71] Fables like the stork tale, math exercises, and the story of Ruben underscored the separate duties of each sex. In an afterward to these tales, the author told boys to "tolerate" girls—because without them there would be no *Volk*. Girls should be patient with boys' "physical and mental discipline, iron control, which alone can restore our nation." Both boys and girls were admonished: "Harden yourselves. Strengthen and empower your bodies. Guard your mind and soul."[72]

With the implementation of the sterilization law in 1934, teachers were ordered to identify students who might have "damaged" genes. Children who had trouble buttoning their coats or taking exams, for example, could be screened for genetic impairment and sterilization. Units on genealogy taught students how to evaluate their own family trees in eugenic terms. "We must also do away with the conception that the treatment of the body is the affair of every individual. There is no freedom to sin at the cost of posterity and hence of the race."[73] Older students memorized the Ten Commandments for Selecting a Mate, which emphasized racial health and compatibility, with the reminder, "Your body does not belong to you; it belongs to your *Volk*." A teacher explained, "The ethnic state puts race at the center of life. It promotes racial purity. It sees in the child the precious commodity of the state." A secondary school teacher told his students to maximize the collective good by "maintaining and increasing the valuable genetic qualities that were handed down to you." If they discovered that they had inherited "racially destructive genetic qualities," he told them willingly to forswear childbearing. He said little about Jews but remarked casually that it was high time for Germans to realize that their blood was more valuable than a criminal's.[74]

For all their superiors' rhetoric about "unswerving will" and "relentless dedication," individual teachers had considerable leeway in applying

Nazi racial values. With fewer than 60,000 Jewish pupils (75 percent of all school-age Jewish children) in public schools in 1933 and about 300,000 teachers, the likelihood of a teacher having a Jewish child in class was quite small. This probability was further reduced by the demographic concentration of Jewish Germans in urban areas, notably Berlin and Frankfurt, and the tradition that teachers taught the same class through the first several years of school. With each passing year, more Jewish schools were constructed and more Jewish families emigrated, so that by 1938 only 27 percent of the 27,500 Jewish children in Germany attended public schools.[75]

The experiences of Jewish students who remained in Germany indicates that civil courage did not vanish entirely from the teachers' ranks. Students' memoirs describe teachers who quietly apologized for not being able to give them the praise they deserved. One mother recalled the Nazi teacher who advised her daughter, Irene, to stay home from school on awards day because she might be upset when she did not receive the recognition she had earned.[76] An American mother (who was not Jewish) lived for twelve years in Hamburg and described the plight of the Jewish children in her daughter's school as "pitiful" because they were humiliated and segregated, but "many teachers were still human enough to hug the little mites in secret, telling them not to mind, but no teacher could run the risk of being caught showing such sympathies."[77] One irate old fighter from Hamburg complained that Hitler Youth members still mingled with "Jewish trash" *(Judengesocks),* as if there were no anti-Jewish policy at all.[78]

A Jewish refugee from Nazi Germany could not remember that anything changed in 1933, except that the students, Jewish as well as Christian, had to raise money for a portrait of Hitler for their classroom. One Nazi teacher treated all students equally, but another Nazi, Fräulein K, tormented Jewish children. When eventually the despised Fräulein K was fired because it turned out that she had a Jewish grandmother, all of her pupils rejoiced.[79] The historian Peter Gay, who grew up in Berlin during the 1930s, cautions against any generalization. He recalls that despite the ambient hostility, "Our teachers were on the whole free of bigotry and did not set out to make their Jewish pupils' lives harder than those of our gentile classmates." But he heard about terrible conditions in other schools, where "every school day the anti-Semitic pressure became more noticeable as teachers joined pupils in verbal, and in some cases, physical attacks on Jewish children."[80]

36. "Behind his glasses, two criminal eyes peer out, and debauched lips smirk." In this chapter of *The Poison Mushroom*, "Inge at the Doctor's Office," an innocent young woman is surrounded by danger: in addition to the threatening doctor and the dark interior of his office, she reads one of the supposedly decadent fashion magazines that litter the table. Signs on the wall indicate that this Jewish physician is allowed to receive reimbursements from the national health program—which would have been highly unlikely in 1938, the year this children's book was published.

It may be that "only" one in three or one in four teachers was an ardent Nazi, but that was sufficient to make life wretched for children who were stigmatized as unwanted. In one school, a Nazi teacher gave ethnic German students a bucket and scrub brushes to wash the benches on which Jewish children sat.[81] As a "practical joke" children in another school gave mock one-way railway tickets marked J (for Jew and Jerusalem) to Jewish classmates.[82] They also played a board game modeled on "Monopoly" which was called "Out with the Jews!" *(Juden raus!).* In her novel *A Model Childhood,* Christa Wolf recalled her beloved teacher, Herr Warsinski, who would command, "May we have silence, please! And I mean right now! Where do you think you are, in a Jew school! . . . Anyone who lets me down when we salute the flag is really going to get it. Our Führer works day and night for us, and you can't even keep your traps shut for ten minutes."[83]

Inveterate Nazi teachers would assign selections from the virulently antisemitic children's book *The Poison Mushroom,* published in 1938 by *Der Stürmer* press, which warned that although many Jews, like mushrooms, appeared attractive on the surface, they were poison underneath.[84] Thus, harming Jewish classmates constituted a good deed.

The wide disparity in accounts of teachers' actions in the Third Reich suggests that educators had more latitude for individual discretion than is commonly assumed. Yet, the net effect of their combined actions was to isolate Jewish students. Hans Winterfeldt, who grew up in an eastern German town, recalled, "Outside our home I only had negative experiences." Although he was not beaten up, his classmates did not want to sit near him and refused to pair up with him when they walked out to recess.[85] Herr Becker, a village schoolmaster in the Mosel Valley, firmly believed in corporal punishment, but one of his Aryan pupils, Alfons Heck, noticed that he rarely beat Jewish pupils and never called on them. Instead, when Jewish boys misbehaved, "he made them sit in a corner, which he sneeringly designated as 'Israel.'"[86] A boy who was the only Jewish student in his class recalled enduring "near-total social isolation. I hadn't been subjected to much overt anti-Semitism by my classmates, and yet I had no friends among them . . . My teachers had been strict, distant and sarcastic."[87]

Occasionally Nazi teachers realized that overt cruelty could be counterproductive. It could happen, for example, that the caricatures in Nazi publications bore so slight a resemblance to actual Jewish classmates that students failed to perceive a connection. Sometimes children felt sorry for an ostracized classmate. "How," one Nazi teacher wondered, "can we convert a collective feeling of togetherness into racial consciousness and racial pride . . . when dangling in front of them is the little appendage, probably quite harmless, of a Jewish child?" The sight of a Jewish classmate fighting back tears of shame after being ridiculed, he wrote, "offends the magnanimous German ethos." Where ridicule backfired, "cool objectivity" was needed to explain the "painful justice" of race laws. Implicitly

"kinder von der Saar besuchen den Fuhrer in der Reichskanzlei," JUGEND UM HITLER

37. When school classes were invited to meet the Führer, they received commemorative photographs like this one. Children who did not personally meet Hitler could vicariously share the experience when they saw photos like this one in Heinrich Hoffmann's illustrated booklet, *Youth Surrounding Hitler.*

criticizing bombastic old-fighter techniques, the author described the model teacher as filled with "fire and knowledge"—who could quote the Talmud, narrate ancient Jewish history, explain racial science, and remind children of Jewish immorality. Only sober facts would disprove the "myth of the decent Jew."[88]

Perceiving themselves as pioneers in ethnic education, Nazi teachers experimented with experience-education in place of book-learning. "Education succeeds when every hour of instruction becomes an experience. Dry, scientific formats don't shape the person. Experience does."[89] Instead of lectures, memory drills, and textbooks, teachers were encouraged to lead their charges out of the classroom and into the larger world. Like Jean-Jacques Rousseau teaching Émile without recourse to books, Nazi educators used nature to instruct students. But, the Nazi pedagogue Krieck boasted, Nazi schools educated students from all economic classes, and not just privileged sons of wealthy parents like Émile. Audiovisual teaching aids also qualified as experience-learning. With economic recovery and larger budgets, the Education Ministry created a special division for educational films and recordings. Its bulletin explained, "Slides and visual experiences unlock the soul, evoke the deepest spiritual visual powers *[Bildekraft]* and prepare us for an entirely new representation *[Gestaltung]* of life."[90]

Even before new national textbooks appeared, educational mass media opened up the possibility of standardizing education. Radio captivated students at first, but its novelty soon wore off.[91] Film offered a more enduring alternative. By 1935, Rust's Education Ministry had purchased over 8,000 projectors and put over 30,000 copies of ORP films in circulation.[92] A special journal kept instructors informed about the latest pedagogical applications of film.[93] Through a program of required films for weekend viewing, the ministry extended its reach to nearly 10 million student viewers. The fact that Jewish students were excluded from these collective experiences reinforced the message posted in restaurants and stores: "Jews not desired here."

Slide lectures and sets of educational charts were also among the modern techniques used to spread Nazism in the schools. Sets of slides, along with an accompanying text to be read out loud, were produced in batches of thousands and loaned to schools. Designed to evoke "Emotions, Faith, and Power" *(Gefühl, Glaube, und Gewalt)*, the images depicted "desirable" and "undesirable" ethnic types.[94] Teaching materials ridiculed supposedly unnatural sexuality, racial dangers, "bossy" women, inter-racial British lesbians, ape-like Jews, and severely crippled children. The Office of Racial Politics distributed poster-size diagrams that applied Mendel's laws to human inheritance and warned against "Jewish-looking" seducers of young maidens. In a nationally distributed set of brightly colored racial education charts, elaborate illustrations used in teaching genetics included only a few images demeaning Jews, but the force of the pictures more than compensated for the relatively scant coverage.[95] Alongside educational media that cast students as passive consumers of racial knowledge, excursions beyond the classroom gave them a chance for more active learning. From the summer of 1933 through the war years, school classes visited traveling exhibits on "degenerate art," ethnic health and hygiene, and "the Eternal Jew." By publicly displaying "harmful" art and "damaged" people, the Nazis introduced menacing images into children's fantasies.

Rassen der Erde I
Europa und seine Grenzgebiete

38. "The teacher uses a racial chart to explain to his students the main traits of the northern man and compares a Nordic boy with the model." The chart illustrated "The Races of the World, Part I: Europe and its Borderlands."

To foster egalitarianism, teachers were instructed to drop normal formalities and become their students' comrades—an alien notion to teachers accustomed to Prussian decorum. Education Minister Rust emphasized teacher-student bonding as a way of reaching students. "Youth will willingly allow themselves to be educated as long as they have a young

National Socialist as a teacher."[96] Dynamic teachers took day trips to strengthen students' healthy Aryan identity. Jewish children were excluded, but even the poorest "racially qualified" students could participate because charitable contributions covered the fees.[97] A visit to an asylum for the mentally ill, physically disabled, or intellectually impaired, for example, reinforced fears of genetic damage. Such outings defied conventional middle-class prohibitions against staring at social outcasts and recalled an earlier era when crowds would flock to public executions and stare at lepers, madmen, deformed people, and flagellants. In addition to appreciating their own good health, spectators at these events felt that their world had become safer since the deviants had been locked up. By the early twentieth century, images of disabled and deformed people appeared only in circumscribed professional environments such as hospitals and medical textbooks.[98] Nazi educators, by contrast, justified public display of the misbegotten because, as one instructor put it, "the sick must provide a school for the healthy. The anonymity of these asylums must end. Every young person, every ethnic comrade of either sex who is interested in marrying must be led at least once through the screaming and nameless misery of an insane asylum, an institution for idiots, a residence for the crippled . . . Here he shall learn to appreciate the sacred genetic inheritance he has received."[99] The message was clear: Don't avert your gaze. Do not yield to pity (*Mitleid,* literally "suffering with"). Do not love this neighbor as yourself.

Other trips took students on excursions to the countryside. "The creation of a communal life is more important than reading," wrote one field trip organizer. "After much experience, I think that the greatest emphasis must be placed on educating participants for collective living."[100] A series of class trips organized during 1934 in the industrialized Rhineland provides a local snapshot of a national program. More than a hundred three-week educational excursions involved 19,000 boys, 9,000 girls, and 2,300 teachers.[101] The days began at 6:30 A.M. with calisthenics, showers, breakfast, and then martial field exercises that lasted from 8:45 until 1:00 P.M. After lunch and rest time came academic study from 3:15 to 6:30. These sessions included racial themes within units on, for example, "National Political Education in Plato's *Republic,*" "Prehistoric Germany," "Cicero's *Scipio's Dream,*" "You and Your Genes," and "Hitler's Service in World War I." At 6:30 P.M. participants stood at attention for inspection. A simple supper at 7:00 was followed by campfires, singing, and storytelling until taps announced lights out at 9:45. In the marching, camaraderie, and collective living students would learn self-discipline and solidarity.[102]

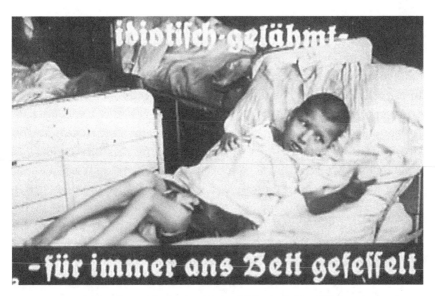

39. "A crippled idiot. Bound forever to his bed." Rather than eliciting viewers' sympathy, this and other images in the Hitler Youth slideshow were intended to incite disgust at helpless people who allegedly diverted resources from more cost-effective members of the *Volk*.

These excursions were popular, even at the universities.[103] In the summer of 1933, for example, Rector Martin Heidegger served on a national committee in Berlin to plan academic retreats that would enhance ethnic rapport between faculty and graduate students and also acquaint academic young people with life outside the ivory tower.[104] Seized with enthusiasm, Heidegger addressed several of these summer retreats. Then for six days in October he directed his own Knowledge Camp *(Wissenschaftslager)* at his mountain ski hut; one biographer described the event as a cross between the Platonic Academy and a Boy Scout camp.[105] In military tones, the great philosopher summoned younger scholars as if he were leading an assault on enemy territory.[106] Attired in Stormtrooper or Steel Helmet uniforms, the all-male, all-Aryan cadre marched in formation from Freiburg to Heidegger's cabin, Todtnauberg. Reveille sounded at 6:00 A.M. and taps closed the day at 10:00 P.M. Extolling the participants' great "courage," Heidegger spoke in his usual elliptical way, a participant recalled, about the "conquest of the new reality" and the "total overturn of our German Existence *[Dasein]*. 'There is no need now to speak any more about it, we merely have to act.'"[107] In seminar-like sessions, participants debated academic structure, university reform, the Führer principle, and philosophy. One participant recalled how easily Heidegger's earlier pop-

ulist instincts took on racial overtones as he attacked "sterile" Christianity and "fact-mongering" positivism. Beyond the specific knowledge imparted at the retreat, Heidegger hoped to "create the appropriate
ambience and attitude" for the Nazi revolution.[108] In his desire to place
universities at the service of the nation, Heidegger as rector approved the
creation of chairs in "military sports" and agreed to award academic credit
for participation in summer military encampments—activities that worried British diplomats as possible violations of the Versailles Treaty.[109] In
Freiburg during August and September, these camps brought together 300
young male students in each session for military drill. Even when Heidegger learned that participants routinely roughed up civilians in the
nearby town who were known to be critics of Nazism, he defended the
program.

In 1934 Education Minister Rust established re-education camps *(Lager)*
to "equip" teachers to, in his words, "fulfill the Führer's desire to alert the
entire German *Volk* spiritually and mentally to the very highest values of
inheritance and race." Rust suggested a core curriculum based on racial
studies, genetics, prehistoric Germany, biology, and geopolitics. Retreat
organizers interpreted this mandate in the most general way possible in
order to attract teachers who remained skeptical of Nazi doctrine. Ethnic
fundamentalism, not Nazi doctrine, provided a common ground for uni-
fying teachers after their ranks had been thinned by racial and political
purges. Rust issued guidelines for indoctrination from Berlin, but local organizers made the restoration of morale—not indoctrination—their top
priority.

The leaders of one retreat (called a "shock troop") wrote a report entitled "Wilderness and Forest in the Anhalt Mountains," which opened
with: "Its impact cannot be described, it must be experienced."[110] A rural
setting was *de rigeur* because, as one leader put it, "the peasant lives totally;
collective feeling is alien to the urban dweller."[111] A wide range of formats
integrated teachers as ethnically *gleich*—the same and equal. Some retreats convened during vacations, while others took place during the
semester; some offered stipends, and others required teachers to pay.[112]
Verena Hellwig, who left Germany in 1939, attended a six-week Drill in
National Socialism on the Baltic seacoast. Among the "thousands and
thousands of teachers, interns, university teachers of all kinds," some
were enthusiastic and others resentful. The physical training was good for
them, she recalled, and despite the dreadful food, the six weeks passed
quickly.[113] By 1937 the NS Teachers League had established 56 regional retreat sites and two national centers, one in the Rhineland and the other

near Berlin. From 1935 to 1938, 11,000 German teachers and a few foreign visitors attended 153 special courses at the two national centers.[114] From 1933 through 1939, 215,000 out of 300,000 teachers participated in at least one regional retreat.[115]

Hundreds of activity reports, syllabi, schedules, participant evaluations, lecture texts, and bibliographies paint a vivid picture of these outings. While these sources may not provide reliable evidence of participants' actual opinions, they do tell us what the authors of these reports believed their superiors expected to hear. Their narratives, redolent with cultural chauvinism and celebrations of Hitler's genius, barely mention racial science and avoid virulent antisemitism altogether. Nevertheless, a consensus in support of Nazi rule—and its racist assumptions—evolved within a less obviously doctrinaire format.

Organizers hardly mentioned academic topics but lavished attention on folklore, logistics, activities, sightseeing, and social gatherings with local residents. A list of topics covered at ten Rhineland retreats featured 31 classes on biology, 14 on language and history, 14 on geography, and 12 on local folkways. The biology courses included subjects that would have figured in any eugenics course in Western Europe or the United States at that time. Among nearly a hundred discussion topics, only one, "Against the Judaization *[Verjudung]* of German Culture," was explicitly antisemitic.[116] Another typical course list included the "Essentials of Racial Thought," the "Racial Fate of the Ancient and Germanic Worlds," "Victory and Decline in Europe," "War and Strategy," the "The Great War," the "Germanic Faith in Destiny," "National Socialism and the Peasant," "Germanic Political Theory according to Ernst Krieck," and the "Saar Question" (which referred to a border region ceded to France by the Treaty of Versailles). Sessions on "great men" celebrated not Nazi martyrs but the same generals, rulers, and writers as in pre-Nazi textbooks.[117]

Very much in the manner of publications from the Office of Racial Politics, racial concepts suffused courses on many topics, and antisemitism was incorporated as only one facet of comprehensive racial studies. The Nazi ideologue Alfred Rosenberg told his staff before their retreat, "Retreats are designed to instruct people on how to interpret the meaning of the radical change that has taken place and how to grasp the formation of a new intellectual attitude and the creation of genuine comradeship."[118] Without mentioning racial or any other dogma, Rudolf Hess admonished instructors of special courses in 1934 to fill their audiences "with passionate devotion" and to "have faith always in the nobility of our *Volk*, and in the goodness of our ethnic comrades because, as you do so, you place your faith in Germany's lucky stars . . . The future will surely bring peace, security, bread and honor."[119]

Speakers from the ORP delivered pantheistic sermons to the *Volk* and waxed eloquent about the spiritual dimensions of race. One teacher's notes on a talk by Walter Gross praised "the uplifting experience of our shared blood and belonging."[120] Evening bonfires featured homilies such as this one: "Everyone can be active wherever he wishes. He must never forget that his comrade who also does his duty is just as indispensable to the nation as he. The nation does not exist because a government rules or because of a class of intellectuals. The nation lives only because everyone works harmoniously together." As one participant observed in 1936, "The promotion of comradeship was the main goal."[121]

In keeping with a folksy populism that fostered ethnic solidarity, an egalitarian ethos brought the end of formal titles, including *Frau* and *Herr*. Wives were no longer called by their husbands' titles, as in *Frau Dr.* or *Frau Professor*. The familiar *Du* form of address replaced the conventional *Sie*, and colleagues became comrades.[122] To underscore egalitarianism, party officials like Schemm, Rust, and Krieck made a point of fraternizing with teachers during weekend retreats. One participant, who wrote ten pages extolling the historical uniqueness of the moment, nevertheless suggested a precedent in the egalitarian medieval monastery, where monks freely "expressed their emotions and desires."[123] Germany too was an ethnic community of like-minded individuals, from whose midst Jewish and leftist colleagues had been expelled. Trainers appealed to ethnic solidarity as the broadest common denominator among teachers, for whom "racial knowledge" would describe an outlook, a worldview, more than a body of facts. In their reports suggesting improvements for future outings, organizers proposed more hiking, sports, vernacular culture, and group singing around campfires to improve morale and strengthen ethnic bonds. These proposals suggest that blatant Nazi indoctrination had proved disappointing.

Another variety of "natural" solidarity promoted in the teacher retreats bonded males with other males across the divides of age and rank, and females with females. Auguste Reber-Gruber, who directed the women's division of the NS Teachers League, believed so strongly in female separatism that she even praised the German bourgeois women's movement (which she otherwise condemned as egotistical) for its celebration of innate feminine traits.[124] Women participants in one group praised the nonhierarchical élan of the retreats, which offset the isolation and "standardization" of everyday life. Organizers of men's retreats built upon the "strong soldierly ambiance" and lauded "the collective spirit that emerged from the strict military operations."[125] Since about half of the male participants were veterans, the older men introduced the younger men to map reading, strategy, nighttime marching, and signal technology. The discipline of a military environment, one trainer commented, created a safe structure "within which participants could yield to collective emotions."

Singing ranked high among participants' favorite activities, but it had to be group singing because individual performances, whether vocal or instrumental, created an unwelcome gap between musicians and audience—a "rupture" between life and song, listeners and performers. Large choruses singing military songs, by contrast, illustrated how diverse voices could "organically" cooperate in a shared purpose. Recognizing the popularity of the "singing hours," many organizers suggested that every retreat should include at least one talented musician. Day hikes provided a chance to enjoy folksinging and avoid disputatious discussions about Nazi dogma.

Behind the detailed schedules that conveyed the impression of strict order, retreats actually allowed wide scope for spontaneity. Participants recalled the cheerful confusion caused by the constant influx of other groups in hostels. After a military drill or exercise class, teachers wandered away from the camp center. "Someone would be blowing a fanfare out in the woods; a group would be singing in the kitchen; while others beat a peasant drum." Sometimes groups of teachers would seek out a local *Bierstube*—"which," one reported, "of course, did not exactly conform to the fundamental intent of the retreat." The casual leisure activities, martial drills, and folkloric settings depoliticized teacher refresher courses and at the same time deemphasized academics. Participants' reports on these retreats suggest that Rust's mandate for thorough politicization fell by the wayside. Comradeship was the order of the day. Effusive descriptions of the setting, excerpts from lectures and conversations, and sentimental evocations of national pride eclipsed specifically National Socialist teachings. Poetic memories were common.

> We sought knowledge and discovered Life.
> We were summoned and became comrades.
> We spoke truth and became friends.[126]

The homely parables and mawkish sentiments of these reports exalted the experience of togetherness and held out the prospect of restoring morale damaged by the dissolution of over a dozen teachers' associations. A revived ethnic spirit promised to compensate for faculty purges and intrusive Nazi bureaucracy. The mellow mood of a campfire, the challenge of a bracing hike, or a beer in the local tavern allowed teachers to relax and look on the bright side of their collective situation.

By scaling back doctrine in the interests of restoring morale, devoted Nazi instructors were emulating Hitler's own avoidance of controversial topics. When he spoke to Hitler Youth at the 1935 Nuremberg Rally, for example, the Führer said nothing about racial danger and much about moral decay. "We must educate a new type of man so that our people is not ruined by the symptoms of degeneracy of our day."[127] At the annual teachers' convention in Bayreuth in 1936, 30,000 participants listened to lectures on character education, watched a 600-man torchlight parade, and attended the dedication ceremony of the House of Education.[128] Although antisemitic slurs were common, vulgar racism had all but disappeared from general teachers' assemblies. In the mid-1930s, ordinary teachers and devoted Nazis arrived at a tacit compromise that highlighted ethnic solidarity and minimized coarse racism.

Ethnic fundamentalism was built on values that already enjoyed unquestioned support among patriotic teachers. The few who dissented were made to feel marginal to a great ethnic purpose—one to which an immense mass of like-minded ethnic citizens had subscribed and from which "unwanted" citizens had been expelled. Open criticism of specifically Nazi doctrine (such as the Führer cult, coarse antisemitism, opposition to Christianity) died out. But teachers discovered that as long as they avoided anti-Nazi remarks in class or in the presence of zealous colleagues, they could deemphasize parts of the curriculum they disliked and, if they had Jewish pupils in their class, shelter them in small ways from Hitler Youth harassment.

This kind of selective compliance assuaged some of the pain suffered by many "unwanted" students at the hands of Nazi colleagues. But it did little to impede the Nazification of German youth because in 1936 all non-Nazi youth organizations were banned and in 1939 membership in Hitler Youth was required of all children with "appropriate" racial backgrounds. Within this vast organization, committed Nazi teachers had ample opportunities to initiate future citizens into the rigors of Nazi ideology: pagan rituals, ethnic arrogance and racist contempt, the Führer cult, and Germany's right to *Lebensraum*. Young—presumably pro-Nazi—teachers were expected not only to join Nazi-affiliated organizations but also to guide

Hitler Youth indoctrination.[129] Twelve thousand males cooperated in this effort to shape boys "who were tough as leather, swift as greyhounds, hard as Krupps steel." Seven thousand five hundred women teachers were charged with producing strong-minded girls who would bear the next generation. In addition to the immense Hitler Youth organization, Labor Service camps and the German Labor Front promoted Nazi ideology. For the students selected to become the elite of the future, the Nazi Party established a network of boarding schools which designed every facet of daily life so as to produce hardened young men prepared to sacrifice for their *Volk*.[130]

As Nazi educators like Rust, Schemm, and Krieck emphasized, the basis of teacher mobilization was emotional, not academic. They railed against the hollow materialism of the "system era," by which they meant Weimar democracy, and they promoted a sentimental vision of the *Volk* rooted in "blood and soil." In the elite Nazi schools, however, the factory-like architecture conveyed a different impression—one of relentless indoctrination. Victor Klemperer heard in the words of the education minister the mechanical sounds of an assembly line: "In every speech Rust emphasizes the overcoming of 'insipid intellectualism,' the precedence given to 'physical and character skills' . . . 'All teachers are to get an annual four-week national political overhaul.' The ever-greater tyranny a sign of ever-greater uncertainty."[131] In verbs appropriate to a factory, teachers were integrated, standardized, lined up, overhauled, and streamlined. Krieck spoke about the "sorting out, integrating every aspect" of Nazi education.[132] Alfred Rosenberg explained, "The point is not to enrich participants' knowledge, but to equip them, physically, spiritually and mentally to grasp and experience National Socialism."[133] As producers of future leaders, teachers were to be "outfitted" or "equipped" as if for an expedition or voyage.[134]

After blunders in the early years of the Third Reich, Nazi pedagogues revamped their approach to deemphasize blatant racial hatred and foreground the creation of a "we-consciousness" from which so-called racial aliens vanished. Behind the language of "utter," "absolute" and "total" loyalty, a fluid consensus evolved on the basis of allegiance to a virtuous leader and his *Volk*. Whether or not they had memorized the verses of the "Horst Wessel Song" or could recite the Ten Commandments for Selecting a Mate, students and teachers imbibed the concepts of Nazism. While this superficially moderate variant of *Gleichschaltung* allowed individual teachers considerable latitude to adapt according to their own situation and predilections, the moral mandate was clear: honor the Führer, expel aliens, sacrifice for the *Volk,* and welcome challenges. Compliant teachers may not have been the heart-and-soul Nazis of whom Nazi leaders boasted in 1933, but they prepared their pupils for induction into Hitler Youth and for sacrifice to the *Volk.*

Law and the Racial Order

National Socialism opposes the theories based on the equality of all men and on the fundamentally unlimited freedom of the individual vis à vis the State. [We support] the harsh but necessary recognition of the inequality of men and the differences between them based on the laws of nature.

—*Hans Globke, coauthor of the Nuremberg Race Laws, 1937*

When Carl Schmitt praised the "total Führer state," he anticipated that decisive leadership would lead to recovery from years of rudderless democracy. Hitler did not disappoint these expectations. Within eighteen months, he unleashed terror against Communists, co-opted conservatives, silenced investigative journalists, banished rival political parties, and purged his own Stormtroopers of dissidents. Having quickly destroyed the last vestiges of democracy, he stunned international opinion by concluding a Concordat with the Vatican and withdrawing Germany from the League of Nations. Ethnic improvement projects also began at once, with incentives for marriage between "desirables" and forced sterilization for others. Unemployment declined. Many Europeans looked on from neighboring countries with envy even if they deplored the Nazi state.

Only with regard to anti-Jewish policy did momentum stall. Between the April 1933 laws that imposed quotas on particular occupational categories and the September 1935 Nuremberg Race Laws, hundreds of local and regional regulations curtailed the rights of Jewish citizens, but no comprehensive national law affected their basic rights across the board.[1] This apparent hiatus, misleadingly called a "grace period," marked a crucial stage in the consolidation of a broad consensus on "the Jewish question" among party men, racial policy experts, seasoned civil servants, and jurists—a category of functionaries aptly dubbed "ethnocrats" by the historian Michael Burleigh. While these men shared an aversion to pogrom-style violence, they disagreed about an orderly alternative. Ethical and legal issues provoked constant friction over the meanings of concepts like community, identity, and citizenship. In the absence of clear orders from

Hitler, ethnocrats had ample opportunity to work out their own patterns of accommodation with the racial order.

Hannah Arendt's portrait of Adolf Eichmann was so compelling that it shaped interpretations of perpetrators at their desks and at killing sites for a generation. Standing trial from the 1960s through the 1990s, hundreds of killers declared they had obeyed orders without believing in them. Reading their testimony, one could easily imagine these mass murderers acting like "cogs" caught up in a machine they neither understood nor controlled.[2] However, archival records of meetings, conferences, task forces, and expert hearings reveal that perpetrators thought carefully about their ultimate aims and often displayed considerable initiative. Even the most relentless among them needed to make sense of their actions. Ethnocrats cared about consistency, coherence, and justice. Accustomed to functioning in a state of law, they took civil rights seriously. In retrospect, their concern for constitutional rights in a police state might seem scarcely credible. But even though free speech and the franchise had lost their meaning, other rights, including the right to participate in civil society, serve in the military, attend public schools, own property, and select sexual partners, mattered more than ever. Ethnocrats in the Third Reich faced pressure from Nazi hardliners who demanded that citizens with Jewish ancestors wear identification badges, that Jews be required to have "typical" Jewish surnames, and that businesses be marked to indicate their owners' racial identity. Many demanded that offspring of mixed marriages lose their citizenship and that sexual relations between people with Jewish and Christian ancestors be criminalized. Public opinion in Germany was not, in 1933, prepared for such radical proscriptions.

While Walter Gross's Office of Racial Politics initiated a massive ethnic-awareness drive with racist components, success at changing basic attitudes would require time. Aside from Gross and activists in Nazi organizations, little was done to prepare public opinion for a thoroughgoing drive against Jews. Even Goebbels, who purged individuals with only one Jewish grandparent from cultural life, avoided coarse antisemitism in Propaganda Ministry productions. Hitler rarely mentioned racial policy in public. Hitler's preoccupation with foreign policy and his finance minister's warning that international boycotts could harm economic recovery contributed to his restraint. But equally important, Hitler and his deputies learned from the disappointing results of the April 1 boycott that intrusive antisemitic sanctions met with apathy or worse. In 1934 opinion surveys by the SS Security Service (*Sicherheitsdienst,* or SD) and the Gestapo made it clear that most Germans disapproved of crude insults,

40. "In the summer of 1935, these two were hauled out of a Hamburg hotel and led through the streets." Like the lynching postcards in the United States, this postcard commemorated a racial assault. The woman wore a placard, "I am the biggest pig in the place and let only Jews enter me." His sign read, "I only take German girls into my room!"

physical violence, boycotts, and vulgar antisemitism. When brown-shirted bullies tormented defenseless Jews, bystanders felt sorry for the victims. Contempt for the Nazi "gutter press" was widespread. Non-Nazis and even some Nazis resented boycotts that interfered with their consumer choices. A series of detailed opinion reports from the state of Hesse, a stronghold of Nazism, noted that while most people harbored pejorative attitudes toward Jewry in the abstract, it did not occur to them to allow their prejudices to interfere with business as usual.[3]

On the other hand, most Germans seemed to accept the ostensibly legal expulsion of Jewish citizens from particular segments of public life as an "adjustment" to offset what many believed were Jews' so-called "special rights" in those areas. The Hindenburg exemption of frontline veterans and their children from the April 1933 laws contributed to the impression of fairness. Even though the exemptions implied that Jewish civil servants, physicians, and lawyers who had not risked their lives for the Fatherland did not deserve job security, the restrictions seemed fair.[4] While most Germans, like other Europeans and North Americans, took cultural antisemitism, or "polite Judeophobia," for granted, only a resolute racist minority approved of sanctions against people who had done no wrong.

From 1933 through 1935, Nazi officials searched for an alternative to both the lawlessness of violence-prone old fighters and conventional "polite" antisemitism. They sought, in effect, a way to translate Gerhard Kittel's superficially nonviolent but actually cruel proscriptions into policy. In hours and hours of meetings and thousands of memos and position papers, ethnocrats struggled to make sense of their obligations to the community, to their profession, and to their *Volk*. At every point, they confronted intractable moral questions. Although a satisfactory solution eluded them, the process of negotiating created a working consensus about methods and a broadly based network of peers. Collaborating with peers who accustomed themselves to a state based on race, not rights, these men suspended the larger moral issues that troubled them during the early years of Nazi rule and focused on the ramifications of immediate questions.

Comments made in 1933 by the Interior Ministry official Achim Gercke to a general audience revealed the racial aims of the Nazi Party. Besides the "positive" goal of "keeping one's own blood pure," Gercke described a "a negative side of our work that, translated into technical racial terms, means *extinction [Ausmerze]*." Against the "false humanitarianism" of a bygone age, he believed, "only one ideal is humane, *the promotion of what is good and the elimination of what is bad*. The will of Nature is God's will. Just look around . . . Nature sides with the strong, the good and the fit and separates the chaff from the wheat. We fulfill her commandment. No more. No less."[5] Gercke hated irresolution. "Against everyone who is incapable of saying a total yes or no to anything, we uphold a hard, masculine, relentless and logical consistency."[6] Because Gercke and other anti-

41. "Encounter in Vienna" insinuated that cosmopolitan Vienna was a site of pronounced racial danger. The woman's brusque rejection of a Jewish man represented the kind of "polite" antisemitism that may have appealed to Germans who were offended by fanatics' coarse racism.

semites in 1933 took for granted the existence of empirical evidence for Jews' "otherness," they exuded confidence. A Nazi jurist declared, "Today it has been recognized that the Jewish race differs considerably from the Aryan race with regard to blood, character, personality and view of life, and that a connection and pairing with a member of this race is not only undesirable for a member of the Aryan race, but also injurious and . . . unnatural."[7] Doctrinaire Nazis believed that a state was not only empowered but also obliged to override individual civil rights in the interest of creating an ethnically homogeneous nation.[8] These impatient Nazis found their plans foiled, however, both by their chaotic conceptual world and by objections from the civil service.

Between the April Laws of 1933 and the Nuremberg Laws of 1935, ethnocrats deliberated about dozens of proposals for ethnic improvement. Without apparent fear of being denounced by zealous colleagues, they expressed doubts about ethics, legal theory, and public opinion. Paradoxically, even as they disagreed, ethnocrats became emeshed in the process of incremental radicalization. As their interagency networks coalesced, experts and policymakers discovered common ground. The pluralism of opinions about "the Jewish question" provided a forum within which the doubtful and the resolute worked out their differences. Although rabid antisemites used terms like "extermination" and "destruction," concrete plans for murder did not exist during these years; when ethnocrats and ideologues used the term "final solution," most of them envisioned ghettoization or expulsion.

How could life be made intolerable for Jews in ways that met radicals' expectations without alienating ordinary citizens? From 1933 through 1935, hundreds of memos and dozens of meetings debated possible answers. While appearing moderate, bureaucratic persecution turned out to be more pernicious than pogroms. Not only did its calm façade mislead victims into believing that the situation was less malign than it was, but policies backed by the state were far more thorough than sporadic violence.

The success of administrative persecution depended on a broader-based complicity than militia-sponsored terror. Small gangs of militant Stormtroopers could intimidate Jews, but laws required bureaucratic organization. Slightly over a million civil servants and tens of thousands of Nazi Party functionaries—together with a veritable army of educators, lawyers, health care professionals, and social workers—would be required to formulate and enforce race laws. Cohesion did not come naturally to these men from three very different backgrounds. In 1933 tens of thousands of old fighters for the Nazi cause with barely adequate educational qualifications received sinecures in the civil service and party offices.[9] A second cohort, recently credentialed careerists (nicknamed "freshly baked Nazis"), joined the Nazi Party and enjoyed rapid promotions. These two groups were greatly outnumbered by civil servants (referred to as "not yet Nazis" in party jargon) who joined the requisite Nazi civil service leagues but did not apply for membership in the party.[10] Support for Nazism among civil servants was high compared with other occupational categories, but two out of three civil servants did not join.[11]

Without widespread assent to white-collar persecution, doubtful officials might use a loophole to protect a Jewish friend or warn Jewish colleagues of impending danger. Two opposing mandates placed functionaries in a quandary. The first was civil servants' commitment to obedience. As the sociologist Max Weber observed over a decade earlier, modern society is governed by rational principles to which individuals must adhere. A professional civil servant, in other words, suspends his own moral sense. "The honor of the civil servant is vested in his ability to execute conscientiously the order of superior authorities exactly as if the order agreed with his own conviction."[12] On the other hand, respect for logic had also been ingrained in civil servants, who held university degrees, usually in law. These men prided themselves on their skill at reasoning within abstract legal categories. Nearly a century after Weber's lecture on bureaucracy, the sociologist Eviatar Zerubavel noted this occupational trait. Punctilious to a fault, bureaucrats despised the intermediate and the anomalous.[13] The "war against Jewry" in Nazi Germany was riddled with precisely the kinds of contradictions that confound the rigid mind.

In 1933 the preconditions for a smoothly functioning bureaucracy were lacking. No clear-cut orders were given, and the conceptual disarray daunted even the resolute. Ethnocrats deplored lawless attacks against Jews and their property, but they could not agree on a lawful alternative.[14] At the most basic level, empirical uncertainty bedeviled their efforts. No one even knew how many citizens counted as Jews. Military statisticians and the Health Bureau in the Interior Ministry estimated that over 2 million Germans had between one and four Jewish grandparents.[15] Some demographers put the total as high as 4 million.[16] By contrast, Friedrich Burgdorfer, the director of the Reich Statistical Office, calculated that only about 800,000 citizens could be defined as all or partly Jewish. His office counted 550,000 "full Jews" (with four Jewish grandparents), 200,000 "half Jews" (two Jewish grandparents), and 100,000 "quarter Jews" (one grandparent), in a population of 65 million.[17]

Trained to reason according to universal principles, ethnocrats found themselves conceptually adrift in a state founded on "racial instinct."[18] One of the first to grasp the implications of a jurisprudence that substituted ethnic identity for legal codes was the minister of justice, Franz Gürtner, who contrasted Nazi law with the liberal doctrine of *Nulla poena sine lege,* "Anything not forbidden is permitted." The Nazi state, he wrote, "considers every attack on the welfare of the ethnic community and every violation of the goals toward which the community is striving as wrong per se. As a result, the law gives up all claims to be the sole source for determining right and wrong. What is right may be learned not only from the law but also from the concept of justice that lies behind the law and may not yet have found expression in the law."[19] Legions of highly educated civil servants confronted a revolution in the axiomatic bedrock of their profession. While their new chiefs still paid lip service to a state based on justice and Hitler refused to officially abolish the Weimar Constitution, in practice a legal system based on race brought chaos.

Nazi ethnocrats were not the first antisemites to encounter cognitive dissonance regarding the definition of "Jewish." In the 1890s, one of twelve Reichstag delegates in the Antisemite Party explained that his party had not proposed a law against Jews because its leaders could not agree on how to define "Jew."[20] Ethnocrats in the Third Reich searched for precedents. According to the April Laws, a citizen with one Jewish grandparent was categorized as Jewish. But military planners favored limiting the definition of Jewish to three or four Jewish grandparents to maximize the pool of draft-age young men. University personnel officers, by contrast, often decided that a non-Jewish professor with a Jewish spouse had been "contaminated" and therefore counted as Jewish. The so-called Jewish question remained without an answer.

After Interior Minister Frick's Committee on Population and Race had expeditiously rendered its opinion on forced sterilization in late 1933, it turned to the Jewish question. Momentum dissipated in rancorous debates about the meaning of "Jewish" and "non-Jewish." Members of the committee disagreed about the percentage of Jewish "blood" that made someone Jewish. When they defined "German-Aryan" as "someone who is of German or predominantly German and at least Aryan descent," a staff member noted in the margin, "This won't do!"[21] This committee, which had deftly pushed through an involuntary sterilization law, did not draft a single antisemitic measure. Several months later, the Nazi jurist Hans Frank established the Academy for German Law to bring the legal code into line with racial values. Experts in its more than forty subcommittees stumbled over the most basic terms such as "Aryan," "mixed blood," "Germanic," and "cognate blood."[22] Proposals to "preserve the purity of German blood" foundered in a semantic swamp.[23]

Zealous Nazis demanded a more aggressive approach to "the Jewish question," even though it became increasingly obvious that no physical marker of the blood they despised could be found. They, too, fell into hair-splitting disagreements about the percentage of Jewish blood that made a citizen Jewish. Brandenburg District Leader Wilhelm Kube suggested 10 percent.[24] The chief of the Nazi Physicians' League, Gerhard Wagner, argued for one eighth. Citing antimiscegenation laws in the United States, Achim Gercke favored one sixteenth because he did not wish to be less rigorous than the Americans.[25] Bernhard Lösener, the expert on Jewish affairs in the Interior Ministry, observed, "Every district and city chief in the Nazi Party made up his own version of 'Jewish,' which might range anywhere from 1/8 to full Jewish background . . . Calls for help pile up in the Interior Ministry asking for advice . . . Total chaos reigns on the question of who counts as Jewish."[26] In the absence of physiological evidence of Jewishness, local baptismal records provided the only "proof" of supposedly biological qualities.

Not surprisingly, Frick and many others feared that conceptual anarchy would discredit racial aims.[27] The chief of the Gestapo despaired at the "collapse of domestic bureaucracy."[28] The director of the Reich Office for People's Health protested, "While logic and consistency have traditionally been a special province of jurists and lawyers, it appears that since the seizure of power, these faculties have escaped them. In looking over our racial laws, the lack of a certain clarity becomes evident."[29] The emotionally powerful rhetoric that categorized people as either ethnically "us" or "them" left officials unprepared for the empirical confusion of day-to-day operations. Nowhere did those doubts reveal themselves more dramatically than in clashes about sexual relations between a Jew and a non-Jew—"racial treason" in Nazi parlance. An important source of indecision stemmed from confusion about the claims of gender as they applied to ethnicity. Against this background of cognitive doubt, state governors registered little support for a marriage ban when Minister of Justice Hans Gürtner polled them in 1933.[30]

Ethnocrats' first task was to clear away the confusion and enunciate the principles that would determine civil status in the ethnic state. Archival records allow us to eavesdrop on conversations about what they called "racial protection" measures. The moral conundrums of racial legislation came into sharp relief on June 5, 1934, when Minister of Justice Gürtner invited seventeen high-ranking civil servants, Nazi Party functionaries, and academics to join Nazi jurist Roland Freisler's committee in charge of reforming the criminal code. The purpose of the meeting was to draft legislation to ban sexual relations between citizens of Jewish and non-Jewish descent. At the outset, Gürtner underscored the magnitude of the meeting by asking whether to transcribe the deliberations. Because participants worried that the record of a meeting without minutes would arouse unwanted suspicion, a 253-page typed account, with marginal comments, was preserved.[31]

Opinion divided sharply along both moral and legal lines. In the first place, the men differed about the scale of the danger. While it was true that over a third of all Jews who married for the first time married Christians, the actual number of these marriages, compared with the roughly 730,000 marriages between Christians each year, was tiny. In 1933, of 15 million existing marriages, only 35,000 unions were between Jews and Christians.[32] Some discussants failed to perceive the danger of "undesirable" marriages as sufficient cause to support state intrusion into private matters. Doctrinaire Nazis like Freisler retorted that because "mixed-race" intercourse constituted an "assault" against communal ethnic health, it was "racial treason." The compromisers dodged both extremes by supporting the aims of harsher laws but counseling more modest means to the desired end. On definitional issues, extremists insisted that one Jewish grandparent made a citizen Jewish, while moderates proposed that three or four Jewish grandparents defined a person as Jewish. Each position evolved from distinctive intellectual and personal elements in the backgrounds of the spokesmen for each option: the Nazi zealot Freisler, the non-Nazi minister of justice Gürtner, and the Nazi race expert Bernhard Lösener.

Freisler's attraction to radical causes had been evident when, as a POW in Russia during the war, he learned to speak Russian fluently and then fought with Lenin's forces in the revolution. Upon his return to Germany, he enrolled in the University of Göttingen and became a Nazi Party member in 1924, at about the same time as his fellow students Walter Gross and Achim Gercke. As a young lawyer, Freisler defended Nazi militiamen against criminal charges by praising their idealistic motives and denouncing democracy as a crime against the *Volk*. In 1933, when Freisler, at age 41, became a state secretary under Gürtner, his attitude toward violence changed.[33] Now that "the state and the *Volk* had fused," he deemed all unsanctioned violence as criminal regardless of motive.[34] Describing the law as "the focused might of the people," he compared it to the "concentrated firepower that could stop a tank attacking the front lines."[35] The "front line" in racial war was a ban on "mixed-blood" sexual relations. In the fall of 1933, the impatient Freisler coauthored a pamphlet calling for the criminalization of sexual relations between "German blooded" individuals and "members of foreign-blooded communities" (including Africans), but the idea was tabled in the face of strong public criticism.[36] The stalemate infuriated Freisler. So did the Führer's silence. For the radical Freisler, ethical questions did not arise. Seized by utopian righteousness, his only concern was to act swiftly. Writing in a law review late in 1933, he fretted that unless key racial questions were settled, "chaos and anarchy would replace unified leadership."[37]

Freisler's superior, the canny 53-year-old minister of justice Franz Gürtner, viewed a law against "racial treason" from a very different standpoint.[38] Like Freisler, Gürtner had served in the war. His heroism as an officer in the Middle East had won him not only a decoration from the kaiser but praise from T. E. Lawrence. As a cosmopolitan intellectual fluent in four languages and an avid reader of English crime novels, Gürtner's background could have scarcely been more different than Freisler's. During the years Freisler defended Nazi criminals, Gürtner served as the Bavarian minister of justice and then accepted the position of reich minister of justice. When Hitler seized power, Gürtner remained at his post. Gürtner's fervent Catholic faith, his refusal to join the party, his criticisms of the libelous Nazi tabloid *Der Stürmer*, and his objections to the inhuman conditions in the Dachau concentration camp enhanced his reputation for integrity outside party circles.[39]

The slightly younger Berhnard Lösener also had fought at the front in the war. After being demobilized in 1920, he received his Ph.D. in law at the University of Tübingen and was appointed to the Prussian customs service. In 1931 he joined the Nazi Party because, he said later, he saw it as a bulwark against Communism.[40] In his memoirs written after the war, Lösener denied having been an antisemite, but documentary evidence suggests otherwise.[41] As a highly educated old fighter with well-placed Nazi connections in Berlin, Lösener was put in charge of Jewish affairs in the Interior Ministry. In the autumn of 1933 and again when briefing his newly appointed supervisor in the spring of 1934, Lösener spoke out in favor of the mildest possible "solutions." When colleagues referred to citizens with one Jewish grandparent as Jewish, Lösener would call them "3/4

Aryans." What was the point, he would ask, of gratuitously alienating loyal German citizens (and their non-Jewish relatives) just because they discovered they had a Jewish grandmother? He insisted on a "hardship paragraph" that took into consideration the "spiritual burden" *(seelische Belastung)* of citizens affected by racial law.[42] As a fillip, Lösener would remind government officials that *"Mischlinge* are unfortunately found in officers and academic families," the very elites with whom Nazi leaders like to identify.[43] Like Gürtner, Lösener questioned the legality of making racial difference grounds for uncontested divorce and reminded his colleagues of Nazis' concern about the family.[44]

At the June 1934 meeting on "racial treason," the determined Freisler faced the laconic Gürtner, while Lösener looked on from the sidelines. The meeting began with participants' affirmation of their support for Nazi aims—and expressions of dislike for Jews, whom one participant described as "an entirely offensive oriental mixture" that had caused mighty nations to disintegrate by "infecting" their racial stock. Another resented Jews who, everyone knew, had "the most beautiful cars and motor boats and frequented all the best vacation spots." Furthermore, because most Germans found intercourse between Germans and Jews "immoral and reprehensible," a legal ban would affect only a tiny number of citizens. Finally, they expressed their endorsement of an ethical order founded not on individual rights but on communal good. "We all agree that we are not considering the protection of individual rights, but rather protecting the purity of our blood community."[45] They lamented the confusion of Nazi racial policy, and they worried about widespread disapproval of uncouth antisemitism. Everyone at the meeting, including Freisler, rejected "emotional antisemitism" because they saw its methods as "unworthy" of a civilized *Volk.* Only Freisler called for immediate and drastic action—because, he said, the "willingness to make hard decisions" (even in the face of hostile public opinion) was a cardinal Nazi virtue. Armed with military jargon, he hurled himself into the verbal fray. "Herr Minister, I cannot bear it that no one supports these proposals . . . If I stood aside [from this debate], I would betray my entire record as a fighter for the cause."

Gürtner countered that such a revision in law and custom had to await a change in attitude among ordinary citizens, and, like many at the meeting, he feared that Nazi racial policy provided fodder for anti-Nazi ridicule. "I remember that not long ago, we were openly laughed at and mocked whenever we would even mention racial thinking." If they erred in making policy, they "would be made fools of" once again. Exasperated, he asked the gentlemen to look around the table at their own racial traits. How many of them measured up? "There already are enough jokes to the effect that top Nazi leaders' skulls should be examined for their Nordic qualities."[46] The rector of Berlin University added that if they acted unwisely their descendents might laugh at their efforts in a hundred years. Freisler's solution to these doubts was to endorse harsh punishments for criticism of racial policy, which he called "intellectual racial treason." Freisler's proposal to criminalize criticism of racial dogma, according to Gürtner, would place Nazis in a class with the sixteenth-century Catholic inquisitors who burned their critics as heretics. The idea did not carry.

Throughout the meeting, Gürtner posed sly questions and turned the conversation to philosophical issues that elicited intense reactions. Three conundrums particularly absorbed the participants: first, the scope of the Criminal Law Commission itself; second, the validity of racial science; and third, the possibility of anomalous hypothetical cases. Gürtner perceived the scope of the commission as being too narrow to allow for a comprehensive law against mixed-race intercourse. In his view, such a law would represent a major change, analogous to the legalization of bigamy. But Freisler compared it to a law passed in the Weimar Republic that, in the interest of curbing the spread of venereal disease, required an infected partner to divulge his or her condition before intercourse. Being Jewish was like having syphilis. Gürtner countered by asking about the status of the many citizens who were unaware of their Jewish ancestors. Unscrupulous researchers (or hostile spouses) could blackmail unsuspecting citizens with forged or real evidence of Jewish blood. Moreover, unwed mothers would never attribute paternity to a Jewish father if their intercourse had been a crime in the first place. Praising the Nazis' support for the family, Gürtner opined that racially based divorce would create "a particularly disagreeable, even revolting, public image."

At several junctures, discussants revealed their doubts about racial science. Given the "absence of roughly reliable objective traits" to identify Jewishness, the potential for corruption was obvious. Freisler suggested that they ignore racial science because it had not furnished clear guidelines. Others defended science but were baffled at the arbitrariness of terms like "hybrid" and "mongrel." The experts at the meeting could not explain the difference between genotype and phenotype, and they disagreed about whether Jews could be considered Caucasians. All of them wondered whether race could be better identified by visible or invisible traits. What would be the tone of a law against racial treason? Zealots wanted the law to reflect their loathing for Jews, but Lösener argued in favor of cool, objective language without "any overtones of emotional racial hatred."

Their lengthy deliberations about tangential issues and meandering hypothetical discussions suggest their unease with the ethical and legal issues engaged by sweeping proposals for racial persecution. Lösener introduced the question of "borderline" ethnic groups (like Turks, Dinarians, Wends [West Slavs], and Poles). Then he raised a more troubling hypothetical: citizens who felt completely German and then discovered a non-Aryan grandparent. How could they be "digested" *(Verdauung)* into the ethnic mainstream? Could the nation afford to lose their talents? When Lösener asked for moderation, Gürtner called his words "the sighs of an oppressed soul" from the only person in the room who actually had to deal with racial questions on a daily basis.

During the meeting and probably over lunch, participants expressed their doubts in the form of anomalies that revealed troubling gender issues, chief among them the infringement of Aryan men's sexual freedom. They agreed, for example, that a Jewish man who disguised his racial identity in order to seduce an unsuspecting non-Jewish woman was committing a crime and deserved punishment; but what about a non-Jewish man who fell in love with a Jewish woman? Did the actual intercourse or the deception constitute his crime? What about "a blond Jewess who spoke flawless French" and seduced a "German-blooded male"—or a blond Jewish man who seduced a "German-blooded female"? What if, one man asked, a mixed-blood couple, both German citizens, left Germany to consummate their relationship? What if a "full German" dated a Jewish woman? Did his knowledge of her racial identity affect his putative crime? When the conversation drifted to what the men called "love for sale," they speculated about females and males as prostitutes and clients.

As trained jurists, these ethnocrats thought analogically and reasoned from precedent. Although they considered the 1928 law against venereal disease and a ban on polygamy, they ignored the antimiscegenation laws passed in German colonies in Africa between 1905 and 1907.[47] Instead, they expressed their admiration for the United States as a model both because antimiscegenation laws and immigration quotas seemed so clear-cut and because public opinion accepted them as natural.

In the early evening, Gürtner concluded, "I think there's a feeling of doubt *[Insuffizienz]*. We stand, between the Syclla of racial protection and the Charybdis of deceit."[48] Freisler came around to the position that public opinion had to be better prepared before a racial treason law could be effective. He also conceded that virulent antisemitic propaganda could backfire. "Hatred," he said, "only weakens us." Gürtner reiterated that unless people felt an "ethical-ethnic obligation *[volksethnisch Verpflichtungen]* to preserve racial purity," racial laws would be moot. After ten hours, the exhausted participants still disagreed "about the kind of law needed, its goals, and its methods." No proposals emerged. "We have been talking past one another," Freisler remarked dismally.

The transcript of this futile meeting elucidates the paradoxical effects of disagreement in a surprisingly open forum. A highly trained group of civil servants and Nazi functionaries aired fundamental differences. Despite the obvious pressure from Freisler, they accomplished nothing. Therein lay the significance of this meeting. The experts forestalled the criminalization of "mixed-race" intercourse, thwarted a law against criticism of racial dogma, and headed off further encroachment on Jews' civil rights. This conscientious and diverse group of public servants were not yet prepared to accede to new levels of persecution, but they nevertheless had become engaged in a process. The fact that their opinions were solicited reassured them that their participation might make a difference, and meeting like-minded peers in other offices embedded them in a network. In the absence of clear orders from Hitler, no sweeping escalation of antisemitic persecution occurred, although the promulgation of hundreds of municipal and state measures, as well as piecemeal national regulations, eroded the position of Jews.[49]

While ethnocrats hesitated on the threshold of radicalization, in regions where Nazism was strong, militia toughs harassed couples they believed to be of mixed race, and local officials required betrothed couples to prove their worthiness to marry *(Ehetauglichkeit)* by presenting proof of Aryan ancestry *(Abstammungsnachweis).*[50] Signs (sometimes written in mock Hebrew letters) warning "Jews not wanted here" appeared at city limits and in restaurants. Hotheads posted traffic signs saying "Dangerous curves! Jews permitted to drive at 120 kilometers per hour."[51] In the Rhineland, Nazis in one village hung up a huge sign saying "Jew Aquarium" in front of a swimming pool from which Jews were not banned.[52] In Breslau, Stormtroopers paraded through the streets shouting obscenities at female Christian "racial traitors" who were married to or even friendly with Jewish men.[53] Where district leaders were powerful, public facilities like parks, libraries, and swimming pools were closed to Jews. In the Franconian village of Treuchtlingen, in which 119 of 4,200 residents were Jewish, Nazis cursed Jews as "Pigs" and "Yids," and boys in Hitler Youth attacked a Jewish businessman in his home and destroyed his furniture. Despite complaints from non-Nazis and petitions from Jewish victims, criminal aggression against helpless citizens was not punished.[54]

By contrast, where support for Nazism was weak, "mixed-race" couples married, teachers treated Jewish children fairly, and many establishments ignored prohibitions against Jewish patrons. Victor Klemperer noted in 1935 that during a national convention of literary scholars, "Not one of all my Romance Language colleagues called on me; I am like a plague corpse." Yet a few friends stood by him and his wife, and one acquaintance who belonged to the Nazi Party continued to treat him cordially.[55] Other memoirists expressed great affection for the few people who helped them despite Nazi pressure. In the spring of 1935, on the anniversary of the death of the Nobel Laureate chemist Fritz Haber in exile, academics held a memorial service that even a few Nazis attended. A few weeks later, the faculty of the University of Berlin held a funeral service for another Jewish Nobel Prize recipient, the microbiologist Robert Koch.[56] Ferdinand Sauerbruch, Germany's leading surgeon, joined the Nazi Party but quietly found positions abroad for his Jewish assistants.[57] The so-called grace period during which incremental persecution continued but major legislation was forestalled facilitated what scholars have called "selective compliance."

As tempting as it might be to generalize about "ordinary" Germans' attitudes toward Jews, any generalization distorts a complex reality. Aside from a hardcore minority of fervent Jew-haters, Germans reacted negatively to what they perceived as unsanctioned violence, but they came to accept measures with an aura of legality. When citizens, whether or not they supported Nazism, ignored one or another antisemitic measure, they may have acted out of empathy with Jews or out of defiance against laws that restricted their consumer choices.[58] Although it is wise to remain agnostic on the topic of motivation, it seems clear that Germans were neither brainwashed nor terrorized. Rather, they conformed to regulations of which they approved and circumvented those they disliked. The memoirs of Jewish Germans who emigrated attest to the existence of both violent antisemites who drove them out and loyal friends whose civil courage enabled them to escape alive.[59]

Foreign journalists filed stories about the wild inconsistencies of a supposedly authoritarian state. A reporter for the London *Fortnightly Review* wrote, "In no other field does the Nazi regime reveal so much muddled and chaotic action as in its dealing with the Jews."[60] According to an editorial in *The New York Times,* "One day the rabble in Munich is given a free hand with Catholics and the Jewish businessmen. The next day it is discovered the hooligans were renegade Nazis and duly arrested."[61] At the University of Tübingen, Georg Weise, an art historian whose wife was alleged to be Jewish, was fired. But when Frau Dr. Weise demonstrated her "Jew-free" pedigree, Weise returned to his post.[62] Optimistic Sopade monitors told of hardcore Nazis' impatience with a regime founded on race that for two years had failed to define Jew, Aryan, or even race.[63] "Of course, external power is in Nazi hands, but . . . as problems multiply, the élan of the movement slackens and the genuine inner influence of the old bureaucracy, economy and feudal rule returns."[64] Another wrote, "Behind the thick veil of closed ranks, the inner oppositions have definitely sharpened."[65] There seemed to be, in 1935, "a kind of nervousness in the regime [suggesting] . . . that something like a conscience is stirring among the people. A public conscience *[öffentliche Gewissen]* is waking up after appearing to be dead for two and a half years."[66]

The Nazi media inadvertently acknowledged widespread indifference to racial values in their shrill admonitions for greater vigilance. "Whenever three educated Germans discuss the Jewish Question, two are sure to bring up a really decent Jew to whom [antisemitic] measures do not apply." Such disregard for racial purity, the author noted, "offended one's sense of justice."[67] Walter Gross chastized fellow Nazis who ignored boycotts: "We cannot find ourselves in the contradictory position of being antisemites who buy handkerchiefs at Simon and Kohn's."[68] Heydrich noted that people everywhere were "unhappy with the inconsistent procedures" in racial political matters.[69] The SS office on Jewish affairs reported in August 1935, "A concerted approach to the Jewish problem is almost impossible in the absence of a clear policy."[70]

Lacking coherent antisemitic laws, Frick sought clarity by issuing linguistic guidelines *(Sprachreglung).* If the meanings of key terms could be regularized, policy might seem clearer. But when his department of genealogy tried to regularize official taxonomy, some experts vetoed "Aryan" on the grounds that it applied to linguistic, not physical, groups; others found "non-Jewish" too vague, and still others believed "race" should indicate an individual's geocultural homeland.[71] According to the last concept, anyone with ancestors from northwestern Europe (including Austria and Iceland, but not Finland) would count as Germanic. The committee talked briefly about a comprehensive Law for the Protection of German

Blood, but participants worried that "such harsh measures against the Jew might well produce a backlash."[72] In June 1935 Frick suggested that "non-Aryan" be replaced by "Jewish" and "of foreign origin" *(Fremdstämig),* but the distinction did not catch on. Exasperated, Frick commented, "'Aryan' and 'Non-Aryan' [are] sometimes not entirely tenable . . . From a racial political standpoint, it is Judaism that interests us more than anything else."[73] A month later, he announced that sweeping racial legislation would be forthcoming, but he produced only a relatively innocuous revision of naturalization procedures.

In the face of government inaction, radical antisemites kept up the pressure throughout the summer of 1935 for a ban on sexual relations between Jews and non-Jews. Nazi Party publications like *The Jewish Expert (Der Judenkenner), Assault (Der Angriff),* Rosenberg's *World Battle against Jewry (Weltkampf),* and Streicher's *The Stormtrooper (Der Stürmer)* featured loathsome caricatures and slanderous reports of Jewish misdeeds. In April 1935 the headlines of *The Stormtrooper* screamed: "Ritual Murder in Lithuania!" "Jewish Doctors, Sexual Criminals, and Murderers!" and "Pesach! Annual Memorial for the Oldest Mass Ritual Murder of All."[74] In July 1935, after a few protesters demonstrated against an antisemitic Swedish film in Berlin, militias and the police savagely beat them up. When militias smashed windows on the Kurfürstendamm in broad daylight, anyone who objected was arrested. Roving bands of Nazi youth systematically vandalized ice cream stands in Berlin—an action that outraged residents who appreciated an evening stroll with a pause for refreshments.[75]

Throughout Germany, roving bands of militiamen beat up people who "looked Jewish" even though local authorities occasionally rebuked them. An article in the April 1935 issue of the new SS weekly *Das Schwarze Korps* demanded criminalization of "racial treason" as an alternative to Stormtroopers' notorious violence.[76] Frick, who in early 1934 had ordered civil servants *not* to ban "inter-racial" marriages on their own initiative, changed his mind and in the summer of 1935 authorized registrars to delay applications from "racially mixed" couples.[77] At the same time, Rudolf Hess ordered restraint. In April 1935 he appealed to "all decent National Socialists . . . not to vent their feelings by acts of terror against individual Jews" because the Führer said he worried that Jews would use atrocities as the pretext for boycotts abroad.[78] The violence did not abate.

In July a demonstration in New York against the German oceanliner *Bremen* that was flying a swastika flag made headlines, and rumors of anti-German boycotts spread. In July Hess insisted, "Lawless outbursts against

Jews must cease at once! The Führer forbids Nazi Party members from undertaking unauthorized actions against individual Jews."[79] On July 27, 1935, Hitler spoke out against graffiti and unauthorized signs and a few weeks later denounced "provocateurs, rebels and enemies of the state."[80] To be "worthy" of Nazism, militias were admonished to remain within the law.[81] Frick admonished his staff to enforce this order from the Führer. The Nazi supervisor of Jewish cultural organizations called for restraint and reminded Nazi militants that Jewish organizations had sworn their loyalty to the regime and therefore operated legally.[82]

SS Security Service surveys of public opinion reflected Germans' mixed reactions.[83] With the German economy in the midst of a slight downturn beginning in late 1934 and consumers complaining about shortages of basic food supplies, the atmosphere was charged. When bands of Stormtroopers, inflamed by Streicher, set off a wave of antisemitic violence in Munich, the foreign media reported "considerable indignation" among bystanders.[84] The Sopade reports from 1935 characterized antisemites as "primitive mentalities" and observed that "four fifths of the population rejects anti-Jewish smear campaigns." In a town on the Rhine, when a drunken Stormtrooper attempted to break into a Jewish home, screaming, "Tonight I'm going to slit your throats!" a crowd of neighbors protested vehemently, and the local police defended the victims. An SS Security Service official lamented that villagers were "still friends of the Jews," and a local Nazi leader called off an antisemitic propaganda campaign because it was counterproductive.[85] In rural areas, peasants maintained longstanding commercial ties with Jewish livestock dealers who offered better terms than their Christian competitors.[86] When shoppers defied Stormtroopers and entered Jewish-owned establishments, "popular sympathy is with the shoppers, and several women made angry remarks at the Stormtroopers."[87] Wilhelm Kube, an inveterate antisemite, complained that far too many people, including Nazi Party members, still patronized Jewish businesses (often placing their orders by telephone to avoid detection).[88]

A minor scandal erupted in Berlin when a zealous bank clerk noticed a canceled check from Lord Mayor Heinrich Salm to a Jewish tailor. At his trial, Salm explained that his large bulk required the special talents of the man who had made his clothes for years.[89] The Nazi Party expelled him, but Hitler reinstated him.[90] A Sopade observer found that "everywhere people grumble. The Nazis are incompetent. Everything is chaotic among leaders of the state and party. Not to mention the lower echelons! Hitler is being pulled this way and that."[91] Reinhard Heydrich, Himmler's second in command, complained to the SS Security Service in August 1935, "Officials who behave according to their consciences and reject mixed-race marriages are often overturned by the courts." The time had come, he insisted, for strict laws governing Jews' citizenship and choice of sexual partners.[92]

The stalemate encouraged Jews and tolerant Germans to take consolation in a peasant adage, "The soup is not eaten as hot as it's cooked." Jews asked themselves, as Klemperer wrote, "Where do I belong? To the 'Jewish nation,' declares Hitler. And I *feel* the Jewish nation . . . is a comedy and I am nothing but a German or German European."[93] A Jewish veterans' association reaffirmed Jews' loyalty to Germany by publishing a book of letters written by Jewish soldiers who had died in the war. Rejecting emigration as an option, they explained their decision to remain in an "ethnic community that rejects us or, at best, only tolerates us . . . [because] We know only one fatherland and one homeland—and it is Germany."[94] Such evidence of Jews' patriotism only incited Nazi radicals to demand harsher laws.[95]

The paradox facing racial policymakers in 1935 lay in the amount of discord among ethnocrats who generally despised Jews and criticized violent attempts to force them out of the country.[96] Foreign news media reported the vacillations in "official" policy.[97] Rumors of impending racial laws circulated so widely that *The New York Times* in August 1935 reported an "anti-Jewish jamboree" and predicted drastic new racial laws.[98] Freisler told the press to expect a new definition of "treason" that encompassed not only crimes against the state but "attacks on the *Volk*," by which he meant sexual relations between ethnic Germans and Jews.[99]

As the annual Nuremberg Party Rally approached, Nazi leaders faced a familiar conundrum: unsanctioned anti-Jewish violence offended public opinion but moderation spawned disaffection among zealots. In late August 1935, Minister of Finance Hjalmar Schacht told leading Nazis, including Minister of Justice Gürtner, that "the present lack of legislation and unlawful activities must stop." Calling extremists' demands "barbarism of the worst kind," Schacht complained that outrages against Jews were ruining Germany's commercial ties.[100] Lest anyone mistake him as a friend of the Jews, he added a few days later, "Jews will have to make their peace with the fact that their influence in our country is permanently at an end."[101] A *Führerstaat* must be consistent in order to enforce its will at the grassroots.[102] By implication, since he did not expect Nazis to modify their antisemitism, he endorsed measures to make it seem legal.

As the high point of the Nuremberg Rally that began on September 8, 1935, Hitler planned a ceremonial Reichstag session as the occasion for a dramatic announcement. But when the rally began, only a rather tepid law making the swastika flag the national flag had been planned.[103] Suddenly, on the evening of Friday, September 13, Hitler summoned three officials from the Interior Ministry to fly from Berlin to Nuremberg. When the telephone call came from Hitler's staff, Lösener was celebrating his recent promotion to the rank of cabinet counselor (which he achieved despite his reputation as a "friend of the Jews").[104] Twelve hours later, in Nuremberg, he and his superiors, State Secretaries Hans Pfundtner and Wilhelm Stuckart, set to work on language for sweeping race laws.[105] For two days, the men worked furiously. Early in the morning of the day Hitler was to deliver his speech, they had finally cobbled together a string of paragraphs. Not being able to agree about how to define Jewish, the experts submitted four versions and left the decision to Hitler.

Hitler's address to the Reichstag at 8:00 P.M. on September 15—his twelfth speech in four days—was uncharacteristically brief. For the first time since drafting the boycott proclamation on the eve of April 1, 1933, Hitler publicly discussed Jewish policy. Before arriving at his main topic, he rambled on about his love of peace, the splendid German army, the plight of ethnic Germans in the Baltic countries, and the Bolshevik menace. This was his segue into the topic of the evening. "We are further compelled to note that here, as everywhere, it is almost exclusively Jewish elements which are at work." Saying nothing about blood, race, or biology, Hitler continued: "Loud complaints of provocative actions of individual members of this race are coming in from all sides, and the striking frequency . . . and similarity of their content appears to indicate a certain method behind the deeds themselves. These actions have escalated to demonstrations in a Berlin cinema directed against a basically harmless foreign film which Jewish circles fancied was offensive to them." Compared to Streicher's slogans or his own language in *Mein Kampf*, Hitler's remarks were pallid. But as on other critical occasions, Hitler closed on an ominous note. "However, should this hope [for a legal solution] prove false and international Jewish agitation proceed on its course, a new evaluation of the situation would have to take place."[106] Distancing himself from the new race laws, Hitler attributed them to "Frick and his comrades" and asked Goering to read them. Although Hitler's speech was broadcast on the radio and over the public address system in Nuremberg, just before Goering read the provisions Goebbels turned off the sound from the Reichstag and played a march. Only the roughly 500 Reichstag delegates inside the hall actually heard the text of the new laws. When the party news media publicized the special Reichstag session, bold headlines announced the flag law, but the race laws appeared in smaller type almost as a side issue. Thus, the race laws Lösener and his colleagues believed would be the high point of the rally actually received relatively muted publicity. But Hitler's endorsement of bureaucratic tactics and rejection of violence was clear. Within days *Der Stürmer* ordered an end of disorder. "The Jewish question will be forcefully solved . . . by a disciplined enlightenment campaign."[107]

The first racial law, The Reich Citizenship Law, deprived Jews of citizenship and defined them as "persons belonging to the Reich" *(Reichsangehörige)*. Next, the Law for the Protection of the German Blood and Honor criminalized marriage and sexual intercourse between Jews and citizens of the Reich. It further forbade Jewish families to employ Christian servants under the age of 45 (a provision not considered by the ethnocrats). But how would "Jewish" be defined? From the four possible definitions, ranging from mild (four Jewish grandparents defined an individual as Jewish) to harsh (only one Jewish grandparent was required), Hitler had selected the mildest version: "valid only for full Jews." But when Goering read out the laws, he noticed that Hitler had crossed out the phrase "valid only for full Jews," without replacing it.[108] No definition was mentioned. After a ceremonial vote, Hitler spontaneously rose to speak, not to vindicate the harsh law but to command "tremendous discipline." To Stormtroopers, he said, "See to it that the nation itself does not stray from the straight and narrow path of the law!" With cynical hypocrisy, Hitler swore "Jews in Germany [have been] granted opportunities in all areas of their own ethnic life such as existed in no other country."[109]

Foreign news media, which routinely deplored outbreaks of violence against Jews, reported the Nuremberg Race Laws almost without comment. The strategy of the cold pogrom worked. As long as the means of persecution appeared orderly, few raised their voices to object. The definition of who counted as a Jew remained as murky as ever. Hitler could not make up his mind. Nine days after his speech at the rally, Hitler convened a meeting with his top deputies, presumably to announce his definition of "Jew."[110] He did not mention the topic.

At the end of September, Hitler summoned Walter Gross along with other race experts to discuss what Hitler termed a "very major reorientation *[ganz gewaltiges Umdenken]* in Jewish policy that will affect all of us."[111] Hitler began by complaining about the lack of racial expertise among the men who had drafted the race laws. Presumably he invited the experts to verify the scientific basis of the new measures.[112] Hitler then acknowledged that gutter antisemitism had been counterproductive and added that Germany had to become "strong, powerful and ready to strike." This meant not only military and economic preparedness but psychological readiness as well. "Right now, we're not discussing utopias, but we're looking the day-to-day reality and the political situation in the eye." The reality that obsessed him was not anti-Jewish policy in general but German citizens who had mixed ancestry (less than half of 1 percent of all Germans). He told Gross and others at the meeting that he wanted a deep social "chasm" to separate "racial full Jews" from non-Jews. "A large category of mixed-race citizens without rights who do not know where they belong" evidently perturbed him. Apparently basing his logic on Mendelian genetic charts derived from crossing strains of peas, Hitler deplored "mixed breeds" and added, "No completely satisfying biological solution exists." He mentioned three potential solutions: (1) emigration, (2) sterilization, and (3) assimilation. He elaborated only on the third—"the absorption *[aufsaugen]* of mixed-race material" by the dominant *Volk*, so that in a few generations Jewish traits would be "liquidated."[113] Hitler, as an ideologically driven autodidact, had little patience with ambiguity. To prepare Germans for war, by implication a race war as well as a territorial war, Hitler told those at the meeting that new methods of persuasion would be required.

It appears that Hitler had been pondering the merits of what he had termed in 1919 "rational" and "emotional" varieties of antisemitism. Besides fretting about the negative fallout from old fighters' crude verbal and physical violence, he revealed his skepticism about Streicher's racial views when he asked Gross whether, after a woman had had intercourse with a Jewish man, her subsequent offspring would be racially tainted, as Streicher claimed. Gross dismissed the notion out of hand. Hitler then complained about the "frequently very strong and not always judicious *[geschikt]* antisemitic propaganda [that] . . . has damaged long-range developments." In contrast to hardcore Nazis' coarse antisemitism, Hitler called for a "fundamentally new direction *[eine grundsätzliche neue Kursrichtung]*" in propaganda—a change that, Hitler added, must not be acknowledged in public. Realizing that moderation would alienate the old fighters, Hitler hoped that non-Nazis in Germany and abroad would appreciate the "humanity" of his restraint. Gross, who all along had lobbied for a rational approach, took Hitler's remarks as a green light for his public relations strategies. As at other crucial junctures, Hitler portentously closed the interview with the warning that in the event of an all-out war, he was "prepared for all consequences [bereit zu allen Konsequenzen]."[114]

Meanwhile, ethnocrats still wondered how the racial terms of the Nuremberg Laws would be defined. With the new regulations in place, the Justice and Interior ministries were swamped with requests for implementation guidelines. Hitler procrastinated. On September 29 he summoned Stuckart and Lösener to Munich, where everyone expected him to side with the extremists. Hitler again said nothing. In October he spoke with Goebbels and consulted with high-ranking functionaries, including Finance Minister Schacht and Justice Minister Gürtner.[115] In his diary on November 7 Goebbels noted that Hitler had made up his mind on the Mischlinge question, but Hitler said nothing.[116] Two days later, at the annual commemoration of the 1923 Putsch, old fighters and high-ranking Nazi leaders must have urged Hitler to decide in favor of the harshest definition. Hitler remained silent.

While their chief procrastinated, Lösener and his colleagues worked feverishly, evaluating proposals, drafting memos, consulting, and debating the merits of over thirty interpretations of the Nuremberg Laws.[117] From Lösener's vantage point, the main stumbling blocks were ethical, not empirical or legal. He published an 18-page article in the October issue of a professional journal for civil servants.[118] Hailing the race laws "that tackle the root of the fundamental evil that threatens the survival of the German Volk," Lösener praised an ethos that valued the well-being of future generations more than its own short-term advantage. "If we were not to wage this war, then our descendents would be plagued with irrevocable and escalating difficulties." Attributing responsibility for the "deplorable state of affairs" in Germany to liberals' belief in universal human rights, he welcomed the healthy National Socialist order, in which citizenship would reflect both racial origin (which Lösener called "objective") and "subjective" commitment to the Volk.

Citing Mein Kampf, Lösener claimed that the laws did not signal the "onset of hatred, but rather of reconciliation." After centuries of maintaining their own "pure blood . . . authentic Jews have not the slightest reason to be indignant." Rejecting proposals for a "geographical ghetto," Lösener advocated instead "dissimilation" (English in the original). In the near future, citizens with one or two grandparents with "Jewish blood" would be "absorbed" by marriage into mainstream culture, and anyone with a preponderance (three fourths or more) of Jewish blood would sever all ties with Germany. Using much the same moral reasoning as Gerhard Kittel, Lösener envisioned a "pure" dominant society in which Jews would live as pariahs. Without denying the suffering of *Mischlinge*, Lösener cast the suffering of this small minority as a temporary injustice on the path to a worthy goal.

While ethnocrats cogitated in October and early November, Hitler kept his thoughts to himself. On November 14 he authorized a subordinate to announce that the race laws would apply to only citizens with three or four Jewish grandparents. Two Jewish grandparents made one a *Mischlinge*. With one Jewish grandparent, a citizen who did not belong to a Jewish community or marry a Jew became virtually Aryan.[119] Perhaps worried about hardship cases, Hitler reserved for himself the authority to upgrade a *Mischlinge* to honorary Aryan status. Goebbels, despite his annoyance that Hitler had sided with Gross and not with Gerhard Wagner,

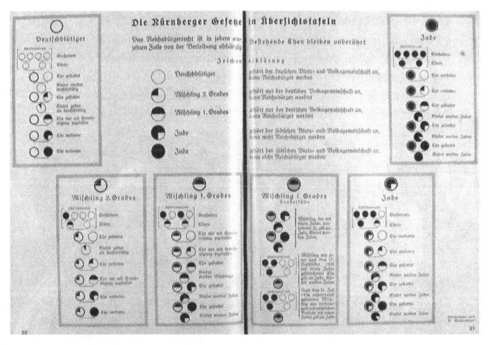

42. "The Nuremberg Laws Summarized in Tables." The complexities of applying state regulation of marriage and intercourse between citizens with different religious backgrounds were illustrated in these charts, in which white represents Aryan and black signifies Jew.

leader of the Nazi physician's association, was relieved to have clarity: "In God's name, let there be peace at last." Acknowledging that hardcore Nazis might perceive Hitler's moderation as a sign of weakness, Goebbels cautioned against publicizing it.[120]

The apparent lull in the Nazis' war against the Jews from the summer of 1933 through the autumn of 1935 had provided an opportunity for ethnocrats to adjust to their role as the administrators of white-collar racial persecution. Like the conscientious and well-educated experts they were, they pondered racial policies in abstract and theoretical discussions—replete with analogy and redolent with logic. Although they functioned within a totalitarian state, they aired their differences openly and over time created a working consensus about the end as well as the means of racial policy.

When Hitler announced "a very major reorientation," ethnocrats were prepared to comply. Three factors conditioned their compliance. First, compared with Stormtroopers' violence in the summer of 1935, ethnocrats could think of themselves as moderates because they endorsed orderly methods and eschewed vulgar racism. Thoughtful ethnocrats like Gürtner and Lösener told themselves that if they resigned from office, the zealots who replaced them would be worse. Tedious meetings about scores of potential racial laws had created, if not unanimity, at least a working consensus that Jews must be severed from the ethnic community by an orderly process sanctioned by the state. Second, when Hitler endorsed both bureaucratic methods and radical goals, ethnocrats behaved as Max Weber had predicted they ought to: they internalized commands from a legitimate authority. Third, although the ethnocrats often disagreed, they had learned by 1936 that not only could they voice their opinions without rebuke but that their opinions might make a difference. Ineluctably, networks had coalesced and collegiality drew them into a shared bureaucratic space. In place of the fundamental ethical questions that plagued them in the early years of the Third Reich, by the late 1930s ethnocrats' moral field narrowed to questions of definitional and procedural consistency.

Lösener, Gürtner, Freisler, and their colleagues managed the bureaucratic restructuring of 1933–1934 and subsequently did their best to make sense of the conceptual chaos created by scores of new laws restricting Jews' rights. Did a Jewish family of four who rented a room to an Aryan constitute a Jewish household?[121] Should a 22-year-old man with three Aryan grandparents and one Jewish grandmother be drafted? Was penetration necessary for sexual relations to be considered racial treason? Although the deluge of queries was daunting, ethnocrats had developed the habits of thinking, the procedures, and the networks within which answers could be formulated. They preserved the appearance of law even as they consigned an entire category of people to civil oblivion. The normalcy of their work was underscored by the fact that after 1945, except for high-ranking officials like Frick and Hans Pfundtner, this army of bureaucrats did not stand trial for their collaboration; most continued their careers with hardly a pause. Stuckart was sentenced to three years in prison. The coauthor of the legal commentary explicating the 1935 race laws, Hans Globke (who had in 1932 lobbied for a law forbidding Jews to change their names to disguise their ethnic origins), became Conrad Adenauer's most trusted advisor. Perceiving themselves as just because of their commitment to the appearance of due process, ethnocrats accommodated themselves to a Nazi conscience appropriate to the tasks ahead. Old fighters and Hitler Youth destroyed Jews' property; bureaucrats liquidated it.[122] Over the next four years ethnocrats met the challenge as the term "liquidate" itself migrated from commerce in material goods to traffic in people.

The Quest for a Respectable Racism

National Socialist scholarship must organize itself across all disciplines into a new totality that will inform policy-making on the Jewish question.

—*C. A. Hoberg, Reich Institute for the History of New Germany*

In 1950 Bernhard Lösener decided to set the historical record straight by writing a memoir about his service as a racial expert in the Interior Ministry. At the center of his account were the 1935 Nuremberg Race Laws. Although the victorious Allies blamed the laws for having unleashed "everything Hitler's Germany has on its conscience," he wrote: "This view is wrong . . . The completely hellish form of the persecution of the Jews in later years became horrible reality *not as the result of, but rather despite the Nuremberg Laws.*" The prohibitions against mixed-race marriage, non-Jewish domestic servants in Jewish households, and Jews displaying the German swastika flag, he wrote, "were meant to bring order into what had become a chaotic situation and to mark the end of the persecution of the Jews."[1]

Lösener's exculpatory words are misleading but instructive. By neglecting to mention the Reich Citizenship Law, which condemned Jews to civil death, Lösener ignored the most devastating provision of the laws. But besides this obvious oversight, by distinguishing between prewar persecution and wartime slaughter, Lösener characterized the Final Solution as an event that occurred beyond his own purview—"out there," "in the East," as Germans said. This misperception was not merely the retrospective rationalization of a troubled ethnocrat but also the result of two widespread perceptions that had been cultivated during the late 1930s. The first was, that decreased physical violence immediately after the laws had been declared. Unsanctioned attacks against Jews and their property declined. After the lawlessness of the previous summer, the SS Security Service reported that the Nuremberg Laws "have been met with great satisfaction and enthusiasm."[2] A few months later the service reiterated, "Even Jews slowly resign themselves to these unpleasant facts and see that the laws were necessary . . . to restore tolerable relations [between Germans and Jews]."[3] With little notice in the German or foreign press, what contemporaries called the cold pogrom gathered force, depriving victims of their legal defenses, stripping them of their property, and eroding their self-respect.

A second source of the misperception embodied in Lösener's memoir was supplied by expert opinion. After Hitler declared his "very major reorientation" in the war against Jews, a veritable academic industry in antisemitic research evolved. News reports, documentary films, exhibitions, and textbooks disseminated the latest scholarly findings that blamed Jews for the existence of "the Jewish question." Thus, the decrease in physical violence after the Nuremberg laws coincided with an intensified disinformation campaign that rationalized white collar persecution. This strategy established the parameters of a genocidal consensus among the planners of the Final Solution and simultaneously reassured the general public that greater vigilance against "Jewish danger" was justified.

The Nuremberg Laws, which redirected antisemitism away from the streets and into offices, neighborhoods, schools, and bedrooms, encroached onto economic and private terrain that had previously been off limits. Before 1935 the Nazi Party had forced some leading Jewish businesses (notably publishers) to sell their assets to Nazi businesses for a small fraction of their worth.[4] After 1935, with military contracts fueling economic recovery, fears of an international boycott against German manufactured goods subsided, and Nazis began to aggressively Aryanize (that is, confiscate) between 75,000 and 80,000 businesses owned by Jews.[5] Jewish stockbrokers were excluded from the bourse. Non-Jewish businessmen, aided by Nazi regulators, expelled Jews from particular sectors of the economy, such as cigarette and textile manufacturing, private banking, second-hand stores, and the cattle market. Knowing their Jewish creditors were legally helpless, many Germans (including the film director Leni Riefenstahl) simply refused to pay their debts to Jews.[6] Local businessmen with Nazi connections arranged for Jews to be jailed on trumped-up charges of "racial defilement" and then offered to release them in exchange for financially advantageous settlements or outright bribes. Facing financial ruin, Jewish owners agreed to sell their property for a pittance. Bank officers denied loans to Jewish borrowers and foreclosed existing mortgages on the most trivial of pretexts. At first, such chicanery succeeded mainly with smaller, local firms. But by the end of 1936, 260 of Germany's largest Jewish-owned firms had been Aryanized by respected industrialists, some of whom did not even belong to the Nazi

Party. Blackmail, extortion, and theft—crimes by any ordinary standard—became legal when sanctioned by the goal of cleansing the *Volk.*

Delusional racists no doubt believed themselves to be the object of Jewish malfeasance and unscrupulous entrepeneurs had ample incentive to exploit Jews' weakness. But ordinary collaborators with "de-Judification" had to make sense of their decisions. In many cases, compliance contradicted self-interest. Resorts and restaurants had to turn away a loyal clientele. Teachers had to ignore or reject talented students. As labor reserves diminished with economic recovery, employers were admonished not to hire the between 30,000 and 40,000 Jewish officeworkers and blue-collar workers who were unemployed. Patients had to stop consulting Jewish physicians they trusted, and shoppers in Jewish-owned stores looked elsewhere. Christian domestic servants under the age of 45, many of whom had worked in Jewish families for years, faced unemployment. Aryans who planned to marry non-Aryans broke off their engagements or emigrated.

Ascertaining individual collaborators' motives for supporting antisemitic regulations is difficult; drawing sweeping conclusions about ordinary Germans' or average citizens' cooperation is impossible. But the public culture within which individuals framed their decisions to either collaborate with or dissent from Nazi persecution can be described. Germans made their peace with regulations against their Jewish fellow citizens, as Lösener's comment suggests, because criminal laws became part of a mirage of law and order, and the perception gradually took hold that Jews were strangers in their own homeland.

In the mid-1930s, the redirection of racial war was accompanied by a dramatic increase in antisemitism in public culture. Because its sources did not usually bear the overt approval of the Nazi Party, they escaped the skepticism engendered by the productions of the Ministry of Propaganda. Books, popular racial science articles, documentary films, exhibits, and educational programs deluged Germans with information about the putative Jewish danger. In the wake of what Hitler called a major reorientation late in 1935, new academic research institutes provided supposedly empirical evidence of Jews' irrevocable otherness. Fraudulent disinformation, stamped with the imprimatur of scholarly sources, footnotes, charts, and bibliographies, offered a respectable alternative to the disreputable Nazi media as a source of knowledge about "Jewry." To people whose consciences may have been troubled by mounting persecution, this seemingly objective evidence for Jews' moral degradation contributed to the expulsion of Jews from the community of moral obligation. In 1933, no credible evidence of Jews' danger was available to proponents of "rational" antisemitism. Starting in the mid-1930s fraudulent research dignified by the hallmarks of conventional scholarship made Jews strangers in the midst of a proud and defiant *Volk*. One refugee, writing in 1940, described the scholarly hate campaign as "intellectual poison."[7]

Victor Klemperer feared the worst in late August 1935: "We are sitting here as *in a besieged fortress, within which the plague is raging* . . . My principles about Germany . . . are beginning to wobble like an old man's teeth." A year later he despaired "that the Jewish dream of being German has been a dream after all. That is the most bitter truth for me."[8] In 1937 a Jewish man whose only friends had been non-Jews before 1933 reported terrible isolation. "Nevertheless," he added, "one has to admit that there are still some who help the Jews . . . But that does not stave off depression . . . One feels as if one is no longer German . . . spiritually *[geistig]* like an immigrant in one's homeland."[9] A Jewish woman recalled that "the blue vanished from my sky . . . Everything became foreign . . . This *Volk* was no longer my *Volk*."[10]

While the overwhelming majority of Germans deplored the wanton destruction of Jews' property and resented boycotts, they gradually came to accept the pariah status of Jews as inevitable.[11] In 1934 an American professor who taught in Germany observed that his colleagues complained a great deal about an outrage here or an injustice there. But, lacking the civil courage to act on their objections, they preferred not to admit their weakness. "There are very few honorable opportunists who openly declare that one has to howl with the wolves without the need to justify their choice."[12] Most needed to rationalize their collaboration.

Within a few years of the Nuremberg Laws, a diverse cross-section of academics collaborated to share with the general public the results of "Jewish research" *(Judenforschung)* that provided a credible basis for "rational" racism. These antisemitic scholars ignored eugenicists' arguments in favor of sterilization, euthanasia, and genetic surveillance. For the most part they ignored Oriental, Nordic, and African ethnic groups, except as their findings reinforced Jews' putative alien nature. They conducted research into Jewish demographics, Hebrew and Yiddish linguistic traditions, religious culture, financial networks, and habitats. With state and party backing, they reformulated old-fighter Nazis' *Judenkoller* (raging antisemitism) into respectable discourse. Using textual criticism, social science, and archival research, they documented the crimes perpetrated by Jewry against

Germanic peoples. During the years when actual Jews emigrated or were reduced to penury in Germany, scholarship coded their vulnerability as a camouflage intended to deceive gullible Germans. As Jews retreated into private life, antisemitic scholars incited not only fear but revulsion. Appropriating the language of peasants who exterminated vermin from their granaries and hunters who stalked their prey, rational antisemites went about their work methodically. In the interests of social hygiene and spurred by the work ethic, academic persecutors did not steal or torment; they "cleansed" and "purified."

Professors had been among the most vocal supporters of the Nazi takeover in 1933.[13] They thanked Hitler for ridding Germany of the triple threat of Bolshevik revolution, cultural decay, and economic decline.[14] Like Heidegger, they welcomed restoration of manly valor in politics and heralded the end of what they called the Judaization of higher education. They included tributes to Hitler in their prefaces and used "Jewish" as a modifier of discredited ideas. When they might have written "nation" a few years earlier, *Volk* slipped into their prose. A musicologist, for example, praised "Karl Maria von Weber as an Educator of the *Volk*," and a medievalist dated the origins of the Führer concept to the twelfth century.[15] In 1934 the rector of Bonn University greeted Nazi rule as the dawn of "a heroic ethic," an age of "moral optimism."[16] The distinguished historian Rudolf Oncken praised, not Germany's rapid industrial growth but the "nameless heroism" of the German peasantry for defending "the soil of the Fatherland."[17] Like Heidegger, many intellectuals who welcomed Hitler's rule railed against the alienation that had severed academe from the *Volk* and denounced the disciplinary divides that trapped specialists in their own narrow enclaves. Heidegger spoke for many when he declaimed, "It's not propositions and concepts that provide the laws of your being *[Sein]*. The Führer himself and only he is Reality in Germany today and in the future."[18]

However welcome these spontaneous accolades may have been to Nazi ideologues, by the mid 1930s the Nazi regime expected more than praise. At a time when Hitler himself remained largely silent about his racial goals, scholars stepped in to make racial science respectable. To win widespread collaboration with the cold pogrom, credible evidence of the so-called Jewish menace was required. The central role of ethnocrats in this process was reflected in Lösener's view of Nazi racism in a grand historical panorama. In a journal for civil servants he wrote that after the medieval "era of the subject" and the liberal "age of the citizen," in 1933 the "epoch of the ethnic comrade *[Volksgenosse]*" dawned.[19] By implication, the laws of history, not Nazi race laws, sanctioned persecution.

As ethnocrats faced mountains of red tape created by the racial laws, and a morass of conceptual confusion, they looked to science for answers. Interior Minister Wilhelm Frick remarked, "From the standpoint of the law as well as public opinion, the possibility of regaining momentum toward a stronger procedure against Jewry . . . depends on clarity."[20] Like modern bureaucrats elsewhere, ethnocrats turned to experts for guidance. At this crucial juncture, racial policy required the services of the academics and intellectuals whom old fighters regularly ridiculed. This meant that academics' general support for Nazi rule no longer sufficed to make them "politically reliable." Genuine support required applying racial biological paradigms in their research.

Writing in 1951 about the Soviet sphere, Czeslaw Milosz described the moment at which intellectuals in a totalitarian regime realize that they must not merely offer generic praise to the regime but also swallow its nonsensical dogma (which he called The Pill of Murti-Bing) "in its *entirety.*"[21] For Nazi academics, this moment came in the mid-1930s when they realized that they were expected to transform their research agendas to conform to biological explanatory schemes. A respected linguist who supported Nazi rule told colleagues, "Today, National Socialism knocks at the door of every scholarly discipline and asks: what have you to offer me?"[22] To those who responded positively, funding, promotions, lecture tours, accolades, and job offers would follow. A few established scholars, like the theologian Gerhard Kittel and the anthropologist Max Hildebert Boehm, incorporated antisemitism into their research program and functioned harmoniously within the new racist orthodoxy. But in Nazi Germany, tenured professors who were willing to forgo these rewards did not have to swallow the racial pill.[23] The Gestapo did not hunt down thought criminals. Although academics who refused to accommodate Nazi racial doctrines found themselves edged out of editorial boards and prestigious associations, they retained their status and salaries (except for Jews, spouses of Jews, and outspoken critics of the regime). As university enrollments dropped and the international prestige of German academic life diminished, the walls of the ivory tower protected its residents.

Dedicated Nazis fretted over what they considered the hypocrisy of professors who pledged support for Nazism but refused to accommodate racial values in their research. After evaluating university racial studies programs, Walter Gross regretted that among the traditionally trained

professors, "virtually none are useful for our cause."[24] When he was depu-
tized to evaluate Martin Heidegger's qualifications for a national position
in 1934, Gross found the philosopher's prose so prolix that he consulted
specialists. They responded, "According to the ordinary common sense
of professionally competent and racially and politically unobjectionable
scholars," Heidegger's work "contained virtually no elements useful for
National Socialism."[25] Heidegger was "a scatterbrained . . . hairsplitter" in
the "worst Talmudic tradition," who wrote in a style so dense that it
might easily be misconstrued. If Heidegger were appointed, "we would
end up with our universities in the grip of an intellectual sickness on an
epidemic scale, a kind of mass psychosis."[26] In the cantankerous world of
Nazi bureaucracy, denunciations could result from academics' failure to
include keywords such as *Volk, Rasse, Judentum,* and *Blut* that old fighters recognized.[27] But denunciation meant exclusion from benefits, not
prison.

Gross fretted that many scholars who claimed to endorse Nazism
actually withheld "inner support" by taking "refuge" in "apolitical" research projects. Support for Hitler in 1933, it became clear, did not auto-
matically mean that a researcher would reorient his scholarship. Although racial studies courses were required in medical schools, too few
professors were qualified to teach them, partly because most respected
biologists did not take Nazi racial science seriously.[28] It infuriated Gross
that a newcomer Nazi like the surgeon Ferdinand Sagebrush received so
much recognition without actually endorsing racial projects. Gross lamented, "Four years after the seizure of power . . . In comparison to what
remains to be accomplished, very little has been achieved."[29]

After much fanfare about a smooth *Gleichschaltung* (switch to Nazism),
hardliners concluded that Nazi thinking barely dented scholarship. The
pedagogue Ernst Krieck wondered why, despite their best efforts, he and
his Nazi colleagues encountered "one mistake after the other and disappointment after disappointment."[30] Another doctrinaire Nazi suspected
that in some academic departments, Nazi credentials actually hindered
promotions.[31] An SS man confided that he was beginning to feel some
sympathy for the French revolutionaries of 1789 (whom the SS routinely
vilified). Like the men of 1789, he wrote, Nazi racial revolutionaries discovered the difficulty of imposing new values on university life. "The year
1933 could not change the [academic] situation with one blow, just as
1789 could not with one blow create a new university." For all the official
expressions of good will, he continued, the old atmosphere persisted.

"The young National Socialist arriving in the university will be reminded in thousands of ways of the gulf between his own outlook and the views he hears in lecture halls and seminars."[32] Sopade reports confirmed these suspicions. "In scholarly seminars, one often hears openly critical voices." Even when professors renamed their courses to stress the *Volk*, they did not always adjust the content. Although vacant university positions were shifted to new racially-oriented fields such as cultural anthropology and Germanic linguistics, these fields attracted the fewest students.[33]

In genetics and physical anthropology, where racial thinking had already taken hold before 1933, collaboration was more common. The internationally respected eugenicist Artur Gütt consulted with the ethnocrats who worked out the Nuremberg Laws. The geneticist Otmar von Verschuer assumed directorship of the University of Frankfurt Institute for Hereditary Biology in 1935 and subsequently trained key SS medical personnel, including Josef Mengele.[34] Working within medical schools and established research laboratories, teams of racial scientists conducted experiments in applied eugenics.[35] Since sickle cell anemia had recently been linked to African blood types, microbiologists searched for distinctive traits in Jewish blood.[36] Writing in a popular magazine published by Gross's Office of Racial Politics, a biologist exulted in 1934, "Think what it might mean if we could identify non-Aryans in the test tube! Then neither deception, nor baptism, nor name change nor citizenship, and not even nasal surgery could help! . . . One cannot change one's blood."[37] Despite significant funding and considerable publicity, success eluded them.[38] Even a taskforce of the Nazi medical association led by Gerhard Wagner admitted failure.[39] No blood type, odor, foot- or fingerprint pattern, skull size, ear lobe or nose shape, or any other physiological marker of Jewishness withstood scrutiny.

The realization that biologists could not identify Jewish blood by physiological traits coincided with Hitler's 1935 "reorientation" of racial policy. With ethnocrats lamenting the empirical vagaries of racial taxonomy, biologists confessed failure. From that point on, cultural stereotypes about Jewish character displaced physical traits in the hunt for sources of Jewishness, and the burden of proof shifted away from the natural sciences to the social sciences and the humanities. Speaking to old fighters who scorned hair-splitting professors, Gross justified the utility of racial research. "Even though the rightness of our racial ideas is absolutely clear to us without additional scientific proof, such proof is indispensable in our struggle against those who oppose racial values."[40] If Nazi doctrine were to convince well-educated people to cooperate with white-collar persecu-tion, Gross implied, scholarly research would have to guide ethnocrats.

Signs of a new approach to racial issues appeared in the party press dur-ing the weeks when Lösener and his colleagues were drafting the guide-lines for the Nuremberg Laws. In August 1935 an article in the Nazi news-paper *Der Völkische Beobachter* heralded the trend. Since the party's earliest days, the author wrote, "racial instinct" had formed the core of National Socialism. But the time had come to modernize longstanding opinions by subjecting beliefs about race to empirical study. A headline, "On the Barri-cades of the Intellect," featured "cutting-edge research into the Jewish danger."[41] A revision in the format and editorship of *The National Socialist Monthly,* a periodical devoted to ideology, heralded the dawn of "the new life-affirming outlook of a young generation of scholars."[42] This cheaply printed journal, founded in 1930, had originally contained articles by self-styled Nazi intellectuals. In the mid-1930s, as legal persecution of Jews escalated, the *NS Monthly* acquired a sedate new look that featured drawings, artistic photographs, poetry, book reviews, and articles with footnotes. Linguists, historians, geographers, literary scholars, psycholo-gists, cultural geographers, and physical anthropologists explained their research in popular formats. Representative titles included "Away with Heinrich Heine!" (the highly esteemed German poet who had been born to Jewish parents) and "Where Can I Find the Jews?" (a guide to scholarly exposés of hidden Jewish influences). Just months after Jewish veterans published a volume of patriotic letters written by Jewish soldiers who had died for Germany in the Great War, a literary theorist performed a close textual analysis of these letters and compared them with letters written by Christian soldiers who had died. His expert opinion on one Jewish letter typified his approach. Reflecting on his earlier antipathy for militarism, in 1914 the Jewish soldier confessed his joy at discovering his authentic self in battle. And yet, he continued, as passionately as he loved Germany, he did not hate French and British soldiers because they had as much claim to honor as he did. The Nazi literary critic denigrated these sentiments (and the style in which they were written) as "characteristically Jewish" because a "dissection of one's feelings is foreign to Germans." Germanic soldiers, he wrote, did not introspect; they volunteered instinctively, ex-hibiting "idealism in its purest form."[43] The Office of Racial Policy's peri-odical *Neues Volk* reflected the new trend both in its doubling of pages per issue and the increase of its coverage of "the Jewish question."

While Nazi publications popularized racial scholarship, specialists in area studies prepared racial planners for military expansion. Younger careerists at university institutes seized the opportunity for funding and status. At the University of Greifswald, for example, social scientists collated demographic information about Jews who inhabited German *Lebensraum* (living space) in Eastern Europe. Researchers at the East European Institute at Königsberg University provided vital information about terrain, industrial infrastructure, agriculture, ethnic composition, demographic structure, and communications networks.[44]

The career trajectory of Peter-Heinz Seraphim, a "freshly-baked Nazi" who was associated with the Königsberg Institute, illustrates the potential for synergy between a resourceful social scientist and party work. As a Nazi Party member and political economist specializing in Central European communication and transportation systems, Seraphim (who was 31 years old in 1933) shifted his research interests to Jewish society. Basing his work largely on testimonials by Jewish authors who celebrated Jews' contributions to German economic, cultural, and political life over the centuries, Seraphim converted their pride into evidence of Jewish subversion. The result, an illustrated 700-page handbook, *Jewry in Eastern Europe,* became a reference work on "alien" populations living in German *Lebensraum.*[45] Together with other area-studies specialists, urban planners, and human geographers, Seraphim fused ethnic idealism with economic utility in support of eastward expansion. Within a few years, Seraphim and his fellow technocrats, along with teams of graduate students, had laid out plans for the colonization of the Slavic frontier.

Other longtime proponents of racial studies found an intellectual home within the prestigious Kaiser-Wilhelm Institute for Anthropology, Human Heredity, and Eugenics (K-WI) in Berlin, which had for decades sponsored research into racial questions.[46] Leading experts associated with the institute collaborated with the involuntary sterilization program and offered advice on euthanasia. Thanks in part to Gerhard Kittel's prestige and his eager collaboration with the institute's director, Eugen Fischer, the K-WI sponsored antisemitic cultural and physical anthropology. Having received generous praise for his 1933 diatribe against "Jew-Christians," Kittel made a midcareer shift away from Biblical exegesis and toward racist scholarship. In 1926 he had remarked that one could prove almost anything by quoting the Talmud, but only ill will would motivate anyone to dwell on its "negative" aspects.[47] Ten years later, he was busily doing just that. Funded by the state-sponsored Foundation for German Research (Deutsche Forschungs Gemeinschaft), which began in 1920 and remained the major academic funding source in West Germany after 1945, he and other anthropologists gathered evidence on national character and physical typologies.[48] The Kittel-Fischer team studied the ancient Middle East, with Kittel documenting the danger posed by Jewish settlements to the Roman Empire and Fischer analyzing the facial bone structure in ancient artifacts to demonstrate the presence or absence of Jewish influence. A sample of the team's findings disclosed that "always the aim [of the Jews] is: world domination. No matter whether the Jewish slave girl, with authentic or forged letters, is the go-between in the relations of the empress and the Jew-princess; or whether the Egyptian tax-collector–high-financier Jew becomes the 'friend' of the emperor and personal banker of the empress . . . always at all times, in the first century as in the twentieth, world Jewry dreams of exclusive world domination on earth and in the hereafter."[49]

Racial studies *(Rassenkunde)* became a required part of the curriculum in many disciplines and produced a market for new textbooks untainted by outmoded humanist values. Fellowships rewarded research projects that reinforced racial thinking. Press conferences, media coverage, and awards ceremonies all enhanced the public status of racial research. Backed by state and party, scholars constructed a simulacrum of a thriving academic endeavor. But a close look reveals that this so-called research served merely to endow traditional Christian stereotypes about "the Jew" with the cachet of modern scholarship. The fury of Hitler's earliest political speeches and *Mein Kampf* reappeared in turgid prose dignified by the accoutrements of scholarship. Social scientists took up the search for distinctive markers of race in mentality, character, and heritage, while literary critics found race in particular genres and themes. Blood and race became master metaphors for the corrosive modernist spirit that had almost destroyed ethnic spiritual health in Weimar Germany.

Taking up a familiar Nietzschean theme, racial revisionists denounced value-free science as symptomatic of a decadent Western, supposedly Jewish, civilization and approvingly quoted Nazi Physicians' League chief Gerhard Wagner, who said only one scholarly question counted: "Am I being useful to my *Volk?*"[50] One enthusiastic graduate student compared himself to a Renaissance humanist fleeing the sterility of Scholastic Paris. Like them, he welcomed the break-up of compartmentalized university life.[51] Combating the "sterile materialism" that informed both individualistic liberals and class-bound Marxists, these proudly partisan scholars set

Die Zahl der Juden betrug in Berlin:	
Jahr	Zahl
1774	4 000
1845	8 000
1855	11 000
1865	24 000
1875	45 000
1885	64 000
1895	86 000
1905	99 000
1910	144 000
1920	350 000
1930	440 000

43. "The number of Jews living in Berlin" from 1774 to 1930. By omitting the increase in the total population of Berlin, these figures vastly overstated the presence of Jews. To add authenticity to the statistics, the photograph of three Orthodox Jewish men was complemented by a quotation from the secular Jew Walther Rathenau, president of the electrical firm AEG, organizer of Germany's economic mobilization in World War I, and foreign minister in 1922 (when he was assassinated by antisemites). "Strange vision!" Rathenau wrote in 1902. "In the midst of German life [dwells] an alienated, self-contained human breed . . . From the sands of the Eastern Marches [comes] an Asiatic horde! . . . So they live, in a half-voluntary ghetto, not a vital member of the *Volk*, but a foreign organism in its body." Antisemitic researchers constructed a veritable subdiscipline on the basis of this kind of Jewish self-criticism.

out to reconfigure every branch of learning according to a third perspective, race.

Starting in mid-1935, five extra-university antisemitic research institutes were created to investigate Jewish influence in the natural sciences, culture, history, jurisprudence, and religion. The first was an institute of physics loosely affiliated with Heidelberg University. Several months later the Reich Institute for the History of the New Germany was established in Berlin. Carl Schmitt launched a drive to expunge Jewish influence from German legal theory, and Alfred Rosenberg established an antisemitic historical institute and library in Frankfurt—The Reich Institute for the Study of the Jewish Question—to rival the one in Berlin. The fifth initiative, the Institute for the Study and Eradication of Jewish Influence in German Religious Life, evolved in the late 1930s under the aegis of the Protestant Church without much official endorsement. Together these institutes provided what passed for empirical evidence of a distinctive Jewish character at a time when racial biologists relinquished the hope of discovering an irrefutable marker of racial identity.

The multidisciplinary approach, high public profile, and policy orientation of these new institutes prefigured what later generations would call think tanks. Founding ceremonies, lavish banquets, and annual meetings became public relations events that enhanced the prestige of racial studies as a separate but capacious field. Headlines announcing the presence of the "men who make history" turned academic conventions into media events at which specialists from many disciplines rubbed elbows with party men and ethnocrats.[52] A typical article in the Nazi media reported that "in deep moral seriousness, Hitler Youth, young German working men and students sat together with women and men of all social backgrounds [and] listened to the words of German scholars."[53] Press releases extolled the achievements of these historical, legal, and theological institutes for racial research. Besides supplying the media with "facts" about evil Jewish influence, the institutes promoted their discoveries in handsomely bound tomes, handy reference books, bibliographies, maps, and lavish coffee-table books.[54]

As the media publicized scholarship documenting the "Jewish peril," Hitler himself maintained his public distance from both the theoretical and practical implications of racism. Although Hitler must have authorized the founding of these institutes, he did not appear at any of their conventions or opening ceremonies. Although the five institutes were not equally successful in attracting funding and prestige, taken together they made the cold pogrom respectable among educated middle-class Germans. Moving beyond biological concepts of blood, they converted racial phobias from ideology to credible knowledge by demonstrating the existence of a corrosive Jewish "spirit." Their scholarly tone, combined with media attention, rationalized the "orderly" removal of Jews from mainstream society and underwrote the consensus that Jews had no place in Germany.

The first of the Nazi think tanks, the so-called Lenard Institute, was founded by two physicists, Johannes Stark and Philipp Lenard, in order to discredit Einstein's "Jewish" physics.[55] During the 1920s both men had been written off by most of their colleagues as personally cantankerous, but after 1933 they attracted the attention of Nazi leaders when they hailed Hitler as a "natural scientist who searches for Truth according to empirical means."[56] Both scientists took pains to disassociate themselves from biological racism because, as Lenard reasoned, it was the "Jewish mentality" (not the blood) that had tainted Aryan scientists (including Werner Heisenberg) with "Jewish traits."[57] Stark and Lenard attacked "primitive antisemites" who believed that Jewish influence could be spread only by people with Jewish ancestors. Germany, they said, could not be made "Jew free" merely by hunting down individuals with physical traits like a "hooked nose or kinky hair." Instead, they incited scholars to expurgate Jewish ideas from the works of non-Jewish scholars.

Das Schwarze Korps, the SS magazine, publicized Stark's and Lenard's attack against "white Jews," their term for any physicist who accepted quantum physics and Einstein's special theory of relativity.[58] Speaking with the imprimatur of Nobel Laureates, Stark and Lenard identified mental traits that were distinctively "Jewish," chief among them being subtle thinking and economic self-interest. In contrast to a Jewish penchant for complexity, the Germanic mind, they asserted, would produce an elegant alternative to Einstein's relativist physical universe. For a variety of reasons, not the least of which were personal, the physics institute did not flourish. In 1936, when Lenard was passed over in the search for a successor to the physicist Max Planck, it became clear that antisemitism had been demoted in the world of experimental physics.

Racial revisionism fared much better in the humanities and social sciences. As the nature of the "deadly enemy" shifted from biological to cultural, character traits displaced physical evidence as indicators of Jewish danger.[59] In a flurry of innovative meta-theories, history came into its own as the queen of the racial sciences. Early in 1935 the Education Ministry and the Propaganda Ministry authorized Walter Frank, an underemployed historian and longtime Nazi, to create the Reich Institute for the History of New Germany.[60] Although he had published monographs on a series of racist themes and written a popular history of the Nazi Party, Frank had failed to secure a university position. Evidently enjoying his newfound eminence, he lashed out against an older generation of academics (whom he ridiculed as "petty Greeks" for their adulation of alien Athenian culture). "During the hard years of struggle, the National Socialist movement received [only] the petty Greeks' unlimited contempt . . . But there was an immediate change as soon as National Socialism triumphed . . . From all sides, the petty Greeks arrived—smart, educated, and devoid of character, generously shouting Heil Hitler and offering 'to establish the intellectual foundation for National Socialist Victory.'"[61]

In his welcome address at the foundation of the Reich Institute for the History of New Germany, Frank pledged to integrate "the proven skills

44. "The Trend in Racial Pollution" blended misleading statistics with photo-graphic images to objectify the supposed danger of marriages between Jews and Christians. Studies produced under the auspices of Nazi-sponsored think tanks quickly found their way into popular print culture, exhibitions, and films.

of the old with the energy of the new" and place his institute "at the forefront" of a battle against both "rootless intellectualism" and reckless "half-educated" activists, by which he meant non-Nazi academics and poorly educated old fighters.[62] "The new type of German scholar will be born into the totality of a National Socialist Weltanschauung and . . . march behind the banner of a new spiritual authority."[63] In the next six years, Frank's Committee of Experts expanded from 25 to 69.[64] The list of publications grew apace.

In the style of research institutes elsewhere, affiliated scholars produced comprehensive bibliographies, critical editions, reports of archival discoveries, and revisionist interpretations of major events. In monographs and articles, racial revisionists bestowed fresh credibility on ancient Christian shibboleths. Compiling large data sets, historical demographers evaluated the negative impact of "inter-racial" marriages on successive generations in several cultures. Quoting the economist Werner Sombart (and criticizing Max Weber's thesis which connected mercantile capitalism with a Protestant ethos), sociologists linked the emergence of capitalism to pernicious Jewish materialism. Comparative historians discovered that nineteenth-century Huguenot emigrants, because of their blood, contributed to Prussia's strength, while Jews' blood damaged it. Unlike conventional histories of the Protestant Reformation that stressed theological issues, Nazi scholars represented religious protest in racial terms.

Viewing historical change within a causal framework that substituted a racial dialectic for Hegel's idealism and Marx's materialism, Frank and his peers revised conventional periodization and added new turning points—for example, the nadir of March 11, 1912 (when the last legal bans against Jews were removed) and the highpoint of September 15, 1935 (when the Nuremberg Laws "reimposed" segregation). Flushed with the thrill of their new paradigm, Nazi historians predicted that the day on which Hitler became chancellor, January 30, 1933, would eclipse July 14, 1789, as a historical watershed.[65] By this, they meant not only that the magnitude of the Nazi Revolution would surpass that of the French Revolution but also that a biologically-based civil order would forever abolish the liberal universalism of 1789. Whereas the French Revolution had promoted the illusion of human equality, the Nazi Revolution marked the dawn of a heroic age that acknowledged the fact of biological inequality.

The historians revived anger at the loss of German colonies after the war and elevated previously forgotten figures to heroic status. The sadistic, misogynist, and racist prewar governor of German East Africa, Carl Peters, became a cult figure, and a film, *Om Kruger,* depicting another colonial governor attracted mass audiences.[66] Where Marxists saw the Russian Revolution as a class conflict, Nazi scholars reinterpreted it as a racial struggle between "inferior" Bolshevik Jews and the "superior" White Russian nobility. Rolf L. Fahrenkrog's massive anthology, *The History of Europe as Racial Destiny,* opened with an introduction by Gross and surveyed major events from prehistory to Hitler, from the Urals to the Atlantic. A concluding essay on "Biological Sociology" summarized the new orthodoxy, according to which racial struggle drove historical change.[67]

Antisemitic historians stumbled over the problem of what Nazi physi-

45. Jewish veterans used Max Liebermann's watercolor, painted in pale reds and grays, as the frontispiece of an anthology of soldiers' letters they published to discredit fraudulent claims that Jewish men had been shirkers in the war. The letters, written by passionately loyal Jewish soldiers who died fighting for their Fatherland, testify to their authors' eloquence and patriotism. Max Liebermann, who had been Germany's most celebrated painter at the turn of the century, painted this image in the hope that viewers would be moved by the woman mourning beside the coffin of a loved one beneath the Imperial German flag. The painterly quality of this pallid image contrasts starkly with the vivid action graphics of Nazi commercial artists.

cists called "white Jews." After Jewish influence had been expunged from historical scholarship, they wondered how to treat Christian writers who had been inspired by Jewish authors. In a 1939 foreword to a racial studies monograph, Walter Frank spelled out the dilemma. "The Jew is of alien blood, and, as such, the enemy. There can be no German Jews. There are, however, millions of German Protestants and German Catholics living out the tradition of the Jewish people."[68] Once race was detached from biology and became identified with moral danger, the logical next step was to identify a distinctively Jewish mentality or character that could infect members of the *Volk*.

Legal theorists joined the hunt for an ineffable Jewish spirit. Perhaps in part because so many lawyers had run up against the pragmatic difficulties of applying ethnic categories to concrete situations, they looked to scholarship for clarity. Like Reich Justice Minister Hans Gürtner, they were caught between their professional respect for a state based on laws *(Rechtsstaat)* and loyalty to a dictatorship *(Führerstaat)* founded on "racial instinct." At the 1935 Nuremberg Rally, the president of the Nazi Lawyers' Guild, Hans Frank, admitted that jurists "stood amidst the rubble of a collapsed justice system." Operating within the legal framework of defunct liberal values, Frank scapegoated Jewish influence for the continuing confusion. In the spirit of Stark and Lenard, he pledged to expunge the lingering Jewish mentality that polluted Germanic law after actual Jews had been driven out and their books removed from libraries.

At the "de-Judaization" conference in October 1936, which was attended by 100 of the 400 professors of jurisprudence at German law schools, Hans Frank praised Aryans' "historic responsibility" for upholding the highest standards of justice. "We must be thankful to the Führer" for supporting an endeavor that was "as respectable as it is objectively justified." The time had come to end the "protective" environment that sustained the "accelerating infection" of the *Volk*. We do not have to listen, Frank concluded, to any other force except our conscience, and "this conscience tells us that it . . . is just to become masters in our own house."[69]

To underscore the significance of the initiative, Hans Frank named Carl Schmitt as the legal institute's director and invited a wide array of celebrities, including Julius Streicher and Martin Heidegger, to the grand opening. Schmitt was a good choice because he had recently praised the Nuremberg Race Laws for restoring "German constitutional freedom." He explained, "For the first time, our conception of constitutional principles is again German. German blood and German honor have become the basic principles of German law, while the State has become an expression of racial strength and unity."[70] In his remarks at the conference, Schmitt endowed the racial purge with a lofty moral purpose and translated the convoluted tirades of crude antisemites into his crisp prose. "The Jew's relationship to our intellectual work is parasitical, tactical, and commercial . . . Being shrewd and quick, he knows how to say the right thing at the right time. That is his instinct as a parasite and a born trader."[71] Praising Nazi leaders' call for "healthy exorcism," Schmitt welcomed "the genuine battle of principles" between Jews' "cruelty and impudence" and Germans' ethnic honor. "The Jew is sterile and unproductive," he has nothing to say to us—no matter how "energetically he assimilates or how shrewdly he assembles information." He is "dangerous" because, like all parasites, he diagnoses our weakness. When borderline cases and anomalies confused jurists, they blamed Jews (and supposedly Jewish attitudes) for their confusion. In keeping with the ethos of white-collar persecution, Schmitt criticized "emotional antisemitism that does not accomplish the task of driving out Jewish influence" and closed the conference by quoting *Mein Kampf,* "In defending myself against the Jew . . . I am doing the

46. "The Jews' Intellectual Invasion," a panel displayed in the Dresden Hygiene Museum. Portraits of important figures in German history who were Jewish, combined with a misleading chart, lent an air of objectivity to the claim that Jews had dominated public life during the Weimar Republic.

work of the Lord."[72] Newscasters and journalists hailed the "cleansing" of Jewish influence from German law as an almost sacred charge.

Conference participants identified textbooks, law review articles, and landmark decisions written by authors with Jewish-sounding names. They fretted over "the white Jew." Legal sleuths confronted a staggering task as they puzzled over questions such as whether to eliminate footnotes to Jewish sources and retain the concepts or to delete both ideas and authors. In order to prevent ethnic German lawyers from plagiarizing the censored texts, the office developed a reference file of purged opinions and articles. Given the sheer scope of this undertaking, it was no wonder that Schmitt fretted about how to "protect law students from confusion." After the 1936 conference, the proceedings were published, but de-Judaization of jurisprudence proceeded on an ad hoc basis, perhaps because the task was so conceptually overwhelming or perhaps because Schmitt himself fell from favor.[73]

A fourth scholarly center, The Reich Institute for the Study of the Jewish Question, was founded in Frankfurt by one of Frank's associates, Wilhelm Grau.[74] The rivalry among Nazi chiefs, combined with the prestige of antisemitic studies, spurred members of both the Berlin and Frankfurt Reich Institutes to confiscate Jewish libraries, produce lavish books, and sponsor public events.[75] A biweekly, *Correspondence on the Jewish Question,* edited by the historian Wilhelm Ziegler, drew together a community of like-minded researchers. Besides recasting Jewish history as a narrative of evil, Grau and his colleagues created a pedigree for Nazi antisemitism that dated back to the Roman emperors and continued through Martin Luther and Goethe. Over a dozen lavishly printed books documented the intellectual and social history of Christians' self-defense against Jewry. In a bourgeois culture where books formed an important index of social standing, the distinguished appearance of these volumes and their non-party publishers were designed to impress.

A typical example of the genre was Theodor Pugel's *Anti-Semitism in Words and Images: The World-Wide Debate about the Jewish Question* (1936), a 324-page 12 × 18 inch hardcover volume printed on glossy paper. The frontispiece celebrated the destruction of the Temple in Jerusalem. A photograph of Titus's Arch (built in 81 CE to commemorate the Roman general Flavius' defeat of the Jews) bore the caption "The Stone Song of Triumph against the Jewish State." With carefully annotated sources and quotations from Shakespeare, Goethe, and other canonical figures, the author surveyed the struggle against Jewish domination throughout European history and in the Americas, Africa, and Eastern Europe. In a diatribe against vulgar antisemites, the author explained that "no cultured person" wants the "Jewish question" answered by "barbaric and culturally alien" tactics. Like a "plague" that infects the world, Jewry must be combated with cold science. The fact, he argued, that Jews cheat and deceive does not entitle the superior Aryans to follow suit. "We do not want to deprive Jews of their civil rights, but merely to give them special rights as visitors," because only a "clean separation" from Jews would leave Germans with a clear conscience.[76]

Antisemitic discoveries were quickly disseminated in textbooks, popular handbooks, and news media. For example, disinformation about the Jewish character appeared in *The Eternal Jew: Visual Documentation,* a book of photographs in which the journalist Hans Diebow took up topics like "the origins of the Jewish nose" and the affinity between nomadic desert Jews and urban ghetto Jews. The book became the basis for a blockbuster exhibition seen by over a half million viewers during the winter of 1937–38. The opening text purported to be a poem by a "self-hating" Jewish author written in 1913, and subsequent pages communicated the message that Germans had sincerely done their best for decades to make Jews feel at home. But "the Jews just did not want to give up! They rejected all opportunities to become German—and the Nation willingly allowed itself to be biologically compromised . . . Jewry remained unassimilated." After the Germans' well-intentioned but futile attempt to treat Jews politely, their patience was finished. "These images of Jewish barbarism warn us to reject further attempts."

Photographs showed Jews in Palestine driving expensive automobiles, Jews in a ghetto, and Jews in New York seated on a stoop next to a Turkish bath. Under the caption "The Visage—Mirror of the Soul," portraits of well-known Jews, one in the company of the celebrated African-American dancer Josephine Baker, depicted "the Great Jewish Hatred." A headline announced: "Germany is the first nation that solved the Jewish Question legally." A Polish journalist described "the crowds of people who before the accumulated facts are strangely quiet—with some terrible implacability in their faces."[77] As people began to take the existence of a "Jewish question" for granted, they watched the civil death of actual Jews.

Two violent episodes in 1938 broke the insidious pattern of government-sanctioned robbery and ostracism: devastating attacks on Jews in Austria when German troops occupied the country in March, and the pogrom that began on November 9, 1938, which the Nazis called "The Night

47. "The Eternal Jew," a poster advertising the 1941 "documentary film about world Jewry" based on Hans Diebow's photograph book and exhibit. Featuring a variety of faces framed by mock Hebrew letters and the Star of David, the poster implied that Jewish men may appear to differ among themselves, but in every guise they undermine the *Volk*.

of Shattered Crystal." After a young Jewish man shot to death a counselor in the German Embassy in Paris, comments by Goebbels, addressing the Nazi Party leadership assembled in Munich for the annual Beer Hall Putsch commemoration, incited Stormtroopers throughout the nation to destroy synagogues, loot stores, and torture individual Jews. Popular opinion overwhelmingly rejected the unrestrained cruelty and destruction of property. As Nazi leaders curbed the worst violence, antisemitic scholars came into their own by providing ex post facto vindication by dredging up fresh evidence of Jewish evil.

The Reich Institute for the History of the New Germany sponsored a series of public lectures on "Judaism and the Jewish Question" in the main lecture hall of the University of Berlin. Walter Frank opened the series with a radio lecture on the Dreyfus Affair in France, attributing Dreyfus's pardon to the power of international Jewry.[78] Antisemitic aphorisms were distributed to local newspapers, and the Nazi press agency directed editors to use the new information to convey this message: "German *Volk*, you have now been able to read how and where the Jews have harmed you!" In an obvious attempt to quell Germans' outrage at the November pogrom, the press depicted "the Jew" as a "typical" black-marketer, assassin, separatist, "architect of [foreign] economic boycotts," and enemy of morality. A headline from the Nazi news service clinched the point: "What kindness did not accomplish must be done with harshness: the clear separation [of Jew and non-Jew]."[79]

Encouraged by local branches of the Office of Racial Policy, historians scavenged municipal and church archives for antisemitic ordinances and evidence of Jewish malfeasance. One of the most active campaigners was Dr. Hans Mauersberg from a northern branch office of the ORP, who complained that previous antisemitic restrictions "were not successful in exterminating the Jews."[80] Journalists had a field day as they concocted headlines like "The Ape of Humanity," "Peasantry Was Once in Jews' Grasp," "Voluptuous Jewish Dames *[Weiber]*," and "Out of the Ghetto and into the World."

The fifth antisemitic institute was organized in 1939. With little encouragement from party or state, Protestant leaders sponsored The Institute for the Study and Eradication of Jewish Influence in German Religious Life. Given Hitler's and Himmler's contempt for organized Christianity, it is not surprising that antisemitic theologians received relatively little recognition despite their efforts.[81] The scholarly initiative to purge the "Jewish spirit" from the Christian *Volk* offered a chance for Protestant theologians to demonstrate their usefulness to a regime that spurned their collaboration. One of their major projects demonstrated that Jesus had been born to Armenian, not Jewish, parents. A subsidiary study showed how "the Jew Paul" had perverted Christ's teachings.[82] Walter Grundmann, a theology professor and the guiding spirit behind the campaign, commented, "The work of the Institute serves the German *Volk* by searching for and defending the German soul."[83] Ernst Krieck's influence secured modest state funding to subvent the publication of the dense and hefty *The De-Judaization of Religious Life as Duty of Theology and the Churches.*[84]

At the organization's second conference in March 1940 (convened at the castle Wartburg where Luther had translated the Bible), participants "de-Judaized" their faith.[85] Not surprisingly, Gerhard Kittel participated avidly in discussions of, among other topics, "Jesus and Jewry," an investigation of a nineteenth-century novelist entitled "Wilhelm Raabe's Views on Jews and Christians," "Methodologies and Essence in Racial Religious History," and "Idealism, Christianity and Jewry." Special taskforces took up topics such as the person of Jesus Christ, early Christianity, Palestine, Jewish influence on Catholicism (divided into "blood-racial and spiritual-religious"), the history of Teutonic Christian faith, archival research, spiritual guidance and cults, and "problems related to the fateful struggle of the *Volk.*"[86] A 400-page volume of the proceedings of its third conference marked the highpoint of the institute's production in 1942.[87] By providing an erudite vindication for the expulsion of the supposedly poisonous Jewish spirit, the Protestant institute supplied Christians with an abstract view of "Jewry" that served as a bromide for consciences troubled by the plight of Jewish friends, neighbors, and colleagues.

In the years before leaders contemplated the wholesale murder of Jews, antisemitic scholars set the stage for genocide by expelling Jews collectively from moral consideration as human beings. Without the encumbrance of eugenics or the sprit of ethnic uplift, this body of venomous scholarship concentrated squarely on the quest for an innate Jewish character. While military strategists prepared to conquer new living space in Eastern Europe, public intellectuals incited contempt for the Jews, as well as Slavs and gypsies, who inhabited the territory that was soon to become German. Their interpretations were skewed and their assumptions biased. They plagiarized source material from victims' texts and built research libraries of stolen books and manuscripts. Their prose was dense to the point of unintelligibility. But these productions appeared to be meticulous, replete with archival documentation, copious footnotes, bibliographies, and methodological discussions. Their findings were incorporated into textbooks and articles for the popular press.[88] Researchers participated in international congresses. Although these scholars usually constituted a minority within their respective fields, the official attention they received, the wide dissemination of their texts, and the variety of their disciplines made them appear representative of the university establishment.

As one contemplates the titles of the hundreds of articles, journals, dissertations, and books this "scholarship" produced, it strains the imagination to think they may have been taken seriously. But the émigré scholar Max Weinreich, writing in 1946, wisely cautioned readers not to dismiss Nazi academics as "merely sham scholars, nobodies elevated in rank by their Nazi friends and protectors, who produced what is described as 'scurrilous literature.'" Weinreich concluded that these "scholars . . . were to a large extent people of long and high standing, university professors and academy members, some of them world famous, authors with familiar names and guest lecturers abroad, the kind of people Allied scholars used to meet and fraternize with at international congresses."[89]

That Nazi scholarship was taken seriously is attested to by the uncritical coverage their activities received in the foreign press. A list of topics related to German racial research from *The New York Times* in 1935 represents a small cross-section: Gercke's call for racial purity; Schmitt's praise for the Nuremberg Race Laws as "entirely German"; the thesis of Nietzsche scholar Alfred Baeumler that Hitler's rule had lifted Germany out of medieval stagnation; Walter Gross's justification for segregating non-Aryan children; Stormtrooper General Victor Lutz's account of his men's interest in philosophy; Eugen Fischer's praise for Hitler at the World Population Congress; and a comment by the wife of the respected historian Hermann Oncken that "Jews caused their own persecution."[90] The academic zealots who became high-profile spokesmen for antisemitic studies enhanced Nazi racism by creating a highly visible academic subculture that underwrote the cold pogrom.[91] Although the lamentable decline of German physics was evident, antisemitic research bore a distant resemblance to paradigms employed by eugenicists and physical anthropologists elsewhere. As German influence expanded in the mid-1930s, Nazi professors like Kittel, Heidegger, Schmitt, the political theorist Hans Freyer, the geographer Karl Haushofer, the historian Hans Naumann, and Walter Gross lectured in Italy and Austria. Wherever German occupation governments set down roots during World War II, most notably in Warsaw, Cracow, Prague, Vienna, and Paris, offshoots of antisemitic research institutes sprang up to carry on their work.

In much the same way that late-nineteenth-century anthropologists amassed information about populations on the brink of annihilation, Nazi scholars examined cultures of the ethnic "enemies" their government was about to exterminate. They photographed their subjects, appropriated their writings, measured their skulls, stole their artifacts, compiled demographic data banks, and studied their customs.[92] Before German armies occupied Eastern Europe, the five Nazi think tanks had produced volumes of scholarship, lavishly illustrated popular books, press releases, films, conferences, and exhibits that prepared the public for harsh treatment of "inferiors." Experts who spoke out forcefully about the "Jewish menace" contributed to the impression that Nazi violence was commensurate with the danger presented by the demonic Jew. After 1939, as the murder of actual Sinti, Roma (gypsies), and Jews began, scholarly output about these "dying races" burgeoned.

The founding statements of institute directors had resonated with promises to achieve empirical clarity; and like most autodidacts, Hitler, Himmler, and their comrades believed that their grand racial synthesis would be sustained by incontestable facts. Ethnocrats, faced with applying racist laws, anticipated rescue by objective information. Until the mid-1930s they did not doubt the physiological basis of racial difference. But when the quest for biological Jewishness proved futile, the search for a "Jewish spirit" held out fresh hope for objective distinctions that would underwrite Nazis' persecution of Jews as a moral danger. But clarity remained as elusive in 1939 as it had been in 1935. Scholars who could find few traces, physical or mental, of Jewishness among Germans with Jewish ancestry attributed their frustration to Jews' capacity for duplicity, which they termed *Mimikry*. Dismissing the visible traits of Jews as "superficial," they attributed Jewish difference to "deeper" qualities that had been implanted by a nomadic Jewish tradition. Like Nazi ethnocrats, antisemitic scholars were obsessed with the conceptual anarchy that dogged the term *Mischlinge*—which referred to less than .03 percent of the population. Key concepts like "Germanic *Volk*," "Aryan," "German blooded" and "of Germanic origin" shifted every few months.[93] Taxonomies based on terms like "Nordic Race" and "non-Nordic Race" or "protected Non-Aryan" and "protected Aryan" presented lawyers and civil servants with endless paperwork.[94] Hitler himself kept talking about Aryan and non-Aryan after this nomenclature had been discredited by state-funded institutes.

Linguistic anarchy dogged the experts' quest for stable classifiers. Technocratic-sounding terminology provided a scientific gloss without actually clearing up doubts raised by how to define "ethnically damaging marriages" *(volksschädlicher Ehen)* and "citizens from nations with related blood" *(artverwandte Staatsangehörigkeit)*. Researchers and bureaucrats pondered "administrative grading" *(Sortierung)*, identified particular individuals' "Jewish portion" *(Judenteil)*, and evaluated "Jewish human material" *(Menschenmaterial)*.[95] Occasionally, academics who approved of Hitler's rule but did not swallow the racial pill appear to have noticed the shortcomings in zealous colleagues' scholarship. Why did they continue to defend Nazism? A conversation between Heidegger and a former student, Karl Löwith, in Rome may contain a partial answer. Heidegger readily acknowledged the lamentable quality of Nazi thinking in his own field but immediately went on to praise great accomplishments in other disciplines about which he knew nothing. Moreover, he added, if only more outstanding philosophers such as himself had supported the new Reich, academic standards would have been higher.[96] Detractors, he implied, had only themselves to blame.

Along with the willful ignorance exemplified by Heidegger, a more subtle rationalization may also account for the palpable failure of racial social science. What seemed like confusion or indecision to outsiders appeared as a legitimate stage of racial revisionism to the faithful. A youthful Nazi theologian explained in late 1935 that in a young science, it was not unusual for disagreements to cause schisms within emerging fields. Doctrinal inconsistencies spurred them to clear away the debris of universal humanism and prepare their minds for a new biological age. Confident that when the racial paradigm matured, evolutionary biologists would discover the genetic racial origins of human nature, antisemitic scholars forged ahead. In the process they convened conferences, sponsored more research, and refined their methods.

Their labile conceptual world evolved in lockstep with a chaotic administrative structure during the 1930s, and antisemitic scholarship burgeoned despite the epistemological fragility of its goal. Credentialed members of the Nazi academic establishment enjoyed considerable freedom to debate without fearing rebuke—provided they did not directly contradict racial dogma or challenge Hitler's authority. No Gulag or concentration camp threatened them.[97] In the rare event of a purge (like the Röhm purge and the dismissal of Generals Fritsch and Blomberg), sexual lapses—not ideological heresies—were cited as pretexts. When the inveterate antisemite researcher Achim Gercke fell from favor in 1935, he lost his position in the Interior Ministry because of his alleged homosexuality, not because of doctrinal lapses.[98] Schmitt and Heidegger's ambitions within the Nazi state were thwarted by the resentment of old fighters, but both men continued their scholarly careers without harmful side effects.[99] Behind strident rhetoric about decisive leadership, ruthless will, and streamlined government, a capacious racial *Weltanschauung* absorbed much confusion and nonconformity. Antisemitic intellectuals' ambiguous mental categories matched the conceptual anarchy facing ethnocrats. Anomalies kept the rumor mill well stocked with the news, for example, that a writer for the tabloid *Der Stürmer* was Jewish and that the champion fencer and *Mischling* Hanni Mayer had accepted a government invitation to return from Los Angeles and compete on the German team in the 1936 Olympics. A researcher at the SS Ahnenerbe (racial heritage) project was himself half Jewish. Eugen Fischer's refusal to dismiss Nobel Laureate Otto Warburg from the Kaiser-Wilhelm Institute because of his Jewish ancestry did not prevent the renaming of the institute as the Eugen Fischer Institute. Over the years, Lösener estimated that Hitler "upgraded" the official racial status of several hundred *Mischlinge* as a reward for loyal service.[100] Germans joked about "honorary" or "nordified" Aryans like General Erich Milch and Leo Killy, a member of the Reich chancery staff.

By interpreting ambiguity as a normal outgrowth of a scholarly paradigm shift, Nazi academics rationalized the cognitive dissonance that dogged both their research and ethnocrats' drive for clarity. Constructing a realm of fact, they functioned within what a contemporary of theirs, the philosopher of science Ludwik Fleck, called a "mental product" *(Denkgebilde)*. Faced with a complex world that resisted their simplistic categories, Fleck observed that passionate believers in one or another *Denkgebilde* fall back on "emotive apriority." Operating on the basis of a fixed belief in Jews' innate depravity, antisemitic researchers applied their considerable skills to constructing an academically credible *Denkgebilde* and insulating it from outside challenges. They arranged their empirical discoveries within a framework that reinforced its own assumptions.[101]

As Max Weinreich put it, these Nazi professors "supplied Nazism with the ideological weapons which any movement . . . needs for its success."[102] More particularly, they provided "facts" that underwrote the hegemonic "rational" antisemitism that gathered force in the mid-1930s, and they secured the moral framework that guided the armies of ethnocrats and police personnel who stripped Jews of their property, dignity, and security. In the years before the onset of battlefield slaughter and industrial mass killing, scholarly discourse habituated bureaucrats and Nazi Party functionaries to what they took to be an empirically sound racial outlook.[103] Klemperer despaired as he witnessed, "again mounting disgusting antisemitism. In Munich the Academic Society for Researching Jewry; a Professor discourses on the *traits éternels* of Jewry: Hate. Passion. Conformity. Cruelty."[104]

During these years, the SS Security Service and clandestine morale surveys reported the growing gulf between Jewish and non-Jewish Germans. A Sopade reporter commented, "Persecution [of Jews] produces no enthusiasm among most people. But on the other hand . . . Although people despise its extreme forms, racial propaganda leaves its traces."[105] While it appeared that only "the most notorious Nazis" *(lautesten Nazischreier)* went out of their way to make life miserable for Jews, almost everyone else avoided contact with Jews. Gradually, the idea took hold that although Jews did not deserve physical mistreatment, their participation in civil society ought to be curtailed. In Nazi strongholds, Jews seldom ventured out onto the streets, and non-Nazis hesitated to object when they witnessed outrages. A Jewish woman wrote, "One lives almost only at home. Going out in Danzig becomes more difficult."[106] People who before 1933 did not think twice about neighbors' and colleagues' ethnic identity came to regard Jews as strangers. For Jews in Germany, as one of them concluded, "the moral, material, and intellectual basis of life has been shattered."[107] Another wrote, "Most people think the Jewish laws are nonsense. Sympathy with Jews is much more common than agreement with the laws." Nevertheless, "The impression that Jews belong to a different race is generally accepted." From Saxony came the observation, "Anti-Semitism has put down roots in wide segments of the *Volk*."[108] By the late 1930s it appeared that most Germans tacitly approved of persecution as long as they did not feel personally threatened or inconvenienced.[109] The apparently objective stereotypes about Jewish nature produced by antisemitic research contributed to Germans' clear consciences as they decided not to return a Jewish friend's greeting, not to shop at Jewish-owned stores, not to shelter a neighbor whose property was Aryanized, or not to comfort an ostracized Jewish pupil.

The final service rendered by racist scholarship, as Lösener's memoir suggests, was to provide complicit Germans with a postwar alibi for their behavior during the Third Reich. A respectable, academically-grounded version of racial hatred provided Germans with an alternative to the bigotry of old fighters like Julius Streicher. Oral histories and memoirs about life in Nazi Germany abound in informants' and authors' denials of their own antisemitism and of knowledge about what happened "in the East." And yet, having denied their racism, many who remember Nazi Germany mention "facts" that they do not identify as antisemitic. For example, they recall as fact that President Roosevelt was Jewish, that Jewish bankers held the mortgages of peasants on the verge of bankruptcy in their village, and that Jewish-led Communist terrorists had almost destroyed Germany in 1933.

Elfriede Fischer, wife of the respected historian Fritz Fischer, told Alison Owings in the late 1980s, "I personally never had an aversion to Jews." The conversation shifted to current events. "My opinion about world Jewry and about the role of the Jew in the world has in no way improved since the war." Frau Fischer especially disliked the way "world Jewry" attacked Kurt Waldheim, who had, first as Secretary-General of the U.N. and in 1986 as a candidate for the presidency of Austria, lied about his war record to disguise suspicions that he served in the Balkans when mass deportations took place. When asked if "German Christians and German Jews are really two different races?" Frau Fischer responded "*Ja*. That we're two races is completely obvious . . . There are features that are specific as to race."[110]

When the geneticist Benno Müller-Hill interviewed Nazi biologists and members of their families in the 1960s, his informants insisted that they did not see themselves as antisemites. The eugenicist Eugen Fischer's daughter set the tone. When asked if one of her father's colleagues had been an antisemite, she responded, "No certainly not. He was just like my father. He never said 'the Jews are bad,' he said 'the Jews are different.' And she smiled at me. 'He supported the segregation *[Trennung]* of the Jews. You know what it was like, when we came to Berlin in 1927. Cinema, theater, literature, it was all in their hands. He was for segregation. But he wasn't an anti-Semite.'"[111] Of course, their denials were suspect. But their failure to identify as antisemitic the opinions they expressed so candidly reveals the enduring influence of anti-Jewish scholarship.

Because so many respectable people accepted fraudulent scholarship as empirical fact, they persisted in their negative opinions about Jews long after the demise of Nazism. Reserving the term "antisemite" for the discredited emotional racism of Streicher and his ilk, they saw themselves as unprejudiced. This *ex post facto* alibi eased their transition into the post-

Nazi cold war world. In the years following World War II, their consciences did not trouble them because they could forget their passivity in the face of white-collar persecution and simultaneously express moral outrage about the violent attacks and coarse language common in the hardcore Nazi subculture.

Perhaps Nazi scholars' betrayal of academic integrity explains the virulence of an image in Klemperer's diary. Writing in 1936, Klemperer indulged in a fantasy that one day he would wield power in post-Nazi Germany: when "the fate of the vanquished lay in my hands," he would "let all the ordinary folk go and even some of the leaders . . . But I would have all the intellectuals strung up, and the professors three feet higher than the rest; they would be left hanging from the lamp posts for as long as was compatible with hygiene."[112]

Racial Warriors

Most of you must know what it means when one hundred corpses are lying side by side, or five hundred or a thousand. To have stuck it out and at the same time . . . to have remained decent fellows. This is a page of glory in our history which has never been written and is never to be written.

—*Heinrich Himmler, Poznan, Poland, October 4, 1943*

Rigorous training transforms ordinary men into soldiers. In basic training, recruits gain technical skills and develop the mental reflexes required to kill enemy soldiers without hesitation or remorse. Murdering helpless civilians, by contrast, violates the warrior's honor as it has been defined throughout Western history. Hunters, not soldiers, decoy and drive their quarry into a vulnerable spot before closing in for the kill. Lynch mobs, not soldiers, gang-murder defenseless victims for putative sexual and other offenses. War parties, not soldiers, set out to massacre women, men, and children as revenge for their victims' alleged crimes. German men on the eastern front committed atrocities not like soldiers but in the manner of hunters, lynch mobs, and war parties. Since the war crimes trials of the postwar era, debates have raged about whether the perpetrators saw their crimes as a "blood sport or noble cause."[1] What combination of peer pressure, obedience to authority, and contempt for their victims drove them?[2]

Emphasizing the importance of situational factors over antisemitism, some historians classify German soldiers' wartime atrocities as crimes of obedience, immoral acts that are "carried out within a hierarchical authority structure and serve the purposes of public policy."[3] Others attribute the slaughter of Jews in particular to a uniquely virulent strain of antisemitism in German history: "The eliminationist anti-Semitism, with its hurricane-force potential, resided ultimately in the heart of German political culture, in German society itself."[4] The focus on either battlefield conditions or on ancient hatreds obscures a crucial stage in the formation of a genocidal consensus. From 1933 through 1939—the so-called peaceful years—racial warriors underwent mental training that prepared them for their subsequent tasks. Whether soldiers went about their work with emotional detachment or frenzied hatred, before they set foot on Polish soil they had imbibed the core elements of Nazi ideology: respect for the Führer, devotion to the *Volk,* a belief in the justice of conquest, and the existence of a Jewish peril.[5] When German troops marched eastward, first into Poland and then into the Soviet Union, Stormtroopers and SS men already belonged to a subculture primed for racial war. When they served with new recruits, their leadership skills endowed them with great influence.

In all likelihood, the men who volunteered for membership in the SA (*Sturmabteilung,* Stormtroopers) or the SS (*Schutzstaffel*) had already experienced the thrill of participating in festivals, mass rallies, and torchlight parades. They had become members of what sociologists of the day called the crowd.[6] The Nobel Laureate Elias Canetti, in a study of crowd formation, described the way a large heterogeneous mass absorbed ever-greater numbers of individuals into its fold. He also observed the formation of packs—small, cohesive, self-contained units that consciously set themselves apart from the crowd. The word "crowd" *(Masse)* implies inertia, while "pack" *(Meute)* retains the overtones of "movement" that are explicit in its Latin root *movita.*[7] Whereas crowds gather strength by adding new members, packs maximize their advantage by eliminating their foes. Crowds are egalitarian, while packs, made up of "males and warriors," cultivate separatism.[8] Participants in a crowd are interchangeable, but in a pack each member is indispensable. Choosing to become an SA man or an SS man constituted an important first step in identifying not just with the *Volk* but with what Canetti called the pack.

In the premodern cultures described by Canetti, packs were bound together by prior kin or tribal ties. In this respect, the contrast between premodern packs and Nazi militias could scarcely have been greater. Members of Nazi paramilitary units hailed from many regions; they were Protestants, Catholics, and nondenominational Christians; they ranged in age from their early twenties to their late forties; their educational achievements varied from vocational school certificates to PhDs. Unit cohesion was not a natural outgrowth of kinship. Rather, tribal identity was forged by sophisticated techniques that merged rigorous Prussian military traditions with a distinctively Nazi concept of racial war. Within this militia subculture, men studied "the enemy," weighed alternative strategies to attack "him," and bonded with fellow soldiers. In an intensely masculine milieu, they were, in military jargon, resocialized and disinhibited.

Since his earliest years as a political agitator, Hitler appreciated the value of all-male packs for political action. A few years after being demobilized in 1919, he reflected on the centrality of masculine identity in his political strategy. "History is made only by political parties with power, strength and ideology. The goal of the National Socialist movement [is] to attract men who are willing to commit themselves, their faith, and their will to the future of the *Volk*. For that, we need masculine discipline, community spirit, and willingness to sacrifice."[9] During the early months of Nazi power, the Nietzsche scholar and Nazi intellectual Ernst Baeumler looked to all-male Nazi formations as the only hope for moral renewal. In Baeumler's view, twelve years of democracy had eroded the masculine altruism exhibited during the war and promoted feminine vices such as egotism, materialism, and decadence. Only all-male fighting units could turn back a decade of indolence.[10] "Man overcomes his doubts and anxiety, not because he sees himself as absolutely good, but because he knows where he belongs, in what community or unit *[Verband]* fate has placed him." In social milieus where men and women mingle (here he disparagingly referred to the society depicted in Gustav Flaubert's *Sentimental Education*), racial pride and masculinity falter because self-indulgence corrupts idealism. Like many Fascist intellectuals of the day, Baeumler paraphrased Nietzsche's *Zarathustra* and *Genealogy* in celebrating "masculine hardness."[11]

Nazi organizers recruited masses of Nazi voters, but packs provided the dynamism of what old fighters called "our freedom movement." In contrast to the amorphous crowd, hunting packs (in Canetti's typology) close ranks against outsiders and divide up predatory tasks among themselves. "The pack is decisive and unshakeable"; it is a "unit of action" pledged to protect the crowd.[12] Nazi militiamen hunted together, honored martyred comrades, and distributed bounty. They also exchanged gossip, competed in sports events, shared leisure activities, and formed personal ties. Rites, ceremonies, and hierarchy enhanced their racial arrogance, even as teamwork created brotherhood among them. In a subculture that praised honor, courage, and loyalty, Nazi militiamen cultivated an elitism that distinguished them from soldiers in the regular army *(Wehrmacht)*.

Although they shared a common enmity for Jews, the two packs that evolved in the mid-1930s—the brown-shirted SA and the black-shirted SS—rivaled one another. Competition sharpened the identities of each and also hardened the men for future tasks. Each had its own distinctive culture, with contrasting ideas about how best to rid Germany of its so-called Jewish problem. The looting, arson, psychological harassment, and physical assaults that provided Stormtroopers with an outlet for their rage contrasted dramatically with the calculating SS men, who systematically destroyed Jews' civil rights, collected intelligence on Jewish organizations, monitored public opinion, and facilitated the legal theft of Jews' property. Whereas SA men defied public opinion, SS men cultivated public trust. Unlike the SA chiefs who appealed to their men's lust for physical violence by tormenting Jews, SS leaders prided themselves on educating men to cleanse the *Volk* of purported danger from any quarter.[13]

Although the duplication of command structures may have appeared inefficient, military trainers have long realized that competition between two forces enhances performance. Like cadets at West Point and Annapolis, rival Nazi Party militias faced off against one another even as they stood apart from ordinary citizens in the crowd. In the aftermath of the Röhm purge in June 1934, the existence of rival Nazi militias proved useful in simultaneously disorienting victims and preparing public opinion for escalating persecution. Three cycles of violence followed by superficial calm illustrate the effectiveness of allowing two tactics to operate in tandem. In the first round during early 1933, Stormtroopers assaulted Jews, vandalized and defaced Jewish-owned property, and humiliated Jews in public. In the wake of this brutality, scores of municipal and occupational restrictions against Jews appeared as the lesser of two evils. After a second upsurge of violence in the summer of 1935, again many bystanders expressed relief at the decrease in lawlessness and anticipated that the Nuremberg Race Laws could provide an acceptable framework of bureaucratic order. Finally, in 1938, the savage attacks that accompanied the annexation *(Anschluß)* of Austria in March and the "Crystal Night" pogrom of November 9–10 increased Jews' desperation, and the ensuing decline in unsanctioned violence created the impression that public policy was being carried out by the appropriate authorities. Because they were accustomed to the rule of law, Germans, whether they were Jews or non-Jews, found it hard to grasp the reality that lawful, orderly persecution would turn out to be more deadly than random cruelty.

Rivalry between the SS and SA also contributed to a competitive radicalization of Nazi policy toward the Jews by connecting the identity of each force with a distinctive "solution" to so-called racial danger.[14] Compared with the vulgar antisemitism of marauding street gangs, for example, an SS man or Auschwitz physician could perceive himself as restrained; on the other hand, a Stormtrooper who beat up a Jewish businessman could think of his act as courageous, in comparison with the lackluster paperwork of an SS racial detective. The popular press and training materials aimed at Stormtroopers and SS men provide a glimpse at contrasting iden-

Der Frontsoldat: „Dein Geist gab mir die Ehre wieder!"

48. "The Front Soldier: Your spirit restores my honor!" With a graveyard in the background, a ghostly soldier spoke to a new generation, and a Stormtrooper pledged revenge against the Treaty of Versailles.

tities taking shape under the aegis of Nazi racial ideology. In the periodicals aimed at the "emotional" SA and the "rational" SS, two markedly different approaches to racial politics took shape. Although it was not the official SA publication, *Der Stürmer (The Stormtrooper),* published by Julius Streicher since 1923, expressed the rough-and-ready ethos of old-fighter

Nazis. Starting in March 1935, Heinrich Himmler's SS published *Das Schwarze Korps (The Black Corps)*, which embodied the élan of a technocratic elite. Because both periodicals were directed at general audiences, they offer an opportunity to assess these two militia packs, as well as their respective admirers in the crowd.

In lively essays and vivid graphics, editors and authors in both periodicals attracted a wide readership that included members of the rival militia. An SS man could laugh at the coarse humor of Julius Streicher's *Der Stürmer,* and an SA man might take pride in his ability to understand a theoretical article in *Das Schwarze Korps.* The cultivation of two militia mentalities with a common goal provided diversity of sorts within the overarching framework of Nazi ideology. Each periodical developed its own concept of racial danger and its own ideal of manhood. The morality invoked to justify both kinds of crime against defenseless victims did not prevent chicanery, theft, blackmail, or corruption. In fact, perpetrators' sense of rectitude most likely enabled crime by rationalizing virtually any immoral act as honorable in the "struggle" against Jews or other targeted groups. Thus, crimes in ordinary circumstances were pushed aside as collateral harm in pursuit of worthy aims.

The separation between the two militia packs became apparent in the aftermath of the Röhm purge in June 1934, when Himmler's SS, which had carried out the murders, closed ranks and gradually detached itself from the discredited Stormtroopers. Although demoralization led to the resignation of over half of all SA members, those who remained performed ceremonial functions, cultivated ties to powerful Nazi functionaries, and instructed members of Nazi associations like the Hitler Youth, the Labor Front, and the Labor Service.[15] Although the actual influence of the SA plummeted after the Röhm purge, its public profile remained high. As Hitler's personal bodyguard in the mid-1920s, this elite group distinguished itself by pledging to uphold the highest standards of virtue *(anerzogenen Tugenden)* appropriate for a superior "union of men"—a *Männerbund,* in Ernst Baeumler's terms. Himmler insisted on rigid selection procedures that included height, weight, physical strength, and his own evaluation of photographic evidence of candidates' racial fitness.[16] In contrast to the SA, over which the suspicion of homosexuality hovered from the beginning, Himmler explicitly encouraged heterosexuality (within marriage and, increasingly, outside it) and fatherhood. And unlike the haphazard indoctrination of Stormtroopers, Himmler prepared his men to carry out a comprehensive racial protection *(Rassenschutz)* program that required study, discipline, and spiritual devotion.[17] From several thousand men in 1935, the SS expanded rapidly as Himmler gained control over the secret police (Gestapo), the criminal police (Kripo), the concentration camps (Death's Head units), and a small female police force. On the eve of the second world war, Himmler commanded about 240,000 men.[18]

Nothing illustrates the contrast between the SA and the SS ethos better than the way each unit regarded public opinion. Whereas the swaggering

Ein Volk steht und fällt mit dem Wert oder Unwert
seiner blutgebundenen rassischen Substanz.

A Volk stands or falls according to the greater or lesser worth of its blood.

Juni   Brachet

11   **12**   **13**   **14**   **15**   **16**   **17**

Sonntag   Montag   Dienstag   Mittwoch   Donnerstag   Freitag   Sonnabend

49. "A *Volk* stands and falls with the value of the racial substance carried in its blood." A model SS man fulfilled his fatherly obligation to the *Volk* in this photograph from the *Neues Volk* calendar.

SA men defied what they derided as petty bourgeois scruples, the SS took great care to cultivate respect beyond Nazi circles. In early 1933, for example, SA men established concentration camps spontaneously, often without any orders or supervision. Oblivious of widespread disgust at their arbitrary cruelty, guards tormented and sometimes murdered their helpless prisoners. The victims, impounded in makeshift camps without facilities, suffered the ravages of disease and malnutrition in addition to torture. After Himmler assumed control of the camps in 1935–1936, most of the inmates were declared rehabilitated, and the incarcerated population dropped from about 90,000 in 1933 to less than 10,000 in the mid-1930s. Under the supervision of the notorious Death's Head Division, strict rules established a semblance of order in the remaining camps. This did not mean an improvement in conditions, but it signaled the replacement of arbitrary violence with systematic cruelty.

Himmler's attention to public relations was evident in a speech to recruits. "The *Volk* must come to understand that if someone has been arrested, he has been arrested justly . . . The members of the Gestapo are men with human kindness, with human hearts, and absolute rightness. We must not forget—beginning with the highest to the lowliest official and employee—that we exist for the *Volk* and not the *Volk* for us." Reminding his men to be "courteous and sociable," he concluded: "Please see yourselves as facilitators and not as dictators."[19] To compensate for the lack of a free press to provide feedback, the SS developed an elaborate secret surveillance system to monitor the popular mood. Starting with just a few thousand "trusted" informers *(Vertrauensmänner)* in 1934, the SS security police received regular analyses of public opinion from over 30,000 men by the late 1930s. Streicher, by contrast, solicited slanderous public denunciations of Jewish crime and "Jewish lackeys" who ignored antisemitic prohibitions.

Der Stürmer epitomized the uncouth style from which Hitler distanced himself as he sought approval from well-educated Germans and foreign powers. Although old fighters' lust for violence could not be suppressed entirely, the Röhm purge and the reduction of violence in late 1935 suggests that it could be controlled. Germans who applauded Nazi rule without being avid followers of specifically Nazi doctrine could tell themselves the Nazi Party had outgrown its disreputable origins. Nevertheless, *Der Stürmer*'s circulation figures, which hovered at around 25,000 in 1933, rose to over 700,000 by the late 1930s. The Nazi Labor Front (DAF) urged its members to subscribe to *Der Stürmer,* and the SS commander of the

Death's Head Division urged his recruits to read it.[20] Subscribers were exhorted to pass their copies on to friends, and about 15 percent of each print run was distributed free of charge. Local SA units built lavish oversized display cases for *Der Stürmer* at bus stops, newsstands, and marketplaces so that casual bystanders could hardly avoid the tabloid's message. Elaborate dedication ceremonies and competitions for the best display design produced ever more outsized and garish publicity. Nine special issues in the 1930s (each one an exposé of an alleged "offense," such as "Jewish Ritual Murder" and "Albert Hirschland, the Race Traitor from Magdeburg") would sell as many as two million copies.

Der Stürmer became, as one of its readers put it, "a fighting tabloid that is loved and hated like no other."[21] Streicher richly deserved his reputation as "Jew-baiter number one," in the words of the indictment at the Nu-

50. "Everything in her has died. She was ruined by a Jew." The rhyme underscores the elements of decadence in this caricature by Fips: a despondent mother who neglects her sobbing child and smokes a cigarette, a lonely rooming house, and, on the floor, the photograph of the Jewish seducer who abandoned her.

remberg Military Tribunal in 1946.[22] Especially from 1933 through 1938, when Hitler and the Propaganda Ministry downplayed the "Jewish question" in public, Streicher's unbridled fury whipped up fanatics' racist rage. Vile caricatures and diatribes against people who felt "false sympathy" for Jews' suffering filled the tabloid's pages.[23] Words like "extermination" *(Ausrottung),* "purging" *(Säuberung),* and "elimination" *(Vernichtung)* stocked the imaginations of hardcore antisemites long before World War II created a context in which mass murder of Jews could become a reality.

Early in his editorial career, Streicher hit on the low-budget formula that achieved notoriety for *Der Stürmer:* eyewitness coverage of scandals involving Jews, sex, and money. In the 1920s the tabloid's only fulltime journalist, Ernst Hiemer, attended trials of Jewish offenders and sent dispatches dripping with repulsive you-are-there details. Lacking funds to hire more reporters, Streicher introduced the "Letter Box" column in which he published readers' accounts of "outrageous" Jewish acts in their neighborhoods. Using the informal *Du* form of address, readers wrote in a chatty style to "Dear *Stürmer.*" In the mid-1930s Streicher claimed to receive hundreds of letters a day.[24] Whether or not they were genuine, the published letters contributed to a frenzy of denunciations by providing readers with appropriate phrases and criminal categories—a veritable menu of accusatory formats for letters to the Gestapo.[25]

These outlandish accusations were reminiscent of the atrocity reports believed so ardently by ordinary citizens during the first world war. In the 1920s, Germans were bitterly disillusioned when they discovered that the atrocity reports had been fabricated by their own government. A lingering sense of betrayal might have rendered reports generated by the Nazi government suspect, but the atrocity reports in *Der Stürmer* purported to come from grassroots, not government, sources, and the coarseness of their style contributed to the image of authenticity. The simple colloquial style of the magazine was, in any case, aimed at a poorly educated readership. As the circulation grew, staff members not only selected letters for publication but also answered them and kept a cross-referenced file of denunciations.[26] A single issue might include as many as a dozen reports of "outrageous" Jewish crimes (putative swindles, rapes, and debauchery), as well as the names, home addresses, and sometimes photographs of defamed Jewish individuals. Knowing that only their initials would be published, letter writers slandered Jews with impunity.

A pillory column denounced "Jew-lackeys" *(Judenknechte)* who ignored antisemitic regulations and patronized Jewish businesses. Interpreted in one way, the continuous stream of complaints about what letter writers called a "lack of racial pride" among their fellow non-Jews suggests widespread rejection of coarse antisemitism. But the indefatigable *Stürmer* writers used disappointment as a spur for greater vigilance. A selection of "news" items conveys the discrepancy between actions that seem trivial to us and the immense outrage they generated: Christians attended a Jew's funeral; a Jewish woman joined the National Socialist Women's Organization; businessmen came to the aid of a Jewish shoe-store owner; a Jewish dentist "was still allowed" to extract the teeth of non-Jews; farmers throughout Germany continued to prefer Jewish livestock dealers; a minister secretly purchased bread from a Jewish baker; Jews sunned themselves on public beaches; and the daughter of a Berlin book publisher "shamed herself" by her friendship with a Jewish man.[27]

Readers were incited to act. After three years of expropriation had devastated Jewish-owned businesses, for example, a reader submitted the names and addresses of 43 Jewish-owned shoe stores in Hamburg and wondered why so many were "still" in business.[28] Nazis would, she hoped, picket the stores. The impact of denunciation could be emotionally as well as financially devastating. Gerta Pfeffer, a Jewish woman who had lived in a small Bavarian town before immigrating to Israel, recalled how she and her co-workers would gather every day after work. As usual, all of them (including Nazis) accepted the invitation to her birthday party. But a neighbor reported them to *Der Stürmer* and threatened to publish snapshots of the party. After the "scandal" broke, Pfeffer remembered, "I now ate my lunch completely alone in the small side room so I would not be noticed."[29] *Der Stürmer* editors created networks of antisemite vigilantes who spied on their neighbors and searched municipal records for evidence of Jewish mischief. They created a virtual community among geographically far-flung individuals which anticipated the call-in radio programs and Internet chatrooms of a later generation. Captioned images— such as a snapshot of a Christian women's association bidding farewell to a Jewish member of the board, with the comment, "You just cannot believe this is possible"—invited readers to share the true believer's moral outrage. "Amid flowing tears, the Jewess resigned from this odd association of dames *[Weiber]*."[30]

The raw paranoia of *Der Stürmer* short-circuited moral considerations by representing Jewry as so potent that even two or three Jews, like rodents in a granary, presented a terrible threat. In the 1920s the periodical likened fanatic antisemites to the early Christians who endured their neighbors' scorn: "Jesus Christ tirelessly struggled during his entire life against the . . . 'children of the devil.' He fought against the same foes we battle today: against the Jewish *Volk*." Biblical phrases consoled them: "Holy are those who are persecuted in the name of justice." Drawings featured altars, crucifixions, and church spires. Not surprisingly, Hitler became a veritable *Volk* messiah who declared, "And even if you all abandon me, and I am left totally alone, I will nevertheless tread along the path for which I have been destined."[31] Against caricatured metaphors of racial danger, a Christian iconography glorified Nazis as steadfast and loyal believers.

Like pioneering advertisers of the day, Streicher's staff grasped the power of visual language in an age of cheap newsprint and colorful graphics. Almost every cover bore oversized red headlines and a full-page caricature by the brilliant graphic artist Philippe Rupprecht, who signed his work "Fips."[32] Like Superman and Batman, Fips's strong-jawed SA men smashed enemies of society whose overdrawn features marked them as unsavory. Unlike most American comics, however, the visual language of *Der Stürmer* was steeped in pornography and saturated with demeaning Jewish stereotypes. Limericks in dialect and slogans like "Jews live by lies and die with the truth" enhanced Streicher's ethnic populism. Boxed quotations from *Mein Kampf* lent Hitler's authority to vile racism, even during the years when he seldom mentioned Jews in public. Fips's leering "Jewish-looking" men stalked blonde maidens. Reptiles, vampires, rodents, and spiders identified by Stars of David attacked healthy Aryan homes. Overweight "Jewish" families looked foolish in Bavarian peasant costumes. Swarthy political orators incited workers to riot, and cigar-smoking bankers conspired to swindle naive Aryans. In 1934 *Der Stürmer* press published an illustrated book of caricatures by Fips entitled "Jews! Introduce Yourselves!"[33] A photo essay about Jews in *Der Stürmer* entitled "Animals, Look at Yourselves!" ridiculed Jewish satirists who had in the past criticized Germany.[34] In every image of "the Jew," exaggerated physiognomy (often enhanced by photo retouching) alerted readers to the connection between inner depravity and external appearance. As part of the 1935 crusade against "inter-racial" sexual relations, Fips drew a series of cartoons stigmatizing not only Jewish male seducers but the Aryan women who yielded to their allure.

In his stolid anti-intellectualism, Streicher personified the SA man. Instead of courting well-educated readers, he played the "bad boy" of the Nazi movement and devised publicity stunts that made headlines in Germany and abroad. A sampling of *New York Times* stories about Streicher in

1935 presents the portrait of an obsessive crackpot who courted ridicule. Speaking in the rhetoric of a priest, Streicher "absolved" anyone who attacked Jews and implicitly likened them (and Hitler) to Christ attacking the moneychangers. As district leader of Nuremberg, he banned wrestling matches between Negroes and whites and threatened to banish any woman who applauded a black athlete. He urged Germans not to use medications discovered by Jews, including diphtheria and tetanus vaccines, digitalis, and salvarsan. At year's end, Streicher made headlines by inviting ten Communist prisoners from Dachau to a lavish Christmas dinner.[35]

Equating Jews with evil, writers for *Der Stürmer* built dehumanization into their vocabulary with nouns like "Jew lawyer" *(Judenanwalt)*, "Jew tenor" *(Judentenor)*, "Talmud Jew" *(Talmudjude)*, and "Jew baggage" *(Judenbagage)*. Women became "filthy Talmud dames" *(Weiber)*. A typical headline announced "Jewish Beast Rapes Viennese Girl."[36] In March 1936 parents were warned about Jewish "perverts"—identified by their photos, names, and addresses—who might molest their sons.[37] Besides linking "Jewish" to unpopular nouns, as in the "Jewish-Liberal era," *Stürmer* editors gave new meanings to verbs associated with sexual acts. "Rape" *(Vergewältigung)* and "molestation" *(Misbrauch)* normally applied to illegal sexual assault, but in *Der Stürmer* they referred to sexual relations between consenting adults of supposedly different races.

As the circulation of *Der Stürmer* grew, so too did its editor's pretensions. Streicher, along with Martin Heidegger and Carl Schmitt, joined the commission to eradicate Jewish influence from Germanic jurisprudence and developed his own research library of Judaica, mainly from donations made by readers who had stolen Jewish books and religious items during raids on synagogues.[38] While avoiding topics related to eugenic improvement projects, like racial science, sterilization, and natalism, *Der Stürmer* articles featured antisemitic passages from Martin Luther, Ben Franklin, Goethe, and other historical figures, to give their tirades the aura of credibility.[39] Expanding the tabloid's foreign coverage, authors cited Henry Ford's *The International Jew: The World's Foremost Problem* and *The Protocols of the Elders of Zion,* and reported news about racism in South Africa, the United States, and Western Europe. Much as antisemites had done for centuries, they also quoted so-called injunctions from the Talmud to demonstrate Jews' immutable moral depravity. Fraudulent quotations from the Talmud—for example, "Jews are human. Non-Jews, however, are not humans, but cattle"—supplied evidence of Jews' inhumanity and

51. "The End . . . Naive, seduced by money, disgraced, poisoned in their souls, infected in their blood—in their wombs disaster festers." In the first issue of *Der Stürmer* to appear after the Nuremberg Race Laws were declared, Fips caricatured "the Jew" as a bestial sexual predator and "the German" as a naive female. After a wave of pogrom-style attacks on Jews and their property in the summer of 1935, readers of *Der Stürmer* were encouraged to avoid physical violence and to increase their psychological torment of Jews and of non-Jews suspected of having sexual or social relationships with Jews.

scripted attacks on Jews as self-defense. In their coarse bombast, *Stürmer* authors popularized the moral reasoning of theological antisemites like Gerhard Kittel.[40]

In the mid-1930s, the *Stürmer* press began to publish books with a scholarly gloss that supposedly documented the existence of a Jewish conspiracy. Among its most ambitious projects was a book by the antisemitic historian Peter Deeg entitled *The Court Jew*—a hefty volume of over 500 pages printed on high-quality paper, with copious scholarly references, glossy photographs, a bibliography, document facsimiles, and a fold-out of the Rothschild family tree that purported to chart the ratlike expansion of the family's financial power.[41] A detailed history of antisemitism, *The Jewish Question through Five Centuries,* dignified antisemitism by quoting great men of history who had spoken out against Jewry. It was not difficult to decipher the subtext: because previous "restrained" tactics had failed, harsher measures were now in order.[42] Rudolf Kummer's *Rasputin: Tool of the Jews* "exposed" the Jewish plot behind the Russian Revolution. Under the title *Struggle against World Jewry,* Streicher's repellent speeches from the early 1920s were reissued. In 1939 the press published a summary of all antisemitic legislation in Greater Germany.

For over two decades, *Stürmer* artists, authors, and readers exchanged

52. "The Execution of the Court Jew Lippold in Berlin. Contemporary print dated 1573." In addition to the execution at the center of the print, the engraver included a portrait of Lippold, the wagon that bore him to his death, and his corpse— flanked by the images of justice and a righteous Old Testament God pointing to the Ten Commandments. The history of antisemitism, made respectable in historical artifacts like this one, established a pedigree for Nazi persecution.

fantasies about how to make German society "Jew-free." According to the prosecution at Streicher's Nuremberg trial, the tabloid on over fifty occasions called for elimination, murder, or annihilation of Jews. News of tragedies that befell Jews was greeted gleefully, as in the case of a Herr Guckenheimer, who was driven by Nazi harassment to commit suicide in 1931. After printing the news, the article added, "The time is coming when other Jews like Guckenheimer will kill themselves."[43] By its relentless fabrication, the tabloid accustomed credulous readers to perceive aggression against Jews as self-defense. In strident "masculine" language devoid of euphemism, Streicher kept hardcore antisemites primed to smash windows, set fire to synagogues, and beat up helpless individuals.[44] Streicher did not mince words in a 1935 lecture to university students at the Bernau leadership-training center. "Actually, one can say that it is not sufficient that we ban the Jew from Germany. No, we must kill him dead *[totschlagen]* everywhere in the world. If Germany solves the Jewish question, then blessed rays will stream out from Germany throughout the world, on other races as well. Hard times definitely lie ahead."[45] If emigration and ostracism did not "solve" the "problem," *Der Stürmer* authors threatened, Jews would be pushed into ghettos.[46] Early in 1934, under a headline, "Jewry Is Organized Crime," the author described Jews as perpetual emigrants who "wander over the entire globe."[47] The moral was simple: since the "nomadic Jew" had no home, expulsion would merely restore his natural state.

Long before Adolf Eichmann and other SS officials proposed that Jews be deported to Madagascar, Streicher wrote, "The contrast between Jew and German is not one of *Volk* and *Volk* but between honor and dirty tricks, between a creative *Volk* and crooked rabble . . . And troublemakers must be sentenced either to hang or be banished to Madagascar."[48] On a vast island concentration camp, Streicher imagined that Jews would remain until "they have gnawed away at one another and devoured one another."[49] The fantasy probably originated with a passage in *Mein Kampf*: "If the Jews were alone in this world, they would stifle in filth and offal; they would . . . exterminate one another."[50] *Der Stürmer* repeatedly advocated the Madagascar solution—sometimes attributing the idea to English or French antisemites and at other times claiming it as a "humane" German idea.[51] Significantly, after the Madagascar scheme became a genuine option in 1940, *Der Stürmer* no longer mentioned it.

As circulation expanded, so did coverage of foreign affairs. In the two years before the invasion of Poland, the tabloid featured hundreds of

53. "Two kinds of children; two kinds of human beings." Fips brutally caricatured not only lecherous Jewish men but overfed and greedy Jewish women and children—suggesting that all Jews, even individuals who had done no wrong, by their very existence posed a moral threat to the *Volk*.

news items that blamed a cabal of Jews—President Franklin Roosevelt among them—for planning war against Germany. Photographs of mass murders and corpses of famine victims from the "Soviet Russian hell" added extermination to readers' imagination before Nazi leaders seriously contemplated mass murder as a realistic option.[52] References to racism elsewhere (notably to lynch mobs in the United States and segregation in South Africa) normalized racial persecution in Germany.[53] Months after the German invasion of Poland, a retouched photograph of Polish Jews standing over the graves of a German Free Corps unit in 1921 implicitly made German mass executions of Jewish civilians seem like reprisals for an earlier crime.[54]

If between three and five adults read each issue, the magazine reached no more than 2 or 3 million readers in a nation of 65 million. But this fanatical minority, emboldened by cooperation from law enforcement agencies, had the power to make life unbearable for the roughly 250,000 Jewish citizens living in Germany during the late 1930s. Ultimately, however, the crude antisemitism of *Der Stürmer* had its limits. The passions that inflamed racist thugs could dissipate. Fraudulent denunciations lacked credibility in educated circles. Crude attacks on helpless Jewish citizens discredited perpetrators and inspired pity for victims.[55] Although *Der Stürmer*'s circulation figures continued to rise and Stormtroopers played a key role in ideological training, it was the ethos of the SS man that established the parameters of a genocidal morality. In contrast to the unruly Stormtrooper, the better-educated SS man was trained to adhere to a restrained, manly ideal. An SS man must never yield to impulse and he must always be ready to ferret out racial danger, which operated in nefarious global networks that included Bolsheviks, financiers, and Free Masons. The "solution" was to outwit, not to terrorize, the enemy; to confiscate his property "legally"; and efficiently to extrude him from the *Volk*.

Surveillance reports from the Gestapo and the SS Security Service (the *Sicherheitsdienst,* or SD) included allegations from loyal Nazis that implied Stormtroopers' vulgarity was damaging the image of antisemitism.[56] A 1934 memo on training explicitly called for every possible tactic to stop intimate ties between Christians and Jews "*except* street methods."[57] SS Führer Himmler's second-in-command, 29-year-old Reinhard Heydrich, openly deplored "vulgar" *(radau)* tactics. A Nazi newspaper reporter complained, "Jews laugh up their sleeves at the disarray" about the Jewish question in Nazi circles.[58] From Frankfurt came a survey of attitudes toward Jews in 1933–1935 that castigated boycotts and physical violence as counterproductive.[59] SS concern with public opinion extended to monitoring the views of foreigners and underground anti-Nazi networks in Germany. Here, too, crude antisemitism backfired, in the opinion of SS analysts. Agents abroad reported their distress at seeing Nazis caricatured as brownshirted bullies.[60]

Accentuating their distance from rival Stormtroopers, SS leaders emphasized the importance of intellectual preparation. As early as 1934, training teams included special consultants on racial matters.[61] Officers were educated at special schools, the *Junkerschulen,* where antisemitism was integrated into routine education about many threats to the *Volk*.[62] In a wide array of instructional materials and in their magazine, SS leaders developed an ethos that was explained on the front page of the first issue of *Das Schwarze Korps,* dated March 6, 1935. The headline announced: "We Volunteers of 1914/15 and National Socialism." Readers understood the implicit insult to the SA in the disparaging references to "arrogant daredevils" and "loudmouthed veterans" as "caricatures of National Socialism" who defiled the memory of the authentic war heroes. The restrained SS man, by contrast, was the heir of the unknown soldiers who

54. This cartoon from the British publication *Time and Tide* mocks thuggish SA men who "protect" a Jewish-owned lingerie shop. The SS Security Service regularly monitored foreign criticism of Nazi policies and often published hostile cartoons (along with instructions on how to refute their criticisms) in *Das Schwarze Korps,* the SS weekly. Perhaps because they found this image particularly damaging, the SS Security Service did not publish it but used it as part of their drive to discredit unsanctioned SA violence.

had so selflessly fought and died. Praising Erich Maria Remarque's *All Quiet on the Western Front,* the author likened SS recruits to the "boy soldiers" in the trenches who became "hardened to iron duty." Readers would have known that during the Weimar Republic, the SA had savagely criticized Remarque's pacifism and that SA riots had prevented the screening of the film based on his novel. By honoring Remarque's trench soldiers, the author implicitly contrasted the self-sacrificing SS man with the swashbuckling and self-indulgent Stormtrooper.[63]

In the style of *Neues Volk,* published by the Office of Racial Politics, each issue of *Das Schwarzes Korps* contained about 16 pages and featured a mélange of photo essays, cultural commentary, news about SS men and their families, SS events, popular racial science, and human-interest stories. Caricatures rarely appeared, and when they did, they usually did not emblazon the front cover and their style fell within ordinary standards of taste. Unlike *Neues Volk, Das Schwarze Korps* included news analysis, foreign policy coverage, theoretical essays about Nazism, and analyses of threats to Nazi rule. Starting with printruns of about 80,000, the periodical expanded quickly to 340,000 in 1937 and 700,000 at the beginning of the war. Its editor, Günther D'Alquen, had joined the Hitler Youth in 1925 at age 15, and in 1931, as a university student and journalist for the Nazi newspaper *Der Völkische Beobachter,* he became an SS man. His youth and middle-class family background made him representative of SS members, two thirds of whom had been too young to fight in World War I.[64] Almost all SS men had completed secondary school, and many had attended technical schools and universities. Nearly 20 percent of all SS generals belonged to the nobility, and aristocrats were over-represented among the lower ranks as well. At a time when 2 percent of all Germans attended universities, 41 percent of the SS officer corps had studied at universities.[65] The SS weekly was designed (as the SS chief of training put it) to win the respect of not only well-educated Nazis but of thoughtful readers everywhere.[66]

In contrast to Himmler's idiosyncratic vision of the SS as a quasi-mystical "elite of the finest blood," Heydrich conceived of an intellectually astute corps of racial detectives. "We in the SS intend to become the ideological *[weltanschaulich]* Shock Troops and the protective honor guard of the Führer's ideal. At the same time, we will fulfill the duties of the state police and become the domestic protective force of the National Socialist state."[67]

In a series of brief articles in 1935 issues of *Das Schwarze Korps,* Heydrich

55. "Who Rules the Soviet Union?" The intellectual pretensions of the SS proscribed the lurid and often pornographic cartoons that appeared on the front pages of virtually every issue of *Der Stürmer*. On occasion, however, *Das Schwarze Korps* featured what the editors judged to be tasteful cartoons like this one.

called on SS men to fashion "a new human type." For the first time in history, a fighting unit would be based on a spiritual revolution that expressed the deepest essence of the German *Volk*. The "political soldier" would inspire non-Nazis and Nazis alike by his exemplary conduct and by his grasp of racial social science. He would be a "*Volk* comrade," distinguished by "character, honor, and racial authenticity." Before converting others, a man had to educate himself, which meant, an article on an SS training camp reported, "We must not only march in the same step, but our hearts must beat to the same rhythm."[68]

The range of opinions expressed in *Das Schwarze Korps* suggests that the editors trusted their readers to think for themselves within the bounds of National Socialism. Despite complaints from Nazis outside the SS, D'Alquen made his periodical the most independent publication in the Third Reich in the 1930s. Assuming that their cosmopolitan readers were acquainted with the hostile foreign press, for example, the editors routinely sampled global opinion and instructed readers how to refute critics' allegations. Vicious caricatures of Hitler from the foreign press were reprinted with captions like, "Just look at how they mock us!" A regular feature entitled "From Where Does Hatred of Germans Come? [*Woher*

Deutschenhass?]" reprinted hostile foreign cartoons and criticism of Nazism. When condemning Einstein's physics, the periodical explained its position with an exposé of ethnic German scientists ("white Jews") who maintained contact with exiled Jewish colleagues.[69]

In an essay entitled "The Struggle against Racial Thinking," the author defended racial theory point by point.[70] When the economy was plagued by dislocations, an article introduced readers to macroeconomic theory. As the SS took control of the concentration camps, criminologists analyzed inmates' racial predispositions to crime. Photographs of SS equestrian teams and advertisements for health spas and vacation hotels enhanced the magazine's elitist image. Despite the official Nazi stand against tobacco, *Das Schwarze Korps* accepted cigarette advertising that depicted gentlemen who appreciated opera, literature, and chess, while ads for another brand featured photographs of gleaming, technologically advanced cigarette-making equipment. An illustrated article denigrating as kitsch the commercialization of Hitler's portrait and the swastika suggested that readers were capable of self-criticism.[71] Photographic essays about concentration camp inmates' faces allowed readers to glimpse a supposedly degenerate and disloyal underworld, which contrasted with the classical elegance of nude sculptures in the art appreciation pages. Abundant praise for family virtues and motherly women was enhanced by attacks on the "Amazons" of the women's movement and pathological "men-women" under the headline "Women Are Not Men!"[72] Illustrated art appreciation essays denigrated nonrepresentational art and used the female nude to explain that "man is the measure of all things."[73]

Whereas racial paranoia drenched *Der Stürmer*, in the pages of *Das Schwarze Korps*, the "Jewish question" was discussed along with Free Masonry, Communism, and "political Catholicism" (that is, any criticism of Nazi rule by the Church). Instructors routinely taught not simply antisemitism but more general "enemy studies" *(Gegnerkunde)*. In the earliest issues of *Das Schwarze Korps*, Heydrich described a world of nefarious conspiracies against Nazi rule. Before 1933, he wrote, Nazis had battled against political ("visible") enemies. But he warned against complacency because the racial ("invisible") enemy remained as strong as ever. Unlike *Stürmer* letter writers who condemned the persistence of social and business ties between Jews and non-Jews as a sign of ordinary Germans' apathy about race, Heydrich imagined subversive networks, redolent with channels, canals, tunnels, and subterranean networks. In his discursive universe, an evil infection connected the diverse "enemies" in the phobic universe of the SS, in which parasites, too lazy to do their own work, mimic their hosts and manipulate their "instincts" so they can effortlessly colonize them.[74] The law establishing the SS political police, the Gestapo, charged it to "carefully supervise the political health of the German ethnic body politic [Volkskörper], which must be quick to recognize all symptoms of disease and germs . . . and to remove them by every appropriate means."[75]

Acknowledging that racial policies had encountered setbacks, Heydrich blamed failure on Nazis' "enemies." Radical Catholics undercut the sterilization program; non-Nazi elements in the civil service undermined restrictions against Jews; recalcitrant professors "attempted through so-called purely scientific discussions to keep the liberal spirit alive"; and social elites spawned malaise among Nazi leaders "by snubbing some and welcoming others into their exclusive circles." Behind them all lurked the "mortal enemy," to be hunted by the "political soldier's" quick wit, knowledge, and ruthless will.

After the Nuremberg Laws, some SS chiefs worried that their men were not intellectually prepared for racial war. At a workshop for SS racial experts, the opening speaker complained, "Jews are being dealt with only as a marginal concern, in a shabby [Stiefmutterlich] manner."[76] Morale surveys by the SD showed an "alarming" lack of anxiety about Jews in the general population. Some ignorant police clerks put Jews in the same category as religious dissenters, while even some Nazi chiefs refused to break off ties to Jewish businesses. To remedy the situation, crash courses on "Jewry" deepened SS men's appreciation of the challenge they faced. Das Schwarze Korps gradually narrowed its "enemy" profile from its multifaceted "superficial" manifestations of evil to its submerged Jewish roots.[77] In scholarly language, articles communicated skewed demographic information about the relative density of the Jewish population in Europe, examined Jews' criminal tendencies, and warned about "malicious" enemies of Nazism.[78] The number of articles on "the Jewish Question" barely increased in the late 1930s, but the tone and the harshness of their proposed solutions intensified. By conjuring up an image of the Jewish enemy as both morally debauched and deviously intelligent instructors presented racial persecution as rational self-defense, not emotional prejudice.[79]

In national training programs and local workshops on "the Jewish menace," SS personnel were presented with detailed accounts of Jewish activity.[80] Although the actual number of Jews in Germany declined steadily and most Jewish businesses had been driven into bankruptcy by the

Preis 15 Pf.

Berlin, 10. Februar 1938
6. Folge · 4. Jahrgang

Das Schwarze Korps

ZEITUNG DER SCHUTZSTAFFELN DER NSDAP
Organ der Reichsführung SS

Wohin mit den Juden?

Man will gar nicht!

Aufn.: Dr. Weskamp.

Der 4. Februar 1938 ist zu einem Markstein in der Geschichte des neuen Deutschlands geworden. Mit der direkten Übernahme des Oberbefehls über die Wehrmacht und der nationalwirtschaftlichen Zentralisierung die Organisation vereinfacht und damit die Schlagkraft erhöht. Über allem aber steht die Persönlichkeit Adolf Hitlers als die Verkörperung der Einheit und Macht eines 70-Millionen-Volkes.

Schnell angepaßt

late 1930s, the government's insistence on cultural separatism provided quotations from Jewish publications and meetings that lent credibility to charges that "the Jew" remained as haughty as ever. Even a modest assertion of Jewish dignity could be twisted to mean "obnoxious." SS spies attended international Jewish congresses to gather evidence of a global conspiracy. No matter how minor an infraction committed by a Jew (for example, a lottery swindle in Hamburg and a vintner in Vienna who mislabeled his wines), it made headlines.[81]

Articles in *Das Schwarze Korps* proposed various "rational" alternatives to the pogrom-style attack, which was bad for public relations.[82] The Nazi Party Program would not be achieved by "smashing windows and scribbling graffiti on walls" but by draining the resources that enable "these parasites" to live in Germany. By their discipline, the article admonished, SS men must set an example for "the little guy" and the ordinary housewife.[83] "The goal of Jewish policy must be the continued *[restlose]* emigration of Jews."[84] While rapacious Nazi officials plundered Jewish-owned property, contributors to *Das Schwarze Korps* thrashed out the pragmatic dilemmas connected to removing Jews and their influence from Germany. Would, for example, other nations accept Germany's "racial discards"? Could a Zionist homeland be created in Palestine, Syria, Ethiopia, Angola, Madagascar, or Bidschen in the USSR? Introducing readers to mass murder as a feasible (although admittedly barbaric) option, *Das Schwarze Korps* (like *Der Stürmer*) printed photos of Soviet soldiers rejoicing on terrain strewn with the corpses of their victims.[85] By implication, Nazi methods were more "civilized" than those of the "uncivilized" Soviet Jews.[86] *Schwarze Korps* authors recommended "polite" but unambiguous signs which stated "Jews not desired here! *[Juden unerwünscht!]*." But behind the pretense of courtesy, a harsh message was clear. If the owners of public establishments suspected a patron of having Jewish blood, they should notify the police at once.[87] Shrewd detective work, not spontaneous pogroms, would "unmask" Germans with Jewish ancestors. While random violence provoked hostility among bystanders and alerted the enemy to danger, a stealth approach caught him off guard. As an SS Jewish

56. "Whither the Jews?" This February 1938 article makes it clear that, one way or another, Jews would be expelled from the German *Volk*. Although Hitler himself at this time avoided public pronouncements about "the Jewish Question," the linkage of his image and antisemitic quotations from *Mein Kampf* implicitly authorized solutions that were both vague and extreme.

expert put it, "One does not hunt rats with a revolver, but with poison and gas."[88]

Between 1933 and 1938, the combination of SA vigilantes and SS racial detectives appeared to function effectively. About 40 percent of the 562,000 citizens defined as Jewish left Germany. In 1938 over half of the 183,000 Jews living in Austria emigrated. Heydrich, however, found emigration too slow, which indicated to him that Jews' "means of making a living had not been sufficiently reduced."[89] Although young men were often among the first to leave Germany, their older relatives were less inclined or able to emigrate. When persecution in small towns escalated, many sought refuge within larger Jewish communities in cities. In the pages of *Das Schwarze Korps* contributors pondered their alternatives. They acknowledged that Nazi rules made emigration financially impossible and worried that impoverished Jews would be a drain on Aryan society. Perhaps the few who remained would be useful hostages; after all, "the Ghetto, in this case the spiritual ghetto, has been the Jewish way of life for 800 years."[90] During the escalation of persecution, SS training materials and *Das Schwarze Korps* familiarized readers with abstract discussions of the goals and methods of racial policy.

In the mix of educational materials assigned to SS recruits, "Jewry" occupied a minor place; much of the material resembled the indoctrination manuals for the regular army at the time.[91] Some historians have seen this lack as evidence that racial indoctrination played a minimal role in SS activities.[92] Precisely because racism was understated, however, it slipped easily into recruits' general philosophy of life *(Weltanschauung)*. "Enemy studies" prepared recruits to perceive even impoverished Jews as a danger to the *Volk*. Because citizens defined as Jewish seemed so harmless and were so vulnerable, their attackers had to be persuaded to perceive them as loathsome as well as lethal; otherwise, attacks against Jews might be seen as bullying of the weak by the strong, which SS men found so objectionable in the rival Stormtroopers. Himmler warned SS men against Christianity, which preached the cardinal sins of "neighborly love, humility, and pity."[93] Instead, he celebrated "hardness and self-discipline."

The showdown between the SS and the SA came in the aftermath of two violent episodes in 1938, the *Anschluß* and the November pogrom. Criticism came not only from the foreign press but from within the Nazi camp. A vocal minority of Austrians expressed its disapproval; one group of Austrian military officers, for example, wrote to the district leader in Vienna, "As enthusiastic National Socialists, the ideals of the party shine through us . . . It is certainly not our intent to defend Jews . . . But graffiti damages our lovely city . . . arbitrary attacks offend our honor as officers . . . We Viennese have always . . . supported orderly regulation and not vigilante justice."[94]

Sopade reporters had commented that people seemed to accept Nazi race laws, but the violence of 1938 disgusted them. Even people who believed Jews deserved harsh treatment did not sanction the senseless destruction of property.[95] Hermann Goering complained, "I have had enough of these demonstrations!" and lambasted the "Chauffeurs and Gauleiters [who] amassed fortunes worth millions overnight." The head of the SS Security Service, Otto Ohlendorf expressed "deep outrage" because lawlessness was unworthy of Nazism, particularly in cases of "racial shame," by which he meant Nazis who raped Jewish women.[96] Because Himmler and Heydrich had not attended the annual November 9 Beer Hall memorial ritual, the SS was not implicated in the fiasco, although individual SS men participated.[97] The editors of *Der Stürmer* and *Das Schwarze Korps* set about controlling the damage in public opinion.

Instead of a loathsome Fips caricature on the cover of *Der Stürmer,* the first issue after the November 9–10 pogrom featured a sober photograph of Deeg's antisemitic book *Court Jews.* Readers were told to study the book so they would understand "how . . . this alien parasite *Volk* gain[ed] such a foothold in Germany." The editors flatly denied reports of violence. "No rational person" would believe such horror stories spread by the foreign, Jewish-controlled media.[98]

Over the next months, however, the magazine justified selective violence, such as the burning of synagogues as centers of conspiracy and the castration of Jewish men who had intercourse with non-Jewish women. Germans who refused to break off ties with Jews were denigrated as dupes and stooges. Hiemer, a *Stürmer* stalwart, was horrified that "there are some women and men who suddenly have been seized with an incomprehensible pity for the criminal Jewish *Volk*." To dissuade them, he did not defend violence directly but argued that one day Germans would understand its necessity. He listed earlier turning points after which Hitler's critics had been proven wrong. Starting with people who once had doubted that an uneducated person like Hitler could lead the nation, he continued through the sterilization program, rearmament, and the bloodless annexation of Austria and the Sudetenland. Ultimately, these timid souls would come to appreciate how "decent" *(anständig)* the Nazis' solution to the Jewish question actually was. With 700,000 and possibly many more Jews living in the Reich (which now included Germany, Austria, and annexed portions of Czechoslovakia), the author prepared readers for "an uncompromising, tough, and relentless" battle.

As they attempted to repair the public image of Nazi racial policy in the wake of the pogrom, the editors of *Das Schwarze Korps* perfected public relations strategies that presaged the wartime press releases that accompanied escalations of violence against Jews living in the Reich. One strategy was denunciation of foreign critics' hypocrisy. Against accusations of German "barbarism," the editors in November 1938 mocked the French for their supposed unwillingness to admit more Jewish-German refugees. In a centerfold photomontage, Churchill and Roosevelt with "balloon quotes" condemning the pogrom were surrounded by images of crimes against civilians in their respective countries.[99]

Expulsion of Jews was a given. Only the pace remained to be decided. Although pogrom-style violence did not recur, a grim fate awaited Jews who remained in the Reich. Later the planners of genocide could tell themselves that Jews had had a chance to leave. In its first post-pogrom issue, *Das Schwarze Korps*'s cover headlines asked, "Well, Jews! What now?" Perhaps, the author speculated, it might have been kinder if, in 1933, Germany had once and for all *(auf Schritt und Tritt)* "totally" dealt with "the parasite *Volk*." In an oblique criticism of Stormtroopers' uncontrolled violence, the editors called on the state to apply "sword and fire" in an "orderly" fashion to achieve the "complete expulsion, relentless ostracism!"

On the second front in its vindication of race war, *Das Schwarze Korps* writers impugned anyone who felt sympathy with Jews' plight by deluging readers with the latest antisemitic research that substantiated the omnipotence of global Jewry. Photographers represented "the Jew" in ways calculated to incite revulsion. In slightly less coarse language than in *Der Stürmer, Das Schwarze Korps* authors intimidated anyone who worried about Jews. These weak-hearted Germans were mocked for their "childish humanitarian silliness." Members of the SS were hailed as "decent and upright men." In the first three issues after the pogrom, the editors ran full pages of mugshots of allegedly Jewish men who were identified by names and crime—for example, "Jew Erich Wolff, born on November 10, 1899 in [the village of] Delitzsch. Sentenced to three years for repeated theft."[100] In the second and third installments, the portraits were identified only by name and occupation, not crime, as in "Jew Samuel Jakobs. Cattle dealer from East Frisia." This so-called sample was meant to convey the impres-

57. "He who digs a pit for others may himself be the first to fall into it." After the November 9–10, 1938, pogrom, *Das Schwarze Korps* featured a centerfold with photographs of Roosevelt and Churchill facing one another. In the balloon, Roosevelt comments that he cannot imagine such brutality occurring in the civilized twentieth century. But photographs of lynchings and race riots in the United States discredit his condemnation as hypocritical.

sion that the roughly 30,000 Jewish men sent to concentration camps and the 90 who were murdered during the pogrom deserved their fate. Addressing "Philosemites and Friends of Jews," an SS reporter explained that the pogrom was appropriate to the nature and extent of the Jewish danger; he went on to ridicule critics as hypocrites and to demand that Jews be eliminated to cleanse "the arteries of German life" of "parasites." The time for "relentless separation" in living quarters and public life had arrived. Over the next few years, make no mistake, the author continued, Germany will have "totally solved" its Jewish problem. He concluded, "No [foreigner] can say that we're unwilling to advise others about constructive solutions to an international problem."[101] Ethical considerations shifted from ends to means, feeding hypocritical assertions of SS men's rectitude.

The November 1938 pogrom was, in effect, the opening battle in what Nazis called "race war" *(Rassenkrieg)*. Its staging replayed the sequence of events in early 1933 and the summer of 1935 and also presaged the sedulous and ultimately murderous strategy of the Final Solution. The veiled threat of another pogrom (which never recurred in the Reich) combined with the stern language of "rational" proposals to solve the Jewish question set the stage for wartime genocide, and the lessons and skillful damage control kept protests at a minimum. Although on the killing fields and in the concentration camps SS brutality came to resemble the SA tactics Heydrich and Himmler had warned against, the cerebral racism of the SS provided the mental armor for mass murderers.

Historians of Nazi genocide conventionally identify the so-called euthanasia program, which began in autumn of 1939, as a training ground for the core personnel who operated the extermination camps. Approximately 100 physicians and their assistants, together with guards, gained experience in medical killing centers; technicians experimented with the most efficient methods for assembly-line homicide; and media specialists developed public relations strategies for "managing" information about the killing operations. A clear line of development connected medical murder with industrial mass killing in the extermination camps. Similarly, the rival subcultures of the SA and the SS prepared a core of key personnel for face-to-face mass murder on the eastern front. Although many SA men were too old for active combat, thousands of them indoctrinated new recruits once the war got under way, and many served in Order Police units charged with exterminating civilians. When German troop strength expanded rapidly after the invasion of Poland in 1939, SS men took com-

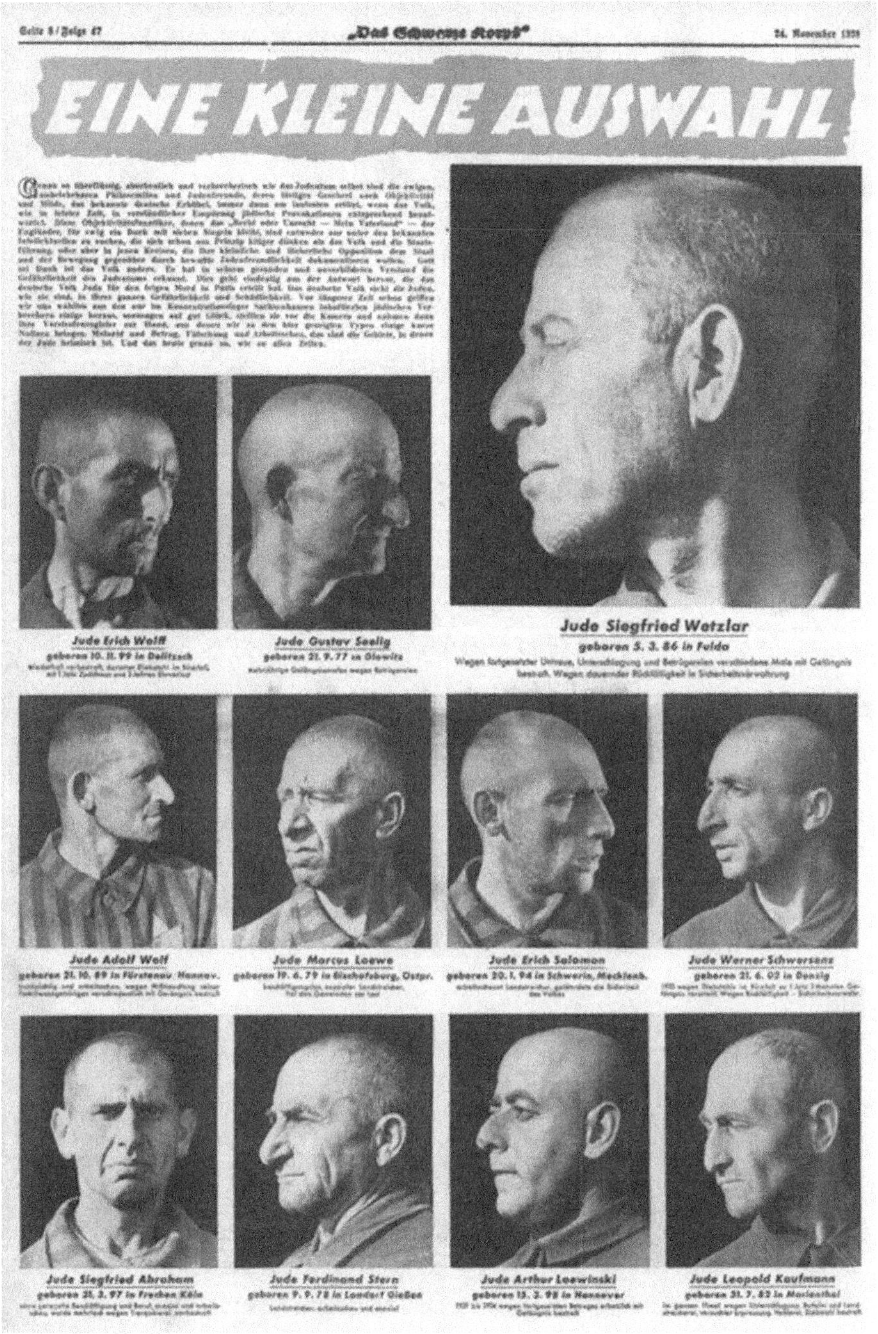

EINE KLEINE AUSWAHL

Genau so überflüssig, oberbenlich und verbrecherisch wie das Judentum erlost sind die ewigen undbelehrbaren Philosemiten und Judenfreunde, deren hötige Gereder noch Objektivität und Milde, den bekannte Beutsche Erbübel, immer dann am lastesten ertönt, wenn das Volk... (text continues, partially illegible)

Jude Siegfried Wetzlar
geboren 5. 3. 86 in Fulda
Wegen fortgesetzter Unzucht, Unterschlagung und Betrügereien verschiedene Male mit Gefängnis bestraft. Wegen dauernder Rückfälligkeit in Sicherheitsverwahrung

Jude Erich Wolff
geboren 10. 11. 99 in Delitzsch

Jude Gustav Seelig
geboren 21. 9. 77 in Olswitz

Jude Adolf Wolf
geboren 21. 10. 89 in Fürstenau Hannov.

Jude Marcus Loewe
geboren 19. 6. 79 in Bischofsburg, Ostpr.

Jude Erich Salomon
geboren 20. 1. 94 in Schwerin, Mecklenb.

Jude Werner Schwersenz
geboren 21. 6. 03 in Danzig

Jude Siegfried Abraham
geboren 21. 3. 97 in Frechen Köln

Jude Ferdinand Stern
geboren 9. 9. 78 in Landorf Gießen

Jude Arthur Loewinski
geboren 13. 3. 98 in Hannover

Jude Leopold Kaufmann
geboren 31. 7. 82 in Marienthal

58. "A Small Sample." In three issues after the November 9–10 pogrom, *Das Schwarze Korps* featured mugshots of purported Jewish criminals. The captions suggested that the men (identified by name, home address, and alleged crime, and marked by shaved heads) were typical of the 90 Jewish Germans who were murdered and the nearly 30,000 who were arrested and held without charge in protective custody during the pogrom.

mand over the new recruits.[102] As in the transition from medical killing to industrial extermination, well-trained and seasoned leaders integrated themselves into new and more powerful positions.

From the mid-1930s, men in these two rival cultures mentally absorbed the image of Jews (including women and children) as not only dangerous but also subhuman. From the pages of Der Stürmer and Das Schwarze Korps they assimilated an imagined world of racial contagion in which technocratic words like "extinction" and "annihilation" became routine.[103] Strengthened by an elitist sense of mission, each militia was equipped not only with rifles but with a conscience that kept to a minimum the psychic stress they might experience when murdering Jews—"undesirables" who had no place on the perpetrators' moral map. When they received their orders on the eastern front, SA and SS militiamen may have been surprised, but they were not unprepared.

Racial War at Home

Every German soldier who dies in this war must be put on the debit account of the Jews. They have him on their conscience and that is why Jews must be made to pay.

—*Joseph Goebbels, November 16, 1941*

On January 30, 1939, the sixth anniversary of his appointment as chancellor, Hitler was in a mood his admirers described as philosophical. Since dictating *Mein Kampf* in prison in 1924, he had divulged little in public about his intentions regarding the Jewish question. To be sure, the adjective "Jewish" had often spiked his verbal jabs, but as chancellor Hitler had avoided programmatic comments. Even at times when his audiences might have expected an antisemitic tirade, he had remained silent. In his eulogy for a Nazi official slain by a Jewish assassin in Switzerland in early 1936, for example, he did not so much as utter the word "Jewish." On the day after the pogrom of November 9–10, 1938, Hitler spoke for over two hours to journalists without mentioning the Jewish question.

Then, on January 30, 1939, Hitler vented his phobic racism as part of his self-congratulatory account of the new moral and geopolitical order he had created. He went out of his way to ridicule "German businessmen devoid of any conscience" who took pity on Jews. "Europe cannot find peace until the Jewish question has been solved." Sarcastically, he sneered at "how the whole democratic world is oozing with sympathy for the poor tormented Jewish People [and yet] remains hard-hearted when it comes to helping these supposedly most valuable members of the human race."[1] With Jews defeated in Germany, Hitler continued, the time had come to "wrestle the Jewish world enemy to the ground." Reminiscing about the days when critics had laughed at his racial views, he mused, "In the course of my life I have been a prophet many times, and this earned me mostly ridicule . . . During the time of my struggle for power it was primarily the Jewish *Volk* who mocked my prophecy that one day I would assume leadership of this . . . entire *Volk*." Hitler portentously added that Jews' "laughter back then may well become stuck in their throats today." Then came the threat: "Today I will be a prophet once again. If the international Jewish financial establishment in Europe and beyond succeeds in plunging the peoples of the world into yet another world war, then the result will not be a Bolshevization of the globe and thus a victory for Jewry, but the annihilation *[Vernichtung]* of the Jewish race in Europe."[2] This warning, so resounding in retrospect, occupied only a few minutes in a very long speech and was barely noticed at the time. Germans might have understood *vernichten* to be merely metaphorical—as in to "smash" or "wipe out" a rival.[3] Foreign reporters were preoccupied with the diplomatic implications of Hitler's speech.[4]

Hitler's January 30th speech can be seen as a virtual declaration of war on two fronts: against Jews and against foreign nations that obstructed German expansion. Indeed, Hitler consistently misdated his threat of extermination to September 1, 1939, to coincide with the date on which Germany invaded Poland. Hitler's speech is significant not only because he predicted that Jews would be annihilated in the event of war but also because he elucidated what he saw as the ethical justification of racial war. In his long-winded discourse about party history, foreign policy, economics, and the *Volk,* Hitler reaffirmed the morality of the four assumptions that underwrote the Nazi conscience.

First, he praised the organic unfolding of German destiny and reminisced about how he had rescued the *Volk* from racial disaster. Boasting about having unified ethnic Germans in Austria and Czechoslovakia into a mighty Reich, he praised his *Volk* "bound together not only by linkage of blood, but by a shared historical and cultural . . . heritage." As a veritable preacher, Hitler noted the second axiom of his ethnic moral code, which enshrined self-denial as its cardinal virtue. Castigating as immoral all "attitudes that cannot be justified in terms of their benefits for the ethnic community," he pointed to the advantages of collectivism. For emphasis, he repeated, "What is unimportant or detrimental to the existence of the *Volk* can never be seen as ethical."[5]

From these two themes a third followed. Condemning the Treaty of Versailles, he shouted, "The rest of the world has looted Germany" and insisted on Germans' right to strike back by claiming the *Lebensraum* they deserved. He returned at several points in his speech to the fourth axiom of the Nazi conscience which justified purifying the ethnic body politic. Among several "unwholesome attitudes" Hitler assailed "phony social morality"—which, by implication, meant a belief in the sanctity of human life. Denying universal morality (and by implication Christian teachings), he appealed to the authority of "the laws and necessities of life, as they reveal themselves to man through reason and knowledge." The subtext was clear: nature's laws allow a strong *Volk* to attack the weak with impunity. He repeated, "German culture is exclusively German; it is not Jewish." Before Nazi rule, liberal politicians' neglect of this truth, he shouted, had led the *Volk* to "squander a large part of its inherent strength on an inner struggle as fruitless as it was senseless." An ethnic ethos, which Hitler did not identify as specifically Nazi, provided the structure of Hitler's January 30th prophecy.

Throughout this landmark performance, Hitler cast himself as the embodiment of harsh, masculine virtue and shouted righteous invective against enemies whom he described as effeminate weaklings. Far from ignoring criticisms of the Nazi regime, Hitler held them up for ridicule as a moral blight, not as political opposition. When he castigated the Catholic Church, for example, he did not object to its doctrine or politics but to its toleration of "pederasty and child abuse." To a cheering Reichstag, he thundered against the perfidious English "apostles of war" and the "useless refuse of Nature," the "hysterical, mean-spirited press . . . Dwarfs . . . [and] the old incorrigible pessimists." In the process of vindicating German territorial expansion and the elimination of Jews, Hitler posed as the sole moral arbiter of his *Volk* at war on two fronts: racial and geopolitical.

Hitler's explicit threat to Jews confirmed what nearly all Jews in Greater Germany had known at least since the pogrom of November 9–10, 1938. "I repeat," wrote a member of the clandestine Sopade network, "The Jews in Germany are lost unless they can emigrate."[6] In February 1939 a horrified German bystander described "the inexorable extermination *[Ausrottung]*" and warned, "What happened to the Armenians in Turkey . . . is, more slowly and efficiently being done to the Jews."[7] Victor Klemperer noted in his diary, "NO HOPE . . . Everything continues with such deadening wretchedness."[8] Where objections occurred, they came from tiny minorities within the Marxist left, dissenting Christian congregations, and the liberal bourgeoisie.[9] But so powerful was the ethnic consensus that even people who privately agonized over Jews' plight barely found the courage to express condolences or perform small acts of kindness. Feeling utterly helpless in the face of a consensus that Jews somehow deserved their fate, Germans who objected could only urge their Jewish acquaintances to flee. When a friend tried to console Klemperer, he wrote, she "spoke to me as to a dying man."

After the November pogrom and Hitler's explicit warning, Germans and foreigners alike could have had no illusions about the danger Nazi rule posed to Jews. Expulsion of Jews from German-held territory was not a secret plot. Moral catastrophe did not take place only on the killing fields and concentration camps in the distant East. It began at home, in the Reich, during the so-called peace years. It was, to use the philosopher Alexandre Koyre's phrase, an "open conspiracy" to commit a vast crime in full view.[10] Rampant criminality against Jews occurred within a public culture that disabled empathy for outcasts. This process was spearheaded not by old-fighter Nazis' coarse hatred of Jews but by a deceptively mild and supposedly objective form of racism that ultimately proved to be far more lethal. Bureaucratically sanctioned persecution was presented as a protective measure against Jewry, depicted as an amorphous moral danger. Individual Jews' evident suffering, however unfortunate, was cast as collateral damage on the crusade for ethnic rebirth. Compared with Stormtroopers' rampages, white-collar persecution could even seem moderate.

During the years of diplomatic success and economic recovery, ethnic Germans lived in an atmosphere of heady collectivism. Hitler's decision in January 1939 to speak openly of Jews and even to predict their extermination in the event of war suggested that he believed public opinion had been sufficiently prepared to accept a harsh solution to the Jewish question. His assessment was well-founded. Nazi-sponsored surveillance teams and anti-fascist clandestine mood monitors alike reported that Germans welcomed full employment and cheered the dismantling of the hated Treaty of Versailles. People seemed enthralled by the pleasures that Nazi popular culture afforded them and appreciated the state-sponsored excursions that allowed millions to enjoy their first real vacations. Even Germans with modest incomes saved to buy the inexpensive *Volkswagen*. Of course, grumblers found fault with one or another corrupt Nazi boss and made jokes about the big shots. But the cult of the Führer remained unblemished. Even when Hitler's diplomatic bombshells seemed reckless and memories of the Great War stoked their fear of another bloodletting, morale monitors registered unflagging support for Hitler. In September 1938, for example, when Hitler had demanded the annexation of the German-speaking region of Czechoslovakia, the Sudetenland, war seemed inevitable. Although the "hurrah patriotism" of 1914 was absent, Germans waited "in honorable readiness to follow their Führer's commands to the utmost."[11] When the Big Four European powers capitulated and signed the Munich Pact a few days later, Hitler acquired the affectionate nickname "General Bloodless."

On the celebration of his fiftieth birthday, April 20, 1939, the nation turned into "a veritable sea of flags." An observer in central Germany described the scene: "Hardly a store window could be seen without a picture of the Führer with victorious symbols of the new Reich."[12] Millions participated vicariously via radio broadcasts and newsreels. Heinrich Hoffmann produced a commemorative album, *A Volk Honors Its Führer,* which allowed readers to glimpse their chief being greeted by foreign dignitaries as well as some of the well-trained troops and modern tanks that marched in a five-hour parade.[13] When Hitler signed the Nazi-Soviet Pact and German armies invaded Poland in the late summer of 1939, Germans again registered anxiety, but a swift victory restored their faith. After Hitler survived an assassination attempt on November 9, 1939, at the annual Beer Hall Putsch commemoration, the media attributed his narrow escape to divine intervention. School children sang the Bach cantata, "Nun danket alle Gott" ("Now Thank We All Our God"), and adults blamed "Brit spies" and "International Jewry" for the attempt on Hitler's life. An SS Security Service report concluded, "Love for the Führer has become even stronger, and the attitude toward war becomes more positive."[14]

During the so-called phony war *[Sitzkrieg]* of 1939–40, when France and Britain were officially at war but took no action, Germans' lives went on as usual. Although three million men served in the military and 8,000 men were killed in the Polish offensive, morale remained high in the homeland. Thanks to a steady influx of foreign workers and POWs, manufacturing and agriculture operated at full capacity, and imported food from conquered lands guaranteed that shortages like those of World War I did not recur. With the swift conquest of Denmark, Norway, Holland, Belgium, and France in the late spring of 1940, "General Bloodless" once again earned his moniker. Goebbels exulted, "We experience the greatest historical miracle ever: a genius is building a new world."[15] So central was the Führer myth to the national euphoria that viewers felt cheated if a newsreel failed to include footage of Hitler.[16] Even when the British Royal Air Force began to bomb Berlin in 1940 (which Nazi leaders had boasted was impossible), Goebbels's staff incited popular outrage against the English by maligning them as cowardly terrorists who murdered innocent women and children.

In the memories of many Germans, the "peace years" continued until June 1941, when German troops invaded the Soviet Union. But similar to the so-called grace period for Jews between mid-1933 and late 1935, the surface calm prepared public opinion and racial policymakers for an approaching storm. The first challenge facing racial persuaders was to provide credible evidence to explain why over 80 million citizens of an invincible Reich ought to believe that less than 1 percent of their countrymen who were Jewish should be deported. Half of all Jews living in the Reich had emigrated; half of those who remained behind in 1939 were over fifty years old, and only 20 percent had jobs. Such an imperiled group of people could not pose a genuine threat to a strong and confident *Volk*. But the dissemination of popularized antisemitic researchers' findings depicted Jews as the last vestiges of a racial plague or the disguised agents of global conspiracy.

As persecution escalated and Jewish Germans' last hopes of rescue faded, the antisemitic think tanks, university institutes, and the Office of Racial Policy supplied fresh evidence of the Jewish peril gleaned from confiscated documents and new research.[17] Even among the victors, one casualty of war is a lower standard of credibility because people eagerly accept almost any information that helps them to make sense of the conflagration that has disrupted their lives. Ordinary readers may well have accepted news media reports produced by the ongoing march of "Scholarship against World Jewry!"[18] Despite paper shortages, an immense outpouring of pamphlets, maps, and booklets deepened ethnic pride and racist panic. *Neues Volk*, the ORP periodical, expanded its coverage of topics designed to incite readers' fear or revulsion, or both. Its experts described the African and Jewish plot to debauch French culture and "The World Racial Struggle."[19] Antisemitic research institutes spawned new affiliates in occupied nations and looted Jewish libraries and archives for evidence of Jewish conspiracies against Aryans.[20] Typical of their findings were books such as *Jewish Self-Portraits,* a compilation of works by Jewish authors who had written critically about their heritage.[21] Other texts, like the sarcastic *The Poor Jews,* ridiculed anyone who sympathized with Jews.[22] Supposedly objective studies by Gerhard Kittel and his collaborator Eugen Fischer exposed the ancient roots of the Jewish peril.[23]

Well in advance of the first feasibility study for mass extermination (commissioned in July 1941), a continuous flow of fraudulent research on the Jewish question shaped the moral context within which desk murderers and field commanders went about their work. These ponderous disquisitions typically had two sections, a long and meticulously footnoted account of Jewish misdeeds throughout history and a brief concluding section that outlined a solution. Having demonstrated, for example, in *The Freedom Fighter,* that Jews had precipitated the Great War in 1914 and the invasion of Poland in 1939, Johann von Leers concluded, "If the Jews had not been granted citizenship but had been left in the ghetto, they would have been unable to hatch the revolt." *Ergo* Jews ought to be re-ghettoized. The Austrian historian Franz Schattenfroh devoted over 400 pages to the history of Jewish aggression before hinting at elimination as a "final" solution.[24] Treatises like these were not likely to have attracted a broad readership, but they were available to the well-educated SS functionaries who drove extermination operations forward as well as to the thousands of ethnocrats responsible for the logistics of persecution, deportation, and murder.[25]

In order to function efficiently, perpetrators needed to maintain a moral self in the face of staggering crime. Scholarly racism facilitated this process in several ways. First, through sober, objective prose, the experts' monographs and articles converted individual Jews into "Jewry," an abstract category into which almost any manner of evil would fit. Second, by projecting their own intentions on to their victims, the perpetrators disavowed their personal responsibility. Seen against an imagined lethal menace, deportation and mass murder became pre-emptive self-defense. The tedious deliberations about which methods of solving the Jewish problem were worthy of an honorable *Volk* placed the honor of the perpetrators, not the suffering of the victims, at the center of the murderous moral calculus. Finally, the endorsement of a manly, unsentimental attitude (and ridicule of emotional, pogrom-style antisemitism) steeled perpetrators against pity.

As they left for the Polish front, soldiers, order policemen, and SS men carried reminders of their ethnic superiority in their packs. Small-format illustrated histories of Germanic art, quotations from *Mein Kampf,* and photographic essays about Nazi Party history and the life of the Führer sanctioned the world historical struggle in which they were engaged. Foreign-language phrase books suggested how to treat "inferior" peoples. In *You and Your Volk*—a nostalgic booklet illustrated with a woodblock print of a peasant family—Walter Gross admonished soldiers to think racially. A pocket guidebook to Warsaw included information about the topography of the city, with a section on the ghetto and a concise history of a centuries-old "infection" by "alien blood."

The relatively small place of antisemitism in the attitude-training these troops underwent does not suggest it was insignificant. On the contrary, as Raul Hilberg explained to the filmmaker Claude Lanzmann in *Shoah,* the most lethal orders were often sent as ordinary memos. If, for example, deportation orders had been marked by red top-secret stamps, they would have attracted attention and provoked debate.[26] Their routine appearance ensured that they would be routinely obeyed. Antisemitism in soldier training was most powerful when it was most insidious—when small doses of poisonous racism were injected into benign information about foreign policy, news from the Reich, the SS honor code, and instructions on selecting racially healthy partners. In letters written by Wehrmacht soldiers as well as SS men, passionate hatred of Jews appears as only one aspect of routine accounts of daily life.[27] Leadership training instructed SS officers to insert racial considerations into all discussions with their men. Racial studies, along with entertainment, culture appreciation, geopolitics, and history, all contributed to what SS trainers called "the maintenance of [soldiers'] spiritual resistance *[Widerstandskraft]*."[28]

Of course, some instructional material, such as the booklet *The Jew on the Eastern Border,* printed for the Seventh Army, focused on Jews.[29] Pamphlets written in a learned style bore titles like *Israel's Ritual Murder of Nations; Are the Roosevelts Jewish?;* and simply *The Jews*.[30] Before they arrived at the front, SS men probably took for granted the "fact" that Jews had turned the United States into their puppet.[31] Later, when the commander of the notorious Order Police Battalion 101 explained to his men that the helpless Jewish civilians they were about to murder were responsible for the terrorist air raids over German cities, he was only reinforcing the common knowledge already implanted by propaganda.[32]

Training material treated the Jewish question as one of many challenges facing German occupation forces. The Office of Racial Politics edited booklets for soldiers entitled *Policy toward Ethnic Aliens,* which conveyed a casual but unmistakably racist message.[33] *Jewish Ghettos . . . between the Baltic and the Black Seas* described the habitat of a *Volk* on the edge of extinction.[34] *That's How They Really Are* and *Jews in France* introduced readers to the allegedly degenerate Jewish culture that had caused the decline of the West.[35] The ethnographer Max Hildebert Boehm wrote a lavishly illustrated book for general audiences, *The Liberated East*.[36] Himmler commissioned a photographic study of *The Subhuman* which featured photographs of ideal racial types and documented the ravages of barbarian races from the days of Attila and Genghis Kahn to massacres in the Jewish-dominated Soviet Union.[37] In this outpouring of print, visual, and aural culture, one message rang out: Jews would soon vanish, and a superior *Volk* would rule the new Europe.

Despite high morale during the early war years, most Germans sensed that the New Order had a dark side. State policies endangered not only

Das ist der Spiegel der sowjetischen „Staatsjugend"! Das sind die Folgen der vom Juden systematisch zertrümmerten Familie! — Dieses Meer geweinter Kindertränen vermögen auch Jahrhunderte nicht auszutrocknen.

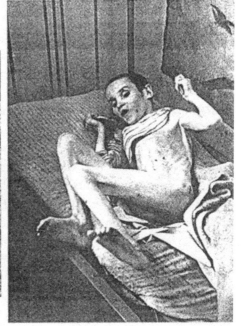

ist die kollektivierte kleine Elendskreatur, die der Jude ohne Bedenken propagierte.

...ses entsetzliche, schmutzstarrende Unglückswesen mit den Totenaugen ist ein sowjetisches Kind, ...

Diese Zehnjährigen im Grauen der sowjetischen Hölle sind wohl die furchtbarste Anklage gegen diesen Fluch der Menschheit.

59. "Here is the hidden side of the Soviet 'bolshevized youth.' Look at the results of the Jews' systematic ruination of the family—a sea of children's tears will take centuries to dry." By implication, *The Subhuman*, a photograph book commissioned by Himmler, justified SS men's barbaric crimes as both retaliatory and preventive.

people in defeated nations but fellow citizens living in the Reich (which included annexed territories as well as Germany and Austria). Rumors circulated about the "euthanasia" of Germans who were diagnosed as incurably ill, severely disabled, or asocial. Gypsies and people labeled as work-shy or sexually deviant were sent to forced labor camps. In 1939 soldiers returned from Poland with the disquieting news that Jewish-German residents of annexed Polish territory (including decorated soldiers from World War I) had been deported to a ghetto in Lodz and many had died or been killed in transit. On the home front, people saw conscripted Jews performing menial tasks such as removing trash, cleaning public toilets, and shoveling snow. Jews in the Reich were reduced to penury because they had to transfer their savings to central exchange banks from which they could withdraw only a pittance.[38] During the winter of 1939–40, Viennese police evicted 60,000 Jews from their homes, sent them to occupied Poland, and transferred their apartments to non-Jewish owners. Shortly after the fall of France, 6,500 German Jews from the Rhineland and 22,000 Alsatian Jews were deported to camps in the south of France. In Berlin, Jews were evicted and sent to "Jew houses" to make way for people displaced by bombing raids and to clear land for Hitler's building projects.

Although opinion surveillance reported widespread apathy about Jews' suffering and even cases of self-pity, a few Germans objected. Employees of *Das Schwarze Korps* and the Nazi publishing company, for example, found it distasteful that they had to witness Jews being tortured in the deportation center next to their building.[39] But others intervened on principle. Some Wehrmacht officers in 1939 objected to massacres of civilians in Poland as both counterproductive and unworthy of Germans.[40] In November 1940 Catholic prelates appealed to Justice Minister Gürtner, a devout Catholic, to halt medical killing. A month later, during an official tour of Nazi-occupied Poland, Hans Frank, governor of the district, noted Gürtner's deep distress, presumably at the treatment of Jews and Poles. Immediately upon Gürtner's return to Berlin, he was hospitalized and died of an undiagnosed illness, amid rumors that he had been poisoned.[41]

Gürtner's fate was unusual. Dissenting ethnocrats and personnel in medical killing centers, like soldiers at the front, found ways to ease their way out of difficult situations. When an associate told Bernard Lösener, the racial expert in the Interior Ministry, about witnessing a gruesome massacre of Jews from Germany, Lösener applied for and eventually received a transfer to another department.[42] Although later he was expelled from the party and arrested, it was because of his alleged participation at

60. A Scene from the Lublin Ghetto, as sketched by a German soldier. Like the hundreds of snapshot albums compiled by soldiers on the Eastern Front and the color slides taken by an accountant in the Lodz ghetto that are featured in the film *The Photographer*, this soldier's drawing suggests his dissociation from the suffering of the subjects he depicted.

the fringes of the July 1944 plot to assassinate Hitler, not because of his dissent on racial questions.

In Nazi Germany, unlike other totalitarian regimes, individuals could dissent from one or another measure, usually without devastating consequences. Ludwig Ferdinand Clauss, for example, an inveterate racial researcher and Nazi Party member, falsified racial identity papers to protect his Jewish co-worker, and Gerhard Kittel sheltered a half-Jewish student from deportation. The existence of a doubter here or a rescuer there did not retard the inexorable process of expulsion and extermination. By treating individual objections as private matters and not as moral protests, Nazi administrators minimized their political fallout.[43]

In occupied Eastern Europe, the corpses of people charged with aiding Jews were hung in public as examples of what happened to traitors. At home in the Reich, that did not happen. Citizens suspected of aiding Jews or malingering could be arrested, but unless they were judged politically dangerous they were not usually sent to concentration camps. News of punishment was spread by rumor but was not publicized in the media. Some Germans took the risk of offering shelter to fellow citizens. In Berlin, between 5,000 and 7,000 Jews (dubbed "Submarines") trusted friends and neighbors to hide them; and despite denunciations and searches, 1,400 of them survived. After the war, over 500 rescuers who lived in Germany, Austria, and the Czech Republic have been honored as righteous gentiles by the Israeli government.[44] Even in his despair, Klemperer noted non-Jews' kindness to him and acknowledged their courage, particularly that of his wife, Eva, and the friend who concealed his diaries. In 1944, when Klemperer was forced to work in a factory, the friendly atmosphere there surprised him. "Again and again, I observe the comradely, easygoing, often really warm behavior of the male and female workers toward the Jews." Even the fear of denunciation did not stop them from "fooling around, yelling, and cheerfully touching."[45]

Some citizens found ways to smuggle food to Jewish neighbors before they were deported, and a few sent food parcels to friends and relatives in the Theresienstadt concentration camp. A Jewish woman in hiding, Ilse Behrend-Rosenfeld, described kindly Herr R., who protected her from the Gestapo as if it were the simplest decision in the world. As the tears welled up in her eyes, he said in thick dialect, "Well, now the first thing you'd better do is stop calling me Herr R and get used to Uncle Karl. You will be my little Maria."[46] The everyday decency of a few magnifies the complicity of the many.

Walter Gross's wartime career was a paradigm of the process that prepared ethnocrats to collaborate with increasingly radical measures. In the ORP newsletter, Gross urged his staff to accelerate secret sterilization (perhaps as a covert reference to medical killing) and "not to become soft" on racial issues.[47] While military strategists early in 1941 planned the invasion of the Soviet Union, Gross contributed his expert opinion to deliberations about the problem that would be created by the addition of millions of Jews to German-controlled territory. Although concrete plans for genocide were formulated later that year, Gross and his colleagues helped to shape the conceptual milieu within which midlevel party functionaries and state employees adjusted their consciences to racial war. They did not, as it is so often assumed, suspend their moral beliefs when they put on their figurative uniforms.[48] Expert opinion vindicated the elimination of Jews as a moral act. For example, Gross's lecture, "Thoughts about a Solution to the Jewish Question," delivered in March 1941 at a conference organized by Alfred Rosenberg's antisemitic think tank, was distributed in three formats: as a brief article in *Neues Volk,* as a mimeographed memorandum circulated to religious and social welfare agencies, and (one year later) as a 32-page booklet.

As was his wont, in his lecture on the Jewish question Gross dredged up putative evidence about the moral depravity of the Jews and cautioned readers against assuming that "harsh treatment had weakened their position." He cast aggression against Jews as "self-defense against a discordant, near-eastern, oriental, Mediterranean Jew *Volk*" and argued for defining as Jewish anyone with two Jewish grandparents (a revision of his milder view in 1935 which required three Jewish grandparents). Thanks to Germans' stunning military successes, Gross said, he could conceive of a Europe-wide extirpation of the Jews that would have been unthinkable only a few years before. Appropriating a metaphor from Kittel's 1933 tirade against Jews, Gross pledged his high-minded dedication to a task that would "bind up a dangerous historical wound" in the ethnic body politic.[49] As a young physician, Gross had seen Jews as a biological threat, but ten years later he admitted that racial science had not produced a coherent body of knowledge and vaguely blamed Jews' "spiritual powers and tendencies."[50] Gross worked unobtrusively to weed out less-than-resolute colleagues. For example, he led the prosecution of party member and racial expert Ludwig Ferdinand Clauss for protecting his Jewish co-worker. "The party cannot conduct a pitiless struggle to exterminate the Jewish contagion if it tolerates this kind of behavior within its own ranks."[51] Although the Jewish woman he sheltered was deported, Clauss's only punishment was expulsion from the SS. Every issue of Gross's newsletter for ORP officials was filled with disinformation that cast the elimination of Jews as a desirable goal. In early 1944, Gross prepared a lecture on "Jewry, the Master of the World Press," for Rosenberg's international conference on the Jewish danger to be held in July in Cracow. Advancing Soviet troops forced its cancellation.

Despite Gross's tireless activity on behalf of racial indoctrination, during the war Joseph Goebbels upstaged him. In the prewar years, Goebbels had concentrated on entertainment, culture, and news, while steering clear of race-related topics. In the late 1930s, his office approved two antisemitic comedies, *Robert and Bertram* and *Irish Linen,* and a rather mediocre antisemitic saga, *The Rothschilds.* With the onset of war and medical killing, Goebbels commissioned a film that defended euthanasia. Then in 1940 he supported the immensely popular historical drama *Jew Süss,* which was seen by 20 million people. Its antisemitic impact was so powerful that Berliners left the theater chanting, "Drive the Jews from the Kurfürstendamn [the major shopping street in Berlin]! Out with the last Jews in Germany!"[52] To popularize antisemitism in occupied Europe as well as at home, *The Eternal Jew* was released with immense fanfare. This lurid documentary horrified audiences with its scenes of cattle being killed in a kosher slaughterhouse, photos of "typical work-shy Jews" who were actually prisoners in ghettos in Poland, and historical maps comparing "the wandering Jew" to rat infestations. The film's climax was a clip of Hitler's January 30, 1939, prophecy. Viewers could hardly escape the message that (as one morale report put it) "the Jew, despite all of his superficial adaptation to states, languages, and regions, still remains a Jew."[53]

As Goebbels understood, wartime audiences wanted diversion more than propaganda. One of his greatest successes was the radio show *Wünschkonzert,* devoted to popular music requested by listeners. Perhaps to offer more sophisticated readers a similar escape from wartime cares, in May 1940 Goebbels launched a new periodical, *Das Reich,* whose erudite tone contrasted with the vile racism of Nazi Party hacks.[54] Among the contributors to *Das Reich* were Carl Schmitt, Theodor Heuss (who became the first president of West Germany), and Rudolf Augstein (who after 1945 edited the prestigious newsweekly *Der Spiegel*). By 1941 the readership of *Das Reich* grew to 1.5 million—almost equal to the circulation of the Nazi daily *Der Völkische Beobachter.*[55] On every Friday evening and Sunday morning until the final month of the war, lead articles from *Das Reich* were broadcast to troops at the front and Germans at home.

By all accounts, contemporaries concurred that "the popularity of Dr. G. was very high."[56] Reviews of theater, films, and literature, occasional columns by Goebbels, news of sporting events, reports on domestic politics in Britain and the United States as well as in Axis countries, art appreciation, and light cartoons filled its pages. Reproductions of great art, dramatic military photographs, and graphics enlivened its fare. As Goebbels put it, *Das Reich* cultivated a respectable image because "the more radical the opinions voiced, the more distinguished and unprovocative it needs to look."[57] Perhaps Goebbels's sense that readers wanted diversion explains why, for over a year, *Das Reich* avoided coverage of his extreme opinions on the Jewish question. During this time, Hitler himself barely mentioned Jews in public and resisted pressure to impose harsh anti-Jewish laws within the Reich even as troops in occupied territories were massacring not only Jews but members of the Polish elite and suspected Communists.

Then in August 1941, as German generals rejoiced at their victory over Soviet forces, Hitler made two decisions about racial policy. He ordered the official end of medical killing in Germany, and he assented to pressure from Goebbels and other zealots that Jews be required to wear a badge in public that would stigmatize them.[58] Even after Hitler's go-ahead, Goebbels wrote, "I am persistently driving the Jewish question forward, but admittedly major resistance in almost every quarter is evident . . . The Jews must not remain as guests of our *Volk* . . . at a time when the German *Volk* is fighting for its future."[59] To prepare public opinion, on September 7, 1941, Goebbels made Hitler's 1939 prophecy that Jewry would be exterminated the "Slogan of the Week." Immense placards with Hitler's words were posted throughout Berlin, in effect investing Hitler's political capital in the war against the Jews. A week later, all Jews over the age of six had to wear a yellow cloth badge with a Star of David and the word "Jew" written in mock Hebrew letters. Failure to do so meant immediate deportation.

In the next few months, Goebbels demonstrated his skill as a hate-monger. In "The Jews Are Guilty!" a front-page article in *Das Reich,* Goebbels reiterated Hitler's prophecy and demanded that Germans show no mercy in "smashing down this colossal filth." Then, in the detached tone of antisemitic research, he asserted that the elimination of Jews conformed to "an elementary law of national and social hygiene," and he mocked anyone "who feels a stir of pity at the sight of an old woman wearing the Yellow Star." Not passion, he wrote, but a sense of duty must guide Germans in their difficult task. "We discuss this without any feelings of resentment . . . There is no room here for sentimental considerations."[60] Perhaps sensing that delay might enable Jews to go into hiding, he added, "The stab will be administered without mercy and without pity."

For Berliners, Goebbels's staff published a four-page leaflet, printed in

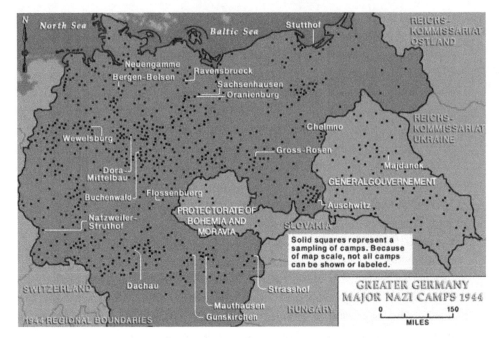

61. As this map of concentration camps in the Reich shows, crimes did not occur only "somewhere in the East," as many Germans claimed after the war, but also at home. Camps within the Reich, such as Buchenwald, Sachsenhausen, Gross-Rosen, Ravensbrück, Neuengamme, Dora-Mittelbau, Dachau, and Stutthof, became the administrative centers of huge networks of subsidiary forced-labor camps in nearby areas.

color on heavy paper stock. On the cover, white headlines against a black field warned, "When you *[Du]* see this badge . . . " and at this point the regulation cloth badge was affixed to the page. The text inside continued, "Then think about this. About what the Jews have done to our *Volk*." Jews had fomented revolution in 1918, deprived seven million Germans of a livelihood in the Depression, poisoned the *Volk*, and debauched morality. Every conceivable crime that antisemitic research had invented during the previous six years took on a new life as part of the litany of dangers attributed to Jewry. The text continued, "Everything that we have done against world Jewry is nothing compared to the future Jews have in store for us." At the bottom of the page, after "Now, for the first time, the Jews' intention is proclaimed out loud," the boldface text breaks off and another yellow cloth badge obliterates the message underneath. Where the text would have read that Jews said "Germans must die," the badge pasted over the words changed the text to read, "The Jew" (symbolized by the

yellow patch) "Must Die." To the right of the cloth badge, the text continued, "Thousands of decent and respectable . . . [elipse in the original] and
children shall be exterminated."

For decades after the war, Germans insisted that, although they may
have sensed terrible things were happening "in the East," they had no
knowledge about the fate of Jews or any other persecuted group. From the
immediate postwar years, however, such professions of ignorance have
not withstood scrutiny.[61] As early as the autumn of 1942, the *Times* of
London published a letter from a German Jew who reported, "The intention of extermination has been professed often enough."[62] Klemperer
heard the drumbeat early; so did other Germans. "Only the Jew is to
blame; we must *exterminate* him in Europe."[63]

In the first study of the concentration camps, published in 1947, Eugen
Kogon, a Viennese journalist who survived five years in Buchenwald,
quoted a credible witness. "The methodicalness of the killing must certainly have become visible even to the totally blind . . . There is no doubt
whatsoever that there was not a single person in Germany who did not
know that the Jews were being harmed, and had been for years."[64] Starting
late in 1942, the BBC broadcast explicit reports of mass murder.[65] In bomb
shelters, Germans' awareness of their culpability emerged in anxieties
that bombardments were reprisals and in fears that invading Soviet troops
would wreak savage vengeance. Knowledge about genocide was available
to anyone who cared to find it.

Anyone who had heard Hitler Youth chanting "When Jewish blood
spurts from the knife" knew Jews were in peril. Witnesses to the public
torment of Jews in Austria after the *Anschluß* or the destruction of the November 9–10, 1938, pogrom could not have doubted Jews' helplessness or
Nazis' ruthlessness. Even without Hitler's explicit prediction of January
30, 1939, no bystander could deny the intention of the Nazi leadership to
eradicate Jews, one way or another. During the war, whether or not they
grasped the full horror of the catastrophic atrocities that occurred "in the
East," Germans observed Jews' anguish firsthand. They may have passed
one of the 38 camps established in 1941 for Jewish forced laborers.[66] In
small towns and cities, coincidence brought people into contact with reality. "I happened to pass a square into which Jews had been herded together . . . I will never forget the shock . . . There were respected businessmen, workers, physicians, aged invalids awaiting deportation."[67] A
Berliner noticed heavily loaded panel trucks in the streets and one day
chanced to see that the back cover of one had not been totally lowered.

DANN DENKE DARAN

was der Jude unserem Volke angetan hat

als er als Urheber und Anführer der Revolte im Jahre 1918 den Zusammenbruch des deutschen Volkes verschuldete,

als er dann die maßgeblichen Positionen in der Staatsführung innehatte und durch die Inflation das Vermögen des deutschen Volkes stahl,

als er durch seine Herrschaft über die deutsche Wirtschaft brutal und rücksichtslos mehr als sieben Millionen Deutsche zu Erwerbslosen machte, um dadurch über billige Arbeitskräfte zu verfügen und so seinen Profit ins Unermeßliche zu steigern,

als er fast die gesamte deutsche Presse in seinen Händen hatte,

als er das Theater, den Film, das gesamte Kulturleben beherrschte und dadurch das deutsche Volk seelisch vergiften und moralisch verderben wollte.

Wie einen bösen Traum

haben viele Volksgenossen diese Erinnerungen an die Zeit der größten Not und tiefsten Erniedrigung des deutschen Volkes beiseite geschoben.

Alles das jedoch, was wir als Folge der Judenherrschaft in Deutschland erlebten, ja alles, was wir bisher von den Plänen des Weltjudentums gehört oder erfahren haben, ist nichts gegen die grauenvolle Zukunft, die Juda dem deutschen Volke tatsächlich bereiten will.

Jetzt wurde ... um ersten Male offen ausgesprochen, was das Weltju... wünscht:

"...uß sterben"

...stehende, fleißige und anständige ... und Kinder sollen ausgerottet werden. ...ie der amerikanische Jude, Theodore ...t der Amerikanischen Friedensver- ...Weltjudentums in seinem Buch „Ger- ...bt.

62. "When you see this badge," read the cover of this pamphlet, "Then Pause to Consider" a detailed list of alleged atrocities perpetrated by Jews against Aryans that had become commonplace in textbooks, exhibitions, and educational films. After these fraudulent accusations, the text read, "Now for the . . . first time it can be openly proclaimed what World Jewry [represented by the yellow cloth badge] intends. The Jew [again represented by the badge] must die!"

The sight of "pretty shoes next to worn shoes, feet wrapped in rags," filled her with horror.[68] Labor camps for POWs and foreign laborers, some of whom were Jewish, dotted the German countryside. Residents of nearby villages and cities knew enough to turn away from their windows when they heard the sound of clogs on the pavement before daybreak and after dusk.

Many did more than turn away. Several thousand maurading men could carry out a national pogrom (as on November 9–10, 1938), but orderly expulsion required hundreds of thousands of compliant ordinary citizens. Over 675,000 Jewish citizens of the Reich had to be identified in municipal files. When they were required to add "Sarah" or "Israel" to their names for identification purposes, files had to be updated. Police routinely searched Jewish households for telephones, radios, cameras, and illegal written material. The non-Jews who "purchased" Jews' property for as little as 10 percent of its market value required banks to sanctify the legal fiction. Postal employees censored Jews' mail. In March 1941, when Jews were conscripted into forced labor, police checked attendance at worksites and dispatched the tardy to concentration camps. Bank clerks verified declarations of financial assets. In October 1941, when Jews' pensions, health insurance, and paid vacation were terminated, records required adjustment. When Jews were moved into "Jew houses" and work camps, residential records were updated. On the eve of deportation, electricity bills and mortgage payments were settled and ration cards cancelled; keys were turned in to superintendents and new "owners." Records were marked, "Address unknown, moved to the East." The saturation of public culture with racist arrogance for "us" and contempt for "them" framed this sequence not as the prelude to wholesale murder but as a continuation of the bureaucratic routines already in place.

Clerks at the Reich Railway scheduled special excursion trains (identified as "Da" for "David"). The SS paid third-class fares for travel in packed cattle trains at rates between 1.5 and 4 pfennigs per kilometer per person, with half fare for children under twelve. SS officers and railway functionaries haggled over round-trip or one-way rates, often settling on a 50 percent rebate for trains carrying more than 400 passengers.[69] Attention to detail preserved a mirage of bureaucratic order as Jewish citizens in the Reich were stripped of their dignity, their rights, their property, and ultimately their lives. Beginning in the late autumn of 1941, 260 trains, each one with over 1,000 Jews packed in boxcars, deported Jews from Germany. Similar transports "cleansed" Austria and other annexed regions of Jews. By late 1943, the Reich had become, in Nazi language, "Jew free."[70]

After the war, survivors and perpetrators, collaborators and bystanders, as well as their offspring, engaged in heated disagreements about how much ordinary Germans had known about the Final Solution. This is a dispute that challenges each generation to confront anew the potential for decent human beings to collaborate in evil. However, questions about precisely what Germans in the Reich knew about the extermination camps and killing fields in the east are irrelevant to these discussions. Millions chose to "decide that they knew enough to know it was better not to know" about these crimes.[71] But Germans living in the Reich knew beyond any doubt that their Jewish fellow citizens desperately needed material and psychological aid. How can we understand civilian compliance— bystanders' callous disregard as well as collaborators' zeal—in the humiliation, impoverishment, persecution, and expulsion of fellow citizens in their midst?

Germans' readiness to expel Jews from their universe of moral obligation evolved as a consequence of their acceptance of knowledge disseminated by institutions they respected. Like citizens in other modern societies, residents of the Reich believed the facts conveyed by experts, documentary films, popular science, educational materials, and exhibitions. What haunts us is not only the ease with which soldiers slaughtered helpless civilians in occupied territories but the specter of a state so popular that it could mobilize individual consciences of a broad cross-section of citizens in the service of moral catastrophe. This persuasive process has little in common with brainwashing, which aims at turning its subjects into mindless automatons. In Nazi Germany, faith in a virtuous Führer and joy at belonging to a superior *Volk* cultivated grassroots initiative and allowed for a margin of choice.

This is not to imply that Nazi Germany was remotely similar to a democracy, but the laxity of its conceptual world distinguished it from the doctrinal rigidity of totalitarian societies such as Stalin's USSR, Pol Pot's Cambodia, and Mao's China. A field policeman in Ukraine explained the difference: "We are not commissars with all their evil ways. We are soldiers of Prussian rearing and stand before a task that demands from us our greatest efforts . . . a task to which the Führer charged us here in the Ukraine; to see something very important and beautiful; something upon which the fate of Germany rests for centuries."[72] German soldiers had been trained to take initiative, to think for themselves in the absence of specific orders. They functioned well because they shared a working consensus, rooted in ethnic pride and self-denial as well as contempt for their victims. Ordinary Germans who were neither politically suspect or racially unwanted had considerable latitude to create their own patterns of selective compliance. Thus, collaborators in racial persecution were ordinary in a different and more frightening way than the image of banal bureaucrats and obedient soldiers suggests.[73] Despite having been raised to believe in the Golden Rule and probably more or less honoring it in their private lives, citizens of the Third Reich were shaped by a public culture so compelling that even those who objected to one or another aspect of Nazism came to accept the existence of a hierarchy of racially based human worth, the cult of the Führer, and the desirability of territorial conquest. The Final Solution did not develop as evil incarnate but rather as the dark side of ethnic righteousness. Conscience, originally seen to protect the integrity of the individual from the inhumane demands of the group, in the Third Reich became a means of underwriting the attack by the strong against the weak. To Germans caught up in a simulacrum of high moral purpose, purification of racial aliens became a difficult but necessary duty.[74]

Nazism offered all ethnic Germans, whether or not they joined the party, a comprehensive system of meaning that was transmitted through powerful symbols and renewed in communal celebrations. It told them how to differentiate between friend and enemy, true believer and heretic, non-Jew and Jew. In offering the faithful a vision of sanctified life in the *Volk,* it resembled a religion. Its condemnation of egotism and celebration of self-denial had much in common with ethical postulates elsewhere. But in contrast to the optimistic language of international covenants guaranteeing universal rights to all people, Nazi public culture was constructed on the mantra: "Not every being with a human face is human."

Until late in the twentieth century, Nazism appeared to have been a retrograde political faith that lacked the potential to outlive its founder. While the idiosyncratic racial fantasies of Nazism seem as dated as the goose-step, the ideology that drove it was the first example of a new and ominous kind of doctrine that based the civil rights of citizens, including the right to live, on ethnic identity as determined by the state. Hitler founded a consensual dictatorship that was "neither right nor left" on the political spectrum but occupied an entirely different political terrain. Like other fundamentalisms, it began with a powerful leader and drew on populist rage against corrupt elites who had betrayed the "common man."

On the basis of a shabby doctrine of racial struggle, Nazi functionaries and academics innovated a political strategy that did not perish with its Führer. In the second half of the twentieth century, the outbreak of ethnic strife and the emergence of populist regionalism during the break-up of colonial empires and the collapse of Soviet power made it clear that Nazism had not been a final atavistic outcropping of tribalism but a harbinger of ethnic fundamentalism, a creed that gathers force when modernizing societies are convulsed by dislocations which threaten conventional systems of meaning. The potential for racial hatred lurks whenever political leaders appeal to the exalted virtue of their own ethnic community. Against a growing commitment to universal human rights, ethnic fundamentalists broadcast alarms about ethnic danger. Evil presents itself as unalloyed ethnic good. Reforging bonds that may be religious, cultural, racial, or linguistic, ethnic fundamentalism merges politics and religion within a crusade to defend values and authentic traditions that appear to be endangered.

In an age of what critics call moral meltdown, when conventional codes governing private morality relax, the struggle between "good and evil" migrates to the political front.[75] Political leaders who appear to embody the communitarian virtues of a bygone age purport to stand as beacons of moral rectitude in a sea of sin. Although they incite hatred against anyone they deem to be ethnic outsiders—whether sexual degenerates, pacifists, defenders of human rights, or simply misfits—their devoted constituencies share a fear of moral and physical pollution so profound it transcends partisan politics. Long after the demise of Nazism, ethnic fundamentalism continues to draw its power from the vision of an exclusive community of "us," without "them."

Abbreviations

BAB	Bundesarchiv Berlin-Lichterfelde
BDC	Berlin Document Center
DBFP	*Documents on British Foreign Policy*
DDF	*Documents diplomatiques français*
FRUS	*Foreign Relations of the United States*
Houghton	Houghton Library, Harvard University
IMT	*Trial of the Major War Criminals before the International Military Tribunal*
NV	*Neues Volk: Blätter des Aufklärungsamtes für Bevölkerungspolitik und Rassenpflege*
RBMSCL	Rare Book, Manuscripts, and Special Collection Library, Duke University
REM	Ministerium für Wissenschaft, Kunst und Volksbildung
RMdI	Reichsministerium des Inneren
SK	*Das Schwarze Korps*
Sopade	*Deutschland-Berichte der Sozialdemokratischen Partei Deutschlands/ Sopade*
StAM	Staatsarchiv Munich
VB	*Der Völkische Beobachter*
ZuW	*Ziel und Weg*

Notes

PROLOGUE

1. Jonathan Glover, *Humanity: A Moral History of the Twentieth Century* (New Haven, Conn.: Yale University Press, 1999), pp. 26–28.

2. Carl Schmitt castigated the "Gleichheit alles dessen, was Menschenantlitz trägt," in "Das gute Recht der deutschen Revolution," *Westdeutscher Beobachter,* May 12, 1933, reprinted in Josef Becker and Ruth Becker, eds., *Hitlers Machtergreifung, 1933: Vom Machantritt Hitlers, 30 Januar 1933, bis zur Beseitigung des Einparteistaates, 14 Juli 1933* (Munich: dtv, 1983), doc. 253, pp. 301–302. The phrase was used in many venues, for example, Hitler, "Ein Kampf um Deutschlands Zukunft," Sept. 18, 1928, in Bärbel Dusik and Klaus A. Lankheit, eds., *Hitler: Reden, Schriften, Anordnung,* vol. 3, part 1 (Munich: Saur, 1992), doc. 26, p. 88, and Bernhard Lösener, "Die Hauptprobleme der Nürnberger Grundgesetze," Oct. 1935, U.S. Holocaust Memorial Museum, record group (hereafter USHMM, RG-) 11.001.M/343/roll 5/343, p. 57.

1. AN ETHNIC CONSCIENCE

1. "Das ist mir geugknusz gebet, das ich mein gewiszen errettet hab am jungsten tage und szagen konde, 'ich hab gehandelt, wie ich sal.'" Quoted in Jacob Grimm and Wilhelm Grimm, *Deutsches Wörterbuch,* vol. 4 (Leipzig: Hirzel, 1911), s.v. "Gewissen."

2. They approvingly cited Cicero on natural law: "There will not be different laws at Rome as at Athens, or different law now and in the future, but one eternal and unchangeable law will be valid for all nations and at all times." George H. Sabine, *A History of Political Theory,* 4th ed. (New York: Dryden, 1973), p. 161.

3. Immanuel Kant, "Conclusion," in *The Critique of Practical Reason* (Cambridge: Cambridge University Press, 1997). P. 473 continues, "I have not to search for them and conjecture them as though they were veiled in darkness or were in the transcendent region beyond my horizon; I see them before me and connect them directly with the consciousness of my existence."

4. Vatican II, "Gaudium et spes," Dec. 7, 1965, in Austin Flannery, ed., *Documents of Vatican II* (Grand Rapids, Mich.: Eardmans, 1975), pp. 903–1001.

5. Explicit injunctions in many other cultures carry the message of the Golden Rule, as enunciated in the Gospels of Matthew 7:12 and Luke 6:31. The *Hadith* guides Muslims, "No one of you is a believer until he desires for his brother that which he desires for himself." The *Mahabharata* commands, "This is the sum of duty: do naught to others which if done to thee would cause thee pain." In the *Talmud* the faithful learn, "What is hateful to you, do not to your fellow men. That is the entire Law, all the rest is commentary." Buddhists learn from the *Udana-Varga,* "Hurt not others with that which pains yourself."

6. The claim of "an inhabitant of the earth," in Freud's words, "like an insect, an earthworm, or a grass-snake," is weak. Sigmund Freud, *Civilization and Its Discontents,* trans. James Strachey, introduction by Peter Gay (New York: W. W. Norton, 1989), pp. 65–67.

7. J. B. Schneewind, *The Invention of Autonomy: A History of Modern Moral Philosophy* (Cambridge: Cambridge University Press, 1998), pp. 345–349. Shakespeare, in *Henry V,* uses "conscience" to mean "opinion": "I will speak my conscience to the King." Thomas Hobbes

wrote: "Mankind, from conscience of its own weaknesse." *Oxford Shorter English Dictionary* (CD-ROM version), s.v. "conscience."

8. Social theorists from Georg Simmel through Jürgen Habermas have analyzed the power of knowledge within the context of Western democracies. Nicos Stehr, *Knowledge Societies* (London: Sage, 1994), pp. 160–203. As Raymond Williams noted, the "expert"—like the "intellectual" and the "professor"—evolved from the status of a mere professional to a more exalted status as the bearer of knowledge in modern society. Raymond Williams, *Key Words* (New York: Oxford University Press, 1983), p. 129. In Germany traditional elites bitterly resented the elevation of the expert. Detlev J. K. Peukert, *The Weimar Republic: The Crisis of Classical Modernity,* trans. Richard Deveson (New York: Hill and Wang, 1987), pp. 134–140.

9. Alfons Heck, *Heil Hitler: Confessions of a Hitler Youth,* Arthur Holch, producer, HBO Knowledge Project Film (New York: Ambrose, 1991). The program was based on Heck's memoir, *A Child of Hitler: Germany in the Days When God Wore a Swastika* (Frederick, Colo.: Renaissance House, 1985).

10. Albert Speer, *The Slave State: Heinrich Himmler's Masterplan for SS Supremacy,* trans. Joachim Neugroschel (London: Weidenfeld and Nicolson, 1981), p. 255.

11. Herbert Spencer: "Progress: Its Law and Causes," *Westminster Review* 67 (Apr. 1857), pp. 445–447, 451, 454–456, 464–465. The distinguished pedigree of the organic analogy can be traced to Alfred Russell Wallace, Peter Kropotkin, William Graham Sumner, Lester Ward, Ernst Haeckel, William Bateson, Andrew Carnegie, L. T. Hobhouse, Konrad Lorenz, Robert Ardrey, E. O. Wilson, Richard Dawkins, and Robert Richards.

12. Oswald Spengler, author of *The Decline of the West* (1922), applied the logic of Ernst Haeckel, *The Evolution of Man* (1897). These internationally best-selling authors explained the organic essence of all creation and infused social criticism with biological metaphors. Peter Weingart, "'Struggle for Existence': Selection and Retention of a Metaphor," in Sabine Maasen, Everett Mendelsohn, and Peter Weingart, eds., *Biology as Society, Society as Biology: Metaphors* (Dordrecht: Kluwer, 1995), pp. 131–136.

13. George L. Mosse, *Toward the Final Solution: A History of European Racism* (New York: Howard Fertig, 1978), p. 168.

14. Joseph Goebbels, *Das kleine abc des Nationalsozialisten* (Bernau: Freyhoff, 1930?), p. 1.

15. L. Frank Baum, quoted in David E. Stannard, *American Holocaust: The Conquest of the New World* (New York: Oxford University Press, 1992), p. 126.

16. In part encouraged by the German example, antisemitic measures were enacted in Poland, Hungary, Romania, Slovakia, and Italy. However, Nazi apologists never cited these parallels when addressing critics. They also ignored the imposition of such racial-religious codes in Latin America as the requirement of pure race *(limpieza de sangre)* designed to bar entry to higher education and the professions to descendants of Moors, Jews, heretics, or *penitenciados* (persons punished by the Inquisition). Duke University, Special Collections Library, Peruvian Collection, manuscript no. 2. "Papeles que pertenecen a Francisco Xavier Montero Bolanos de los Reyes" (Caracas, 1765–1770). The author thanks Elizabeth Dunn for suggesting this precedent.

17. A politician declared, "On Greek soil there should remain nothing that's not Greek." Mark Mazower, *Dark Continent: Europe's Twentieth Century* (New York: Knopf, 1999), p. 42. Norman M. Naimark, *Fires of Hatred: Ethnic Cleansing in Twentieth-Century Europe* (Cambridge: Harvard University Press, 2002), pp. 17–35.

18. Internal debates among policymakers included frequent references to race in the United States. Strafrechtskommission, 37th sitting, June 5, 1934, Bundesarchiv Berlin-Lichterfelde (hereafter BAB) R3001/852. See also *Der Stürmer* 14 (Mar. 1936), and Walter Gross, "National Socialist Racial Thought," in *Germany Speaks! Twenty-One Leading Members of the National Socialist Party,* foreword by Joachim von Ribbentrop (London: Butterworth, 1938), p. 75. For scholarly studies, see Judy Scales-Trent, "Racial Purity Laws in the United

States and Nazi Germany: The Targeting Process," *Human Rights Quarterly* 23 (2000): 259–307.

19. "Begriff 'Mischehe,'" Apr. 26, 1935, Interior Ministry, Reichsministerium des Inneren (hereafter RMdI) to State Governments *(Landesregierungen)*, BAB/R4901/521/Bl. 32. Cornelia Essner, "Zwischen Vernunft und Gefühl: Die Reichstagdebatten von 1912 um koloniale 'Rassenmischehe' und 'Sexualität,'" *Vierteljahrshefte für Zeitgeschichte* 45 (1997): 503–519.

20. William I. Brustein, *Roots of Hate: Anti-Semitism in Europe before the Holocaust* (Cambridge: Cambridge University Press, 2003), chap. 6. The author thanks Dr. Brustein for making this book available in manuscript form. Albert S. Lindeman, *Esau's Tears: Modern Anti-Semitism and the Rise of the Jews* (Cambridge: Cambridge University Press, 1997), pp. 457–460, 481–503.

21. Statistisches Reichsamt, ed., *Statistisches Jahrbuch für das Deutsche Reich*, vol. 51 (Berlin: Hobbing, 1932), part 2, pp. 29–30, and *Statistisches Jahrbuch für das Deutsche Reich*, vol. 55 (Berlin: Sozialpolitik, 1936), part 2, p. 41. Between 1931 and 1932 roughly 36 percent of all new Jewish marriages were mixed; and in 1933 the percentage increased to 44. One in four children born to "mixed-race" parents were raised Jewish. Bruno Blau, *Das Ausnahmerecht für die Juden in Deutschland, 1933–1945* (Düsseldorf: Allgemeine Wochenzeitung der Juden in Deutschland, 1965), pp. 7–10. Jeremy Noakes, "Wohin gehören die 'Judenmischlinge?' Die Entstehung der ersten Durchführungsverordnungen zu den Nürnberger Gesetzen," in Ursula Buttner, ed., *Das Unrechtsregime: Internationale Forschung über den Nationalsozialismus*, vol. 2 (Hamburg: Christians, 1986), pp. 70–74.

22. Michael Burleigh and Wolfgang Wippermann, *The Racial State: Germany, 1933–1945* (Cambridge: Cambridge University Press, 1991), pp. 23–43. Williams, *Keywords*, pp. 119–120, 248–250.

23. William Sheridan Allen, *The Nazi Seizure of Power in a Single German Town*, rev. ed. (New York: Watts, 1965), p. 77. Allen does not deny that antisemitism existed, but he found that it did not contribute to the appeal of the Nazi Party. Peter Fritzsche, *Germans into Nazis* (Cambridge: Harvard University Press, 1998), pp. 208–209. Ulrich Herbert, "New Answers and Questions about the History of the 'Holocaust' in German Historiography," in Herbert, ed., *National Socialist Extermination Policies: Contemporary German Perspectives and Controversies* (New York: Berghahn, 2000), pp. 4–27.

24. Raul Hilberg, *The Destruction of the European Jews*, student ed. (New York: Holmes & Meier, 1985), p. 63, and Raul Hilberg, *The Politics of History: The Journey of a Holocaust Historian* (Chicago: Ivan R. Dee, 1996), p. 64. Peter J. Haas, *Morality after Auschwitz: The Radical Challenge of the Nazi Ethic* (Philadelphia: Fortress, 1988), pp. 13–21. Avraham Barkai, "The German *Volksgemeinschaft*," in Michael Burleigh, ed., *Confronting the Nazi Past: New Debates on Modern German History* (New York: St. Martin's, 1996), pp. 84–88.

25. Omer Bartov, *Hitler's Army: Soldiers, Nazis, and War in the Third Reich* (New York: Oxford University Press, 1992), p. 148. Bartov notes that "the moral values these young men had internalized before their recruitment" conditioned their reactions at the front, p. 7. Omer Bartov, "The Lost Cause," *New Republic*, Oct. 4, 1999, pp. 47–50, and "The Penultimate Horror," *New Republic*, Oct. 13, 1997, pp. 48–53.

26. Browning, concerned to explore the motivation of face-to-face killers, finds that indoctrination "still did not offer the prospect that the 'onlookers' of 1938 would become the genocidal killers of 1941–1942." Although he notes that "a surprisingly high percentage had become Party members," he adds: "These were men who had known political standards and moral norms other than those of the Nazis." In Browning's view, adults resist cultural pressure to change their moral values. Christopher R. Browning, *Ordinary Men: Reserve Police Battalion 101 and the Final Solution in Poland*, 2nd ed. (New York: Harper Perennial, 1998), pp. 200, 48. Other historians who emphasize situational factors over ideology have placed the generational cohort at the center of their research. Michael Wildt, *Generation des Unbedingten: Das Führungskorps des Reichssicherheitshauptamtes* (Hamburg: Hamburger Edi-

tion, 2002), pp. 23–29, 137–142. For an explicit analysis of the production of morality among killers, see Bronwyn McFarland-Icke, *Nurses in Nazi Germany: Moral Choice in History* (Princeton, N.J.: Princeton University Press, 1999), pp. 128–172.

27. Hettie Shiller, "Es geschah in einer Generation!" Houghton Library, Harvard University (hereafter Houghton), bMS Ger 91 (210). Victor Klemperer, diary entry of June 17, 1934, *I Will Bear Witness: A Diary of the Nazi Years*, vol. 1, trans. Martin Chalmers (New York: Random House, 1998), p. 72. Rudolf Steiner, "My Life in Germany," Houghton, bMS Ger 91 (227), p. 50. Joseph B. Levy, "Die guten und die bösen Deutschen," and Hilde Honnet-Sichel, "Jeden Tag neue Angst," in Margarete Limberg and Hubert Rübsaat, eds., *"Sie durften nicht mehr Deutsche sein": Jüdischer Alltag in Selbstzeugnissen, 1933–1938* (Frankfurt am Main: Campus, 1990), pp. 130–139, 178–180, 182–186. Marion A. Kaplan, *Between Dignity and Despair: Jewish Life in Nazi Germany* (New York: Oxford University Press, 1998), pp. 17–49.

28. Hanna Bernheim, "Mein Leben in Deutschland," Houghton, bMS Ger 91 (25).

29. Karl Löwith, "Mein Leben in Deutschland," Houghton, bMS Ger 91 (161), published as *My Life in Germany before and after 1933*, trans. Elizabeth King (Champaign-Urbana: University of Illinois Press, 1986), pp. 52–53.

30. Heinemann Stern, "Einsam in vertrauter Umwelt," in Limberg and Rübsaat, *"Sie durften nicht,"* pp. 172–173.

31. Hannah Arendt, *The Origins of Totalitarianism* (New York: Meridian: 1958), pp. 465–466.

32. Robert Gellately, *The Gestapo and German Society: Enforcing Racial Policy, 1933–1945* (Oxford, Eng.: Clarendon, 1990), 135–140. B. Dörner, "Gestapo," in Gerhard Paul and Klaus-Michael Mallmann, eds., *Die Gestapo: Mythos und Realität*, foreword by Peter Steinbach (Darmstadt: Primus, 1996), pp. 332–334, 341–342. Eric A. Johnson, *The Nazi Terror: The Gestapo, Jews, and Ordinary Germans* (New York: Basic Books, 2000), pp. 253–301.

33. In his chapter on racist propaganda, David Welch cited no evidence of Hitler's role. *The Third Reich: Politics and Propaganda* (London: Routledge, 1993), 72–82. On the paucity of racism in film, see Sabine Haake, *Popular Cinema of the Third Reich* (Austin: University of Texas Press, 2001), pp. 14–17, 34–36, 53–54. Despite Hitler's caution in public, as Peter Longerich conclusively demonstrated, Hitler was the "decisive instigator" of each escalation in antisemitism. *The Unwritten Order* (London: Tempus, 2001), p. 28.

34. Joseph Goebbels, *Signale der neuen Zeit* (Munich: Eher, 1934), p. 34. Gerd Albrecht, *Nationalsozialistische Filmpolitik: Eine soziologische Untersuchung über Spielfilme des dritten Reiches* (Stuttgart: Ferdinand Enke, 1969), p. 468.

35. Michael Ignatieff, *The Warrior's Honor: Ethnic War and the Modern Conscience* (New York: Metropolitan, 1998); Benjamin Barber, *Jihad vs. McWorld: How Globalism and Tribalism Are Reshaping the World* (New York: Ballantine, 1996); Omer Bartov and Phyllis Mack, *In God's Name: Genocide and Religion in the Twentieth Century* (New York: Berghahn, 2001). Bruce B. Lawrence, *Defenders of God: The Fundamentalist Revolt against the Modern Age* (San Francisco: Harpers, 1989). In the American context, see George M. Marsden, *Fundamentalism and American Culture* (New York: Oxford University Press, 1980).

36. Ian Kershaw, *The "Hitler Myth": Image and Reality in the Third Reich* (New York: Oxford University Press, 1987). Kershaw investigated Hitler's capacity to integrate rivals into the Nazi Party and give the appearance of standing above factions. He did not, however, analyze the techniques by which the Hitler myth was produced. Joseph Peter Stern analyzed the deployment of charisma in his *Hitler: The Führer and the People* (Berkeley: University of California Press, 1975), pp. 35–42. 92–97.

37. "Deutsches Requiem," *Labyrinths*, trans. D. A. Yates and J. E. Irby (New York: New Directions, 1964), p. 144. George Steiner, *The Portage to San Cristóbal of A. H.* (New York: Simon and Schuster, 1981). Harry Mulisch, *Assault*, trans. Claire N. White (New York: Pantheon, 1985), and Don DeLillo, *White Noise* (New York: Viking, 1985), in very different ways, relativize the evil of Nazi rule.

2. THE POLITICS OF VIRTUE

1. Adolf Hitler, *Mein Kampf*, trans. Ralph Mannheim, Sentry Edition (Boston: Houghton Mifflin, 1962), p. 469. Hitler adopted the narrative mode as the most effective way to communicate his message of virtue. In Classical Greek culture, oral narratives had transmitted "moral scriptures" and "moral fictions," as the philosopher Alasdair McIntyre calls them. He notes that "the chief means of moral education is the telling of stories." Alasdair MacIntyre, *After Virtue: A Study in Moral Theory*, 2nd ed. (Notre Dame, Ind.: Notre Dame University Press, 1984), pp. 120, 75.

2. Hitler, *Mein Kampf*, p. 466.

3. Ibid., pp. 470–471.

4. Hitler, speech to party leaders of June 12, 1925, in Clemens Vollnhals, ed., *Hitler: Reden, Schriften, Anordnung*, vol. 1, Feb. 1925 to June 1926 (New York: Saur, 1992), doc. 50, pp. 93–94, 96–97.

5. Hitler, *Mein Kampf*, p. 468.

6. Werner Jochmann, ed., *Adolf Hitler: Monologe im Führerhauptquartier, 1941–1944* (Hamburg: Albrecht Knaus, 1980), pp. 175–176; Jacques Attali, *Noise: The Political Economy of Music* (Minneapolis: University of Minnesota Press, 1985), p. 87.

7. Hitler to Adolf Gemlich, Munich, letter of Sept. 16, 1919, in the series Quellen und Darstellungen zur Zeitgeschichte, vol. 21: *Hitler: Sämtliche Aufzeichnungen, 1905–1924*, Eberhard Jäckel, ed., with Axel Kühn (Stuttgart: Deutsche Verlags-Anstalt, 1980), doc. 61, pp. 88–90.

8. The catalogue of Hitler's hatreds included Jewry, Marxism, Liberalism, parliamentarism, capitalism, the "stab in the back," and the "November criminals" who signed the Versailles treaty. Karl Dietrich Bracher, Wolfgang Sauer, and Gerhard Schulz, *Die nationalsozialistische Machtergreifung: Studien zur Errichtung des totalitären Herrschaftssystems in Deutschland, 1933/34* (Cologne: Westdeutscher, 1960), p. 23. Too much has been made of Hitler as a purely oppositional politician. The "anti's" in his speeches served primarily to enhance his praise of the *Volk*.

9. Apr. 6, 1920, in Jäckel, *Hitler*, doc. 91, pp. 119–120.

10. Josef Hell, 1922, quoted by Gerald Fleming in *Hitler and the Final Solution* (Berkeley: University of California Press, 1984), p. 17. In many passages, Hitler expressed his hatred without divulging what "solution" he suggested; see speeches "Der Jude als Arbeitführer," Munich, June 24, 1920, doc. 112, pp. 151–152; "Die Hetzer," Apr. 22, 1922, Munich, doc. 377, p. 620; and "Die Politik der Vernichtung unseres Mittelstands," Munich, Sept. 28, 1922, doc. 408, pp. 696–699, all in Jäckel, *Hitler*.

11. Hitler, "Der Weltkrieg und seine Macher," speech at an NSDAP meeting, Munich, Apr. 17, 1920, in Jäckel, *Hitler*, doc. 93, pp. 123–124. Square brackets added. See also, "Deutsch nationale Logik," Munich, May 29, 1921, in Jäckel, *Hitler*, doc. 254, p. 419.

12. "Rede auf einer NSDAP Versammlung," Jan. 9, 1922, in Jäckel, *Hitler*, doc. 341, p. 544. In this speech, Hitler reworked the Nativity as an incitement to antisemitism and closed with "Amen."

13. "Maifeier," "Politik und Rasse," and "Stichwörte zu Reden," in Jäckel, *Hitler*, doc. 501, pp. 853–854, doc. 517, pp. 906–909.

14. Hitler, speech, Munich, Feb. 24, 1924, in Jäckel, *Hitler*, doc. 605, p. 1068. References to Hitler's speeches at his trial in 1924 cite sometimes the German and sometimes the English version. The German transcript of his speeches is complete. The English transcript of the entire trial (including other defendants' statements) includes some summaries. Where the English matches the German, I have cited *The Hitler Trial before the People's Court in Munich*, trans. H. F. Freniere, L. Karcic, and P. Fandek, introduction by Harold J. Gordon, vol. 3 (Arlington, Va.: University Publications of America, 1976). Where a passage appears only in the German, I have cited Jäckel, *Hitler*.

15. Hans von Hülsen, *Zwillings-Seele: Denkwürdigkeiten aus einem Leben zwischen Kunst und Politik* (Munich: Funck, 1947), vol. 1, pp. 207–209. The author noted also that these same judges expelled left-wing cartoonists and journalists from the court. Quoted in John Toland, *Adolf Hitler* (New York: Doubleday Anchor, 1976), p. 191.

16. Joachim Fest, "The Drummer," in *The Face of the Third Reich: Portraits of the Nazi Leadership*, trans. Michael Bullock (New York: Pantheon, 1970), pp. 15–26; Ian Kershaw, *Hitler, 1889–1936*, vol. 1 (New York: W. W. Norton, 1999), pp. 118, 169–220. Kershaw mentions the appeal of "moral revival" in passing but does not develop the theme.

17. Hitler, "Vor dem Volksgericht: Erster Verhandlung," Feb. 26, 1924, in Jäckel, *Hitler*, doc. 605, p. 1065. In the same passage he referred dismissively to Hottentots. He suggested that more than the "deportation of 60 or 70 East Jewish families" would be necessary to "solve the Jewish question" (doc. 605, p. 1079; see also *Hitler Trial*, vol. 1, p. 51). On March 1, 1924, the chairman inquired about his views on the Jewish conspiracy. Hitler, speech of Mar. 3, 1924, in Jäckel, *Hitler*, doc. 610, pp. 1123–1124. When an attorney inquired on March 7 about Hitler's diatribes against "foreigners and Jews," Hitler evaded the question (doc. 613, p. 1131). On March 27 Hitler referred again to "international Jewry" as a "racial tuberculosis" (doc. 625, p. 1209). The more than 150 closely printed pages of Hitler's trial speeches contain fewer than half a dozen references to Jews.

18. Erster Verhandlungstag, in Jäckel, *Hitler*, doc. 605, p. 1072.

19. Hitler compared the German right of self-determination to that of "every Negro tribe," and his lawyer spoke of the "Pacifist-Marxist-Jewish" threat. *Hitler Trial*, Negro reference, vol. 3, p. 354; Hitler's talk about "Jewish-Marxist-International" danger, p. 124; for his lawyer Höll's reference to "Pacifist-Marxist, let's say Jewish" threat, pp. 137, 188, 225.

20. "From the first day of its existence" the political movement aiming at power must "feel itself a movement of the masses and not a literary tea-club or a shopkeepers' bowling society." Hitler, *Mein Kampf*, pp. 342–343.

21. Hitler, speech, "an internal German conflict between two philosophies," *Hitler Trial*, vol. 3, p. 139.

22. *Hitler Trial*, vol. 3, p. 357.

23. Ibid., p. 359.

24. Ibid., pp. 137, 139, 355.

25. Ibid., p. 353. "On the day when the German Emperor received his crown in Paris, high treason was legalized before the German people and the entire world."

26. Hitler, speech of Mar. 27, 1924, in Jäckel, *Hitler*, doc. 625, pp. 1215–1216, and *Hitler Trial*, vol. 3, p. 366.

27. The "prison" was a castle converted into a detention center for wayward sons of wealthy families. Kershaw, *Hitler*, vol. 1, pp. 240–253. Hitler recalled that prison had given him "the chance of deepening various notions for which I had only an instinctive feeling . . . I acquired the fearless faith, the optimism, the confidence in our destiny that nothing could shake afterward."

28. Emil J. Gumbel, *Vier Jahre politischer Mord: Denkschrift* (Berlin: Malik, 1924), pp. 67–68, 118–124, 183. Between the end of the war and the opening of the Hitler trial, 376 political murders had been committed in Germany—of 354 right-wing perpetrators against leftists, 326 went free. Of 22 leftist murders, 10 were executed. Arthur D. Brenner, *Emil J. Gumbel: Weimar German Pacifist and Professor* (Boston: Humanities Press, 2001), pp. 69–74. Hitler, speech to Berlin district leaders, Jan. 20, 1932, in Christian Hartmann and Klaus A. Lankheit, eds., *Hitler: Reden, Schriften, Anordnungen, Februar 1925 bis Januar 1933*, vol. 5, part 2, Apr. 1932 to Jan. 1933 (Munich: Saur, 1998), doc. 143, p. 384. John Toland, *Adolf Hitler* (New York: Doubleday Anchor, 1976), p. 103.

29. Hitler, Conversation with Kugler, Landsberg, July 29, 1924, in Jäckel, *Hitler*, doc. 654, p. 1242.

30. Hitler, *Mein Kampf*, p. 305.

31. The Jew was an "eternal bloodsucker"—never a nomad "but only and always a *parasite*" embedded in his host. "The nationalization of our masses will succeed only when . . . their international poisoners are exterminated." Hitler, *Mein Kampf*, pp. 304, 310, 338.

32. "Hitler Frei," *Der Nationalsozialist* (Munich) 1 (Dec. 25, 1924): 1.

33. During Hitler's months in prison, the Nazi Party fragmented. In July 1924 Hitler broke personal contact with his followers outside Landsberg and skillfully engineered the refoundation of his movement after his release. Kershaw, *Hitler*, vol. 1, pp. 232–259. Hitler, "Deutschlands Zukunft und unsere Bewegung," in Vollnhals, *Hitler*, vol. 1, Feb. 27, 1925, doc. 6, pp. 14–28. In this lengthy speech, Hitler deplored the Jewish young men *(Judenjunge)* walking arm in arm with "German girls" on the streets of Berlin, and the Jewish organizers of mass public opinion, p. 18.

34. Hitler, "Rede auf der Generalmitgliederversammlung der NSDAP/NSDAV," Aug. 31, 1928, in Bärbel Dusik, ed., *Hitler: Reden, Schriften, Anordnungen, Februar 1925 bis Januar 1933*, vol. 2, part 2, Aug. 1927—May 1928 (Munich: Saur, 1992), doc. 13, pp. 35–47.

35. Hitler, "Volkskampf . . . Gegen die jüdischer Weltpressevergiftung," in Vollnhals, *Hitler*, vol. 1, Sept. 17, 1925, doc. 65, p. 153. "Fortsetzung," Jan. 23, 1928, in Dusik, *Hitler*, vol. 2, part 2, doc. 222, p. 646.

36. Hitler, "Nationalsozialismus und Kunstpolitik," Jan. 26, 1928, in Dusik, *Hitler*, vol. 2, part 2, doc. 224, p. 651.

37. Hitler, "Geist und Doktor Stresemann?" Munich speech to NSDAP meeting, May 2, 1928, published in a special edition of *Der Völkische Beobachter* (hereafter *VB*), in Dusik, *Hitler*, vol. 2, part 2, doc. 268, p. 824.

38. Hitler, "Der Kampf, der einst die Ketten bricht," Nov. 16, 1928, Berlin, in Bärbel Dusik and Klaus A. Lankheit, eds., *Hitler: Reden, Schriften, Anordnungen, Februar 1925 bis Januar 1933*, vol. 3, part 1, July 1928–Sept 1930 (Munich: K. G. Saur, 1994), doc. 50, p. 238.

39. Hitler, "Freiheit und Brot," June 26, 1927, in Dusik, *Hitler*, vol. 2, part 1, doc. 152, pp. 386–403, 395.

40. About 1,200 people attended each speech, which occurred in the evening at the Bürgerbrau beer hall. Hitler, "Die Stützen von Thron und Altar," Feb. 29, 1928, *VB*, special issue, in Dusik, *Hitler*, vol. 2, part 2, doc. 237, pp. 681–716. Hitler, "Rede auf der NSDAP *Führertagung,"* Aug. 31, 1928, in Dusik and Lankheit, *Hitler*, vol. 3, part 1, doc. 13, pp. 35–47. Saul Friedländer, *Nazi Germany and the Jews*, vol. 1, *The Years of Persecution, 1933–1939* (New York: 1997), pp. 102–103.

41. Hitler, "Rede auf NSDAP-Versammlung in Zwickau," July 15, 1925, in Vollnhals, *Hitler*, vol. 1, doc. 57, pp. 126–128. Hitler, "Zukunft oder Untergang," Mar. 6, 1927, doc. 83, p. 165, "Rede auf Generalmitgliederversammlung der NSDAP/NSDAV," to 1,400 party members, Munich, July 30, 1927, doc. 159, pp. 413–437, and "Wesen und Ziele des Nationalsozialismus," Freilassing, July 3, 1927, doc. 153, pp. 405–408. All references are to Dusik, *Hitler*, vol. 2, part 1.

42. These images are from "Zukunft oder Untergang," Mar. 6, 1927; "Aufgaben und Aufbau der S.A.," May 18, 1927; and "Freiheit und Brot!" June 26, 1927, in Dusik, *Hitler*, vol. 2, part 1, doc. 83, pp. 165–179; doc. 124, pp. 302–308; doc. 135, pp. 386–403.

43. Hitler, "Zukunft oder Untergang," Vilsbiburg, Mar. 6, 1927, Dusik, *Hitler*, vol. 2, part 1, doc. 83, p. 168.

44. "Die Hitlerversammlung in Memmingen," excerpted from *Memminger Zeitung*, Jan. 20, 1928, BAB/NS26/51/Bl. 1–4. "Die deutsche Not und unser Weg," Jan. 18, 1928, in Dusik, *Hitler*, vol. 2, part 2, doc. 221, pp. 619–639.

45. "This was a campaign speech. The Jew baiting was only to be revealed in its real dimensions after they were in power." Hilda Henneh Siche, "My Life in Germany," Houghton, bMS Ger 91 (212), p. 57.

46. The original 683 essays are preserved in the Hoover Institution, Stanford University. Theodor Fred Abel, *Why Hitler Came to Power: An Answer Based on the Original Life Stories of Six Hundred of His Followers* (New York: Prentice-Hall, 1938), pp. 172–176, 166–168. Peter Merkl, *Political Violence under the Swastika: 581 Early Nazis* (Princeton, N.J.: Princeton University Press, 1975), pp. 67–94, 713–715.

47. Hilde Boehm Stoltz, party number 429,341. Nr 44. Abel Collection, Hoover Institution. Abel, *Why Hitler Came to Power*, pp. 13–31, 78–79.

48. Gustav Skrieme, essay no. 70. Abel Collection, Hoover Institution. Merkl, *Political Violence*, p. 98. The thirty-seven essays by women are analyzed in Claudia Koonz, *Mothers in the Fatherland* (New York: St. Martin's, 1987), pp. 60–66. These essays written after 1933 indicate what their authors believed would be convincing essays. That idealism, not partisan politics, figures so large in the answers suggests that the authors were politicized to see themselves as apolitical.

49. From his earliest writings Hitler had distinguished between two solutions to "the Jewish problem." If he came to power via nonviolent, or "legal," means, then an administrative solution would be found. But if the Nazis staged a successful armed revolution, then violent measures would be appropriate. Karl A. Schleunes, *The Twisted Road to Auschwitz: Nazi Policy toward German Jews, 1933–1939* (Champaign-Urbana: University of Illinois Press, 1970), p. 70. On other occasions Hitler differentiated between vulgar and rational antisemitism, saying he preferred the latter (although his diatribes suggested that he was motivated by the former). Werner Jochmann contends that programmatic planning to solve the "Jewish question" began in 1930: Werner Jochmann, *Gesellschaftskrise und Judenfeindschaft, 1870–1945* (Hamburg: Christians, 1988), pp. 222–239.

50. Apr. 2, 1932, "Mein Programm: Erklärung," in Lankheit, *Hitler*, vol. 5, part 1, doc. 1, pp. 7–8. The phrases "Befehl meines Gewissens" and "Ich verstehe, daß meine Gegner mich hassen" drew wild cheers from audiences.

51. In the Reichstag, Nazi delegates held a plurality of 196 seats, as compared to the Social Democrats' 121 and the Communists' 100.

52. Quoted in Hannah Vogt, *The Burden of Guilt: A Short History of Germany, 1914–1945*, trans. Herbert Strauss (New York: Oxford University Press, 1964), p. 118.

53. Feb. 10, 1933, speech at the Sportpalast, in Max Domarus, ed., *Hitler Speeches and Proclamations, 1932–1945: The Chronicle of a Dictatorship*, vol. 1, trans. Mary Fran Gilbert (Wauconda, Ill.: Bolchazy-Carducci, 1990), pp. 245–249.

54. Sir Horace Rumbold to Sir John Simon, dispatch 171, Feb. 22, 1933, Foreign Office, Great Britain, *Documents on British Foreign Policy, 1919–1939*, ser. 2 (London: His Majesty's Stationery Office, 1950), (hereafter *DBFP*), vol. 4, doc. 243, pp. 423–424.

55. Leon Dominian to secretary of state, no. 899, Stuttgart, Feb. 21, 1933, *Foreign Relations of the United States* (Washington, D.C.: U.S. Government Printing Office, 1949), (hereafter *FRUS*), vol. 2, doc. 899, p. 195.

56. Rudolf Steiner, "Mein Leben in Deutschland," Houghton, bMS Ger 91 (227), pp. 86–89.

57. Until March 12, Hitler appeared only once in uniform. While Göring, Goebbels, Hitler, and other leaders praised the Nazis' "iron discipline" and "iron broom," militias unleashed terrible violence. "Die Nationale Revolution war von eiserner Disziplin," *VB* 46 (Mar. 28, 1933), and "Boykottpause bis Mittwoch," *VB* 46 (Apr. 2–3, 1933).

58. Rumbold to Simon, dispatch 171, Feb. 22, 1933, *DBFP*, vol. 4, doc. 243, p. 426.

59. On February 10, 1933, Hitler pledged to "do justice to God and our own conscience, we have turned once more to the German *Volk*." Sportpalast, in Domarus, *Hitler Speeches*, vol. 1, p. 246.

60. Hitler had used this rhetoric at his trial. *Hitler Trial*, vol. 3, p. 364.

61. Hitler, speech, Feb. 10, 1933, in Domarus, *Hitler Speeches*, vol. 1, p. 249.

62. Hitler, Reichstag speech, Mar. 23, 1933, ibid., p. 279.

63. Hitler, speech to Associated Press, Feb. 3, 1933, ibid., p. 241. Ian Kershaw emphasizes Hitler's private comments to a powerful group of conservative insiders that evening. "Those unwilling to be converted must be crushed." Kershaw, *Hitler*, vol. 1, pp. 441–442.

64. Hitler, speech, Mar. 23, 1933, in Domarus, *Hitler Speeches*, vol. 1, p. 276.

65. Hitler, speech, Jan. 30, 1934, ibid., p. 429.

66. A. François-Poucet, Feb. 8, 1933, DDF, 1st series, vol. 2, no. 275, p. 581. Rumbold, dispatch 143, Feb. 14, 1933, *DBFP*, vol. 4, doc. 240, p. 415.

67. Rumbold reported, "The police are told that when in doubt their safest policy is to shoot, because 'if they fail to do so and anything happens they may expect disciplinary punishment.'" Inaction, in other words, could bring severe consequences, while a careless murder counted for nothing. Sir Horace Rumbold to Sir John Simon, Feb. 22, 1933, *DBFP*, vol. 4, doc. 243, p. 423. In 1930, 100,000 men belonged to the SA; by 1934 the total approached two million because of the influx of new members from the rival Steel Helmet association.

68. Hitler, speech, Mar. 23, 1933, in Domarus, *Hitler Speeches*, vol. 1, pp. 277–278. Hitler claimed that 350 Germans had been murdered by communists and announced that "equality before the law" would not protect the perpetrators.

69. Hitler, speech to the German press, Berlin, Feb. 8, 1933. The prediction does not appear in the English translation; see Max Domarus, ed., *Hitler Reden und Proklamationen, 1932–1934*, vol. 1 (Munich: Süddeutscher, 1963), p. 202.

70. Sidney B. Fay, "The Hitler Dictatorship," *Current History* 38 (May 1933): 230–232. Joachim Fest mentions that the minister of the interior (and Nazi Party member) Wilhelm Frick announced that 100,000 had been taken into custody by early March. Domarus, *Hitler Speeches*, vol. 1, p. 401. The American Embassy estimated that 260 Germans lost their citizenship because they fled from Germany.

71. Rumbold, Feb. 22, 1933, *DBFP*, vol. 4. doc 243, p. 423. Dodd, July 28, 1933, ,FRUS vol. 3, p. 251. According to Joachim Fest, between 500 and 600 political murders were committed in the first several months of Nazi rule. *Hitler*, trans. Richard Winston and Clara Winston (New York: Vintage, 1975), p. 401.

72. Diary entry of Mar. 25, 1933, in Walter Tausk, *Breslauer Tagebuch, 1933–1940*, ed. Ryszard Kincel, afterword by Henryk M. Broder (Leipzig: Reclam, 1995), p. 25. Like many contemporaries, Tausk believed rumors of catacombs and secret tunnels. He commented disparagingly on the "Heroes of the Third Reich" who clubbed innocent bystanders and beat up the helpless (p. 25).

73. Rudolf Diels, *Lucifer ante Portas* (Zurich: Interverlag, 1949), pp. 190–197.

74. Daniel Guérin, *The Brown Plague: Travels in Late Weimar and Early Nazi Germany*, trans. with an introduction by Robert Schwartzwald (Durham, N.C.: Duke University Press, 1994), p. 139.

75. Hermann Göring, speech in Frankfurt, Mar. 3, 1933, doc. 78, in Josef Becker and Ruth Becker, eds., *Hitlers Machtergreifung, 1933: Vom Machantritt Hitlers, 30 Januar 1933, bis zur Beseitigung des Einparteistaates, 14 Juli 1933* (Munich: dtv, 1983), p. 117.

76. Ralf Georg Reuth, *Goebbels*, trans. Krishna Winston (New York: Harcourt Brace, 1993), p. 170. Goebbels, diary entry of Mar. 4, 1933, in Elke Fröhlich, ed., *Die Tagebücher von Joseph Goebbels: Sämtliche Fragmente*, part 1, *Aufzeichnungen, 1924–1941*, vol. 2 (Munich: Saur, 1987), pp. 385–386. During these months, Hitler privately made it clear that if he came to power, he had no intention of leaving. In Domarus, *Hitler Speeches*, vol. 1, pp. 249–250.

77. Correspondent in Germany, *Spectator*, Apr. 7, 1933, p. 496.

78. Heinz Höhne, *Die Zeit der Illusionen: Hitler und die Anfänge des Dritten Reiches, 1933–1936* (Düsseldorf: Econ, 1991), p. 69.

79. "Nun wird die rote Pest mit Stumpf und Stiel ausgerottet. Widerstand zeigt sich

nirgendwo," Goebbels, diary entry of Feb. 28, 1933, in Fröhlich, *Tagebücher,* part 1, vol. 2, p. 384.

80. "Hitler in Power," *New York Times,* Mar. 7, 1933.

81. With an 89 percent turnout, Nazi candidates received 10,312,000 votes (43.9 percent) and 211 seats. Communists (despite being illegal) received 4,848,199 votes (12.3 percent) and 81 seats. The majority Socialists received 7,181,600 votes (18.3 percent) and 120 seats. In 1928 the Nazi vote had been 1,445,300 (4.8 percent) and 4 seats. By July 1932 it rose to 13,745,800 (15.5 percent) and 230 seats. Koppel S. Pinson, *Modern Germany: Its History and Its Civilization,* 2nd ed. (Prospect Heights, Ill.: Waveland, 1989), pp. 603–604.

82. Hitler, Mar. 10, 1933, in Domarus, *Hitler Speeches,* vol. 1, p. 208.

83. Hitler, Feb. 10, 1933, ibid., pp. 244–249.

84. Hitler, Mar. 20, 1933, ibid., pp. 270–274.

85. Y. K. W. "The Nazi Terror," The author, a resident of Germany, withheld his or her name. *New Republic,* Apr. 12, 1933, p. 235. "Nazis and Jews," *Times* (London), Apr. 4, 1933.

86. Hitler, campaign speech, Mar. 11, 1933, in Domarus, *Hitler Speeches,* vol. 1, p. 264. Hitler, speech to party leaders in Munich, Apr. 22, 1933, ibid., p. 308. "We are not working for the moment, but for the judgment of millenniums."

87. Dr. Ernst Deissmann, "Terror in Germany," *Spectator,* Mar. 10, 1933, p. 337. George Gordon, a U.S. chargé d'affaires, stressed both the "real revolution" and the absence of violence. "If one considers that during the last weeks a revolution was witnessed, one will have to admit that it passed with very little bloodshed." Berlin, Apr. 9, 1933, *FRUS,* vol. 2, doc. 61, pp. 216–218.

88. Hitler to the foreign press, Berlin, Apr. 6, 1933, in Domarus, *Hitler Speeches,* vol. 1, p. 304. He pledged to "bring about the moral and political, and hence also the economic ascent without which the press cannot exist for long."

89. "If God is for us, who can be against us," Romans 8:31. Otto Dibelius, sermon at the Nikolaikirche, on Mar. 21, 1933, quoted in Becker and Becker, *Hitlers Machtergreifung, 1933,* doc. 114, p. 156. The parallel between August 1914 and March 1933 inspired him to recall: "This was a time when the German *Volk* shared the highest experience a nation can have . . . They felt an upsurge *[Aufschwung]* of patriotic feeling that expelled all else; a new faith flamed up in millions of hearts!"

90. Dispatch, Mar. 28, 1933. Perhaps Jews served, in the words of one U.S. diplomat, as a "safety valve." National Archives record group (henceforth NA/RG) 59/862.4016/no. 1210.

91. Hitler to SA men, Mar. 10, 1933, in Domarus, *Hitler Speeches,* vol. 1, pp. 263–264.

92. Jochmann, *Gesellschaftskrise,* pp. 236–238.

93. Uwe Dietrich Adam, *Judenpolitik im Dritten Reich* (Düsseldorf: Droste, 1972), pp. 47–48.

94. Diary entries of Apr. 1 and Apr. 14, 1933, in Tausk, *Breslauer Tagebuch,* pp. 36–38. In Breslau, Nazi candidates captured over 50 percent of the vote, about 10 percent above the national average.

95. Diary entry of Feb. 2, 1933, in Tausk, *Breslauer Tagebuch,* pp. 1–2. See also Hermann Tuggelein, "Prügel"; Edwin Landau, "Schützengräbern"; Gerta Pfeffer, "Terror"; and Paul Barnay, "Menschenjagd," all in Margarete Limberg and Hubert Rübstaat, eds., *"Sie dürften nicht mehr Deutsche sein": Jüdischer Alltag in Selbstzeugnissen, 1933–1938* (Frankfurt am Main: Campus, 1990), pp. 28–430, 31–35, 36–37, 43–46.

96. Fritz Stern, *Dreams and Delusions: The Drama of German History* (New Haven, Conn.: Yale University Press, 1987), p. 121.

97. George Messersmith, report, NA/RG59/862.4016/no. 1205, Mar. 25, 1933, p. 14. Seventeen Jewish lawyers (out of a total of seventy-two) in Breslau were restored to their po-

sitions. Schleunes, *Twisted Road,* pp. 72–73. Bundesarchiv Koblenz, Sammlung Schumacher, 240, folder 1, BDC. Adolf Heilberg, "Pro Memoria 1933," Leo Baeck Institute Archives, p. 4. Otto Tolchius, "Rulers in Silesia to Wipe Out Reds," *New York Times,* Apr. 30, 1933, p. 28.

98. Dorothy Thompson and Benjamin Stolberg, "Hitler and the American Jew," *Scribner's Magazine* 94 (Sept. 1933), p. 136.

99. *The Yellow Spot: The Outlawing of a Half a Million Human Beings—A Collection of Facts and Documents Relating to Three Years' Persecution of German Jews,* introduction by the bishop of Durham (London: Victor Gollancz, 1936), pp. 33–46.

100. The *New York Times,* in March and April 1933, printed 75 articles on political violence in Germany and more than 450 reports of antisemitic assaults and policies.

101. "Goering Says Communists, Not Jews Get Attacked," *New York Times,* Mar. 26, 1933, pp. 1–4.

102. To discredit news of violence, pamphlets supposedly published by the non-Nazi press spread disinformation. *Die Greuelpropaganda ist eine Lügenpropaganda sagen die deutschen Juden selbst* (Berlin-Charlottenburg, Trachtenberg, 1933).

103. Messersmith, Mar. 25, 1933, NA/RG59/862.4016/no. 1205, Bl. 14. Gordon, Berlin, Mar. 25, 1933, *FRUS,* vol. 2, doc. 47, pp. 331–332.

104. *New York Times,* Mar. 4, 1933, p. 4.

105. Hitler, speech to the Reichstag, Mar. 20, 1933, in Domarus, *Hitler Speeches,* vol. 1, p. 273.

106. These excerpts are from Hitler's speeches on March 12, March 20, and March 23, 1933. Ibid., pp. 265, 267, 271, 273, 280.

107. Hitler, "Proclamation," Mar. 28, 1933, ibid., p. 299. Throughout the week before the boycott, the non-Nazi press carried information obviously supplied by Nazi press agents: "Die Gegenaktion," *Vossische Zeitung,* Mar. 25, 1933, and "Die Durchführung des Boykotts," *Vossische Zeitung,* Mar. 31, 1933. Messersmith, Mar. 31, 1933, *FRUS,* vol. 2, doc. 1214, pp. 338–341.

108. Goebbels noted, "Panic among the Jews!" diary entry of Mar. 28, 1933, in Fröhlich, *Tagebücher,* part 1, vol. 2, pp. 398–399.

109. Adam, *Judenpolitik,* pp. 60–62. Lothar Gruchmann, *Justiz im Dritten Reich, 1933–1945: Anpassung und Unterwerfung in der Ära Gürtner* (Munich: Oldenbourg, 1988), pp. 124–133.

110. Wolf Telegraph Bureau, Apr. 1, 1933, quoted in Comité des Délégations Juives, ed., *Die Lage der Juden in Deutschland, 1933* (1935; Frankfurt am Main: Ullstein, 1983), p. 65.

111. Joseph Goebbels, *Revolution der Deutschen* (Oldenburg: Stalling, 1933), p. 15. Friedländer, *Nazi Germany and the Jews,* vol. 1, pp. 20–24.

112. Viktor Klemperer, *I Will Bear Witness: A Diary of the Nazi Years, 1933–1941,* trans. Martin Chalmers (New York: Random House, 1998), p. 9.

113. Leonard Baker, *Days of Sorrow and Pain: Leo Baeck and the Berlin Jews* (New York: Macmillan, 1978), p. 150.

114. Gordon describes the "wild men" in the Munich old guard from the Brown house as the "lower strata." In his opinion, "Goebbels is one but Goering is not." Berlin, June 23, 1933, *FRUS,* vol. 2, doc. 107, p. 233. Messersmith reported that the Nazi Party was "in complete control" and "order [had] been completely reestablished in a comparatively short time." Apr. 10, 1933, *FRUS,* vol. 2, doc. 1231, pp. 222–227; Richard Breitman, "American Diplomatic Records Regarding German Public Opinion," in David Bankier, ed., *Probing the Depths of German Anti-Semitism: German Society and the Persecution of the Jews, 1933–1941* (New York: Berghahn, 2000), pp. 501–510.

115. Hans Mommsen and Dieter Obst, "Die Reaktion der deutschen Bevölkerung auf die Verfolgung der Juden, 1933–1943," in Hans Mommsen, ed., *Herrschaftsalltag im dritten*

Reich: Studien und Texte (Düsseldorf: Schwann, 1988), pp. 374–378; David Bankier, *The Germans and the Final Solution: Public Opinion under Nazism* (Oxford, Eng.: Blackwell, 1992), pp. 67–83.

116. Michael Müller-Claudius, *Deutsche und jüdische Tragik* (Frankfurt am Main: Knecht, 1955), pp. 158–164. Evelyn Wrench, "Letter," *Times* (London), Apr. 25, 1933. The author arrived at his conclusions after three extended lecture tours.

117. Eric A. Johnson, *Nazi Terror: The Gestapo, Jews, and Ordinary Germans* (New York: Basic Books, 2000), p. 89.

118. William E. Beitz, Berlin, Apr. 6, 1933: "Tame affair. 20 percent or so Jewish stores boycotted, so people thought fewer Jews than had been predicted." Dispatch, Department of State, NA/RG59/862.4016, microfilm reel 21. The American Consul in Hamburg observed, "If it were not for the gathering of the curious, one would hardly have realized that a serious boycott was in progress." Hamburg, Apr. 4, 1933, NA/RG59/862.4016/635.

119. Quoted in Johnson, *Nazi Terror*, p. 90. Bankier, *The Germans and the Final Solution*, pp. 67–77. Avraham Barkai, *From Boycott to Annihilation: The Economic Struggle of German Jews, 1933–1943*, trans. William Templer (Hanover, N.H.: University Press of New England, 1989), pp. 59–69.

120. Headlines: "Ganz Deutschland Boykottiert die Juden," *VB* 46 (Apr. 2, 1933), and "Die jüdische Weltmacht weicht zurück," *VB* 46 (Apr. 3, 1933). Streicher, "Zentralkommittee für Boykottbewegung," BDC, folder 21. "Der jüdische Machtkampf gegen Deutschland," *VB* 46 (Mar. 28, 1933), north German edition.

121. Interview with Sir Walter Layton, quoted in *Vossische Zeitung*, Apr. 7, 1933, reprinted in Comité des Délégations Juives, *Die Lage der Juden*, p. 317.

122. The violent acts included attempts on Hitler's life and vehement anti-Nazi protests. Barkai, *From Boycott to Annihilation*, pp. 16–25, 56–59. Barkai called the relaxation of antisemitic violence after the failed boycott "the illusion of a grace period" that proved both false and fatal.

123. "Strange Interlude," *Businessweek*, Apr. 12, 1933, p. 5. Correspondent in Germany, "Can Hitlerism Last?" *Spectator*, Apr. 7, 1933, p. 496.

124. "News of the Week," *Spectator*, Apr. 21, 1933, p. 558.

125. Luise Solmitz, diary, entry of Apr. 28, 1933, in the Archiv der Forschungsstelle Hamburg 11/11, quoted in Jochmann, *Gesellschaftskrise*, p. 242.

126. Frederic Sackett, Berlin, Mar. 21, 1933, *FRUS*, vol. 2, doc. 2261, p. 210.

127. The police report "justified" the dismissals. "We . . . have more important duties for our SA and SS men than providing protection for Herr Klemperer," implicitly from angry anti-Jewish mobs. Comité des Délégations Juives, *Die Lage der Juden*, p. 416.

128. Stern, *Dreams and Delusions*, p. 170.

129. Reports in Comité des Délégations Juives, *Die Lage der Juden*, 121–139, 175, 204–206, 249–261. Klemperer, diary entries of Aug. 19, 1933, and May 2, 1935, *I Will Bear Witness*, vol. 1, pp. 29–30, 119.

130. Hindenburg to Hitler, Apr. 4, 1933, in *Ursachen und Folgen: Vom deutschen Zusammenbruch 1918 und 1945 bis zur staatlichen Neuordnung Deutschlands in der Gegenwart*, vol. 9 (Berlin: Dokumenten-Verlag Wendler, n.d. [1959–1979]), doc. 2159, p. 393. Lothar Gruchmann points to Hitler's clever use of restrained antisemitism in his letter to the president—and in the letter he drafted for Hindenburg to sign in response. Gruchmann, *Justiz*, pp. 132–135. The strongest protest against expelling Jews from government service came from the military, which defended 5 percent of its officer corps against expulsion. Erich von Manstein, Apr. 21, 1933, in Klaus-Jürgen Müller, *Das Heer und Hitler: Armee und nationalsozialistisches Regime, 1933–1940* (Stuttgart: Deutsche Verlags-Anstalt, 1969), doc. 4, pp. 593–598.

131. On the April Laws, see Adam, *Judenpolitik*, pp. 51–75. About one third of more than

3,000 lawyers, less than half of the 717 non-Aryan judges, and about a quarter of the 4,500 Jewish physicians were affected by the law. Schleunes, *Twisted Road,* p. 109. The law preventing non–ethnic Germans from being naturalized affected about 15,000 people. Dodd, Berlin, Aug. 12, 1933, *FRUS,* vol. 2, doc. 66, pp. 252–255.

132. May 4, 1933. He was describing responses to Nazi students' slogan "The Jew can only think Jewish." NA/RG59/862.4016/no. 1282/folder 10; Breitman, "German Public Opinion," in Bankier, *Probing the Depths,* pp. 503–513.

133. "News of the Week," *Spectator,* Apr. 14, 1933, p. 521.

134. McReynolds virtually ignored Benjamin Cardozo and Louis B. Brandeis. Edward Lazarus, *Closed Chambers: The First Eyewitness Account of the Epic Struggles inside the Supreme Court* (New York: Random House, 1998), p. 284.

135. Rumbold described the "Alice in Wonderland" atmosphere to Simon, Apr. 12 and 13, 1933, *DBFP,* vol. 5, docs. 28, 30, p. 36.

136. Correspondent in Germany, *Spectator,* Apr. 7, 1933, p. 496.

137. Messersmith reported that an "American Jewess" fired from the Leipzig opera did not regain her post even though he demonstrated that she was not Jewish. Mar. 28, 1933, Berlin, NA/RG59/862.4016/1210,2274.

138. Bankier, *The Germans and the Final Solution,* pp. 71–73.

139. Friedländer, *Nazi Germany and the Jews,* vol. 1, p. 29. Schleunes, *Twisted Road,* pp. 107–110. Two accounts illustrate the potential for anger and shame: Siegfried Neumann, "My Life," Houghton, bMS Ger 91 (165); writing for the same "contest," Karl Löwith deplored the exemption, *My Life in Germany* (Champaign-Urbana: University of Illinois Press, 1994), pp. 50–51. By late 1933, instead of the 1 percent quota stipulated by the law, 16 percent of all lawyers in Germany were Jews.

140. Hilda Henneh Siche, "My Life in Germany," Houghton, bMS Ger 91 (212), pp. 63–65.

141. When caricatures of Jews warned them, "The Jew's Father is the Devil," the image did not remind them of any Jews they knew. Why, they wondered, should they forego a profitable business with Jewish merchants? Falk Wiesmann, "Juden auf dem Lande: Die wirtschaftliche Ausgrenzung der jüdischen Viehhändler in Bayern," in Detlev Peukert and Jürgen Reulecke, eds., *Die Reihen fast geschlossen: Beiträge zur Geschichte des Alltags unterm Nationalsozialismus* (Wuppertal: Hammer, 1981), pp. 381–387.

142. Michael Wildt, "Violence against Jews in Germany, 1933–1939"; Bankier, *Probing the Depths,* pp. 184–185. Michael H. Kater, "Everyday Anti-Semitism in Prewar Nazi Germany: The Popular Bases," *Yad Vashem Studies* 16 (1984): 134–146. Kater assumes that violence by about 10 percent of the German population "must have gained the approval of a much larger, inactive section of the entire German population." Security Service and clandestine reports from subsequent years suggest a different interpretation.

3. ALLIES IN THE ACADEMY

1. Karl Jaspers, *Philosophische Autobiographie: Erweiterte Neuausgabe* (Munich: Piper, 1977), pp. 100–101. See also Hans Saner, ed., *Karl Jaspers: Notizen zu Martin Heidegger* (Munich: Piper, 1978), pp. 23–43. Wolfgang J. Mommsen, "'Der Geist von 1914,'" in Mommsen, ed., *Der Autoritäre Nationalstaat: Verfassung, Gesellschaft und Kultur in deutschen Kaiserreich* (Frankfurt am Main: Fischer, 1990), pp. 407–412.

2. Reinhold Niebuhr, "Religion in the New Germany," *Christian Century* 50 (Apr. 5, 1933): 451.

3. Sir H. Rumbold to Sir J. Simon, no. 171, Feb. 22, 1933, in *DBFP,* vol. 4, doc. 243, p. 423.

4. Rumbold added, "It will be interesting to see how far the cautious and diffident ele-

ment can be won over in time by the new propaganda machine." Rumbold to Simon, Berlin, Mar. 21, 1933, *DBFP,* vol. 4, doc. 268, p. 472.

5. Saul Friedländer, *Nazi Germany and the Jews,* vol. 1, *The Years of Persecution, 1933–1939* (New York: HarperCollins, 1997), pp. 38–39.

6. Michael Kater, *The Nazi Party: A Social Profile of Members and Leaders, 1919–1945* (Cambridge: Harvard University Press, 1983), p. 71.

7. Ericksen's concept of "accidents of biography" describes shared experiences more effectively than does the concept of generation. Robert P. Ericksen, *Theologians under Hitler: Gerhard Kittel, Paul Althaus, and Emanuel Hirsch* (New Haven, Conn.: Yale University Press, 1985), pp. 25–26.

8. Albrecht Mendelssohn-Bartholdy, *The War and German Society* (1937; New York: Howard Fertig, 1971), pp. 280–295.

9. "We will not be able to find our way any more. And men will not understand us—for the generation that grew up before us, though it has passed these years with us here, already had a home and a calling. Now it will return to its old occupations, and the war will be forgotten." Erich Maria Remarque, *All Quiet on the Western Front,* trans. A. W. Wheen (New York: Fawcett Crest, 1958), p. 174. References to the hardened spirit of 1914 were ubiquitous in the press. André François-Poncet, Berlin, Feb. 8, 1933, *Documents diplomatiques français, 1932–1939* (Paris: Imprimerie Nationale, 1963) (hereafter *DDF*), 1st ser. (1932–1935), vol. 2, doc. 275. Berlin, Apr. 5, 1933, *DDF,* 1st ser., vol. 3, doc. 93, p. 171. Heide Gerstenberger, *Der revolutionäre Konservatismus* (Berlin: Dunker & Humblot, 1969), pp. 30–64.

10. Dieter Langewiesche, "The Deliberalization of the 'Middle Class Centre,'" *Liberalism in Germany,* trans. Christiane Banerji (Princeton, N.J.: Princeton University Press, 2000), pp. 257–303. Hans Mommsen, *Beamtentum im Dritten Reich* (Stuttgart: Deutsche Verlags-Anstalt, 1966), pp. 26–30. Jerry Z. Muller, *The Other God That Failed: Hans Freyer and the Deradicalization of German Conservatism* (Princeton, N.J.: Princeton University Press, 1987), pp. 17–18, 30–36, 223–226.

11. Hannah Arendt wrote that no philosophy is "Hitler-proof." Collaborators came from every political and religious faith. Hannah Arendt, *The Origins of Totalitarianism* (New York: Meridian, 1958), pp. 2, 163.

12. There were about 3,000 regular professors in Germany. Karl Dietrich Bracher, Wolfgang Sauer, and Gerhard Schulz, *Die nationalsozialistische Machtergreifung: Studien zur Errichtung des totalitären Herrschaftssystems in Deutschland, 1933/34* (Cologne: Westdeutscher, 1960), pp. 317–321. Rumbold deemed the "intelligentsia" solidly anti-Nazi, Berlin, Feb. 22, 1933, *BDFP,* vol. 4, doc. 243, p. 423. Party membership grew from 130,000 in 1930 to 850,000 in late 1932 to 2,500,000 in May 1935 and 5,300,000 in 1939. Kater, *Nazi Party,* fig. 1, p. 263.

13. Dietrich Orlow, *The History of the Nazi Party, 1933–1945* (Pittsburgh, Pa.: University of Pittsburgh Press, 1973), vol. 2, pp. 2, 18–19.

14. Kater, *Nazi Party,* pp. 69, 91. Kater suggests that academics' membership rates were roughly equivalent to the participation of civil servants. After 1937 their number declined. Medicine was the field with the highest membership rates among academics.

15. Martin Heidegger, "Die Lehre vom Urteil im Psychologismus," 1914. His *Habilitation* (second dissertation) thesis was "Die Kategorien und Bedeutungslehre des Duns Scotus" (1916). Hugo Ott, *Martin Heidegger: A Political Life,* trans. Allan Blunden (New York: Basic Books, 1993), pp. 49–83.

16. "Gethsemane hours of my life, / in the dim light / of doubt and despair / how oft have you seen me! / My tearful cries were never in vain. / My youthful being, / weary of lamentation, / trusted only in the angel of mercy," quoted in Ott, *Martin Heidegger,* p. 68. Archbishop Conrad Gröber, who was an enthusiastic Nazi supporter in the 1930s and a dissident after 1940, was Heidegger's mentor.

17. Robert Wollenberg, "Nervöse Erkrankungen bei Kriegsteilnehmern," *Münchener medizinische Wochenschrift* 1 (1914): 2181–2183. Quoted in Paul Lerner, "Hysterical Men: War, Psychiatry, and the Politics of Trauma in Germany, 1890–1930" (Ph.D. diss., Columbia University, 1996), pp. 84–92.

18. He dedicated his *Habilitation* to a fellow philosopher who was killed in battle. Ott, *Martin Heidegger,* pp. 103, 154.

19. Heidegger's friend Emil Lask must have discussed with Heidegger his decision to enlist during the early months of the war, in terms similar to those he used to express his sentiments in a letter to his mother: "It's unbearable not to be able to contribute, not even in the smallest way." Rüdiger Safranski, *Martin Heidegger: Between Good and Evil* (Cambridge: Harvard University Press, 1998), p. 57.

20. Heidegger's entry for *Das Deutsche Führerlexikon* (Berlin: Otto Stollberg, 1934–1935), p. 180, claims he volunteered but was "demobilized owing to illness." But in 1927, when university administrators asked five times for his military records to work out his pension plan, Heidegger did not respond. Safranski, *Martin Heidegger,* pp. 37–38. Victor Farias, *Heidegger and Nazism,* trans. Paul Burrell and Gabriel R. Ricci (Philadelphia: Temple University Press, 1989), pp. 48–50.

21. "This unheroic personal fate probably contributed to the mythical transfiguration of the experience at the front in Heidegger's thinking." Max Müller added that in skiing and hiking Heidegger demonstrated considerable skill and courage. Müller, "Martin Heidegger: A Philosopher and Politics," in Günther Neske and Emil Kettering, eds., *Martin Heidegger and National Socialism: Questions and Answers,* trans. Lisa Harries, with an introduction by Karsten Harries (New York: Paragon, 1990), pp. 175–196, quotation on p. 192. Ott, *Martin Heidegger,* p. 154.

22. Although she was a Protestant, in 1917 the two were married in the Catholic Dom in Freiburg. But the marriage was annulled when Catholic authorities learned that the couple had also been married in a Protestant church. Ott, *Martin Heidegger,* pp. 100–103.

23. Quoted by Alan Milchman and Alan Rosenberg, "Martin Heidegger and the University as a Site for the Transformation of Human Existence," *Review of Politics* (Winter 1997), pp. 78–83. Safranski examines the longing for an authentic conscience in his *Martin Heidegger,* pp. 168–170. Mark Lilla takes up "the call of conscience" in relation to his "rhetoric of authenticity and resoluteness" in *The Reckless Mind: Intellectuals in Politics* (New York: New York Review of Books, 2001), p. 27.

24. Müller, "Martin Heidegger," in Neske and Kettering, *Martin Heidegger and National Socialism,* pp. 178–179.

25. Ursula Ludz, ed., *Hannah Arendt/Martin Heidegger, Briefe, 1925 bis 1975* (Frankfurt am Main: Klostermann, 1998), p. 11. Elzbieta Ettinger notes the sentimental tone of Heidegger's letters to Hannah Arendt at this time. Ettinger, *Arendt/Heidegger* (New Haven, Conn.: Yale University Press, 1995).

26. Miguel de Beistegui, *Heidegger and the Political Dystopias* (London: Routledge, 1998), pp. 45–46, 60–61. Ott, *Martin Heidegger,* pp. 169–170.

27. Karl Löwith, *My Life in Germany before and after 1933,* trans. Elizabeth King (Champaign-Urbana: University of Illinois Press, 1986), p. 28.

28. Hermann Mörchen, quoted in Safranski, *Martin Heidegger,* pp. 226–227. Ott, *Martin Heidegger,* pp. 192–193. Heidegger received party number 3,125,894. After 1945 Heidegger shrewdly attributed his support for Hitler to his fear of Communism.

29. Neske and Kettering, *Martin Heidegger and National Socialism.* Before 1933, Heidegger commented, there were only two non-Jews. Shortly thereafter, only two professors were not Jews. Ettinger, *Arendt/Heidegger,* pp. 36–37.

30. Farias, *Heidegger and Nazism,* p. 149; Safranski, *Martin Heidegger,* pp. 235, 224.

31. On election day, 14 of 93 regular faculty members entitled to vote did not attend.

Thirteen others had been dismissed because of their racial identity, leftist opinions, or both. All but one of those who attended voted for Heidegger. Ott, *Martin Heidegger*, p. 146. Safranski, *Martin Heidegger*, p. 240.

32. In early May, he asked Hitler to postpone an upcoming meeting so that Nazi academics would have the chance to eliminate possible opponents. The meeting was not delayed, but the telegram provides evidence of Heidegger's willing participation in the nationwide drive to impose the "leadership principle" on university life. Ott, *Martin Heidegger*, pp. 187–209.

33. Safranski, *Martin Heidegger*, p. 242. Heidegger distorted the speech in his interview with Rudolf Augstein of *Der Spiegel;* see Neske and Kettering, *Martin Heidegger and National Socialism*, pp. 50–51.

34. Translation from Neske and Kettering, *Martin Heidegger and National Socialism*, p. 12.

35. De Beistegui, *Heidegger and the Political Dystopias*, pp. 39–46.

36. Jaspers, *Philosophische Autobiographie*, p. 101. "Heidegger selbst schien sich verändert zu haben." Safranski, *Martin Heidegger*, p. 232. Despite profound disagreements with Heidegger, Jaspers thanked him a few months later for the lavishly printed copy of his rector's address.

37. Farias, *Heidegger and Nazism*, pp. 136–148. Heidegger told students that the Nazi takeover was but a "prelude to true combat" and called for "a tough struggle to the end in the spirit of National Socialism." He justified the time taken up by National Socialist paramilitary drill and other activities because "the struggle that is beginning is the struggle for the new Teacher and the new *Führer* of the university."

38. *Bekenntnis der Professoren an den deutschen Universitäten und Hochschulen zu Adolf Hitler und dem nationalsozialistischen Staat überreicht vom Nationalsozialistischen Lehrerbund* (Dresden: Limpert, 1933), pp. 36–37. I used the rather awkward English translation of the original edition—lavishly printed in English, French, and Italian translations of the German. Compare Max Weinreich, *Hitler's Professors: The Part of Scholarship in Germany's Crimes against the Jewish People* (1946; New Haven, Conn.: Yale University Press, 1999), pp. 14–15. Ott, *Martin Heidegger*, p. 205. Hellmut Seier, "Der Rektor als Führer," *Vierteljarhshefte für Zeitgeschichte* 2 (Apr. 1964): 105–145.

39. Löwith, *My Life in Germany*, pp. 31–33. Heidegger wrote of "freedom for death" and Schmitt of "sacrifice of life" in the case of war. "Thus it is no mere chance that one finds a political 'decisionism' in Carl Schmitt which corresponds to Heidegger's existentialist philosophy."

40. Heidegger to Schmitt, *Telos* 72 (Summer 1987): 132.

41. Johannes Negelinus, *Schattenrisse* (Leipzig: Maier, 1913). Raphael Gross, *Carl Schmitt und die Juden: Eine deutsche Rechtslehre* (Frankfurt am Main: Suhrkamp, 2000), pp. 31–42.

42. Paul Noack, *Carl Schmitt: Eine Biographie* (Frankfurt am Main: Propyläen, 1990), p. 38. Schmitt was 1.59 meters, or about 5 feet 3 inches, tall.

43. Schmitt called the work a total work of art, *Gesamtkunstwerk*, a *pitura poesis*. Carl Schmitt, *Theodor Däubler's "Nordlicht": Drei Studien über die Elemente, den Geist und die Aktualität des Werkes* (Munich: Müller, 1916), pp. 41, 36.

44. "The *Volk* urges itself on, instinctively submits and allows itself to be whipped." Schmitt, *Däubler's "Nordlicht,"* pp. 35–36.

45. He despised the "nauseating flood of approaching materialism and the pernicious values" as the *Ungeist*. Carl Schmitt, afterword to Johannes Arnold Kanne, in *Aus meinem Leben: Berenhorst, Selbstbekenntnis* (Vienna: Karolinger, 1918), pp. 57–58.

46. Schmitt, *Däubler's "Nordlicht,"* p. 59. Like his peers, Schmitt also echoed Nietzsche's complaints about life as a meaningless void, a "grinding machine" (*Zarathustra*, Aphorism no. 61).

47. Schmitt, *Däubler's "Nordlicht,"* pp. 64–65.

48. George Schwab, *The Challenge of the Exception: An Introduction to the Political Ideas of*

Carl Schmitt (New York: Greenwood, 1989), p. 15. Paul Noack, Carl Schmitt, pp. 83–86. Todorovic was fifteen years his junior and bore a striking physical but not personal resemblance to Dorotic. Colleagues registered their surprise at hearing him address his wife in the polite Sie form long after the practice had been dropped even in most upper-class families.

49. Earlier he had also rejected his youthful romanticism on the grounds of its hypocrisy. "Everything romantic stands in the service of other, unromantic energies." Carl Schmitt, Political Romanticism, trans. Guy Oakes (Cambridge: MIT Press, 1986), p. 144.

50. Schmitt, Däubler's "Nordlicht," pp. 64–65. The impact of war on Sigmund Freud's vision of philia and neikos bears striking parallels; see Jacques Derrida, Politics of Friendship, trans. George Collins (London: Verso, 1997), p. 112.

51. Quoted in Mark Lilla, "The Enemy of Liberalism," New York Review of Books 44 (May 15, 1997): 40.

52. In discussing morality, Dostoevsky, and Hobbes, Schmitt commented, "Tell me who your enemy is and I will tell you who you are" ("Nenne mir Deinen Feind, und ich sage Dir, wer Du bist"). Carl Schmitt, Glossarium: Aufzeichnungen der Jahre 1947–1951, ed. Eberhard Freiherr von Medem (Berlin: Duncker & Humblot, 1991), pp. 243, 4–5.

53. Leo Strauss, "Notes on the Concept of the Political," reprinted in Heinrich Meier, Carl Schmitt and Leo Strauss: The Hidden Dialogue (Chicago: University of Chicago Press, 1995), pp. 100–110.

54. Dirk Blasius, Carl Schmitt: Preußischer Staatsrat in Hitlers Reich (Cologne: Vandenhoeck & Ruprecht, 2001), pp. 86–105.

55. In his diary, Schmitt noted the April 1 boycott and mentioned having heard from his wife, who was at that time visiting Jewish friends in Hamburg, about its impact. But he registered no particular reaction. Noack, Carl Schmitt, 170–171.

56. Quoted in Noack, Carl Schmitt, p. 178. Schmitt became party member number 2,098,860. Blasius, Carl Schmitt, p. 10.

57. Carl Schmitt, "Aus Deutschland." Perhaps because he had once admired the theorist Julius Stahl, Schmitt singled him out for ridicule. "Prussian nobles and theologians praised a man named Joelsohn, who called himself Friedrich Julius Stahl." Westdeutscher Beobachter, May 31, 1933, reprinted in Josef Becker and Ruth Becker, Hitlers Machtergreifung: Vom Machtantritt Hitlers, 30. Januar 1933, bis zur Beseitigung des Einparteienstaates, 14. Juli 1933 (Munich: Deutscher Taschenbuch Verlag, 1983), doc. 280, pp. 323–325. On Schmitt's antisemitism, see Gross, Carl Schmitt und die Juden, pp. 43–50.

58. Schmitt's pamphlet is often cited in works on dictatorship, for example, Karl Dietrich Bracher, Wolfgang Sauer, and Gerhard Schulz, Die nationalsozialistische Machtergreifung: Studien zur Errichtung des totalitären Herrschaftssystems in Deutschland, 1933/34 (Cologne: Westdeutscher, 1960), pp. 372–374, 1001; Arendt, Origins of Totalitarianism, p. 262.

59. Carl Schmitt, Staat, Bewegung, Volk: Die Dreigliederung der politischen Einheit (Hamburg: Hanseatische, 1933), pp. 17, 35.

60. Blasius, Carl Schmitt, pp. 153–155.

61. Carl Schmitt, Westdeutscher Beobachter, May 12, 1933, reprinted in Becker and Becker, Hitlers Machtergreifung, 1933, doc. 253, p. 301. Schmitt equated national character with "a sense of order and discipline."

62. Schmitt, Staat, Bewegung, Volk, pp. 8, 17–21, 44.

63. Kittel's father praised Jewish soldiers' courage in World War I. Ericksen, Theologians under Hitler, p. 207, n. 88. Rudolf Kittel, Leipziger akademische Reden zum Kriegsende (Leipzig: Lorentz, 1919), and Judenfeindschaft oder Gotteslästerung (Leipzig: Wiegand, 1914).

64. For a theological historicization of Kittel's antisemitism, see Eleanor Siegele-Wenschkewitz, Neutestamentliche Wissenschaft vor der Judenfrage: Gerhard Kittels theologische Arbeit im Wandel deutscher Geschichte (Munich: Kaiser, 1980), pp. 7–33.

65. "Stimmen aus der deutschen christlichen Studentenbewegung," in Ericksen, Theologians under Hitler, pp. 25–26.

66. Ibid., p. 54.

67. Robert P. Erickson, "Assessing the Heritage," in Susannah Heschel and Robert P. Erickson, eds., *Betrayal: The German Churches and the Holocaust* (Minneapolis, Minn.: Fortress, 1999), p. 24.

68. Siegele-Wenschkewitz, *Neutestamentliche Wissenschaft*, p. 63.

69. Ibid., pp. 64–66.

70. Ericksen, *Theologians under Hitler*, p. 205, n. 22.

71. Heinrich Stern surveys how widespread this assumption was, in *Angriff und Abwehr: Ein Handbuch der Judenfrage*, 2nd ed. (Berlin: Philo, 1924).

72. Siegele-Wenschkewitz, *Neutestamentliche Wissenschaft*, p. 69. Gerhard Kittel, *Die Judenfrage* (Stuttgart: Kohlhammer, 1933), 3rd ed. Kittel dedicated the volume to "Meinen Bundesbrüdern" on the fiftieth anniversary of the founding of the Verein deutscher Studenten in Tübingen.

73. Kittel, *Die Judenfrage*, p. 7.

74. Ibid., p. 9. He quoted Gottfried Feder, *Das Programm der NSDAP und seine weltanschaulichen Grundlagen* (Munich: Eher, 1933), p. 30.

75. "A forced extermination of Jews cannot be seriously considered . . . the idea in any case is so absurd it is not worth the effort to respond." Kittel, *Die Judenfrage*, p. 14.

76. In the 1934 edition, Kittel added that other nations might want to absorb Jews from Germany, although it was clear he doubted that this would happen. Kittel used the term "eine gewaltsame Ausrottung des Judentums." *Die Judenfrage*, pp. 14, 115, n. 4.

77. Ericksen, *Theologians under Hitler*, pp. 55–57. Kittel, *Judenfrage*, pp. 13–27.

78. Kittel, *Die Judenfrage*, p. 51.

79. Hitler, "Rede auf einer NSDAP-Versammlung," Nuremberg, Jan. 3, 1923, in Eberhard Jäckel, ed., *Hitler: Sämtliche Aufzeichnungen, 1905–1924* (Stuttgart: Deutsche Verlags-Anstalt, 1980), doc. 454, pp. 776–780. He railed against "christlichen Juden" who betrayed Christ; he condemned their "whore selfishness" and demanded "not neighborly love" toward the Jews but the "gallows."

80. Kittel, *Die Judenfrage*, p. 105.

81. Ibid., p. 108 (emphasis in the original). On September 27, 1933, 2,000 Protestant ministers endorsed the introduction of the Aryan paragraph, which expelled ministers with Jewish ancestors from the ministry.

82. Kittel, *Die Judenfrage*, p. 68. Weinreich, *Hitler's Professors*, p. 41.

83. Kittel, *Die Judenfrage*, p. 67.

84. A Protestant theologian wrote, "No one in England, Jew or Christian, troubles about the views of Nazi professors who have given themselves to Hitler and sinned against the light. It is just not worthwhile . . . But about you we are troubled and grieved because we reckoned you to be on the side of the angels," quoted in Ericksen, *Theologians under Hitler*, p. 29.

85. Kittel insisted that, because of their "visitor status and foreign, alien nature" *(Gastsein, Fremdlingsein, Andersartigkeit)*, Jews were outsiders, and his motives had nothing to do with hatred. He reasoned, for example, that claiming that too many mediocre Jews were overpopulating particular occupations was not "defamation." It would have been "defamation" if he had said race made Jews mediocre. Kittel, *Die Judenfrage*, p. 95. His remarks to Buber later became the basis of *Die Behandlung des Nichtjudens nach dem Talmud;* see Weinreich, *Hitler's Professors*, pp. 216–218. On Buber's response, compare Jonathan C. Friedman, *The Lion and the Star: Gentile-Jewish Relations in Three Hessian Communities, 1919–1945* (Lexington: University Press of Kentucky, 1998), pp. 143–144.

86. His theologian colleagues were astonished that a Christian could write such things. To one critic (whom Kittel cited in the notes to the second edition), it seemed as if Kittel refrained from advocating murder, or *totschlagen,* only because "it might have seemed a bit inhuman." A British critic asked, "Is it not significant that when this theologian considers the

policy of pogroms . . . he rules [them] out not because they are wicked but only because they are impracticable?" *Judenfrage,* p. 115, n. 4.

87. Apr. 22, 1933, cited in Joseph W. Bendersky, *Carl Schmitt: Theorist for the Reich* (Princeton, N.J.: Princeton University Press, 1983), p. 203.

88. Weinreich, *Hitler's Professors,* pp. 41–42.

89. Joseph B. Levy, "Die guten und die bösen Deutschen," Houghton, bMS Ger 91 (135), reprinted in Margarete Limberg and Hubert Rübsaat, eds., *"Sie durften nicht mehr Deutsche sein": Jüdischer Alltag in Selbstzeugnissen, 1933–1938* (Frankfurt am Main: Campus, 1990), pp. 178–182.

4. THE CONQUEST OF POLITICAL CULTURE

1. William Shirer, *The Nightmare Years, 1930–1939* (New York: Bantam, 1984), p. 121. Ralph Georg Reuth, *Joseph Goebbels,* trans. Krishna Winston (New York: Harcourt Brace, 1993), p. 187. Hitler, speech of Jan. 3, 1933, Lippe, in Max Domarus, ed., *Hitler Speeches and Proclamations, 1932–1945: The Chronicle of a Dictatorship,* vol. 1, trans. Mary Fran Gilbert (Wauconda, Ill.: Bolchazy-Carducci, 1990), pp. 213–214. Claudia Koonz, *Mothers in the Fatherland* (New York: St. Martin's, 1987), pp. 136–138. Diary entry of Aug. 30, 1933, in Bella Fromm, *Blood and Banquets: A Berlin Social Diary* (New York: Harper & Brothers, 1942), p. 55.

2. Letter to Erika Mitterer, Apr. 28, 1933, Josef Becker and Ruch Becker, eds., *Hitlers Machtergreifung: Vom Machtantritt Hitlers, 30. Januar 1933 bis zur Beseitigung des Einparteienstaates, 14. Juli 1933* (Munich: dtv, 1983), doc 219, p. 272. "Steamroller" was a common metaphor for the Nazi takeover; see, for example, "Racial Hygiene," *Times* (London), Apr. 7, 1933; George Gordon, Berlin, June 24, 1933, *FRUS,* vol. 3, doc. 2496, p. 239.

3. Walter Thomas (Andermann; pseud.), *Bis der Vorhang fiel* (Dortmund, Schwalvenberg, 1947), p. 51.

4. Roger B. Nelson, "Hitler's Propaganda Machine," *Current History* 38 (June 1933): 287–294. Goebbels, diary entry of Apr. 6, 1933, in Elke Fröhlich, ed., *Die Tagebücher von Joseph Goebbels: Sämtliche Fragmente,* part 1, *Aufzeichnungen, 1924–1941,* vol. 2 (Munich: Saur, 1987), p. 403,

5. Günther S. Stent, *Nazis, Women, and Molecular Biology: Memoirs of a Lucky Self-Hater* (Kensington, Calif.: Briones, 1998), p. 51.

6. Goebbels, diary entry of Apr. 6, 1933, in Fröhlich, *Tagebücher,* part 1, vol. 2, p. 403. Georg Stark, *Moderne politische Propaganda* (Munich: Eher, 1930), p. 6. "Adolf Hitler Pass—Named," *New York Times,* Apr. 17, 1933.

7. "Nazis Ban Song 'Lorelei' Because Heine Wrote It," *New York Times,* Nov. 14, 1933. *Frankfurter Zeitung,* Aug. 5, 1933.

8. Hitler, press conference of Apr. 27, 1933, in Domarus, *Hitler Speeches,* vol. 1, p. 309. The editor noted that streets and squares named after Hitler nevertheless appeared everywhere over the next twelve years. Goebbels, diary entry of Apr. 6, 1933, in Fröhlich, *Tagebücher,* part 1, vol. 2, p. 403; Hitler's birthday speech, Domarus, *Hitler Speeches,* vol. 1, p. 257. Ian Kershaw, *Hitler, 1889–1935,* vol. 1 (New York: W. W. Norton, 1999), p. 484. Sabine Behrenbeck, "Der Führer: Die Einführung eines politischen Markenartikels," in Gerald Diesener and Rainer Gries, eds., *Propaganda in Deutschland: Zur Geschichte der politischen Massenbeeinflussung im 20. Jahrhundert* (Darmstadt: Primus, 1996), pp. 51–78.

9. *Deutschland-Berichte der Sozialdemokratischen Partei Deutschlands/ Sopade* (Frankfurt am Main: Petra Nettelbeck, 1937–1940) (hereafter *Sopade*), May/June 1934, p. 152.

10. Alan E. Steinweis, "Cultural Eugenics: Social Policy, Economic Reform, and the Purge of Jews from German Cultural Life," in Glenn R. Cuomo, ed., *National Socialist Cultural Policy* (New York: St. Martin's, 1995), pp. 23–37.

11. "Betteln polizeilich verboten . . . Gebt alles dem Winterhilfswerk!" Poster from 1933, reprinted in Wolfgang Ayaß, *'Asoziale' im Nationalsozialismus* (Stuttgart: Klett-Cotta,

1995), p. 28. Publicity attacked the "asocial," a category that included beggars, hoboes, homeless, and sexual "deviants"—that is, sex offenders and homosexuals.

12. Announcements on July 14 and July 20, 1933. Herbert Michaelis and Ernst Schraepler, eds., *Ursachen und Folgen: Vom deutschen Zusammenbruch 1918 und 1945 bis zur staatlichen Neuordnung Deutschlands in der Gegenwart*, vol. 9 (Berlin: Dokumenten-Verlag Wendler, n.d. [1959–1979]), doc. 2103, p. 301; docs. 2077 and 2078, pp. 233–234.

13. Hitler, press conference of Oct. 18, 1933, in Domarus, *Hitler Speeches*, vol. 1, pp. 378–380. Hitler explained why legal methods were more effective than violence to journalist Ward Price on February 13, 1934, Domarus, *Hitler Speeches*, vol. 1, pp. 433–435.

14. Sidney B. Fay "The Hitler Dictatorship," *Current History* 38 (May 1933), pp. 230–232.

15. Siegfried Kracauer, *From Caligari to Hitler: A Psychological History of the German Film* (Princeton, N.J.: Princeton University Press, 1947), pp. 8–11, 267–269, 250–259. Heidi E. Faletti, "Reflections on Weimar Cinema," in Robert C. Reimer, ed., *Cultural History through a National Socialist Lens* (Rochester, N.Y.: Camden House, 2000), pp. 11–36.

16. Hans Dieter Schäfer, *Das gespaltene Bewußtsein: Über deutsche Kultur und Lebenswirklichkeit, 1933–1945* (Munich: Carl Hanser, 1982), pp. 115–121. Peter Reichel, *Der schöne Schein des Dritten Reiches: Faszination und Gewalt des Faschismus* (Munich: Hanser, 1991). Leny Yahi, "Double Consciousness," in David Bankio, ed., *Probing the Depths of German Anti-Semitism: German Society and the Persecution of the Jews, 1933–1941* (New York: Berghahn, 2000), pp. 35–53.

17. Rudolf Jordan, *Erlebt und Erlitten: Weg eines Gauleiters von München bis Moskau* (Leoni am Starnberger See: Druffel, 1971), p. 117.

18. "The chief preoccupation of the new régime has been to press forward with the greatest energy the creation of uniformity throughout every department of German life." Rumbold to Simon, no. 421, Apr. 26, 1933, *DBFP*, vol. 4, appendix, pp. 864–865. Gordon Craig, *Germany, 1966–1945* (New York: Oxford University Press, 1978), p. 578.

19. Correspondent in Germany, "Die Erneuerung der Universität," *Spectator*, June 9, 1933, pp. 831–832.

20. Victor Klemperer, *LTI: Notizbuch eines Philologen* (Frankfurt am Main: Röderberg, 1987), pp. 18, 164–165.

21. Klemperer, *LTI*, pp. 101, 21 (quotation). Rumbold emphasized two characteristics of the Nazi regime: first, the immense variety in ideas and personalities in the leadership and, second, the "amorphous, absorptive and even absorbable nature" of the Nazi movement. *DBFP*, vol. 4, Appendix, p. 889.

22. Karl Dietrich Bracher, Wolfgang Sauer, and Gerhard Schulz, *Die nationalsozialistische Machtergreifung: Studien zur Errichtung des totalitären Herrschaftssystems in Deutschland, 1933/34* (Cologne: Westdeutscher, 1960), pp. 207–209. Hitler, Speech to SA and SS Men and Young Steel Helmets, June 26, 1933, in Domarus, *Hitler Speeches*, vol. 1, pp. 337–339.

23. "Die Jugend im Dritten Reich," *Sopade*, Sept./Oct. 1934, p. 573.

24. George Gordon, no. 2350, Berlin, May 1, 1933, *FRUS*, vol. 2, p. 229.

25. Louis Lochner interview, Mar. 25, 1934, in Domarus, *Hitler Speeches*, vol. 1, pp. 444–446.

26. Willi A. Boelcke, *The Secret Conferences of Dr. Goebbels: The Nazi Propaganda War, 1939–1945*, trans. Ewald Osters (New York: E. P. Dutton, 1970), pp. 7–31. Marlis G. Steinert, *Hitlers Krieg und die Deutschen: Stimmung und Haltung der deutschen Bevölkerung im Zweiten Weltkrieg* (Düsseldorf: Econ, 1970), pp. 11–13.

27. Introduction, in Heinz Boberach, ed., *Meldungen aus dem Reich: Die geheimen Lageberichte des Sicherheitsdienstes der SS,* 17 vols., vol. 1 (Herrsching: Pawlak, 1984), pp. 11–31. David Bankier, *The Germans and the Final Solution: Public Opinion under Nazism* (Oxford, Eng.: Blackwell, 1992), pp. 5–13. D. Welch, *The Third Reich*, p. 51. Klaus Drobisch, "Die Judenreferate des Geheimen Staatspolizeiamtes und des Sicherheitsdienstes der SS, 1933 bis 1939," *Jahrbuch für Antisemistimusforschung* (Frankfurt am Main: Campus, 1992), pp. 230–

247. Steinert, *Hitlers Krieg*, pp. 17–51. Ian Kershaw, *The "Hitler Myth": Image and Reality in the Third Reich* (New York: Oxford University Press, 1987), pp. 97–104.

28. See, for example, the Monatsbericht from Feb. 1937, BAB/R58/266. See also Boberach, *Meldungen*, p. 533.

29. Aryeh L. Unger, "The Public Opinion Reports of the Nazi Party," *Public Opinion Quarterly* 29 (1965): 565–582. O. D. Kulka and A. Rodrigue, "The German Population and the Jews," *Yad Vashem Studies* 16 (1985): 421–424.

30. "Bericht über die Lage," report no. 7 (May 1934), in Bernd Stöver, ed., *Berichte über die Lage in Deutschland* (Bonn: Dietz, 1996), doc. 6, pp. 140–148. Bankier, *The Germans and the Final Solution*, pp. 70–72. Max Weber described the process by which charismatic leadership solidifies into bureaucratic rule, in "Politics as a Vocation," in Hans Gerth and C. Wright Mills, eds., *From Max Weber: Essays in Sociology* (New York: Galaxy, 1960), pp. 90–96.

31. *Sopade*, May/June 1934, p. 169. Dietrich Orlow confirms these reports in *The History of the Nazi Party, 1933–1945* (Pittsburgh, Pa.: University of Pittsburgh Press, 1973), vol. 2, p. 99.

32. *The Yellow Spot: The Outlawing of a Half a Million Human Beings—A Collection of Facts and Documents Relating to Three Years' Persecution of German Jews*, introduction by the bishop of Durham (London: Victor Gollancz, 1936), p. 283.

33. Rudolf Steiner, "My Life in Germany," Houghton, bMS Ger 91 (227), 99–101.

34. Fritz Stern, *Dreams and Delusions: The Drama of German History* (New Haven, Conn.: Yale University Press, 1987), p. 170. "It, *Selbstgleichschaltung*, signifies voluntary, preemptive acceptance of the conformity . . . expected by the regime."

35. Erich Ebermayer, *Denn heute gehört uns Deutschland: Persönliches und Politisches Tagebuch* (Hamburg: Paul Zsolnay, 1959), pp. 46–51. Fromm describes a similar conversation, on April 3, 1933, in *Blood and Banquets*, p. 102.

36. *Sopade*, Sept. 1934, p. 477.

37. François-Poncet, dispatch 715, Berlin, July 4, 1933. *DDF*, 1st ser., vol. 2, doc. 449, pp. 324–325.

38. Representative activities blended leisure and ideology. A sample from mid-July in Munich included "Die zweite Reihe Schulungskurse," "Theaterabend," "Schulungsabend—Pflicht," *VB* 46 (July 17, 1933), and public lectures "Der Staat aus Blut und Boden," "Adolf Hitler wie ein Seher," a torchlight parade, and "Kulturpolitischer Abend," *VB* 46 (July 30, 1933).

39. Ella B. Christoffers, "My Life in Germany," Houghton, bMS Ger 91 (43).

40. Margot Littauer, "My Life in Germany," Houghton, bMS Ger 91 (412).

41. *Sopade*, July/Aug. 1934, p. 275.

42. Cigaretten-Bilderdienst, ed., *Adolf Hitler: Bilder aus dem Leben des Führers* (Altona-Barhrenfeld: Cigaretten-Bilderdienst, 1935). Seven hundred thousand copies were printed in the first edition.

43. Simonetta Falasca-Zamponi, *Fascist Spectacle: The Aesthetics of Power in Mussolini's Italy* (Berkeley: University of California Press, 1997), pp. 45–88.

44. Heinrich Hoffmann, *Hitler abseits vom Alltag: 100 Bilddokumente aus der Umgebung des Führers* (Berlin: Zeitgeschichte, 1937), and *Adolf Hitler wie ihn Keiner kennt: 100 Bilddokumente aus dem Leben des Führers*, with 100 photographs and an introduction by Baldur von Schirach (Munich: Zeitgeschichte, 1933).

45. Heinrich Hoffmann, ed., *Deutschland Erwacht: Werden, Kampf und Sieg der NSDAP* (Altona-Bahrenfeld: Cigaretten-Bilderdienst, 1933). The military theme was taken up in *Die deutsche Wehrmacht* (Dresden: Cigaretten-Bilderdienst, 1936).

46. This is part of the series "Kampf ums Dritte Reich." Heinrich Hoffmann, *Der Staat der Arbeit und des Friedens: Ein Jahr Regierung Adolf Hitlers* (Altona-Bahrenfeld: Cigaretten-Bilderdienst, 1934).

47. *Die Reden Hitlers für Gleichberechtigung und Frieden* (Munich: Eher, 1934).

48. *Die Reden Hitlers als Kanzler: Das junge Deutschland will Arbeit und Frieden,* 4th ed. (Munich: Eher, 1934). Eighty thousand copies were published in four editions.

49. Velhagen & Klasing published 300 booklets ranging from 130 to 150 pages in length between 1933 and 1939. A typical example is Martin Iskraut, ed., *Nationalsozialistische Weltanschauung: Auswahl aus Schriften und Reden des Führers Adolf Hitler und seiner Mitkämpfer Gottfried Feder, Alfred Rosenberg, Dr. Joseph Goebbels, Walter Darré und Hanns Johst* (Bielefeld: Velhagen & Klasing, 1934), p. 1935.

50. George S. Mosse, *The Fascist Revolution: Toward a General Theory of Fascism* (New York: Fertig, 1999), pp. 158–173.

51. For summaries of *Der Wanderer* and *Brüder,* see Joseph Wulf, *Theater und Film im Dritten Reich: Eine Dokumentation* (Gütersloh: Mohn 1964), pp. 190–192. Goebbels' *Michael* was a morality play that praised sacrifice to the *Volk* as the highest virtue.

52. The "voice of the blood" creates ethnic unity out of divisive class, religious, and regional allegiances. Kurt Kölsch, "Nationalsozialistische Kulturpolitik in der Grenzmark," *Unser Wille und Weg* 4 (June 1934): 161.

53. Hedda Lembach, "Hier hört eben die Vernunft auf," *Nationalsozialistische Monatshefte* (Sept. 1933), p. 464.

54. Bernd Stöver, *Volksgemeinschaft im Dritten Reich: Die Konsensbereitschaft der Deutschen aus der Sicht sozialistischer Exilberichte* (Dusseldorf: Droste, 1993), pp. 35–55, 115–174.

55. "Das Reich sorgt für die Kämpfer der nationalen Bewegung," *VB* 46 (July 22, 1933); "Versöhnung," *VB* 46 (Oct. 18, 1933). To administer a party of 2,600,000 by the mid-1930s, the Nazi Party appointed 373,000 functionaries; by comparison, the Social Democratic Party in the 1920s, with 1,000,000 members, employed only 10,000 functionaries. Orlow, *History,* vol. 2, pp. 91–95.

56. Jordan, *Erlebt und Erlitten,* p. 121. Kater, *Nazi Party,* p. 262 and fig. 1.

57. Peter Longerich, *Die braune Battalionen: Geschichte der SA* (Munich: Beck, 1989), pp. 83, 188, 196ff. Conan Fischer, *Stormtroopers: A Social, Economic, and Ideological Analysis, 1925–1935* (London: Allen & Unwin, 1983), pp. 148–169, demonstrates the lack of concern with ideology among Stormtroopers.

58. "As a group, the party's local leaders, *Kreisleiters,* in 1933 were typically frustrated, lower-middle-class individuals." Of the 776 district leaders in 1935, 58.5% described themselves as white-collar or civil service employees, who seemed to think, "As a National Socialist I express the feelings of the people; I am not concerned with legal niceties." Orlow, *History,* vol. 2, pp. 38–39.

59. Orlow, *History,* vol. 2, p. 33.

60. Hitler, "Großer SA Appell vor dem Führer," speech to 45,000 SA men, Kiel, May 7, 1933, *VB* 46 (May 8, 1933).

61. Jordan, *Erlebt und Erlitten,* pp. 125–126. Domarus, *Hitler Speeches,* vol. 1, p. 456. Kater, *Nazi Party,* pp. 92, 329.

62. Hitler's speech to the *Reichsstaathalter,* governors, July 6, 1933, in Domarus, *Hitler Speeches,* vol. 1, pp. 342–343.

63. "Die Macht haben wir," *VB* 46 (July 11, 1933), Munich edition. Hitler, speech to SA in Dortmund, July 9, 1933, in Domarus, *Hitler Speeches,* vol. 1, p. 345.

64. Hitler, July 6, 1933, Berlin speech to *Reichsstaatshalter,* in Domarus, *Hitler Speeches,* vol. 1, p. 343. "Wir haben die Aufgabe eine eherne Front zu bilden!", *VB* 46 (Sept. 3, 1933), edition A, Nord. Gordon, no. 2529, Berlin, *FRUS,* July 10, 1933, vol. 2, p. 246.

65. Hitler, Oct. 15, 1933, in Domarus, *Hitler Speeches,* vol. 1, p. 378.

66. Domarus, *Hitler Speeches,* vol. 1, p. 432. Hitler placed top priority on selecting men who would be capable and utterly obedient ("Menschen die einerseits fähig, andersseits in blindem Gehorsam die Maßnahmen der Regierung durchsetzen"). Hitler speech to

Gauleiter-Tagung, Berlin, Feb. 2, 1934, and Hitler letter to Röhm of Dec. 31, 1933, doc. 2365 in *Ursachen und Folgen: Vom deutschen Zusammenbruch 1918 und 1945 bis zur staatlichen Neuordnung Deutschlands in der Gegenwart,* vol. 10 (Berlin: Dokumenten-Verlag Wendler, n.d. [1959–1979]), doc. 2365, pp. 133–135.

67. Quoted in David Welch, *Propaganda and the German Cinema, 1933–1945* (Oxford, Eng.: Clarendon, 1983), p. 67. Jay W. Baird, *To Die for Germany: Heroes in the Nazi Pantheon* (Bloomington: University of Indiana Press, 1990), p. 84. Linda Schulte-Sasse, *Entertaining the Third Reich: Illusions of Wholeness in Nazi Cinema* (Durham, N.C.: Duke University Press, 1996), pp. 258–268. Goebbels emphasized high production values and entertainment over narrow Nazi dogma. Monika Speer, ed., *Schlager: Das große Schlager-Buch* (Munich: Rogner & Bernhard, 1978), pp. 179–180. Rudolf Steiner described the scandal when Goebbels canceled the premier of the first version. Houghton, bMS Ger 91 (100).

68. Interview with Hanns Johst, BAB/R43/2/387. Kershaw discusses Hitler's new image in "The Führer Image and Political Integration: The Popular Conception of Hitler in Bavaria," in Gerhard Hirschfeld and Lothar Lettenacker, eds., *Der "Führerstaat": Mythos und Realität* (Stuttgart: Klett-Cotta, 1981), pp. 139–141.

69. Goebbels commented at the opening of the Propaganda Ministry in March 1933, "Anyone who had no firm political conviction could become a Bolshevik after seeing the film. It shows very clearly that a work of art can be tendentious . . . if it . . . is an outstanding work of art." Welch, *Propaganda and the German Cinema,* pp. 12–13. A *Sopade* report on film-making from 1937 noted that the "simplistic political propaganda" films ("eindeutig politische Tendenzfilme") proved to be "aesthetically worthless," and distributors requested not to be supplied with more like them—and, the author noted, radio and stage producers registered the same opinion. *Sopade,* June 1937, pp. 908–909. "Filmschau," *National-sozialistische Monatshefte* 7 (1936): 85–86.

70. Hitler, "Großer SA Appell," speech of May 7, 1933, in Domarus, *Hitler Speeches,* vol. 1, p. 319; *VB* 46 (May 8, 1933).

71. On Hitler's rewriting of party history, see Willi Münzenberg, *Propaganda als Waffe* (Paris: Éditions du Carrefour, 1937), pp. 198–201.

72. Hitler in Saarbrücken celebrating the return of the Saar, speech of Mar. 1, 1935, in Domarus, *Hitler Speeches,* vol. 2, pp. 643–648.

73. Interview with Ward Price, Feb. 14, 1934, in Domarus, *Hitler Speeches,* vol. 1, p. 433.

74. "Feierliche Einweihung der Reichsführerschule durch Adolf Hitler," *VB* 46 (June 17, 1933).

75. Hitler, "Revolutionary Roll Call," Mar. 19, 1934, in Domarus, *Hitler Speeches,* vol. 1, p. 441.

76. "Adolf Hitler über Fürhrung und Führertum," *VB* 46 (June 18–19, 1933).

77. Door-to-door collections, leafletting, street-corner speaking, fundraising, and postering were all forms of *Kleinarbeit.*

78. "Kämpfer ohne Schwert," *VB* 46 (July 20, 1933). Kurt Rittweger, *Der unbekannte Redner der Partei: Tagebuchskizzen eines Redners* (Munich: J. B. Lindl, 1939). Josef Sebastian Viera, *SA.-Mann Schott* (Leipzig, Schneider, 1933); *Männer gegen Schnüffler* (München, Zentralverlag der NSDAP, Eher, 1937). Adolf Hitler, *Zehn Jahre unbekannter S.A.-Mann* (Oldenburg: Gerhard Stalling, 1933); *Der Unbekannte S.A.-Mann: Ein guter Kamerad der Hitler-Soldaten* (Munich: Eher, 1934); Hermann Gerstmayer, *SA.-Mann Peter Müller,* 3rd ed. (Berlin, J. Beltz, 1933); *A.B.C. für den SA-Mann: Grundlagen für den S.A. Dienst* (Frankfurt am Main: Kolb, 1934); Friedrich Wilhelm Hillmann, *Kampf an der Unterweser* (Bremerhaven: Morisse, 1934).

79. Rittweger called on the "shock-troop orators" (*Stoßtruppredner*) not to break the law. *Der unbekannte Redner,* pp. 13–14. And he dignified *Kleinarbeit* as an honor, p. 10.

80. Walter Tießler, "Neue Wege der Propaganda," *Unser Wille und Weg* 4 (July 1934): 204–208. Hugo Ringler, "Der Redner, der aktivste Träger der nationalsozialistischen Propa-

ganda," *Unser Wille und Weg* 4 (July 1934): 234–249; Ringler, "Zum Aufklärungsfeldzug," *Unser Wille und Weg* 41 (Jan. 1934): 6–7.

81. *Aufklärungs- und Redner-Informationsmaterial der Reichspropagandaleitung der NSDAP und des Propagandaamtes der Deutschen Arbeitsfront* (Munich: Der Partei, 1935–1944). Fischer, *Stormtroopers*, pp. 65–70.

82. Dr. Günther Frohner, "Die Durchführung von öffentlichen Versammlungen in geschlossenen Räumen: Skizzen für den Entwurf einer Dienstvorschrift." *Unser Wille und Weg* 4 (July 1934): 230–232.

83. Kurt Pfeil, "Wie wir unsere Aktion gegen Miesmacher und Kritikaster organisierten," *Unser Wille und Weg* 4 (July 1934): 226–228. Mordehoff, "Propaganda einer Ortsgruppe," *Unser Wille und Weg* 5 (July 1935): 231–234.

84. William Edward Dodd, memo of Sept. 12, 1933, NA/RG59/862.401/1.

85. Max Weinreich, *Hitler's Professors: The Part of Scholarship in Germany's Crimes against the Jewish People* (1946; New Haven, Conn.: Yale University Press, 1999), pp. 20–21.

86. *Sopade*, May/June 1934, p. 117.

87. *Kreisleiter*, Munich East, Bericht über den ersten politischen Schulungsabend. Feb. 27, 1934, Staatsarchiv Munich (hereafter StAM)/NSDAP 981.

88. Party member Dr. Passow, "Vortrag über 'Rassenkunde,'" Oct. 12, 1933, Bertram. BAB/R1501/26246/Bl. 146–153. Passow, a fanatical old fighter, assembled a series of Hitler quotations to demonstrate that the Führer actually did remain true to his racist ideas. *Ja aber . . . was sagt Hitler selbst? Eine Auswahl* (Munich: Eher, 1931). Among the topics discussed at the indoctrination evenings in Munich were the experiences of SA unit 2VR16, "the National Socialist spirit in the Postal Service," a musical evening for the Women's Association, an enlightenment evening, a guest appearance by pilot Hannah Reitsch, and a National Socialist garden concert. *VB* 46 (July 16, 1933); *VB* 46 (July 19, 1933), Munich edition.

89. Walter Gross, "Schwierigkeiten mit der 'deutschen Rasse,'" memo to the Office of Racial Politics, Oct. 24, 1934, in Léon Poliakov and Josef Wulf, eds., *Das Dritte Reich und seine Denker: Dokumente* (Berlin: Arani, 1959), p. 411.

90. F. O. Bilse, "Die sittliche Förderung im Nationalsozialismus: Nationalsozialismus eine Revolution," *Nationalsozialistische Monatshefte* 4 (June 1933): 263.

91. Röhm praised the "disciplined brown Storm Battalions" under his command, Ernst Röhm, "S.A. und deutsche Revolution," *Nationalsozialistische Monatshefte* 4 (June 1933): 251–254. Wolfgang Horn, *Führerideologie und Parteiorganisation, 1919–1933* (Düsseldorf: Droste, 1972), pp. 332–333.

92. "Braunhemden in Hannover: Die Romreiter beim S.A.-Appell," *VB* 46 (July 20, 1933).

93. Otto Gohdes, "Das Prinzip der weltanschaulichen Schulung," *Schulungsbrief* (Reichsschulungsamt der NSDAP und der DAF, Berlin), 1 (Mar. 1934): 4.

94. Hermann Schäfer, "Der Funkwart und seine Aufgaben," *Unser Wille und Weg* 4 (Apr. 1934): 105.

95. Eugen Hadamowsky quotes Wolf Zeller, "Propaganda und National Macht," trans. Daniel Lerner, typescript (1954), pp. 67, 83. Bracher, Sauer, and Schulz, *Die Machtergreifung*, pp. 296–297. Roland Marchand, *Advertising the American Dream: Making Way for Modernity, 1920–1940* (Berkeley: University of California Press, 1985), p. xxi.

96. "Was sendet Berlin?" *Vossische Zeitung*, Apr. 20, 1933.

97. Neu-Beginnen report, June 1935, in Stöver, *Volksgemeinschaft*, p. 298.

98. Hadamovsky to Hitler, Mar. 23, 1935, in Josef Wulf, ed., *Presse und Funk im Dritten Reich: Eine Dokumentation* (Gütersloh: Mohn, 1964), p. 309. The Nazis, the first political organizers to appreciate film as a political weapon, made their first film in 1927, which was released on Hitler's birthday in 1929. The Reichsfilmstelle was founded in November 1930. Konopath, Apr. 1, 1931, NA/T-580/33/Ordner 228. G. Koch, "Der NS-Film-Institutiónen," in Bernd Sösemann, ed., *Nationalsozialismus* (Stuttgart: DVA, 2002), pp. 214–220.

99. Goebbels, diary entry of Apr. 8, 1933, in Fröhlich, *Tagebücher,* part 1, vol. 2, pp. 404–405.

100. Dr. Goebbels, Reichsminister, Sept. 22, 1933, BAB/R43/2/387/Bl. 30. Goebbels, *National-sozialistischer Rundfunk* (Munich: Eher, 1935).

101. Inge Marssolek and Adelheid von Saldern, *Radio im Nationalsozialismus: Zwischen Lenkung und Ablenkung* (Tübingen: Edition Diskord, 1998). Kate Lacey, *Feminine Frequencies: Gender, German Radio, and the Public Sphere, 1923–1945* (Ann Arbor: University of Michigan Press, 1996). On the financial background for programming changes, see Hans Bausch, *Rundfunk in Deutschland* (Munich: DTV, 1980), pp. 142–205.

102. Speeches by Goebbels, May 3, 1934; Göring, June 26, 1934; and Hitler, June 17, 1934, in Domarus, *Hitler Speeches,* vol. 1, pp. 455, 466, 464.

103. Lothar Machtan, *Hidden Hitler,* trans. John Brownjohn (New York: Basic Books, 2001), pp. 216–224. Among those murdered who may have had such information were Gregor Strasser, ex-chancellor general Kurt von Schleicher, and his close adviser General Ferdinand von Bredow, conservative critic Edgar Jung, Prussian Interior Ministry police chief Erich Klausener, Munich journalist Fritz Gerlich, ex–Bavarian premier Gustav Ritter von Kahr, and Karl Zehnter, the owner of a reputedly homosexual "hangout" of the SA. Even the top Nazi attorney, Alfons Sack, was jailed for a month while Gestapo officials searched his documents. It was also during this time that Ernst Hanfstangel and Kurt Leudeke were suggesting that they knew more about Hitler's sexual proclivities than was publicly known.

104. Klaus-Jürgen Müller, *Das Heer und Hitler: Armee und nationalsozialistisches Regime, 1933–1940* (Stuttgart: Deutsche Verlags-Anstalt, 1969), pp. 122–135. Heinz Höhne, *Mordsache Röhm: Hitlers Durchbruch zur Alleinherrschaft* (Rheinbek: Rowohlt, 1984), pp. 297–298, 306–316.

105. Hitler, July 13, 1934, in Domarus, *Hitler Speeches,* vol. 1, p. 487. Hitler circulated a press release and wrote his orders for Röhm's successor Victor Lutze on June 30, ibid., pp. 472–477. Only a passing comment about "international Jewish well-wishers [*Menschheitsbeglücker*]" referred to Jews. Machtan, *Hidden Hitler,* p. 215. Kershaw, "The Führer Image," pp. 142–144.

106. About a fifth of the lower officials in the Nazi Party were removed at this time. Orlow, *History,* vol. 2, pp. 118–126.

107. Hitler, speech of July 13, 1934, in Domarus, *Hitler Speeches,* vol. 1, p. 432. As in his 1924 trial, Hitler rhetorically addressed mothers with his appeals to virtue.

108. Hitler to party comrades, Berlin, Aug. 20, 1934 (after the plebiscite), in Domarus, *Hitler Speeches,* vol. 1, p. 526.

109. Carl Schmitt, "Der Führer schützt das Recht: Zur Reichstagsrede Adolf Hitlers vom 13. Juli 1934," *Deutsche Juristen-Zeitung* 39 (1934): 945–950.

110. Alexandre Koyre, "The Political Function of the Modern Lie," *Contemporary Jewish Record* (June 1945), pp. 294–296, 298.

111. Hitler, speeches made on September 13, 1935, Domarus, *Hitler Speeches,* vol. 2, pp. 703–708; September 13, 1937, ibid., vol. 2, pp. 936–942; and January 30, 1939, ibid., vol. 3, pp. 1446–1449.

112. Hitler, speech to NS Frauenschaft, Nuremberg, Sept. 8, 1934, in Domarus, *Hitler Speeches,* vol. 1, p. 532.

113. Otto D. Tolischus, "The German Book of Destiny," *New York Times Magazine* (Oct. 18, 1936) "Die Geburtstaggabe der deutschen Beamtenschaft," *VB* magazine section, 49, no. 111 (Apr. 20, 1936).

5. ETHNIC REVIVAL AND RACIST ANXIETY

1. The committee included racial scientists like Bodo Spiethoff, Alfred Ploetz, Fritz Lenz, and Ernst Rüdin, ideologues like Baldur von Schirach, Walter Darré, Hans F. K.

Günther, Paul Schultze-Naumberg, and Nazi racial bureaucrats like Friedrich Bartels, Arthur Gütt, Bernhard Lösener, Falk Ruttke, and Gerhard Wagner. BAB/R1501/26248, 266249. Paul Weindling and Christian Gansmüller, *Die Erbgesundheitspolitik des Dritten Reiches: Planung, Durchführung, und Durchsetzung* (Cologne: Böhlau, 1987), pp. 36–46.

2. Wilhelm Frick, *Bevölkerungs- und Rassenpolitik* (Langensalza: Beyer, 1933), p. 9. Hans-Walter Schmul, *Rassenhygiene, Nationalsozialismus, Euthanasie: Von der Verhütung zur Vernichtung 'Lebensunwerten Lebens,' 1939–1945* (Göttingen: Vandenhoeck & Ruprecht, 1987), pp. 23–40. Paul Weindling, *Health, Race and German Politics between National Unification and Nazism, 1870–1945* (Cambridge: Cambridge University Press, 1989), pp. 521, 454–457, 462–484; Gabriele Cznarnowski, "Hereditary and Racial Welfare," *Social Politics* 4 (Spring 1997): 114–135. "Niederschrift über die Beratung," Nov. 14–15, 1933, BAB/NS10/34/Bl. 38–61.

3. "Verhütung erbkranken Nachwuches, Minister Frick legt dem Rasserat sein neues Gesetz vor," *Vossische Zeitung* 306 (June 28, 1933), evening ed.

4. Hitler, "Aufruf an die Kraft!" *VB* 42 (Aug. 7, 1929).

5. "Kabinettesberatung vom 14. July 1933." (Secret!) BAB/1501/25248/Bl. 311. The policy was announced in *VB* 46 (June 29, 1933), sec. 2. Jeremy Noakes, "Nazism and Eugenics: The Background to the Nazi Sterilization Law of 14 July, 1933," in R. J. Bullen, H. Pogge von Strandmann, and A. B. Polonsky, eds., *Ideas into Politics* (London: Croom-Helm, 1984), pp. 75–94.

6. Hitler, July 6, 1933, in Max Domarus, ed., *Hitler Speeches and Proclamations, 1923–1945*, vol. 1, trans. Mary Fran Gilbert (Wauconda, Ill.: Bolchazy-Carducci, 1992), pp. 342–344. Hess acknowledged that the measure would be unpopular. Hitler remarked that any measures that maintained the *Volktum* were justified. Karl-Hinz Minuth, ed., *Die Regierung Hitler,* part 1, *1933/1934,* in *Akten der Reichskanzlei* (Boppard am Rhein: Boldt, 1983), vol. 1, pp. 664–665. Weindling, *Health,* pp. 397–398.

7. Holmes elaborated, "We have seen more than once that the public welfare many call upon the best citizens for their lives. It is better for all the world, if instead of waiting to execute the degenerate offspring for crime, or to let them starve for their imbecility, society can prevent those who are manifestly unfit from continuing their kind . . . Three generations of imbeciles are enough." This decision of upheld a Virginia law. Only one justice dissented from Holmes's majority opinion. Quoted in Jacob P. Landman, *Human Sterilization Movement: The History of the Sexual Sterilization Movement* (New York: Macmillan, 1932), pp. 10–14.

8. The issues that framed the 1933 law can be found in BAB/R1501/26248. Jonas Robitscher, ed., *Eugenic Sterilization* (Springfield, Ill.: Thomas, 1973), p. 123.

9. Walter Darré, *Neuadel aus Blut und Boden* (Munich: Lehmann, 1930), pp. 170–172.

10. Hans-Ulrich Brändle, as quoted in Sheila Weiss, "The Race Hygiene Movement in Germany," *Osiris,* 2nd ser., 3 (1987): 230. Wilhelm Frick, BAB/1501/26248/Bl. 422.

11. The Law for the Prevention of Progeny with Hereditary Diseases authorized physicians to order sterilization; it did not mandate them to do so. Weiss, "Race Hygiene," pp. 228–230; and Robert Proctor, *Racial Hygiene: Medicine under the Nazis* (Cambridge: Harvard University Press, 1988), pp. 95–117. Although 1,700 "genetic health courts" were planned, about 300 were subsequently established.

12. Hitler, *Mein Kampf* (Boston: Houghton Mifflin, 1962), pp. 404–405.

13. Their birth years were as follows: Speer, 1905; Scholtz-Klink, 1902; Riefenstahl, 1902; Heydrich, 1904; Best, 1903; Höß, 1900; Eichmann, 1906; and Frank, 1900. Michael Burleigh, *The Third Reich: A New History* (New York: Hill & Wang, 2000), p. 315. Ulrich Herbert, "The National Socialist Political Police," in Hans Mommsen, ed., *The Third Reich between Vision and Reality: New Perspectives on German History, 1918–1945* (New York: Berg, 2001), pp. 95–101. Men of this generation provided the driving force of wartime extermination as well, as demonstrated by the biographies of a random sample compiled in Michael

Wildt, *Generation des Unbedingten: Das Führungskorps des Reichssicherheitshauptamtes* (Hamburg: Hamburger Edition, 2002), pp. 143–191.

14. Max Weinreich, *Hitler's Professors: The Part of Scholarship in Germany's Crimes against the Jewish People* (New Haven, Conn.: Yale University Press, 1999), pp. 79–81, 174–175.

15. Proctor, *Racial Hygiene*, 89. Robert Wistrich, *Who's Who in Nazi Germany* (London: Routledge, 1995), pp. 87–88. Michael H. Kater, *Doctors under Hitler* (Chapel Hill: University of North Carolina Press, 1989), pp. 181–182.

16. Reinhard Bollmus, *Das Amt Rosenberg und seine Gegner: Studien zum Machtkampf im nationalsozialistischen Herrschaftssystem* (Stuttgart: Deutsche Verlags-Anstalt, 1970), p. 274.

17. Richard Breitman, *The Architect of Genocide: Himmler and the Final Solution* (New York: Knopf, 1991), p. 86.

18. Roger Uhle, "Neues Volk und Reine Rasse: Walter Gross und das Rassenpolitische Amt der NSDAP" (Ph.D. diss., Rheinisch-Westfälische Technische Hochschule Aachen, 1999), pp. 44–53. The author thanks Hans Mommsen for recommending this valuable work. Reichsorganisationsleiter der NSDAP, ed., *Organisationsbuch der NSDAP* (Munich: Eher, 1936), pp. 330–334. Gross worked closely with the Nazi Teachers League, NSLB; see Leckler, "Aufbau," Nov. 17, 1933, BAB/NS22/827.

19. Heinrich Becker, Hans-Joachim Dhams, and Cornelia Wegeler, eds., *Die Universität Göttingen unter dem Nationalsozialismus* (Munich: Saur, 1987), pp. 16–21. Among the members of the Deutschvölkischen Schutz- und Trutz-Bundes who became influential Nazis were Julius Streicher, Fritz Saukel, Walter Buch, Werner Best, Leonardo Conti, Reinhardt Heydrich, Friedrich Mennecke, Viktor Lutze, Karl Florian, and Joseph Grohé. Uhle, "Neues Volk und Reine Rasse," p. 77.

20. Walter Gross, "Die biologische Lage des deutschen Volkes," *Der Weltkampf: Monatsschrift für Weltpolitik, völkische Kultur und die Judenfrage aller Länder* 4 (Sept. 1927): 393–409. Hitler, speech to party faithful, Nov. 9, 1927, and speech in Hof, Oct. 16, 1927, in Bärbel Dusik, ed., *Hitler: Reden, Schriften, Anordnungen*, vol. 2, part 2, *August 1927 bis Mai 1928* (Munich: Saur, 1992), docs. 187, 190, pp. 520–521, 533–535.

21. Report on a ten-hour meeting on July 30, 1932, Reichorganisationsleitung (ROL), sec. 3, Aug. 1, 1932, BAB/NS22/445. For biographical information, see NA/BDC/OPG Akten, NA/BDC/A3340-MFOK-G029/frame 1010; BDC/A3345-DS-J008. Gross's birthday was listed as both October 21, 1904, and January 20, 1904. Reichserziehung Ministerium [REM] Personalakte, G 211. Wistrich, *Who's Who in Nazi Germany*, pp. 87–88. Bollmus, *Das Amt Rosenberg*, pp. 220, 274. Roger Uhle, "Neues Volk und reine Rasse," pp. 73–79.

22. Walter Gross, "Braunschweig: Bericht und Sinndeutung," *Ziel und Weg* (hereafter *ZuW*) 2, no. 5 (Nov. 1932): 4.

23. Walter Gross, "Die Propheten: Friedrich Nietzsche, Paul de Lagarde und Houston Stewart Chamberlain in ihrer Bedeutung für uns," *Nationalsozialistische Monatshefte* 1 (Apr. 1930): 29–33.

24. Dr. Groß, Braunschweig, "Kritik der 'Gesellschaft,'" *Nationalsozialistische Monatshefte* 1 (Nov. 1930): 393–384.

25. Walter Gross, "Warum Antisemitismus?" *Weltkampf* 8 (Mar. 1931): 109.

26. Uhle, "Neues Volk und reine Rasse," pp. 78–79. Although Gross claims to have served in the SA, he did not receive the official recognition that he normally would have, and as late as 1935 he refused to join the SS.

27. More than three dozen proposals arrived at Nazi Party headquarters. "Anregung zur Rasseforschung Privat 1933," BAB/R39/102. Several specialists expressed their ideas in the press. Martin Staemmler, "Rassenhygiene im Dritten Reich," lecture, Dec. 5, 1931, at the Leipzig Convention of the NS Doctors' League, *ZuW* 2, no. 1 (Jan. 1932): 7. "Amt für Rassenpflege," *Vossische Zeitung* 234 (May 18, 1933), evening ed.

28. Ludolf Haase, "Vorschlag zur Errichtung des Reichsrassenamtes," *ZuW* 3, no. 11 (Aug. 1933): 286. Uhle, "Neues Volk und reine Rasse," pp. 78–80.

29. Gross, speech to NS Frauenschaft, Cologne-Aachen, Oct.13, 1934, NA/T-81/22/ 19682.

30. Charlotte Köhn-Behrens, *Was ist Rasse? Gespräche mit den größten deutschen Forschern der Gegenwart* (Munich: Eher, 1934), p. 74. This brief book, published by the Nazi Party publisher, was evidently written by an author with Jewish ancestry. The chaotic state of racial thinking subsided quickly and Köhn-Behrens relocated to the United States.

31. Walter Gross, *Rassenpolitische Erziehung* (Berlin: Junker & Dünnhaupt, 1934), pp. 28–29. Gross often worried about "Scorn and hostility." "Die Aufgabe," *ZuW* 3, nos. 1/2 (Mar. 1933): 3–6.

32. Gross called for the "training of the Will, Heart, and Mind": see Walter Gross, *Rassenpolitische Erziehung* (Berlin: Junker & Dünnhaupt, 1934) p. 6. This volume appeared in the series of the Deutsche Hochschule für Politik. Franz Alfred Six, "Die politische Propaganda der NSDAP im Kampf um die Macht" (Ph.D. diss., Heidelberg University, 1936), pp. 60–64. Organisationsabteilung, Munich, Sept. 20, 1932, BAB/NS22/445/folder 1.

33. "Das Aufklärungsamt für Bevölkerungspolitik und Rassenpflege," *Neues Volk: Blätter des Aufklärungsamtes für Bevölkerungspolitik und Rassenpflege* (henceforth *NV*) 1, no. 1 (July 1933): 10.

34. Walter Gross repeated his appeal often during these months. See Gross, "Die ewige Stimme des Blutes im Strome deutscher Geschichte," *NV* 1 (Aug. 1933); "Diesen Blutstrom gilt es rein zu halten," *VB* 46 (Sept. 2, 1933), sec. 3. Physicians were advised to prepare for the administrative and technical challenges of the sterilization law in "Sterilisierungsgesetz ist da!" *ZuW* 3, no. 11 (Aug. 1933): 257–258, and "Politik und Rassenfrage," *ZuW* 3, no. 14 (Sept. 1933): 409–415.

35. Walter Gross, "Die ewige Stimme des Blutes im Strome deutscher Geschichte," *NV* 1 (Aug. 1933): 2–3; Gross, "An die Mitglieder," *ZuW* 3 (July 1933): 257–258.

36. "Politik und Rassenfrage," *ZuW* 3, no. 14 (Oct. 1933): 409–415. Weinreich, *Hitler's Professors,* p. 27.

37. Walter Gross, "Die ewige Stimme des Blutes im Strome deutscher Geschichte," *ZuW* 3, no. 10 (July 1933): 257.

38. Bernd Rüthers, *Carl Schmitt im Dritten Reich: Wissenschaft als Zeitgeist-Verstärkung?* (Munich: Beck, 1990), pp. 31–34.

39. Walter Gross, "An die Mitglieder des Nationalsozialistischen Deutschen Ärztebundes!" *ZuW* 3, no. 7 (June. 1933): 149.

40. "Zur Berufsethik des Arztes," *ZuW* 3, no. 7 (June 1933): 157–158.

41. Gross, "Politik und Rassenfrage," *ZuW* 3, no. 14 (Oct. 1933): 409–415. "Diesen Blutstrom gilt es rein zu halten!" *VB* 46 (Sept. 2, 1933), sec. 3. NA/BDC/A3345-DS-B030/ 2894–2897. "Dr. Walter Gross," in Léon Poliakov and Josef Wulf, eds., *Das Dritte Reich und seine Denker: Dokumente* (Berlin: Arani, 1959), p. 410.

42. Goebbels, diary entry of Sept. 2, 1933, in Elke Fröhlich, ed., *Die Tagebücher von Joseph Goebbels: Sämtliche Fragmente,* part 1, vol. 2 (Munich: Saur, 1987), p. 463.

43. Goebbels, diary entry of Oct. 28, 1937, ibid., vol. 3, p. 316.

44. Goebbels, diary entry of Oct. 27, 1937, ibid., vol. 3, pp. 314–315.

45. Himmler, Order no. 4, Apr. 23, 1934, NA/T-611/19, and memo, Sept. 27, 1934, BAB/ 4901/521/Bl. 10.

46. Rudolf Hess, NSDAP Reichsleitung, letter, May 15, 1934, and "Rassenpolitisches Amt, Aufbau, Organisation," Nov. 17, 1933, BAB/NS22/827, and NA/BDC/A3345-DS-J005/ 1444/Ordner 212. "Zehn Monate Aufklärungsamt," with a photograph of Gross and Helmut Unger, *ZuW* 4, no. 4 (Apr. 1934): 133.

47. Rudolf Hess, "Sonderlehrgang der Reichsschule Bernau," Summer 1934, NT/T-81/ 22/19711–19717/5.

48. Uhle, "Neues Volk und reine Rasse," pp. 4–6, 44–45. Alice Rilke, "Die Frau am

Werk," *ZuW* 7, no. 22 (1937): 612. Gross laid out ambitious plans for popularizing sterilization. Oct. 17, 1933, BAB/1501/26249.

49. Walter Gross, *Der deutsche Rassengedanke* (Berlin: Juncker & Dünnhaupt, 1939), pp. 26–27. "Die Dresdener Versammlung der deutschen Naturforscher: Rückblick und Kritik," *ZuW* 6, no. 19 (1936): 538–542.

50. Walter Gross, "An die Mitglieder," *ZuW* 3, no. 7 (Spring 1933): 149. Gross, Nov. 17, 1933, speech to the Interior Ministry Blue Ribbon Committee, *ZuW* 3, no. 12 (Dec. 1933): 606. Ulrich Herbert, *Best: Biographische Studien über Radikalismus, Weltanschauung und Vernunft, 1903–1989* (Bonn: Dietz, 1996), pp. 199–203, 206–209.

51. Walter Gross, speech in Cologne, Oct. 13, 1934, *Nationalsozialistische Rassenpolitik: Eine Rede an die deutschen Frauen* (Dessau: Dünnhaupt, n.d.), p. 18.

52. Walter Gross, "Du bist nichts, Dein Volk ist alles!" *NS Frauenwarte*, BAB/NSD47/3.

53. NA/A3345-DS-J005/Bl. 41. "Opfern und Dienen," and "Das Aufklärungsamt für Bevölkerungspolitik und Rassenpflege," *NV* 1 (July 1, 1933): 10. Weindling, *Health, Race*, pp. 520–521. Weinreich, *Hitler's Professors*, pp. 30, 171.

54. Dr. Curt Thomalla lecture, *Vossische Zeitung*, June 1, 1933, quoted in Comité des Délégations Juives, *Die Lage der Juden in Deutschland, 1933: Das Schwarzbuch—Tatsachen und Dokumente* (1934; Frankfurt am Main: Ullstein, 1983), pp. 452–453.

55. Gercke, memo of July 22, 1933, Reichsleitung NSDAP and distributed to all *Gauleiter.* "Grundsätzliches zur Mischlingefrage," BAB/NS22/827/Bl. 45–51. Achim Gercke, *Die Aufgaben des Sachverständigen für Rasseforschung beim Reichsministerium des Innern* (Leipzig: Zentralstelle, 1933). For Gercke's proposals on the "Jewish question" at this time, see Gercke's "Lösung der Judenfrage" and other Reichssippenamt (Reich Kinship Bureau) papers in BAB/R1509/35, and an article in *Der Jüdische Rundschau*, May 30, 1933, quoted in Comité des Délégations Juives, *Die Lage der Juden*, pp. 454–455. Diana Schulle, *Das Reichssippenamt: Eine Institution nationalsozialistischer Rassenpolitik* (Berlin: Logos, 2001), pp. 54–59.

56. Gross, *Rassenpolitische Erziehung*. Walter Gross, "Der Rassengedanke des Nationalsozialismus," *Die Schulungsbrief* 1 (Apr.1934): 6–8.

57. Walter Gross, "Charakter," *ZuW* 3, no. 7 (Aug. 1933): 330–350; Gross, "Hütet die Flamme," *ZuW* 3, no. 16 (May 1933): 114–115; Gross, "Arzt und Judenfrage," *ZuW* 3, no. 8 (May 1933): 186–187.

58. Gercke, radio address, July 7, 1933, "Die Erziehung zu rassischem Denken," BAB/R39/49/Bl. 1–7. The proposals he expressed privately were considerably more ruthless. See, for example, Achim Gercke, "Soll man den deutsch-jüdischen Bastarden die vollen Staatsbürgerrechte geben?" BAB/1509/35/Bl. 64–68.

59. Gross's office published a magazine devoted to popular health, *Die Volksgesundheitswacht* (People's Health Watch) from 1933 to 1944 in editions of more than 100,000. Proctor, *Racial Hygiene*, p. 78.

60. "Zum Gleit," with statements and the handwritten signatures of Gross, Arthur Gütt, Gerhard Wagner and other leading eugenicists and racists, *NV* 1 (July 1933), cover.

61. A. von Rohden, "Verstößt das Gesetz zur Verhütung erbkranken Nachwuches gegen das Gebot der Nächstenliebe?" *NV* 2 (Jan. 1, 1934): 8. Gross, *Der deutsche Rassengedanke*, p. 17. "Grenzen des Mitleids," *NV* 1 (July 1933): 18–20. Georg Usadel, "Nationalsozialistische Ethik," *NV* 3 (June 1935): 21–23.

62. The following is typical of these articles: "Von der äußeren zur inneren Revolution," *NV* 2 (Aug. 1, 1934): 4.

63. "Der Jude kriminell," *NV* 3 (Dec. 1935): 22–23.

64. Kopp von Hofe, "Frankreich und die schwarze Gefahr," *NV* (Oct. 1934): 7; Walter Gross, "Wert der Rasse?" *NV* 2 (June 1934): 20–26.

65. "Wohin wollt Ihr Deutschland? So? oder So?" *NV* 1 (Nov. 1933): 14–15. Two photos

without a headline juxtaposed an African-American hobo with healthy German youth looking out a train window.

66. "Vom Sinn der Familien Forschung," *NV* 2 (Nov. 1934): 10–11.

67. "Wie wollt Ihr Deutschland?" NV (Aug. 1933) and "Nicht Snobs, Gents, Tanzjunglinge und Barsitzer," ibid., (Sept 1933).

68. "Geschmachlosigkeit oder Rassevergessen?" *NV* 4 (July 1936): 22–27.

69. "Erbkrank," *NV* 1 (Jan. 1934): 16–17.

70. "Emigranten in Paris," *NV* 4 (June 1936): 19–25. "La Vie Pariesienne," *NV* 3 (July 1935): 33.

71. "Judenverfolgung in Deutschland?" *NV* 2 (Dec. 1934): 32–33.

72. Margot Littauer, "My Life in Germany," Houghton, bMS Ger 91 (412).

73. William Dodd, Feb. 27, 1935, NA/862.401/13. The course took place February 5–7, 1935. See also Gütt, letter to the CA Innere Mission, Jan. 14, 1935, StAM Gesundheitsämter 498.

74. *ZuW* 5, no. 7 (July 7 1935): 152.

75. Walter Gross, *N.S. Schul- und Tageszeitung,* Aug. 24, 1935.

76. Reiner Pommerin, *Sterilisierung der Rheinlandbastarde: der Schicksal einer farbigen Minderheit, 1918–1937* (Dusseldorf: Droste, 1979), pp. 72–78. Peter Weingart, Jürgen Kroll, and Kurt Bayert, *Rasse, Blut, und Gene: Geschichte der Eugenik und Rassenhygiene in Deutschland* (Frankfurt am Main: Suhrkamp, 1988), pp. 43–44.

77. Walter Gross, "Die deutsche Bevölkerungspolitik und das Ausland," *ZuW* 5, no. 7 (Apr. 1935): 152.

78. "Arbeitstagung RPA," June 20–29, 1935. NA/T-81/9/17448–17459.

79. Walter Gross, "Blut und Rasse," Cologne, Aug. 1935, NA/T-81/22/19682–19686.

80. "Eröffnung der 4. staatsmedizinischen Lehrgangs," *VB* 48 (Sept. 20, 1935). Falk Ruttke, "Rassen- und Erbpflege in der Gesetzgebung des dritten Reiches," *Die Schulungsbrief der DAF,* 1 (Oct. 1934): 7–17.

81. "Verantwortung und Freiheit," *NV* 3 (Aug. 1935): 5–8.

82. "Dr. Gross im Ärztekursus," Nov. 11, 1935, *Presseberich des Rassenpolitischen Amtes, Reichsleitung der NSDAP,* Nov. 28, 1935, BAB/NS2/155.

83. "Errichtung eines Rassenmuseums," *Frankfurter Zeitung,* June 17, 1939.

84. "Rassenmuseum Berlin," *ZuW* 9, no. 20 (Oct. 1939): 418.

85. Helmut Schubert, interview about Dr. Gross, Jan. 5, 1956, quoted in Uhle, "Neues Volk und Reine Rasse," pp. 227–228. For a survey of RPO activities at the local level, see Johnpeter Horst Gill, *The Nazi Movement in Baden* (Chapel Hill: University of North Carolina Press, 1983), pp. 357–362.

86. Proctor, *Racial Hygiene,* pp. 87–88, 285–286. Walter Gross, "Die Familie: Tagung des Rassenpolitisches Amtes," *ZuW* 8, no. 18 (Oct. 1938): 533–541.

87. Gross, "Die Familie," *ZuW* 8, no. 18 (Oct. 1937): 533–541.

88. Apr. 18, 1935, BAB/4901/521/Bl. 39–41.

89. "Internationaler Anthropologen- und Ethnologen-Kongress in Kopenhagen," Aug. 1–9, 1938. *Informationsdienst* 56 (Aug. 30, 1938), and "Tagung," *ZuW* 8, no. 20 (Dec. 1938): 531.

90. Neither Gross nor his colleagues mentioned the anti-miscegenation laws in former German African colonies. See, for example, Walter Gross, "National Socialist Racial Thought," G. Kurt Johannsen, ed., *Germany Speaks! Twenty-One Leading Members of the National Socialist Party,* foreword by Joachim von Ribbentrop (London: Butterworth, 1938), pp. 66–78; Wilhelm Frick, *Wir bauen das Dritte Reich* (Oldenburg: Stalling, 1934), pp. 64–67; Köhn-Behrens, *Was ist Rasse?* pp. 55–56.

91. William Dodd, dispatch, Feb. 27, 1935. NA/862.401/13.

92. "Dr. Gross Speaks before the Foreign Students of the Berlin University," *Raciopolitical Foreign Correspondence* (Oct. 1, 1936), pp. 1–6.

93. BAB/R1501/RMdI/25482. The Hoover Institution Library includes a large selection of single issues. Gross, "Die Familie," *ZuW* 8, no. 19 (Oct. 1938): 533–541.

94. Frank Dikörrwe, "Race Culture: Recent Perspectives on the History of Eugenics," *American Historical Review* 101 (Apr. 1998): 467–478.

95. Walter Gross, *Blood and Race: Radio Address to the Youth of the German Nation* (Milwaukee, Wis.: n.p., n.d.), p. 7.

96. Walter Gross, "Adolf Hitler zur Rassenpflege," *ZuW* 4, no. 4 (Feb. 1934): 118, cover.

97. Aaron Gilette, "Guido Landra and the Office of Racial Studies in Fascist Italy," *Holocaust and Genocide Studies* 16 (Winter 2002): 365–368.

98. Herbert Obenaus, "The Germans: 'An Anti-Semitic People.'" In David Bankier, ed., *Probing the Depths of German Anti-Semitism: German Society and the Persecution of the Jews, 1933–1941* (New York: Berghahn, 2000), pp. 166–173. The author highlights the successful efforts of a Hannover district leader to spread disinformation about Jews after the pogrom.

99. Walter Gross, "Grundsätzliche Bemerkungen zur Propaganda," *ZuW* 3, no. 13 (Sept. 1933): 384–386; Gross, "Zur Schulung und Propaganda," *ZuW* 3, no. 19 (Dec. 1933): 611.

100. Coverage of the International Film Festival in Berlin, *VB* 50 (Aug. 19, 1937). Walter Gross, "Der zweite Etappe," *ZuW* 7 (Apr. 1937): 310. Erich Berger, "Filmbetrachtungen: Filme sollen dem Leben dienen," *ZuW* 8, no. 22 (1938): 622; see also "Wir verzeichnen," *ZuW* 7, no 22 (1937): 477.

101. Walter Gross, "Diesen Blutstrom gilt es rein zu halten!" *VB*, Sept. 2, 1933, 3rd sec. Gernot Bock-Stieber, director, *Opfer der Vergangenheit: Die Sünde wider Blut und Rasse*, BAB/NS2/63/folder 1, "Geistige Wettkampf."

102. Memo of Mar. 3, 1936, BAB/R1501/25482/Bl. 51. "Filme zur Volksaufklärung," *NV* 4 (Feb. 1936): 12–16. Karl Ludwig Rost, *Sterilisation und Euthanasie im Film des 'Dritten Reiches': Nationalsozialistische Propaganda in ihrer Beziehung zu rassenhygienischen Maßnahmen des NS-Staates* (Husum: Matthiesen, 1987), pp. 59–85.

103. Parteigenosse [party member] Dietel, lecture, Bernau, July 1935, NA/T-81/75/Bl. 24.

104. Walter Gross, "Arzt und Judenfrage," *ZuW* 3, no. 8 (May 1933): 186. Jews, he said, were not "bad," or *schlecht*, but profoundly alien in the "deep recesses of their soul."

105. "Gross urges Germans to be constantly anti-Jewish minded," *New York Times*, July 2, 1935, p. 6, col. 3.

106. Leuschner, a staff member of the RPO, memo to *Reichsorganisationsleiter*, Munich, Aug. 18, 1937, BAB/NS22/287. Walter Gross, memo, "Btr: 'Deutsche Rasse,'" Rassenpolitisches Amt der NSDAP, Oct. 24, 1934, reprinted in Poliakov and Wulf, *Denker*, p. 411. Gross accused Gercke and Bartels of misusing "race."

107. Gross had already demonstrated his academic cantankerousness against, for example, Karl Saller during his student days. Becker, *Göttingen*, p. 32. Gross turned on racial extremists in "Feststellung," *ZuW* 4, no. 22 (Nov. 1934): 860. Despite Gross's objections, *Ziel und Weg* published an article by one of them, Lothar Gottlieb Tirala, "Medizin und Biologie," *ZuW* 5, no. 6 (Apr. 1935): 136–138.

On disputes among racial scientists during the 1930s, see Weindling, *Health*, pp. 509–522, and Kater, *Doctors under Hitler*, pp. 143–1544, 157–161.

108. The material was identified as "vertrauliche Mitteilungen" and "nur für den Dienstgebrauch" ("confidential" and "only for in-house use"), both of which labels were low on the classification scale. NA/T-175/229 and BDC/3345-DS-J005/Bl. 55ff. On the role of the RPO in training the Order Police, see Karl-Heinz Heller, "The Reshaping and Political Conditioning of the German Ordnungspolizei, 1933–1945" (Ph.D. diss., University of Cincinnati, 1970), pp. 180–192.

109. Gütt to Interior Ministry, Jan. 14, 1935, StAM, Gesundheitsämter 498. Gütt insisted that Gross justify the law in secular, National Socialist terms.

110. Two reports entitled "Staatsmedizinische Akademie" (in Munich and Berlin), *ZuW* 7, no. 6 (1937): 156–157.

111. "Die erste Lehrgang der Reichsfachsgruppe Medizin auf der Ordensburg Vogelsang," *ZuW* 7, no. 20 (1937): 518–520.

112. Notice in *ZuW* 5, no. 12 (1935): 256. Gross, "Grundsätze der nationalsozialist-ischen Rassenpolitik," Program of the Nationalpolitischer Lehrgang, 1938/1939, reprinted in Klaus-Jürgen Müller, *Das Heer und Hitler: Armee und nationalsozialistisches Regime, 1933–1940* (Stuttgart: Deutsche Verlags-Anstalt, 1969), doc. 38, p. 649. The lectures in this series, which covered every Nazi organization, included Gertrud Scholtz-Klink's lecture on the women's organizations and Arthur Gütt's lecture on pragmatic approaches to demographic improvement.

113. Nationalsozialistischer Lehrerbund, Reichsfachgebiet Rassenfrage, ed., *Shrifttum über Familie, Volk und Rasse, für die Hand des Lehrers und Schülers* (Berlin: Eher, 1938).

114. Walter Gross, "Der geistige Kampf um die Rassenpflege," *ZuW* 5, no. 18 (1935): 412.

115. K. D. Erdmann, "Lebensunwertes Leben," *Geschichte in Wissenschaft und Unterricht* 26 (1975): 215–225. For extensive records of protest, see BAB/4901/REM/964; BAB/R36/1380; and NA/T580/104/Ordner folder 9.

116. When Gross burned the ORP files, he destroyed a valuable source of information on public opinion. We can assume that the attitudes of those files were similar to that of other primary sources. See, for example, Frick to REM and Berlin Polizeipräsidenten, Dec. 27, 1935, BAB/R4901/REM/964/Bl. 12–42, and "Der Terror," *Sopade*, Jan. 1936, pp. 79–80.

117. NA/T-81/9/17224–172230. Marga Gifhorn, a local representative of the ORP, re-ported: "Gegen das Sterilizationsgesetz," *Pressedienst des Rassenpolitischen Amtes,* July 25, 1935.

118. Rundschreiben, 22/39, July 8, 1939, NA/T-81/9/17170ff. Otto Dov Kulka, "Die Nürnberger Rassengesetze und die deutsche Bevölkerung im Lichte geheimer NS-Lage- und Stimmungsberichte," *Vierteljahrshefte für Zeitgeschichte* 32 (1984): 582–624; David Bankier, *The Germans and the Final Solution: Public Opinion under Nazism* (Oxford, Eng.: Blackwell, 1992), pp. 67–88. Johnson, *Nazi Terror*, pp. 433–485. Nevertheless, many Germans came to accept the necessity of segregation after 1935. Bernd Stöver, *Volksgemeinschaft*, pp. 35–54, 173–184, 263–265, 413–428.

119. Uhle, "Neues Volk und reine Rasse," pp. 280–281. Party activists complained of *Überfütterung* because they had to buy more books than they had time to read.

120. Walter Gross, "Tagung des Rassenpolitischen Amtes," *ZuW* 8 (Nov. 1938): 532–535; Gross, "Um die Rassenhygiene als Lehr- und Forschungsfach," *ZuW* 7, no. 7 (1937): 166. See also Knorr, "Eine noch nicht genügend beachtete . . ." *ZuW* 7, no. 22 (1937): 570.

121. Walter Gross, "Entartete medizin: 'Künstliche Befruchtung' treibt tolle Blüten," *Der Angriff* 196 (Aug. 22, 1937). The possibility that women who rejected men's sexual ad-vances could bear children added force to his reactions.

122. "Wir verzeichnen," notice in *ZuW* 7, no. 19 (Nov. 1937): 556.

123. Walter Gross, "Rassengedanke und Wissenschaft," *ZuW* 6, no. 21 (Mar. 1936): 566–568.

124. Walter Gross, "Abschrift," undated, stamped "received" Nov. 5, 1937, BAB/NS22/827.

125. Gross to *Gau* representatives, Berlin, Oct. 24, 1934, quoted in Poliakov and Wulf, *Denker*, pp. 411–412.

126. Gross to the Reichsorganisationsleiter, "Abschrift," received on Nov. 5, 1937, BAB/NS22/827. Gross favored Nazi Party neutrality "vis-à-vis the *Unmenge* of scientific problems. "Wegbereiter," *Informationsdienst*, June 20, 1941.

127. "Die Idee muß rein und unverändert bestehen sonst bricht jede Bewegung in sich zusammen." Gross, "Ein neuer Abschnitt," *ZuW* 4 (Sept. 1934): 634.

128. Gross, "Grundsätzliche Bemerkungen zur Propaganda," *ZuW* 3 (Sept. 1933): 385–386.

129. Konrad Lorenz, "Disturbances of Species-Specific Behavior Caused by Domestication," 1940, quoted in Benno Müller-Hill, *Murderous Science: Elimination by Scientific Selection of Jews, Gypsies, and Others, Germany, 1933–1945*, trans. George R. Fraser (New York: Oxford University Press, 1988), pp. 14, 56.

6. THE SWASTIKA IN THE HEART OF THE YOUTH

1. Hitler to the Hitler Youth, Sept. 8, 1934. This speech was immortalized in *Triumph des Willens*, but it has been omitted from the Domarus edition of Hitler's speeches. The text appeared in *VB* 253 (Sept. 10, 1934). See also the report in *Sopade*, Sept./Oct. 1934, p. 551.

2. "Leitgedanken für den Geschichtsunterricht," *VB* 46 (July 14, 1933). Wilhelm Frick, *Kampfziel der deutschen Schule* (Langensalza: Beyer, 1933), pp. 4–7, 17–20. Frick, edict (*Erlaß*) of Dec. 18, 1934, *Ursachen und Folgen: Vom deutschen Zusammenbruch 1918 und 1945 bis zur staatlichen Neuordnung Deutschlands in der Gegenwart*, vol. 9 (Berlin: Dokumenten-Verlag Wendler, n.d. [1959–1979]), doc. 2179, p. 452.

3. Verena Hellwig, "Mein Leben," 1940 or 1941, Houghton, bMS Ger 91 (93).

4. Rolf Eilers, *Die nationalsozialistische Schulpolitik: Eine Studie zur Funktion der Erziehung im totalitaren Staat* (Cologne: Westdeutscher, 1962), p. 77. On teachers' political allegiance before *1933*, see Rainer Bölling, *Volksschullehrer und Politik: Der Deutsche Lehrerverein, 1918–1933* (Göttingen: Vandenhoeck & Ruprecht, 1978), pp. 195–225.

5. Michael Kater, *The Nazi Party: A Social Profile of Members and Leaders, 1919–1945* (Cambridge: Harvard University Press, 1983), pp. 68–69. In 1936, of 1,200,000 civil servants, 206,000, or 17 percent, belonged to the party. Of these, 5.8 percent were Nazi Party officials. Eilers, *Schulpolitik*, p. 74.

6. Michael Kater, "Hitlerjugend und Schule im Dritten Reich," *Historische Zeitschrift* 228 (1979): 572–623. Thirty-two percent of all recently graduated physicians joined the Nazi Party between 1933 and 1939. Michael Kater, *Doctors under Hitler* (Chapel Hill: University of North Carolina Press, 1989), pp. 67–69; Kater, *Nazi Party*, pp. 199, 383–384. Late in 1934 about 49 percent of all district leaders (*Kreisleiter*) were teachers; and the percentages among local leaders were roughly the same—42 percent of all *Ortsgruppenleiter* and 70 percent of all neighborhood organizers (*Stützpunktleiter*). The high percentages of Nazi officials resulted not so much from teachers' special devotion as from the lack of trustworthy Nazis with adequate literacy skills for office jobs.

7. Teachers' associations relented only after the Reichstag granted Hitler dictatorial power in March 1933. Marjorie Lamberti, *The Politics of Education: Teachers and School Reform in Weimar Germay* (New York: Berghahn, 2002). With 250 separate professional journals for teachers, it was not difficult for editors to change the masthead and article titles without transforming the content. Most of these periodicals were outlawed. Eilers, *Schulpolitik*, pp. 9–11.

8. The high percentage of teachers in the Nazi elite reflects the paucity of adequately trained Nazis to fill high positions, much as the fact that 14.2 percent of all teachers held high party offices resulted from a shortage of qualified Nazis. Heinz Sünker and Hans-Uwe Otto, eds., *Education and Fascism: Political Identity and Social Education in Nazi Germany* (London: Falmer, 1998).

9. Charles E. McClelland, *The German Experience of Professionalization* (Cambridge: Cambridge University Press, 1991), pp. 212–213. Thomas Childers, *The Nazi Voter: The Social Foundations of Fascism in Germany, 1919–1933* (Chapel Hill: University of North Carolina Press, 1983), p. 169. One educator warned of "an army of 120,000 jobless scholars." Jarausch and Gerhard Arminger, "The German Teaching Profession and Nazi Party Membership," *Journal of Interdisciplinary History* 20 (1989): 197–225. Jürgen Falter and Michael H.

Kater, "Wähler und Mitglieder der NSDAP: Neue Forschungsergebnisse zur Soziographie des Nationalsozialismus, 1925 bis 1933," *Geschichte und Gesellschaft* 19 (1993): 155–177.

10. Eilers, *Schulpolitik,* p. 74; McClelland, *Professionalization,* pp. 222–223. Jarausch, *Unfree Professions,* pp. 140–142. See BAB/NS12/1317.

11. Quoted in Delia Nixdorfand Gerd Nixdorf, "Politisierung und Neutralisierung der Schule in der NS-Zeit," in Hans Mommsen, ed., *Herrschaftsalltag im dritten Reich* (Düsseldorf: Schwann, 1988), pp. 226–227. "Die Zentralisierung des Bildungswesens," edict *(Erlaß)* by Hindenburg of May 1, 1933, and edict *(Erlaß)* by Adolf Hitler of May 11, 1934, on centralization, *Ursachen und Folgen,* vol. 9, doc. 2178, pp. 451–452.

12. More than 30 percent of all female head teachers were dismissed, as compared to 15 percent of their male peers. Eilers, *Schulpolitik,* pp. 68–71. By the end of 1933, 16 percent of all Prussian school administrators had been dismissed on one or another pretext. Of the 529 *Schulräten* (school inspectors) in Prussia, 118, or 22 percent, were fired pp. 227–228. Nixdorf and Nixdorf, in Hans Mommsen, *Herrschaftsalltag,* pp. 227–228. Of 596 tenured *Oberstudienräten* and *-rätinnen,* 47 (8 percent) were fired; of 13,023 male Studienräten, 355 (3 percent) lost their jobs. Eilers, *Schulpolitik,* p. 68. Ottwilm Ottweiler, *Die Volksschule im Nationalsozialismus* (Weinheim: Beltz, 1979), pp. 52–56.

13. Edward Yarnall Hartshorne, Jr., *The German Universities and National Socialism* (Cambridge: Harvard University Press, 1937), pp. 94–96; Helmut Heiber, *Universität unterm Hakenkreuz,* part 1, *Der Professor im Dritten Reich* (Munich: Saur, 1991), pp. 150–152; "Die Säuberung," Apr. 13, 1933, *Ursachen und Folgen,* vol. 9, doc. 2180, pp. 453–454.

14. An unsigned letter to the Interior Ministry, July 30, 1933, BAB/R1501/26246. Hartshorne, *German Universities,* pp. 56–71. Birgit Vezina, *"Die Gleichschaltung" der Universität Heidelberg im Zuge der nationalsozialistischen Machtergreifung* (Heidelberg: Winter, 1982), pp. 28–29. Fritz Stern, *Dreams and Delusions: The Drama of German History* (New Haven, Conn.: Yale University Press, 1987), pp. 158–165.

15. Ernst Krieck, *Erziehung im nationalsozialistischen Staat* (Berlin: Spaeth & Linde, 1935), p. 32; Krieck, *Nationalpolitische Erziehung* (Leipzig: Armanen, 1934), p. 47. Krieck criticized social Darwinism because competition among ethnic Germans would undercut the power of the *Volk* as a whole to compete against rivals.

16. Quoted in Ottwillm Ottweiler, *Die Volksschule im Nationalsozialismus* (Weinheim: Beltz, 1979), p. 58.

17. Ernst Krieck, *Volk unter dem Schicksal.* Published lecture (Heidelberg, 1939), pp. 9–10.

18. Erich Klinge, *Die Erziehung zur Tat, zu Mut, und zur Tapferkeit* (Dortmund: Crüwell, 1936).

19. Hans Schemm, "Das Haus der deutschen Erziehung," *Hans Schemm spricht* (Bayreuth: Kahl-Furthmann, 1942), pp. 297, 290.

20. Quoted by Karl Dietrich Bracher, "Die Gleichschaltung der deutschen Universitäten," *Universitatstage, 1966* (Berlin: De Gruyter, 1966), pp. 127–128.

21. Stephen H. Roberts, *The House That Hitler Built* (London: Methuen, 1937), p. 256. Robert S. Wistrich, *Who's Who in Nazi Germany* (London: Routledge, 1995), pp. 214–215.

22. "Der Sinn der nationalpolitischen Schulungslehrgänge," *Die deutsche höhere Schule* (Frankfurt am Main: Diesterweg) 2 (15 July, 1935): 497.

23. Rundschreiben des MfWKuV, Berlin, Sept. 13, 1933, in *Ursachen und Folgen,* vol. 9, doc. 2127, pp. 450–451. Between October 4, 1933, and December 15, 1933, Rust created a national program of student and teacher camps lasting between two and three weeks. The REM provided funding and required teachers' education in racial studies. Dr. Zühlke, Marburg, report of 12–14/Nov. 1934, BAB/4901/4607/Bl. 348.

24. "Halte dein Blut rein, / es ist nicht nur dein, / es kommt weit her, / es fliesst weit hin, / es ist von Tausend Ahnen schwer / und alle Zukunft ruht darin! Deiner Unsterblichkeit." Gretel and Karl Blome, *Ein Wort an junge Kameradinnen,* vol. 18, Schriftenreihe des Rassen-

politischen Amtes der NSDAP und des Reichsbundes Deutsche Familie (Berlin: Verlag Neues Volk, 1941?), 3rd ed.. Erika Mann, *School*, pp. 66–68.

25. The publisher Beyer, in Langensalza incorporated older titles into the new era and added three new topics: *Weltanschauung*, Education, and Race—and offered a 10 percent reduction in price. Reichsschulungsamt der NSDAP und der deutschen Arbeitsfront, *Der Schulungsbrief*.

26. Memo from district leader Trier, July 4, 1936, Franz Josef Heyen, *Nationalsozialismus im Alltag* (Boppard: Harald Boldt, 1967), doc. 134, p. 257. A good example of a relatively lavish booklet is Franz Lüke's eighty-three-page *Rassen ABC* (Bochum: Kamp, 1934).

27. *Kreisleiter*, Munich East, "Bericht über den ersten politischen Schulungsabend," Feb. 27, 1934, StaM/NSDAP 981.

28. The series title was *Schriften zu Deutschlands Eneuerung* (no. 54 a/b). The only title that remained in print was Curt Hermann's thirty-two-page *Der Jude und der deutsche Mensch: Was jedermann im Dritten Reich vom Judentum wissen müsste*, 2nd ed. (Breslau: Handel, 1935).

29. Günther Hecht, *Kannst Du rassisch denken?* (Hamburg: Berg & Otto, 1938).

30. Dr. Rudolf Benze and Alfred Pudelko, eds., *Rassische Erziehung als Unterrichtsgrundsatz der Fachgebiete* (Frankfurt am Main: Diesterweg, 1937).

31. "Die Jugend im Dritten Reich," *Sopade*, Feb. 1936, p. 199.

32. Ottwilm Ottweiler, *Die Volksschule im Nationalsozialismus* (Weinheim: Beltz, 1979).

33. In May 1933, 28,000 Bavarian Catholic teachers demonstrated in defense of their rights. Bredow to Kammerer, Apr. 7, 1938, StAM/NSDAP 351. For an account of the crucifix dispute, see Kershaw, *Popular Opinion and Political Dissent in the Third Reich: Bavaria, 1933–1945* (Oxford, Eng.: Clarendon, 1983).

34. Barbara Maier memos, especially "Bericht der Abteilung Weibl. Erziehung im Gau Mü-Obb 1. Vierteljahr 1936," StAM/ NSDAP 981. For more complaints by women, see BAB/NS12/temporary 844. Auguste Reber-Gruber, StAM/NSDAP 994, 998–999.

35. "Die Jugend," *Sopade*, Sept./Oct. 1934, p. 568.

36. "Die Jugend," *Sopade*, Feb. 1935, pp. 202–203.

37. The wide variation in treatment of Jewish students is obvious, for example, in the memoirs of Marcel Reich-Ranicki, Wolf-Dietrich Schnurre, and Walter Jens, in Marcel Reich-Ranicki, ed., *Meine Schulzeit im Dritten Reich: Erinnerungen deutscher Schriftsteller* (Cologne: Kiepenheuer & Witsch 1988); Max von den Grün, *Wie war es eigentlich? Kindheit und Jugend im Dritten Reich* (Darmstadt: Luchterhand, 1979); Wolfgang Keim, *Erziehung unter der Nazi-Diktatur* (Darmstadt: Wissenschaftliche Buchgesellschaft, 1995–1997); Marion A. Kaplan, *Between Dignity and Despair: Jewish Life in Nazi Germany* (New York: Oxford University Press, 1998), pp. 94–118; Clemens Vollnhals, "Jüdische Selbsthilfe bis 1938," in Wolfgang Benz, ed., *Die Juden in Deutschland, 1933–1945: Leben unter nationalsozialistischer Herrschaft* (Munich: Beck, 1988), pp. 330–341.

38. Eilers, *Schulpolitik*, pp. 54–58. Hojer, *Ernst Krieck*, p. 71.

39. "The Case of Hermann Staudinger," in Hugo Ott, *Martin Heidegger: A Political Life*, trans. Allan Blunden (New York: Basic Books, 1993), pp. 210–224. A similar fate befell Eduard Baumgarten; Rüdiger Safranski, *Martin Heidegger: Between Good and Evil* (Cambridge: Harvard University Press, 1998), pp. 271–273.

40. Schemm, like Krieck, was suspicious of established academics. Kater, *Nazi Party*, p. 161; Hojer, *Ernst Krieck*, pp. 55–57. Nazi pedagogues struggled to reconcile their praise of struggle in the biological world with their dislike of competition within the *Volk*. If a *Volk* was to prevail against its rivals, individuals would have to collaborate.

41. Ernst Krieck, "Über Nationalsozialismus," *Nationalpolitische Erziehung* 1 (Sept. 1934): 36–38. Ernst Hojer, *Nationalsozialismus und Pädagogik: Umfeld und Entwicklung der Pädagogik Ernst Kriecks* (Wurzburg: Königshausen, 1997), pp. 125–129.

42. Rudolf Benze, "Umschulung der Erzieher im Lager," *Deutsche Schulerziehung: Jarhbuch des Deutschen Zentralinstitut für Erziehung und Unterricht* (Berlin: Mitler, 1940), p. 347. *Sopade*, 1936, p. 198. Between 1933 and May 1935, for example, 66 percent of all teachers in Magdeburg, 90 percent in Silesia, and 88 percent in Hannover participated in training encampments. Ottweiler, *Volksschule*, pp. 55–57.

43. E. Tiersch, "Rassenfrage Betreffend!" Dec. 3, 1934, BAB/R1501/26246.

44. Elisabeth Evenius, Kurmark, Oct. 1934, BA/NS12/temporary 844. One teacher explained, "By the false application of the *Führer* principle, too many stand aside and await explicit instructions from above." An observer described the "mountains of forms that bury administrators in chaos." *Sopade*, Sept./Oct. 1934, p. 568.

45. Nixdorf, "Politisierung und Neutralisierung," in Mommsen, *Herrschaftsalltag.*, pp. 227–229.

46. Auguste Reber-Gruber, letters, 1935–1937, StAM/ NSDAP/994, 998.

47. Ley to Rust, Jan. 22 1937, in Hans-Jochen Gamm, *Führung und Verführung: Pädagogik des Nationalsozialismus* (Munich: List, [1964]), doc. 21, p. 133.

48. Kater, *Nazi Party,* pp. 93–94, 110, 132.

49. Melita Maschmann, *Account Rendered: A Dossier on My Former Self,* trans. Geoffrey Strachan (London: Abelard-Schuman, 1965), p. 31. Gregory Paul Wegner, *Anti-Semitism and Schooling in the Third Reich* (New York: Routledge-Falmer, 2002), pp. 66–93.

50. Lisa Pine, "The Dissemination of Nazi Ideology and Family Values through School Textbooks," *History of Education* 25 (1996): 91–109.

51. Hitler, quoted in Jay Baird, *To Die for Germany: Heroes in the Nazi Pantheon* (Bloomington: Indiana University Press, 1990), p. 202.

52. Christa Kamentsky, *Children's Literature in Hitler's Germany: The Cultural Policy of National Socialism* (Athens: Ohio University Press, 1984), pp. 207–209.

53. Karl Dilg, *Die deutsche Bauernsage in der Schule* (Leipzig: Harrassowitz, 1935), p. 106.

54. Heinz Schreckenberg, ed., *Erziehung, Lebenswelt und Kriegseinsatz der deutschen Jugend unter Hitler* (Münster: LIT, 2001), pp. 84–98, 145–163. Reiner Lehberger, "Neusprachlicher Unterricht," and Andreas Fritsch, "Die altsprachlichen Fächer," in Rheinhard Dithmar, *Schule und Unterricht im Dritten Reich* (Neuwied: Luchterhand, 1989), pp. 117–134, 163–186.

55. *Gau* inspector party member Thiel, Feb. 27, 1934, Wahn-Heide, NA/T-81/22/19516–19523.

56. Fritz Brennecke, *Vom deutschen Volk und seinem Lebensraum,* trans. Harwood L. Childs, in *The Nazi Primer,* commentary by William E. Dodd (New York: Harper, 1938), pp. 75–83.

57. Hans Berendes, "Die Körperliche Erziehung in der neuen Schule," *Die deutsche höhere Schule* 2 (July 1935): 456–459; Dr. Auguste Reber-Gruber, "Die Mädchenschule und die Parteigliederungen," *Die deutsche höhere Schule* 2 (July 1935): 480–485.

58. "Wenn ich die Stimme Adolf Hitlers höre," in Léon Poliakov and Josef Wulf, eds., *Das Dritte Reich und seine Denker: Dokumente* (Berlin: Arani, 1959), p. 48. Schreckenberg, *Erziehung,* pp. 112–116.

59. Alfons Heck, *A Child of Hitler: Germany in the Days When God Wore a Swastika* (Frederick, Colo.: Renaissance House, 1985), p. 8. Werner T. Angress, *Generation zwischen Furcht und Hoffnung: Jüdische Jugend im Dritten Reich* (Hamburg: Christians, 1985).

60. Cordelia Edvardson, *Gebranntes Kind sucht das Feuer,* trans. (from Swedish) Anna-Liese Kornitzky (Munich: Carl Hanser, 1987), pp. 37–38. Dagmar Reese, "Emancipation or Social Incorporation: Girls in the Bund Deutscher Mädel," in Sünker and Otto, *Education and Fascism,* pp. 102–120.

61. Maschmann, *Account Rendered,* pp. 26, 35. Memoir of Hans Bender, "Willst du nicht beitreten?" in Reich-Ranicki, *Meine Schulzeit,* pp. 37–38. *Sopade* reporters conceded that the young were seized by a "joy in sacrifice" *(Opferfreudigkeit),* Feb. 1936, pp. 170–171.

62. Christa Wolf, *A Model Childhood*, trans. Ursule Molinaro and Hedwig Rappolt (New York: Farrar, Straus and Giroux, 1980), p. 135.

63. Quoted in *The Yellow Spot: The Outlawing of a Half a Million Human Beings—A Collection of Facts and Documents Relating to Three Years' Persecution of German Jews*, introduction by the bishop of Durham (London: Victor Gollancz, 1936), pp. 245–246.

64. Martin Staemmler, *Der Sieg des Lebens: Lesestücke zur Rassenkunde* (Berlin: Verlag für Soziale Ethik und Kunstpflege, 1934). Other story titles include "Victory of the Strong," "The Elephant and the Flea," a rewriting of the Great War as seen from 1980, and "Fate."

65. "Rechenaufgabe," ibid., pp. 28–29. "Wie hoch wären dann die Gesamtausgaben für Tabak und Alkohol?"

66. "Nach Berlin," ibid., pp. 27–29.

67. Hans Schemm, *Hans Schemm Spricht: Seine Reden und sein Werk*, G. Kahl-Furthmann, ed. (Bayreuth: Gauverlag Bayerische Ostmark, 1936), pp. 108–113.

68. Rudolf Benze, *Erziehung im Großdeutschen Reich: Eine Überschau über ihre Ziele, Wege und Einrichtungen* (Frankfurt am Main: Diesterweg, 1939), p. 64.

69. Franz Kade, *Die Wende in der Mädchenerziehung* (Dortmund & Breslau: Crüwell, 1937), pp. 6–8. Gamm, *Führung und Verführung*, p. 298. Walter Gross, *Rassenpolitische Erziehung*, Sonderausgabe für das Rassenpolitische Amt der NSDAP (Berlin: Junker & Dünnhaupt 1935).

70. Gretel und Karl Blome, *Ein Wort an junge Kameradinnen*, 3rd ed., vol. 18 in Schriftenreihe des Rassenpolitischen Amtes der NSDAP und des Reichsbundes Deutsche Familie (Berlin: Verlag Neues Volk, 1940).

71. Elizabeth Lenz, "Mädchenbildung in der Volksschule des Dritten Reich," Gamm, *Führung und Verführung*, p. 273.

72. Staemmler, *Der Sieg des Lebens*, pp. 32, 83.

73. Hitler, *Mein Kampf* (Boston: Houghton Mifflin, 1962), p. 254.

74. *Studienrat* Dr. Jakob Graf, *Die Bildungs- und Erziehungswerte der Erblehre, Erbpflege und Rassenkunde* (Munich: Lehmanns, 1933), p. 34.

75. In 1933, 60,000 Jewish children attended public schools. "Gesetz gegen die Überfüllung," Apr. 22 and 25, 1933, *Ursachen und Folgen*, vol. 9, docs. 2181, 2182, p. 456. "Runderlaß über die Einrichtung gesonderter jüdischer Schulen, 10. September 1935," and "Auswirkungen des Reichsbürgergesetzes . . . vom 2.7.1937," in Gamm, *Führung und Verführung*, pp. 139–143. At the university level, whereas nearly 4,000 Jewish students were enrolled in 1932, by 1934 only 656 (486 men and 170 women) remained. Kaplan, *Between Dignity and Despair*, p. 98.

76. Kaplan, *Between Dignity and Despair*, p. 95.

77. Elsie Axelrod (Mrs. Adolf Axelrod), "My Life in Germany," Houghton, bMS Ger 91 (89), p. 32.

78. "Since we unfortunately cannot simply throw the Jews out of school, . . . the Hitler Youth must treat them in such a way that they will not want to remain at the school." A Super's Observations, letter to Hitler Youth leadership, Altona, Nov. 10, 1936, reprinted in Hans Mommsen, *Herrschaftsalltag*, pp. 285–286.

79. Margarete Littauer, "Mein Leben," Houghton, bMs Ger 91 (142).

80. Peter Gay, *My German Question* (New Haven, Conn.: Yale University Press, 1998), p. 64, 65, 108.

81. Kaplan, *Between Dignity and Despair*, p. 96.

82. Maschmann, *Account Rendered*, p. 39.

83. Wolf, *A Model Childhood*, p. 98.

84. For a translation and full color reproduction of this rare book, see Ronald Bytwerk's website: *www.calvin.edu/academic/cas/gpa/images/giftpilz*

85. Hans Winterfeldt, "Ein Kind erlebt die Ausgrenzung," in Margarete Limberg and

Humber Rübsaat, eds., *"Sie durften nicht mehr Deutsche sein": Jüdischer Alltag in Selbst-zeugnissen, 1933–1938* (Frankfurt am Main: Campus, 1990), pp. 212–217.

86. Heck, *A Child of Hitler*, p. 8.

87. Gunther S. Stent, *Nazis, Women, and Molecular Biology: Memoirs of a Lucky Self-Hater* (Kensington, Calif.: Briones, 1999), pp. 73, 59. As late as 1942, a school inspector in an East German province was writing to Jewish parents to tell them their children had been barred from classes. "Entlassung eines 'nichtarischen' Schülers," in Gamm, *Führung und Verführung*, doc. 24, p. 145.

88. Walther Scharrer, "Judengegnerschaft und höhere Schulen," *Der Weltkampf* 10 (1933): 245.

89. Party member Leutloff, speech of Feb. 8, 1935, NA/T-81/22/19695.

90. "Förderung des Lehrfilmwesens," *VB* 46 (Apr. 2–3, 1933): 3. A. Hubnhäuser, "Die nationalpolitische Lehrgänge im Rheinland," in *Die deutsche höhere Schule* (Frankfurt am Main: Diesterweg) 2, no. 13 (July 1935): 445. Kurt F. K. Franke, "Medien im Geschichts-unterricht der national-sozialistische Schule," in Dithmar, *Schule und Unterricht*, pp. 59–87.

91. *Sopade*, Feb. 1935, p. 205. "Bericht über die Lage," report no. 4 (Feb. 1934), in Bernd Stöver, ed., *Berichte über die Lage in Deutschland* (Bonn: Dietz, 1996), pp. 64–66.

92. Hartshorne, *German Universities*, p. 33; Eilers, *Schulpolitik*, pp. 28–33. Ten million school children were required to attend films for which they had to pay an admission fee, which produced a profit for the Ministry of Propaganda, report from *Sopade*, Sept./Oct. 1934, pp. 571–572.

93. *Film und Bild in Wissenschaft, Erziehung und Volksbildung: Zeitschrift der Reichsstelle für den Unterrichtsfilm* (Berlin: Kohlhammer) 1 (Jan. 10, 1939).

94. Gerhard Paul, *Aufstand der Bilder: Die NS-Propaganda vor 1933* (Bonn: Dietz, 1990), pp. 53–57.

95. Alfred Vogel, *Erblehre und Rassenkunde in bildlicher Darstellung* (Stuttgart: National Literatur, 1938). I am indebted to Dr. Barbara M. Kelly, Hofstra University Library Services, for guiding me through the large sample of these charts in the Kroul Collection before it was catalogued.

96. Quoted in *Die deutsche höhere Schule*, 1935, p. 521. See *Sopade*, Feb. 1936, p. 200. Rust, "Umschulung," Aug. 1923, BAB/490/4607/Bl. 101–110.

97. *Nationalpolitische Lehrgänge für Schüler* provides suggestions for student excursions. Suggested topics included the goals of special outings, finances, hostels, the teacher as leader, health questions, hiking, and evening entertainment.

98. Saul Friedländer describes Julius Schreck's tour of one such institution, in *Nazi Germany and the Jews*, vol. 1, *The Years of Persecution, 1933–1939* (New York: HarperCollins, 1997), p. 209. A similar experience was remembered by a Jewish child, Reich-Ranicki, *Meine Schulzeit*, pp. 37–38.

99. Albert Friehe, *Was muß der Nationalsozialist von der Vererbung wissen? Die Grundlagen der Vererbung und ihre Bedeutung für Mensch, Volk und Staat* (Frankfurt am Main: 1936), pp. 52–53.

100. Rheinland Excursion. Hunhäuser, "Die nationalpolitischen Lehrgänge im Rhein-land," *Die deutsche höhere Schule* 2 (July 1935): 433–437.

101. A hundred three-week educational excursions with 19,000 boys, 9,000 girls, and 2,300 teachers. R. Schaller, lecture, Wahn School, Apr. 18, 1935, NA/T81/22/frames 10779–19784.

102. *Nationalpolitische Erziehung* (Berlin: Juncker & Dunnhaupt, 1936), pp. 7–21.

103. Volker Losemann, "Zur Konzeption der NS-Dozentenlager," in Manfred Heinemann and Helmut Engelbrecht, eds., *Erziehung und Schulung im Dritten Reich* (Stutt-gart: Klett-Cotta, 1980), p. 21.

104. Ott, *Martin Heidegger*, pp. 224–226.

105. Safranski, *Martin Heidegger*, pp. 261–262.

106. Ott, *Martin Heidegger,* pp. 35–57.

107. Tübingen lecture of Nov. 30, 1933, in Ott, *Martin Heidegger,* pp. 238–243.

108. Safranski, *Martin Heidegger,* p. 262. Heidegger, "Facts and Thoughts," in Günther Neske and Emil Kettering, eds., *Martin Heidegger and National Socialism: Questions and Answers,* trans. Lisa Harries, with an introduction by Karsten Harries (New York: Paragon, 1990), p. 27.

109. Colonel Thorne to Rumbold, Berlin, Apr. 25, 1933, *DBFP,* vol. 4, doc. 36, pp. 874–878.

110. Schulungslager in Anhalt, "Shocktroop 1935," report, BAB/4901/REM/4607/Bl. 168.

111. Schulungslager "Selketal" der anhaltischen Lehrer, 1935. BAB/4901/REM/4607/Bl. 183. On camps as the paradigmatic Nazi social form, see Jürgen Schiedeck and Martin Stahlmann, "Totalizing of Experience: Educational Camps," in Sünker and Otto, *Education and Fascism,* 54–80.

112. "Aus der Schule," report from Saxony, *Sopade,* Feb. 1936, pp. 190–191.

113. Hellwig, "Mein Leben," Houghton, bMS Ger 91 (93).

114. Rudolf Benze, "Umschulung der Erzieher im Lager," reprinted in Gamm, *Führung und Verführung,* p. 132. The *Sopade* reporter said that participants hated the overwhelmingly military atmosphere of these courses. But 3,000 teachers applied for 150 openings, all the same. "The intellectual level was so low, that especially Catholic teachers engage in animated conversations during the lectures" (*Sopade,* Feb. 1935, p. 210). Ottweiler, *Volksschule,* pp. 128–130. The SS Security Service Report came to similar conclusions. "Erziehung," in Heinz Boberach, ed., *Meldungen aus dem Reich, 1938–1945: Die geheimen Lageberichte des Sicherheitsdienstes der SS.,* 17 vols., vol. 2 (Herrsching: Pawlak, 1984), pp. 133–140.

115. Eilers, *Schulpolitik,* pp. 87–91. Jeremy Noakes and Geoffrey Pridham, *Nazism: A History in Documents,* vol. 1 (New York: Schocken, 1984), doc. 312 pp. 432–435.

116. Vorbereitung der Lehrgänge, BA/4901/4607/Bl. 320–322.

117. *Nationalpolitische Lehrgänge,* pp. 197–203. "Lehrgang in Vererbungslehre und Rassenkunde in der Adolf-Hitler Schule zu Marburg." On Bavaria, see Streicher, "Grosse Veranstaltungen," StAM/NSDAP 981.

118. Schulungslager "Selketal" der anhaltischen Lehrer 1935. BAB/4901/4607/Bl. 183.

119. Rudolf Hess to the Sonderlehrgang der Reichsschule Bernau, Summer 1934, NA/T81–22/19711–19717/1–6.

120. Manuscripts on racial education in Donndorf-Bayreuth, BAB/NS12/temporary 817.

121. *Sopade,* Feb. 1935, p. 216.

122. *Sopade,* Feb. 1936, p. 192, and memos in StAM/NSDAP/993. Eilers, *Schulpolitik,* pp. 3–6.

123. Georg Burkhardt Kolb, "Wie sehe ich die Gestaltung der Schulungslager des nationalsozialistischen Lehrerbundes?" BAB/4901/REM/4607/Bl. 290–301.

124. Reber-Gruber specifically singled out Helene Lange as a role model and welcomed women teachers from liberal pre-1933 associations: StAM/NSAP/994.

125. "Vorbereitung der Lehrgänge," BAB/4901/4607/Bl. 305.

126. Count [Freiherr] von Lünick, Vorbereitung der Lehrgänge, BAB/4901/4607/Bl. 327.

127. Hitler, speech to 54,000 Hitler Youth, Sept. 14, 1935, in Domarus, *Hitler Speeches,* vol. 2, pp. 700–701.

128. Notice in column "Kritik der Zeit," *Nationalsozialistische Monatshefte* 7, no. 77 (Aug. 1936), p. 749.

129. Quoted in Marlis G. Steinert, *Hitlers Krieg und die Deutschen: Stimmung und Haltung der deutschen Bevölkerung im Zweiten Weltkrieg* (Düsseldorf: Econ, 1970), p. 60.

130. Elke Fröhlich, "Die drei Typen der nationalsozialistischen Ausleseschulen," in Johannes Leeb, ed., *Wir waren Hitlers Eliteschüler: Ehemalige Zöglinge der NS-Ausleseschulen brechen ihre Schweigen*, 2nd ed. (Hamburg: Rasch & Röhling, 1998). Barbara Feller and Wolfgang Feller, *Die Adolf-Hitler-Schulen: Pädogische Provinz versus ideologische Zuchtanstalt* (Munich: Juventa, 2001), pp. 29–36, 109–145.

131. Victor Klemperer, diary entries of June 13, 1934, and Apr. 17, 1935, *I Will Bear Witness: A Diary of the Nazi Years, 1933–1941*, trans. Martin Chalmers (New York: Random House, 1998), pp. 70, 118.

132. Krieck, *Nationalpolitische Erziehung*, p. 36. Gamm, *Führung und Verführung*, p. 102.

133. Schulungslager "Selketal" der anhaltischen Lehrer, 1935. BAB/4901/4607.

134. Gamm, *Führung und Verführung*, pp. 31–32.

7. LAW AND THE RACIAL ORDER

1. Joseph Walk, *Das Sonderrecht für die Juden im NS-Staat: Eine Sammlung der gesetzlichen Maßnahmen und Richtlinien, Inhalt und Bedeutung*, 2nd ed. (Heidelberg: Müller, 1996), pp. 1–128. Scores of measures went into effect at the national and regional level between early February and late April 1933. Bruno Blau, *Das Ausnahmerecht für die Juden in Deutschland, 1933–1945* (Düsseldorf: Verlag Allgemeine Wochenzeitung der Juden in Deutschland, 1965), pp. 23–41.

2. Michael Thad Allen, *The Business of Genocide* (Chapel Hill: University of North Carolina Press, 2002), p. 276.

3. Thomas Klein, "Marburg-Stadt und Marburg-Land in der amtlichen Berichterstattung, 1933–1936," in Klaus Malettke, ed., *Der Nationalsozialismus an der Macht: Aspekte nationalsozialistischer Politik und Herrschaft* (Göttingen: Vandenhoeck & Ruprecht, 1984), pp. 123–127.

4. Karl Löwith, *My Life in Germany before and after 1933*, trans. Elizabeth King (Champaign-Urbana: University of Illinois Press, 1994), p. 10.

5. Emphasis in the original. Gercke despised the disorder and insisted on an efficient "cleansing process [*Säuberungsvorgang*]." "Die Lösung der Judenfrage," BAB/R1509/35/Bl.43–55.

6. Achim Gercke, "Ausmerze und Auslese," *VB* 46, nos. 190/191 (July 9–10, 1933). Gercke, "Die Lösung der Judenfrage," and "Grundsätzliche zur Mischlingsfrage," *Nationalsozialistische Monatshefte* 4 (June 1933): 195–196. To Gercke it was perfectly obvious that civil rights "should not be given" to German citizens with Jewish ancestors (whom he called bastards)–as if they had already been taken away. "Soll man den deutschen Bastarden die vollen Staatsbürgerrechte geben?" BAB/1509/35/Bl. 64–71. For an excellent analysis of the Reich Kinship Bureau, see Diana Schulle, *Das Reichssippenamt: Eine Institution nationalsozialistischer Rassenpolitik* (Berlin: Logos, 2001).

7. German superior court ruling "Höchstrichterliche Rechtsprechung," 489 (1934), quoted in Ingo Müller, *Hitler's Justice: The Courts of the Third Reich*, trans. Deborah L. Schneider (Cambridge: Harvard University Press, 1991), p. 95. Karl Saller, *Die Rassenlehre des Nationalsozialismus in Wissenschaft und Propaganda* (Darmstadt: Progress, 1961), p. 119. Carl Jung and Ernst Kretzschmer held similar views: Robert Proctor, *Racial Hygiene: Medicine under the Nazis* (Cambridge: Harvard University Press, 1988), pp. 161–163.

8. Carl Schmitt, *Staat, Bewegung, Volk: Die Dreigliederung der politischen Einheit* (Hamburg: Hanseatische, 1933), p. 17.

9. Christoph Schmidt, "Zu den Motiven 'alter Kämpfer' in der NDSAP," in Detlev Peukert and Jürgen Reulecke, eds., *Die Reihen fast geschlossen: Beiträge zur Geschichte des Alltags unterm Nationalsozialismus* (Wuppertal: Hammer, 1981), pp. 21–31. Joachim Fest, *The Face of the Third Reich: Portraits of the Nazi Leadership*, trans. Michael Bullock (New York: Pantheon, 1970), pp. 136–139. "Old Nazis to Get Posts," *New York Times*, May 9, 1935, p. 9.

To guarantee an ideological presence, at least 10 percent of all appointments were reserved for Nazi Party members. Christopher R. Browning, "The Government Experts," in Sybil Milton and Henry Friedlander, eds., *The Holocaust: Ideology, Bureaucracy and Genocide* (Millwood, N.Y.: Kraus, 1980), p. 184. Hans Mommsen, *Beamtentum im Dritten Reich* (Stuttgart: Deutsche Verlags-Anstalt, 1966), pp. 39–40.

10. The new office holders were "a group of alienated political fanatics with few administrative or technical skills." Dietrich Orlow, *The History of the Nazi Party, 1933–1945* (Pittsburgh, Pa.: University of Pittsburgh Press, 1973), vol. 2, pp. 19–21. Martin Broszat, *The Nazi State: The Foundation and Development of the Internal Structure of the Third Reich*, trans. Richard Hiden (New York: Longman, 1981), pp. 244–253. In 1935, approximately 307,000 civil servants had joined the party. Jeremy Noakes and Geoffrey Pridham, eds., *Nazism: A History in Documents*, vol. 1 (New York: Schocken, 1984), doc. 62, pp. 86–87. Eighty-one percent of Nazi Party joiners between February and May 1933 were civil servants. Charles McClelland, *The German Experience of Professionalization* (New York: Cambridge University Press, 1991), pp. 221–222.

11. Thomas Childers, *The Nazi Voter: The Social Foundations of Fascism in Germany, 1919–1933* (Chapel Hill, N.C.: University of North Carolina Press, 1983), pp. 178, 239–242. Because their services were so essential, even if they joined the party, senior officials could carry on with "quiet defiance." Michael Kater, *The Nazi Party: A Social Profile of Members and Leaders, 1919–1945* (Cambridge: Harvard University Press, 1983), pp. 8–9, 107–110. About 10 percent of all civil servants supported the Nazi Party before 1933, as compared to less than 4 percent of the population. William Brustein, *The Logic of Evil: The Social Origins of the Nazi Party, 1925–1933* (New Haven, Conn.: Yale University Press, 1996), pp. 109–119.

12. Max Weber, "Politics as a Vocation," in Hans Gerth and C. Wright Mills, *From Max Weber: Essays in Sociology* (New York: Galaxy, 1960), p. 95.

13. Eviatar Zerubavel, *The Fine Line: Making Distinctions in Everyday Life* (New York: Free Press/ Macmillan, 1991), pp. 33–60.

14. Discussions, Reichssippenamt, Genealogy Department, Dec. 1934 through Apr. 1935, BAB/R1509/35/Bl. 35–41. Discussion *(Besprechung)*, BAB/NS2/143/Bl. 28, Dec. 20, 1934. Uwe Dietrich Adam, *Judenpolitik im Dritten Reich* (Düsseldorf: Droste, 1972), pp. 115–120.

15. The 1939 census reported 72,740 citizens with two Jewish grandparents and 43,000 with one Jewish grandparent. Jeremy Noakes, "'Wohin gehören die 'Judenmischlinge?' Die Entstehung der ersten Durchführungsverordnungen zu den Nürnberger Gesetzen," in Ursula Buttner, ed., *Das Unrechtsregime: Internationale Forschung über den Nationalsozialismus*, vol. 2 (Hamburg: Christians, 1986), pp. 70–74. See also Pfundtner to Hossbach, Apr. 3, 1935, BAB/R432/602/Bl.170–171.

16. Bernhard Lösener, comments, June 5, 1934, BAB/R3001/852/Bl. 182.

17. "Anti-Semitic campaigns were retarded by the fact that other countries could not absorb 2,100,000 Jews, half-Jews and quarter-Jews" (*New York Times*, Aug. 10, 1935, p. 6). Leonardo Conti, state councilor and physician, declared that there were 2,500,000 Jews in Germany, or 2.3 percent of the population (*New York Times*, June 14, 1935, p. 7). Schlosser reported statisticians' far lower estimates, in Friedrich Burgdorfer, *Aufbau und Bewegung der Bevölkerung: Ein Führer durch die deutsche Bevölkerungsstatistik und Bevölkerungspolitik* (Leipzig: Barth, 1935). Karin Magnussen, *Rassen- und Bevölkerungspolitisches Rüstzeug, Statistik, Gesetzgebung und Kriegsaufgaben* (1936; Munich: Lehmann, 1943).

18. Ralph Angermund, "Die geprellten 'Richterkönige': Zum Niedergang der Justiz im NS-Staat," in Hans Mommsen, ed., *Herrschaftsalltag im Dritten Reich: Studien und Texte* (Düsseldorf: Schwann, 1988), pp. 312–317.

19. Noakes and Pridham, *Nazism*, vol. 1, doc. 355, pp. 483–485.

20. Raul Hilberg, *The Destruction of the European Jews* (New York: Holmes & Meier, 1985), p. 27.

21. Lösener memos of July 24, 1933, and Oct. 30, 1933, Institut für Zeitgeschichte/F71/ 1, cited in Jeremy Noakes, "The Development of Nazi Policy towards the German-Jewish 'Mischlinge,' 1933–1945," *Leo Baeck Institute Yearbook* 34 (1989): 303. For important examples of early proposals circulating among Nazi leaders, see "Material zum Judengesetz" and "Einführung zum Judengesetz," Apr. 6, 1933, and "Entwurf," in USHMM, RG-11/11.001/ 379/roll 5, pp. 1–7.

22. "Der Neubau des deutschen Rechts," *VB* 46 (Apr. 23–24, 1933): 2. Max Weinreich, *Hitler's Professors: The Part of Scholarship in Germany's Crimes against the Jewish People* (1946; New Haven, Conn.: Yale University Press, 1999), p. 38.

23. Pfundtner's law of July 4, 1933, in Adam, *Judenpolitik*, p. 84.

24. Kube had joined the Nazi Party years before and served as the governor of Brandenburg after 1933: Werner Jochmann, *Gesellschaftskrise und Judenfeindschaft in Deutschland, 1970–1945* (Hamburg: Christians, 1988), pp. 243–246. Peter Hüttenberger, *Die Gauleiter: Studie zum Wandel des Machtgefüges in der NSDAP* (Stuttgart: Deutsche Verlags-Anstalt, 1969), p. 215.

25. After generations, a black family could be "whited out." Edgar von Schmidt-Pauli, *Die Männer um Hitler* (Berlin: Verlag für Kulturpolitik, 1933), p. 33. Judy Scales-Trent, "Racial Purity Laws in the United States and Nazi Germany," *Human Rights Quarterly* 23 (May 2001): 259–307.

26. Bernhard Lösener, "At the Desk for Racial Affairs in the Reich Ministry of the Interior," in Karl A. Schleunes, ed., *Legislating the Holocaust: The Bernhard Loesener Memoirs and Supporting Documents*, trans. Carol Scherer (Boulder, Colo.: Westview, 2001), pp. 33–104. About 750,000 Germans counted as *Mischlinge*. Jeremy Noakes, "The Development of Nazi Policy," 292–299.

27. Memo of Jan. 17, 1934, BAB/R1501/3746. Frick used the terms "ethnic" and "political." Günter Neliba, *Wilhelm Frick: Der Legalist des Unrechtsstaates—Eine politische Biographie* (Munich: Schöningh, 1992), p. 191.

28. Diels to Göring, Nov. 5, 1934, quoted in Heinz Höhne, *The Order of the Death's Head: The Story of Hitler's S.S.*, trans. Richard Barry (New York: Coward-McCann, 1969), p. 180. The "Zerbröselung der inneren Verwaltung" occasioned much dissatisfaction. Adam, *Judenpolitik*, p. 108.

29. Falk Ruttke complained about confusion (*Verwirrung*) in *Deutsches Recht*, Jan. 25, 1935, pp. 25–27, quoted in Schleunes, *Twisted Road*, p. 120.

30. BAB/R4909/968 and BAB/R3001/1389, cited in Benno Müller-Hill, *Murderous Science: The Elimination by Scientific Selection of Jews, Gypsies, and Others, Germany, 1933–1945*, trans. George R. Fraser (New York: Oxford University Press, 1988), pp. 33, 178.

31. Participants included racial researchers Klee, Dahm, and Rudolf Möbius, Hans von Dohnanyi, Count Gleispach, and minister directors Schäfer and Mezger. The quotations from this section are from BAB/R3001/1389.

32. *Statistisches Jahrbuch für das Deutsche Reich* 55 (1936): 40. Noakes, "The Development of Nazi Policy," p. 291. Marion A. Kaplan, *Between Dignity and Despair: Jewish Life in Nazi Germany* (New York: Oxford University Press, 1998), pp. 74–93.

33. *Das deutsche Führerlexikon* (Berlin: Stollberg, 1935), p. 130.

34. "The demands of the individual conscience express the ideals of the *Volk* state." Roland Freisler, "Recht, Richter und Gesetz," *Deutsche Justiz: Rechtspflege und Rechtspolitik* 95 (1933): 694–696. "Nazi Holds Popular View Is Test of Law's Sanctity," *New York Times*, May 31, 1935, p. 2.

35. Müller, *Hitler's Justice*, p. 71.

36. Lothar Gruchmann, "'Blutschutz' und Justiz: Zur Entstehung und Auswirkung des Nürnberger Gesetzes vom 15. September 1935," *Vierteljahreshefte für Zeitgeschichte* 31 (1983): 418–441. Philippe Burrin, *Hitler and the Jews: The Genesis of the Holocaust*, trans. Patsy Southgate, with an introduction by Saul Friedländer (London: Edward Arnold, 1994), pp. 41–64.

37. Roland Freisler, "Recht, Richter und Gesetz," p. 694, quoted in Müller, *Hitler's Justice*, p. 95.

38. Lutz Schwerin von Krosigk, *Es geschah in Deutschland: Menschenbilder unseres Jahrhunderts*, 3rd ed. (Tübingen: Wünderlich, 1952), pp. 517–525. Lothar Gruchmann, "Franz Gürtner: Justizminister unter Hitler," in Ronald Smelzer, Enrico Syring, and Rainer Zitelmann, eds., *Die Braune Elite: 21 weitere biographische Skizzen* (Darmstadt: Wissenschaftliche 1993), pp. 128–136.

39. Gürtner wrote, "Brutality and cruelty are totally alien to German values . . . Such cruelty, reminiscent of oriental sadism, cannot be explained or excused . . ." Robert Wistrich, *Who's Who in Nazi Germany* (London: Routledge, 1995), pp. 92–93. Schwerin von Krosigk, *Es Geschah in Deutschland*, pp. 517–525.

40. Schleunes, *Legislating the Holocaust,* pp. 23–25.

41. Cornelia Essner, "Das System der Nürnberger Gesetze' (1933–1945) oder der verwaltete Rassismus" (Ph.D. diss., Free University of Berlin, 1999), pp. 118–135. Thanks to Cornelia Essner for allowing me to cite her dissertation and to Hans Mommsen for calling it to my attention. Loesener, "At the Desk," in Schleunes, *Legislating the Holocaust,* pp. 35–55.

42. Lösener, Oct. 30, 1933, five-page letter. He also suggested that distinguished Jewish Germans be exempted from racial laws. BAB/R1501/3746. Adam, *Judenpolitik,* pp. 88, 113, 34–36.

43. Because most *Mischlinge* belonged to the middle classes, Lösener appealed for empathy among his colleagues.

44. Lösener, "Anwendung der Arierbestimmung auf Abkömmlinge aus Mischehen," a five-page memo, Oct. 30, 1933, BAB/R1501/3746. Even the virulent antisemite Achim Gercke in the Reich Kinship Bureau *(Reichssippenamt)* argued for exceptions in the case of "undeserved hardships" *(unbillige Härten)* of the law.

45. Stenographic record of the 37th session of the Criminal Law Commission, Reich Justice Ministry. BAB/R3001/852/Bl. 118, 249, 307, 323. Lothar Gruchmann, *Justiz im Dritten Reich 1933–1940: Anpassung und Unterwerfung in der Ära Gürtner* (Munich: Oldenbourg, 1988), pp. 866–871, and Gruchmann, "'Blutschutzgesetz' und Justiz," *Vierteljahrshefte für Zeitgeschichte* 31 (July 1983): 418–42; Hermann Graml, *Antisemitism in the Third Reich,* trans. Tim Kir (Oxford, Eng.: Blackwell, 1992), pp. 108–111; Müller-Hill, *Murderous Science,* pp. 32–33.

46. Criminal Law Commission (Strafrechtscommission), Stenographic record, Straf BAB/R3001/852/Bl. 75–328.

47. Lorna Wildenthal, *German Women for Empire, 1884–1945* (Durham, N.C.: Duke University Press, 2001), pp. 84, 92–99. The term "racial treason" was originally used in connection with colonial men having sexual relations with colonial subjects. These laws punished offending men by disallowing their rights as citizens and preventing their offspring from acquiring civil status.

48. Criminal Law Commission (Strafrechtscommission), BAB/R3001/852/Bl. 276, 325. Essner, "Das System," p. 105.

49. Walk, *Das Sonderrecht,* pp. 129–251. Adam discusses the multiplicity of offices and opinions in *Judenpolitik,* pp. 104–106.

50. Robert Gellately, *Backing Hitler: Consent and Coercion in Nazi Germany* (New York: Oxford University Press, 2001), pp. 132–141.

51. "Die Judenverfolgung," *Sopade,* Sept. 1935, pp. 1027–1029, 1037. These reports include dozens of instances of cattle dealers and shopkeepers who retained their customers' loyalty.

52. "Im Judenaquarium Herweck," Mannheim *Hakenkreuzbanner,* Aug. 1, 1933, in Comité des Délégations Juives, ed., *Die Lage der Juden in Deutschand, 1933: Das Schwarzbuch—Tatsachen und Dokumente* (1935; Frankfurt am Main: Ullstein, 1983), p. 460.

53. Otto Dov Kulka, "Die Nürnberger Rassengesetze und die deutsche Bevölkerung im

Lichte geheimer NS-Lage und Stimmungsberichte," *Vierteljahrshefte für Zeitgeschichte* 32 (1984): 594.

54. Michael Wildt, "Violence against Jews in Germany, 1933–1939," in David Bankier, ed., *Probing the Depths of German Antisemitism: German Society and the Persecution of the Jews, 1933–1941* (New York: Berghahn, 2000), pp. 187–194.

55. Klemperer, diary entries of Oct. 5, 1935, and Feb. 11, 1936, *I Will Bear Witness: A Diary of the Nazi Years, 1933–1941*, trans. Martin Chalmers (New York: Random House, 1998), vol. 1, pp. 134–135, 153.

56. "Scholars Show Manhood," *New York Times*, May 28, 1934, p. 24.

57. Personal communication from Barbara Hell, the daughter of one of those physicians. On Sauerbruch's ambivalent status, see Michael H. Kater, *Doctors under Hitler* (Chapel Hill: University of North Carolina Press, 1989), p. 138.

58. David Bankier, *The Germans and the Final Solution: Public Opinion under Nazism* (Oxford, Eng.: Blackwell, 1992), pp. 67–88. Michael H. Kater, "Everyday Anti-Semitism in Prewar Nazi Germany: The Popular Bases," *Yad Vashem Studies* 16 (1984): 129–159.

59. Victoria J. Barnett, *Bystanders: Conscience and Complicity during the Holocaust* (Westport, Conn.: Praeger, 1999), pp. 118–131.

60. "The only remedy for the Jewish problem in Germany is a large Jewish mass emigration until the entire group is liquidated." William Zuckerman, "Nazis without A Jewish Policy," *Fortnightly Review* 144 (new ser. 138, July 1935), pp. 86–94.

61. "Playing Both Ends," *New York Times*, May 28, 1935.

62. Saul Friedländer, *Nazi Germany and the Jews*, vol. 1, *The Years of Persecution, 1933–1939* (New York: HarperCollins, 1998), p. 50. Adam, *Judenpolitik*, pp. 28–38.

63. "Term 'Aryan' Abandoned," *New York Times*, Nov. 16, 1935; and "Term 'German-Blooded' Replaces 'Aryan,'" *New York Times*, Dec. 4, 1935.

64. *Sopade*, May/June 1934, docs. 1, 2/3, p. 168.

65. Reports "Bericht über die Lage," report nos. 1 (Dec. 1933) and 2 (Jan. 1934), Gruppe Neu Beginnen, in Bernd Stöver, ed., *Berichte über die Lage in Deutschland* (Bonn: Dietz, 1996), pp. 40–44.

66. *Sopade*, Sept. 1935, p. 900.

67. Heinrich Olms, "Anständige Juden," *VB* 48, no. 215 (Aug. 3, 1935): 3.

68. "Reich Court Spurs Boycotting of Jews," *New York Times*, July 2, 1935.

69. Jochmann, *Gesellschaftskrise*, p. 246. One source of their concern may have been the cases of successful legal appeals by Jews against persecution. Daniel Frankel, "Jewish Self-Defense," in Bankier, ed., *Probing the Depths*, pp. 339–359.

70. Report by SD-Hauptamt Ji 6 (Juden), Aug. 17, 1935; Michael Wildt, "Before the 'Final Solution': The Judenpolitik of the SD, 1935–1938," *Leo Baeck Institute Yearbook* 43 (1998): 246–247.

71. Reichssippenamt, "Lösung der Judenfrage," BAB/1509/35/Bl. 75/Bl. 75–76. Draft *(Entwurf)*, "Vertraulich!" (Secret!), May 17, 1935, BAB/R18/5513/Bl. 1–32. Weinreich, *Hitler's Professors*, p. 36.

72. "[Kränkende] Maßnahmen gegen große Völkerstaaten fremder Rasse," June 25, 1935, BAB/NS2/143/Bl. 11–13, and BAB/R3001/1389/Bl. 190. Müller-Hill, *Deadly Science*, p. 10.

73. May 27, 1935, BAB/R4901/521/Bl. 42. Frick responded to "pressure from the streets." Adam, *Judenpolitik*, p. 106. By August, he defended race laws. "Reich Won't Reform," *New York Times*, Aug. 4, 1935.

74. "Ritualmord in Litauen: Ein jüdischer Blutmord im März 1935," *Der Stürmer* 13, no. 16 (Apr. 1935); "Judenärzte Frauenschändler," und "Mörder erstickt," *Der Stürmer* 13 (Apr. 1935); "Pesach, alljährliche Gedenkfeier des ältesten Massen Ritualmords," *Der Stürmer* 11, no. 14 (Apr. 1933).

75. "Einzelheiten der Berliner Juden-Aktion," report no. 16 (July 1935), in Bernd Stöver, ed., *Berichte über die Lage in Deutschland* (Bonn: Dietz, 1996), doc. 15, pp. 576–577.

76. Dr. Kurt Plitschke, S. S. Oberscharführer, "Kommt das Strafgesetz gegen Rassever-rat?" *Das Schwarze Korps* (hereafter *SK*) 6 (Apr. 10, 1935): 6. "Gegen Rassenschändung wird durchgegriffen," *VB* 48 no. 199 (July 18, 1935). Wilhelm Frick, announcement of Aug. 20, 1935, BAB/R18/5513/Bl. 2.

77. Gruchmann, "'Blutsschutzgesetz' und Justiz," pp. 435–440. BAB/R58/276/Bl. 26.

78. Hess, order dated Apr. 11, 1935, reprinted in Jeremy Noakes and Geoffrey Pridham, *Nazism: A History in Documents*, vol. 1 (New York: Schocken, 1988), doc. 400, p. 530. "Eine Warnung an Staatsfeindliche Elemente," *VB* 48 (July 17, 1935).

79. "Verkehr mit Juden—Anordnung des Stellvertreters des Führers," July 20, 1935. See also USHMM, RG-11/260/roll 4. Graml, *Antisemitism*, pp. 116–118.

80. July 27, 1935, warning against "Einzelaktionen," including graffiti and signs: "Aus-länder berichten über Kurfürstendamm-Erlebnisse," *VB* 48, no. 200 (July 19, 1935). Burrin, *Hitler and the Jews*, p. 45. Jochmann, *Gesellschaftskrise*, p. 246.

81. "Die Judenfrage," *Frankfurter Zeitung*, July 27, 1935. "Zurückweisung der jüdische Herausforderung," *VB* 48, no. 196 (July 15, 1935); and "Jüdische Frechheiten!" *VB* 48, no. 200 (July 19, 1935).

82. "Die Judenfrage," *Frankfurter Zeitung*, July 27, 1935; Hans Hinkel, "Strohmänner des Judentums," *Der Angriff* 173 (July 27, 1935).

83. A. Rodrigue and O. D. Kulka, "German Popular Opinion and the Jews," *Yad Vashem Studies* 16 (1985): 421–423. David Bankier, *The Germans and the Final Solution*, pp. 74–75. Cologne *Gauleiter* Grohé, reports of Mar. 7 and Apr. 9, 1935, BAB/NS22/583.

84. "Anti-Jewish Drive in Munich Failure: Much Indignation Aroused by Campaign, Which Collapses When Streicher Leaves," *New York Times*, Feb. 1, 1935, p. 7.

85. Anton Doll, ed., *Nationalsozialismus im Alltag: Quellen zur Geschichte der NS-Herr-schaft im Gebiet des Landes Rheinland-Pfalz* (Speyer: Landesarchiv, 1983), p. 139.

86. Falk Wiesemann, "Juden auf dem Lande: Die wirtschaftliche Ausgrenzung der jüdischen Viehhändler in Bayern," in Detlev Peukert and Jürgen Reulecke, *Die Reihen fast geschlossen*, pp. 380–396.

87. In one village, Nazis put up a road sign reading, "This Way to Palestine" on the street leading to a local Zeppelin field, and in the central square they hung a banner pro-claiming, "A Heart for Germany. A Fist for Jews." In another town, stormtroopers paraded with a Jew and a Marxist in a cage. *Sopade*, Aug. 1935, p. 923.

88. Werner T. Angress, "Die 'Judenfrage' im Spiegel amtlicher Berichte," in Ursula Buttner, ed., *Das Unrechtsregime: Internationale Forschung über den Nationalsozialismus*, vol. 2 (Hamburg: Christians, 1986), p. 25.

89. Frederick T. Birchall, "Berlin Mayor Put on Trial by Nazis," *New York Times*, Nov. 14 and 26, 1935.

90. Angress, "Die 'Judenfrage,'" in Buttner, *Das Unrechtsregime*, vol. 2, pp. 19–23. See the informal survey of forty-one Nazis' attitudes to antisemitism, carried out after November 10, 1938, in Michael Müller-Claudius, *Der Antisemitismus und das deutsche Verhängnis* (Frankfurt am Main: Knecht, 1955), pp. 157–163.

91. "Die allgemeine Situation in Deutschland," *Sopade*, July 1935, p. 759.

92. "Lagebericht des SD-Hauptamtes J I/6 (Juden)," Aug. 17, 1938, in Michael Wildt, ed., *Die Judenpolitik des SD, 1935 bis 1938: Eine Dokumentation* (Munich: Oldenbourg, 1995), doc. 2, pp. 69–70.

93. Klemperer, diary entry of Oct. 5, 1935, *I Will Bear Witness*, vol. 1, p. 134. Franz J. Jürgens, *Wir waren ja eigentlich Deutsch: Juden berichten von Emigration und Rückkehr* (Berlin: Aufbau, 1997), pp. 138–140, 188–189.

94. "Wir kennen nur ein Vaterland und eine Heimat, das ist Deutschland." Quoted in Angress, "Die 'Judenfrage'," in Buttner, *Das Unrechtsregime*, vol. 2, p. 23. The leading Jewish-German periodical reprinted Hitler's reassurance that, "National Socialist understanding of race does not lead to contempt [*Geringschätzung*] for other *Völker*," *Die Judische Rundschau*, Feb. 2, 1934.

95. An Interior Ministry official worried, "These [returning] Jews are doing business again in Germany, which is causing a great stir." Draft *(Entwurf)*, BAB/R18/5513. RMdI, Schnellbrief, May 17, 1935, "Vertraulich!" (Confidential!), to AA (Foreign Office) and Gestapo.

96. "Lagebericht des SD-Hauptamptes J 1/6 (Juden)," Aug. 17, 1935, in Wildt, *Die Judenpolitik*, p. 69.

97. An editorial in the *New York Times* pointed out: "Berlin has no difficulty in staging anti-Jewish riots and then denouncing such riots as the work of enemies of the Nazi regime." "Nazis to Define Citizenship," *New York Times*, Aug. 11, 1935, p. E4.

98. "Goebbels Warns of Greater Drive on Foes of Nazis," and "'Mixed'" Weddings Barred . . . Ghettos Are Advocated," *New York Times*, Aug. 5, 1935; "Nazis to Define Citizenship," *New York Times*, Aug. 11, 1935; "Breed Inspectors Urged in Germany," *New York Times*, Aug. 18, 1935.

99. "Volksverrat—das schwerste Verbrechen: Staatssekretär Freisler über Aufbau und Ausgestaltung des kommenden Strafrechts," *VB* 48 (Aug. 3, 1935).

100. BAB/R4901/521/Bl. 52–53. Schacht, Aug. 18, 1935. Königsberger Ostmesse, Jochmann, *Gesellschaftskrise*, p. 246. For the Aug. 20, 1935, meeting, see Noakes and Pridham, *Nazism*, vol. 1, doc. 402, pp. 531–535. USHMM/RG11.001M.01/379.

101. Wildt, "Before the 'Final Solution,'" pp. 248–250.

102. BAB/R18/5513/Bl. 4. That Gürtner became the prisoner of this rationalization is suggested by his dismissal of the only judge who protested against medical killing, Lothar Kreyssig.

103. Hitler planned to declare the swastika the national flag and to make a major foreign policy statement in connection with the Italian invasion of Ethopia. Following advice from his foreign minister, however, Hitler canceled his statement on Ethiopia. See Jeremy Noakes, "Wohin gehören die 'Judenmischlinge'? Die Entstehung der ersten Durchführungsverordnungen zu den Nürnberger Gesetzen," in Buttner, *Das Unrechtsregime*, vol. 2, pp. 69–89.

104. Bernhard Loesener, "At the Desk," in Schleunes, *Legislating the Holocaust*, pp. 43–53.

105. Lösener, "Das Reichinnenministerium," pp. 262–276. Schleunes, *Legislating the Holocaust*, pp. 53–65. Walter Sommer from the Nazi Party headquarters in Munich was present, but according to Lösener, he spent his time playing with a new toy introduced at the rally, a mechanical tank that fired sparks. Adam, *Judenpolitik*, pp. 125–140.

106. Hitler, speech of Sept. 15, 1935, in Domarus, *Hitler Speeches*, vol. 2, pp. 703–708.

107. "Historische Beschlüße. Hackenkreuzbanner alleinige Staatsflagge," *VB* 48 (Sept. 16, 1935); "Jeder muß es wissen!" *Der Stürmer* 13 (Sept. 1935).

108. Since printed copies of the version with those words had been distributed to the Reichstag members and the press, Lösener and his colleagues lost another night's sleep redrafting publicity for the new law.

109. Friedländer, *Nazi Germany and the Jews*, vol. 1, pp. 87–99, interprets this speech as being primarily directed against Jews—although less than half of it concerned the "Jewish question" and Hitler avoided diatribes against infectious Jewish danger.

110. "Führertagung," *VB* 48 (Sept. 25, 1935). No record of the speech was published. Ian Kershaw, *Hitler, 1889–1936*, vol. 1 (New York: W. W. Norton, 1999), p. 571. The term "cold pogrom" appeared in the foreign press. "Jews in Germany: Persecution at a New Pitch," *Times* (London), Nov. 8, 1935.

111. Draft *(Entwurf)*, "Vertraulich!" (Confidential!), May 17, 1935, BAB/R18/5513/Bl. 1., report by Gütt, "Abt. Volksgesundheit des RMdI," Sept. 25, 1935, Bl. 33. Bernhard Lösener, "Die Hauptprobleme der Nürnberger Grundgesetze und ihre ersten Ausführungsverordnung," *Reichsverwaltungsblatt* 56 (1935): 264–268, USHMM, RG-11.001M.01/343/roll 5.

112. Dr. Vellguth, Saxon district racial expert, Dresden, "Über die Entstehung der

Judengesetze vom 15.9.1935," Oct. 12, 1935. Vellguth further noted Hitler's inquiries about Streicher's "Impregnation theory" and ordered an end to support for Zionism. He also discussed state-funded legal aid for "Aryan" women servants who claimed lifelong payments as damages against their abusive Jewish employers, marking Jewish-owned businesses, and "limiting the anti-Jewish boycott!!" This file also contains a Mendelian inheritance chart, presumably supplied by Artur Gütt. USHMM, RG-11.001M.01 (Reichssicherheits-hauptamt—SD Berlin), 1993/343/roll 5, pp. 53–54.

113. "Aufsaugung des Mischlingsmaterials durch das Haupt Volk." "Hitler's rigorism," it appeared, fed his dread of intermediate categories. H. A. Adler, *Der verwaltete Mensch: Studien zur Deportation der Juden aus Deutschland* (Tübingen: Mohr, 1974), pp. 280–301.

114. The remarks at this meeting are based on the secret transcript of the meeting [*Abschrift, Geheim!!*], "Bericht des mit der Führung der Geschäfte beauftragten SS-Sturm-mann Dr. Schlösser über die Besprechung im Rassenpolitischen Amt," Sept. 25, 1935, BAB/NS2/143/Bl. 4–7. Schlösser speculated that Hitler's "new course" might actually be just a tactical choice, and he cautioned that the SS should make its own long-range plans.

115. Joseph Goebbels, *Goebbels-Reden*, ed. Helmut Heiber (Düsseldorf: Droste, 1971), p. 520.

116. Goebbels noted pressure from Streicher and Kube for stronger measures against Jews. "A compromise is absolutely essential and a completely satisfactory solution is not possible." Diary entry of Nov. 7, 1935, in Fröhlich, *Tagebücher*, vol. 2, pp. 536–537. Burrin, *Hitler and the Jews*, pp. 46–56.

117. Lösener, "At the Desk," in Schleunes, *Legislating the Holocaust*, pp. 56–58.

118. Werner Best, legal chief in the SS, praised the memo and distributed it to the relevant SS offices. "Die Hauptprobleme der Nürnberger Grundgesetze," "Abschrift aus dem Reichsverwaltungsblatt," USHMM, RG-11/343/roll 5, pp. 56–77. From memory, Lösener listed his twelve major arguments in "At the Desk," in Schleunes, *Legislating the Holocaust*, 57–58. The arguments, however, appear to be based more on his Oct. 30, 1933, internal memo, "Anwendung der Arierbestimmung auf Abkömmlinge aus Mischehen," BAB/R1501/3746, than on his 1935 position paper. After the intense three-month pressure to clarify the "Jewish question," Lösener suffered a nervous collapse and returned to his desk in the early spring of 1936.

119. "Abt. Volksgesundheit des RMdI," Sept. 25, 1935, BAB/R18/5513/Bl. 33–39.

120. Goebbels, diary entry of Nov. 15, 1935, in Fröhlich, *Tagebücher*, part 1, vol. 2, p. 540. Stuckart, memo of Nov. 6, 1935, BAB/R18/5514/Bl. 86–90. Noakes, "Wohin gehören die 'Judenmischlinge?'" pp. 80–82. Hitler upgraded approximately 600 *Mischlinge*, 339 Jews to *Mischlinge*, 238 *Mischlinge* to first-degree *Mischlinge* because they served in the military. And 394 *Mischlinge* became Aryan. Lösener, "At the Desk," in Schleunes, *Legislating the Holocaust*, pp. 84–85, 90.

121. Memo of Mar. 27, 1936, Reichsanstalt für Arbeitsvermittlung, BAB/R58/276, Bl. 40.

122. Adler, *Der verwaltete Mensch*, pp. 281–297.

8. THE QUEST FOR A RESPECTABLE RACISM

1. Bernhard Lösener, "Als Rassereferent im Reichsministerium des Innern," *Vierteljahr-shefte für Zeitgeschichte* 9 (1961): 262–313, trans. as "At the Desk for Racial Affairs in the Reich Ministry of the Interior," in Karl A. Schleunes, ed., *Legislating the Holocaust: The Bernhard Loesener Memoirs and Supporting Documents*, trans. Carol Scherer (Boulder, Colo.: Westview, 2001), pp. 55–56. Emphasis in original.

2. Otto Dov Kulka, "Die Nürnberger Rassengesetze und die deutsche Bevölkerung im Lichte geheimer NS-Lage- und Stimmungsberichte," *Vierteljahrshefte für Zeitgeschichte* 32 (1984): 602.

3. "Lagebericht J/IA" (Situation report, Jewish section), Jan. 1936, USHMM, RG-11.001M.01/343/roll 5, pp. 77–80.

4. The *Frankfurter Zeitung* was "sold" to the chemical giant I. G. Farben in 1933. The Ullstein empire, valued at between fifty and sixty million marks, was "sold" for ten million to the Nazi publishing house, and the Mosse chain was "sold" for under five million marks. Norbert Frei and Johannes Schmitz, *Journalismus im Dritten Reich* (Munich: Beck, 1989), pp. 20–39.

5. Helmut Genschel, *Die Verdrängung der Juden aus der Wirtschaft im Dritten Reich* (Göttingen: Musterschmidt, 1966), p. 125.

6. She asked Streicher to dispatch "that Jew Bela Balacs" who had billed her. Riefenstahl to Streicher, July 7, 1937, Riefenstahl file, BDC.

7. Anna Siemsen, "My Life in Germany," Houghton, bMS Ger 91 (213).

8. Victor Klemperer, entries of July 21, 1935, and Sept. 27, 1936, *I Will Bear Witness: A Diary of the Nazi Years, 1933–1941*, vol. 1, trans. Martin Chalmers (New York: Random House, 1998), pp. 129, 192.

9. Report quoted in *Sopade,* June 1937, pp. 941–942.

10. Hilde Honnet-Sichel, "Jeden Tag neue Angst," in Margarete Limberg and Hubert Rübsaat, eds., *"Sie durften nicht mehr Deutsche sein": Jüdischer Alltag im Selbstzeugnissen, 1933–1938* (Frankfurt am Main: Campus, 1990), p. 182.

11. In more than two decades of research on German public opinion in the Third Reich, historians have reached a consensus that most Germans deplored physical violence and coarse insinuations but gradually accommodated themselves to bureaucratically sanctioned persecution. Ian Kershaw, "The Persecution of the Jews and German Public Opinion," *Leo Baeck Institute Yearbook* 26 (1981): 261–289; Otto Dov Kulka, "Public Opinion in Nazi Germany," *Jerusalem Quarterly* 25 (1982): 121–144; David Bankier, *The Germans and the Final Solution: Public Opinion under Nazism* (Oxford, Eng.: Blackwell, 1992); Bankier, "German Social Democrats," Yehuda Bauer, "Overall Explanations," Alf Lüdtke, "German Work," and Otto D. Kulka, "The German Population," all in David Bankier, ed., *Probing the Depths of German Anti-Semitism: German Society and the Persecution of the Jews, 1933–1941* (New York: Berghahn, 2000), p. 318. Avraham Barkai, "German Volksgemeinschaft," in Michael Burleigh, ed., *Confronting the Nazi Past: New Debates on Modern German History* (New York: St. Martin's, 1996), pp. 85–88, 90, 193–194.

12. Rudolf Heberle, "Zur Soziologie der Nationalsozialistischen Revolution: Notizen aus dem Jahre 1934," *Vierteljahrshefte für Zeitgeschichte* 13 (1965), p. 459.

13. "National Socialism succeeded more rapidly and effectively in its assault on people's minds than in its seizure of political and social power." Karl Dietrich Bracher, in Bracher, Wolfgang Sauer, and Gerhard Schulz, eds., *Die nationalsozialistische Machtergreifung: Studien zur Errichtung des totalitären Herrschaftssystems in Deutschland, 1933/1934* (Cologne: Westdeutscher, 1960), pp. 22–24. Jeremy Noakes discusses the "crisis of values" that hastened acceptance of Nazi rule. "The Ivory Tower under Siege: German Universities in the Third Reich," *Journal of European Studies* 23 (Dec. 1993): 371–375. Ronald Forman, "Scientific Internationalism," *ISIS* 64 (June 1973): 151–180.

14. Helmut Seier, "Universität und Hochschulpolitik im nationalsozialistischen Staat," in Klaus Malettke, ed., *Der Nationalsozialismus an der Macht: Aspekte nationalsozialistischer Politik und Herrschaft* (Göttingen: Vandenhoeck & Ruprecht, 1984), pp. 143–165. Among those who collaborated early in the Nazi regime were Max Hildebert Boehm (Jena), Hans Freyer (Leipzig), Ernst Jaensch (Marburg), Willy Andreas (Heidelberg), Max Wundt (Tübingen), Ernst Rothacker (Bonn), Otto Koellreuther (Munich), Karl Haushofer, president of the "Deutsche Akademie" (Munich), Hans Naumann (Bonn), and Karl Alexander von Müller (Munich).

15. Paul Zschorlich, "Karl Maria von Weber als Volkserzieher," *VB* 48 (Aug. 4, 1935): 5.

16. Hans Naumann, *"Der hohe Mut und das freie Gemüte," Rede beim Antritt des Rektorats* (Bonn: Universitäts-Drückerei, 1934), pp. 4–5.

17. Hermann Oncken, "Die nationale Werte der Geschichte," June 1934, quoted in Ingo Haar, *Historiker im Nationalsozialismus: Deutsche Geschichtswissenschaft und der "Volkstumskampf" im Osten* (Göttingen: Vandenhoeck & Ruprecht, 2000), pp. 225–226.

18. Martin Heidegger, "German Teachers and Comrades!" in *Bekenntnis der Professoren an den deutschen Universitäten und Hochschulen zu Adolf Hitler und dem nationalsozialistischen Staat überreicht vom Nationalsozialistischen Lehrerbund* (Dresden: Limpert, 1933), p. 13; official English trans., 36–38.

19. Bernhard Lösener, "Die Hauptprobleme der Nürnberger Grundgesetze und ihrer ersten Ausführungsverordnungen," typescript copy of an article published in the *Reichsverwaltungsblatt*, USHMM, RG-11.001M.01/343/roll 5, pp. 57ff.

20. Wilhelm Frick and Artur Gütt, *Nordisches Gedankengut im Dritten Reich* (Munich: Lehmann, 1936), pp. 5–8.

21. Czeslaw Milosz, "The Pill of Murti-Bing," *The Captive Mind*, trans. Jane Zielonko (New York: Random House, 1990), p. 17. Emphasis in the original.

22. Quoted in Max Weinreich, *Hitler's Professors: The Part of Scholarship in Germany's Crimes against the Jewish People* (1947; New Haven, Conn.: Yale University Press, 1999), p. 68. For examples of Nazi demands, see "Wissenschaft ohne die richtige Weltanschauung für die Nation schädlich," *VB* 46 (May 24, 1933): 2, and "Der Hochschullehrer und nationale Revolution," *ZuW* 5, no. 7 (May 1935): 151–154.

23. Saul Friedländer contrasts their lack of courage (or was it empathy) with the slightly better behavior of the clergy: Friedländer, *Nazi Germany and the Jews*, vol. 1, *The Years of Persecution, 1933–1939* (New York, HarperCollins, 1997), pp. 59–60. Jeremy Noakes, "The Ivory Tower," *Journal of European Studies* 23 (1993): 371–420.

24. Quoted in Hellmut Seier, "Universität und Hochschulpolitik im nationalsozialistischen Staat," in Malettke, *Der Nationalsozialismus an der Macht*, p. 151. "Old fighters" often complained about younger "apolitical" colleagues: BAB/R58/1094/106, 1095/6, M. Kater, *Ahnenerbe*, p. 283.

25. Gross to Thilo von Trotha, Außenpolitisches Amt der NSDAP, probably late 1933 or early 1934, reprinted in Léon Poliakov and Josef Wulf, eds., *Das Dritte Reich und seine Denker: Dokumente* (Berlin: Arani, 1959), p. 548. Here Gross says he has "kein eigenes Urteil" and has relied on Jaentsch in Marburg. He suggests that Rosenberg rule on this "offenbar gefährlichen Angelegenheit." Hugo Ott, *Martin Heidegger: A Political Life*, trans. Allan Blunden (New York: Basic Books, 1993), p. 392.

26. Ibid.

27. Michael Grüttner, "Das Scheitern der Vordenker: Deutsche Hochschullehre und der Nationalsozialismus," in Reinhard Rürup, Michael Grüttner, et al., eds., *Geschichte und Emanzipation* (Frankfurt am Main: Campus, 1999), pp. 460–461. Michael Kater, *The Nazi Party: A Social Profile of Members and Leaders, 1919–1945* (Cambridge: Harvard University Press, 1983), pp. 108–113.

28. Walter Gross, "Um die Rassenhygiene als Lehr- und Forschungsfach," *ZuW* 7, no. 7 (Apr. 1937): 166. Memo, Nov. 23, 1937, and the subsequent *Rundschreiben* 19/1938, ROL, Hauptschulungsamt, May 7, 1938, BAB/NS22/827.

29. "Die Dresdener Versammlung der deutschen Naturforscher und Ärzte: Rückblick und Kritik," *ZuW* 6, no. 20 (1936): 538–542.

30. Ernst Krieck, "Führertum und Hochschulreform," *Volk im Werden* 5 (1937): 58.

31. Seier, "Universität und Hochschulpolitik," in Malettke, *Der Nationalsozialismus an der Macht*, pp. 145–147. Seier notes three stages of Nazification: The first months of Nazi rule, in which Nazi academic leaders complained that they had too few followers, was followed by two years of *Gleichschaltung* during which most academics gained job security by

complying with the new order, but up to a third of all academics left Germany (including fifteen Nobel Prize winners, eleven of whom were physicists). The third phase of consolidation, 1935–1939, was marked by normalization of university life. Nevertheless, Rosenberg and others perceived an acute shortage of qualified academics. "Draft" *(Entwurf)*, to Göring, June 17, 1941, NA/T-81/52/54938–54942.

32. "Eigenlob stinkt! Die Grundlage fehlt! Der Kampf um die Hochschulen" (Self-promotion stinks. The basis does not exist. The struggle for the universities), *SK* 2 (Feb. 27, 1936): 6.

33. "Die Jugend unterm Hakenkreuz," *Sopade*, June 1935, pp. 704–705.

34. BAB/R4901/965/Bl. 13. The institutes and their directors were the Kaiser-Wilhelm Institut in Berlin (Fischer); anthropological institutes in Munich and Breslau (Mollison and Eickstedt); genetic research in Frankfurt (Verschuer); racial political research at Königsberg (Löffler); human genetics and racial politics at Jena (Astel); racial studies and ethnology in Leipzig (Reche); and racial biology in Hamburg (Scheidt). Giessen, Hamburg, Leipzig, and Tübingen expanded previous programs, while Frankfurt, Jena, and Königsberg created new programs. Paul Weindling, *Health, Race and German Politics between National Unification and Nazism, 1870–1945* (Cambridge: Cambridge University Press, 1989) p. 513. Weinreich, *Hitler's Professors*, pp. 77–78, 107–110, 27. Michael H. Kater, *Doctors under Hitler* (Chapel Hill: University of North Carolina Press, 1989), p. 116. On the Eugenic and Population Biological Research Station of the Reich Health Office (Rassenhygienische und Bevölkerungsbiologische Forschungsstelle des Reichsgesundheitsamtes), see Henry Friedlander, *The Origins of Nazi Genocide: From Euthanasia to the Final Solution* (Chapel Hill: University of North Carolina Press, 1995), p. 250.

35. Uwe Dietrich Adam, *Judenpolitik im Dritten Reich* (Düsseldorf: Droste, 1972), p. 107. The issue was raised in *Der Erbarzt*, June 14, 1935, Verschuer's supplement to the *Deutsches Ärzteblatt*. Robert Proctor, *Racial Hygiene: Medicine under the Nazis* (Cambridge: Harvard University Press, 1988), p. 104.

36. Franz Boas, Earnest Albert Hooton, Sir Arthur Keith, Robert Yerkes, and Wolfgang Koehler were among the dozens of researchers outside Germany who searched for connections between physiological markers and ethnic or racial character.

37. Dr. Eugen Stähle, *Die Volksgesundheit* (Oct. 1934), quoted in Proctor, *Racial Hygiene*, pp. 78–79.

38. "At no time was there a National Socialist biology with a uniform ideological objective. The work of most biologists remained commmitted to scientific criteria . . . Mainly jurists and physicians did the work of racial research." Ute Deichmann, *Biologists under Hitler*, trans. Thomas Dunlap (Cambridge: Harvard University Press, 1996), p. 322.

39. Karl A. Schleunes, *The Twisted Road to Auschwitz: Nazi Policy toward German Jews, 1933–1939* (Champaign-Urbana: University of Illinois Press, 1990), p. 119.

40. "Deutsche Rasse," Gross to *Gau* district racial consultants. (Confidential!) Oct. 24, 1934, Centre de Documentation Juive Contemporaine, Paris, doc. CXLV–628, quoted in Poliakov and Wulf, *Denker*, pp. 411–412.

41. Alfred Rosenberg, NS Jurists' League president Hans Frank and *Stürmer* editor Julius Streicher took the leadership in this initiative. "Die Arbeitstagungen auf dem Parteitag," *VB* 48 (Sept. 17, 1935). Weinreich, *Hitler's Professors*, pp. 36–40.

42. "Rassenkundliche Begründung der Geisteswissenschaften," *VB* 48 (Aug. 9, 1935): 5.

43. J. Murgowsky, "Jüdisches und deutsches Soldatentum," *Nationalsozialistische Monatshefte* 76 (1936): 633–638. Hans Hinkel, "Was heute die Juden sagen: Kleine Erlebnisse aus der praktischen Arbeit," *Die Lage* 1 (Jan. 1939). For a discussion of the issues raised, see Ulrich Sieg, *Jüdische Intellektuelle im Ersten Weltkrieg* (Berlin: Akademie, 2001), pp. 257–264.

44. Susanne Heim and Götz Aly, *Vordenker der Vernichtung: Auschwitz und die deutschen Pläne für eine neue europäische Ordnung* (Hamburg: Hoffmann & Campe, 1991), pp. 9–36,

151–168. Michael Burleigh, *Ethics and Extermination: Reflections on Nazi Genocide* (Cambridge: Cambridge University Press, 1997), pp. 91–101, 222–257.

45. Alan Steinweis, "Ideology and Infrastructure: German Area Science and Planning for the Germanization of Eastern Europe, 1939–1944," *East European Quarterly* 28 (Fall 1994): 335–350, and Alan Steinweis, "Antisemitic Social Science and Nazi Policy: The Case of Peter-Heinz Seraphim," presented at the American Historical Association annual meeting, Washington D.C., 1999. Burleigh, *Ethics and Extermination*, p. 177. Michael Fahlbusch, "Die 'Südostdeutsche Forschungsgemeinschaft,'" and Hans Mommsen, "Der faustische Pakt der Ostforschung," in Winfried Schultze and Otto Gerhard Oexle, eds., *Deutsche Historiker im Nationalsozialismus* (Frankfurt am Main: Fischer, 1999), pp. 241–164, 265–293.

46. Carola Sachse and Benoît Massin, "Biowissenschaftliche Forschung an Kaiser-Wilhelm-Instituten und die Verbrechen des NS-Regimes" (Berlin: Max-Planck Gesellschaft zur Förderung der Wissenschaften, research report no. 3, 2000). Deichmann, *Biologists*, pp. 206–250.

47. Robert P. Ericksen, *Theologians under Hitler: Gerhard Kittel, Paul Althaus, and Emanuel Hirsch* (New Haven, Conn.: Yale University Press, 1985), p. 65.

48. Hannsjost Lixfeld, "The Deutsche Forschungsgemeinschaft and the Umbrella Organizations of German Volkskunde during the Third Reich," *Asian Folklore Studies* 50 (1991): 95–116. James R. Dow and Hannsjost Lixfeld, eds., *The Nazification of an Academic Discipline: Folklore in the Third Reich* (Bloomington: Indiana University Press, 1994).

49. Quoted in Weinreich, *Hitler's Professors*, pp. 216–217.

50. Quoted in Robert Proctor, *Value-Free Science? Purity and Power in Modern Knowledge* (Cambridge: Harvard University Press, 1991), p. 171.

51. Dr. Peter Winkelnkempner, NA/T-81/22/19525–19532. Quoting the humanist Ulrich von Hütten at the May 10, 1933, book burning, Goebbels rejoiced, "Oh This Century! Oh Science! What a joy to be alive," "Oh Jahrhundert! Oh Wissenschaften, es ist eine Lust zu leben!" *Der Angriff*, May 11, 1933.

52. The University for Political Theory [Hochschule für Politik] in Berlin was reorganized by the state "to disseminate and strengthen the formation of knowledge and will in the spirit of National Socialism." Weinreich, *Hitler's Professors*, p. 68.

53. *VB* 52 (Feb. 2, 1939).

54. Joachim Fest, "Professor NSDAP," in *The Face of the Third Reich: Portraits of the Nazi Leadership*, trans. Michael Bullock (New York: Pantheon, 1970), pp. 256–258.

55. Alan Beyerchen, *Scientists under Hitler: Politics and the Physics Community in the Third Reich* (New Haven, Conn.: Yale University Press, 1977), pp. 141–150. Weinreich, *Hitler's Professors*, p. 13. Johannes Stark, *Nationalsozialismus und Wissenschaft* (Munich: Eher, 1934), defended his views. Johannes Stark, "Philip Lenard als Naturforscher," *Nationalsozialistische Monatshefte* 71 (1936): 106–112.

56. German natural scientists' reputations plummeted in the international community. Beyerchen, *Scientists under Hitler*, pp. 71–83, 158, 187–193.

57. Quoted by Ernst Jaensch, "Der Kampf um die Wahrheit," in Poliakov and Wulf, *Denker*, p. 95.

58. "'Weiße Juden' in der Wissenschaft," *SK* 28 (July 13, 1937): 6. Karl Ferdinand Werner, *Das nationalsozialistische Geschichtsbild und die deutsche Geschichtswissenschaft* (Stuttgart: Kohlhammer, 1967); Haar, *Historiker im Nationalsozialismus*, pp. 224–255.

59. Only one scholar before the 1990s seriously investigated the field of history. Werner, *Das nationalsozialistische Geschichtsbild*, pp. 45–54. See "Die unfrohe Wissenschaft," *Süddeutsche Zeitung*, Sept. 14, 1998, and Karen Schönwälder, "Akademischer Antisemitismus: Die deutschen Historiker in der NS-Zeit," in *Jahrbuch für Antisemitismusforschung*, vol. 2 (Frankfurt am Main: Campus, 1993), pp. 200–229.

60. Account of meeting of Apr. 27, 1935, W. Frank, Vermerk, btr: Historische Reichs-kommission, BAB/R4901/2591/Bl. 64–68. Helmut Heiber, *Walter Frank und sein Reichs-institut für Geschichte des neuen Deutschlands* (Stuttgart: Deutsche Verlags-Anstalt, 1966), pp. 257–278. Klaus Schreiner, "Führertum, Rasse, Reich," in Peter Lundgreen, ed., *Wissen-schaft im Dritten Reich* (Frankfurt am Main: Suhrkamp, 1985), pp. 163–252. On Frank's ca-reer, see, NA/BDC/Ordner 212/A3345-DS-J005/frame 1717ff., A3345-DS-B029. Karl Heinz Roth, "Heydrichs Professor," and Willi Oberkrome, "Geschichte, Volk und Theorie," in Pe-ter Schöttler, ed., *Geschichtsschreibung als Legitimationswissenschaft, 1918–1945* (Frankfurt am Main: Suhrkamp, 1997), pp. 262–341, 104–127.

61. Walter Frank, *Kämpfende Wissenschaft* (Hamburg: Hanseatische, 1934), pp. 34–35. Rüdiger Hohls, Konrad Hugo Jarausch, and Torsten Bathmann, eds., *Versäumte Fragen: Deutsche Historiker im Schatten des Nationalsozialismus* (Stuttgart: Deutsche Verlags-Anstalt, 2000), pp. 9–13, 37–39. Frank criticized senior historians for being merely nationalistic and summoned his colleagues to the battlefield, "Ready, Aim, Fire!" with "seriousness, scholar-ship, and conscience" (*Ernst, Gründlichkeit und Gewissen,*) in Walter Frank, *Zunft und Nation* (Hamburg: Hanseatische, 1935), pp. 15–20.

62. Adam, *Judenpolitik*, p. 107. Walter Frank, Rundschreiben an alle Mitglieder, Nov. 22, 1935, BAB/R4901/2591/Bl. 64. Not surprisingly, he blamed Jews driven into exile for the chaos! Weinreich, *Hitler's Professors*, pp. 46–47, 53. In 1938 it became the Hauptreferat für Judenfrage under Frank's leadership.

63. Frank, Reichsinstitut für Geschichte des neuen Deutschlands, 4th annual conven-tion, Dec. 1938. NA/A3345-DS-J005/folder 212.

64. Patricia von Papen, "'Scholarly' Anti-Semitism during the Third Reich: The Reichs-institut's Research on the 'Jewish Question,' 1935–1945" (Ph.D. diss., Columbia University, 1999), p. 63. The committee was a "who's who" of humanities scholarship: Ernst Krieck, Al-fred Baeumler, Erich Marcks, Heinrich Ritter von Srbik, Karl Alexander von Müller, Hans F. K. Günther, and Ottokar Lorenz.

65. The *homme nouveau* of the French Revolution bore the same traits as the New Nazi Man; see Mona Ozouf, "La Révolution française et l'idée de l'homme nouveau," in Colin Lucas, ed., *The Political Culture of the French Revolution*, vol. 2 of *The French Revolution and the Creation of Modern Political Culture* (New York: Pergamon, 1987–1994), pp. 214–219. On the link between 1914 and new conservatism, see Heide Gerstenberger, *Der Revolutionäre Konservatismus* (Berlin: Duncker & Humblot, 1968), pp. 32–37, 40–43.

66. W. Frank, Reichsinstitut, to Rust, Reichsminister für Wissenschaft, Erziehung und Volksbildung, Jan. 27, 1941, BAB/R4901/2592/Bl. 12–14. For an examination of the role of gender in Nazi colonial nostalgia, see Laura Wildenthal, *German Women for Empire, 1884–1945* (Durham, N.C.: Duke University Press, 2000), pp. 175–202.

67. Walter Gross, "Rassiche Geschichtsbetrachtung," in Rolf L. Fahrenkrog, ed., *Europas Geschichte als Rassenschicksal: Vom Wesen und Wirken der Rassen im europäischen Schicksals-raum* (Leipzig: Hesse & Becker, n.d.).

68. Walter Frank, foreword, in Karl Richard Ganzer, *Der heilige Hofbauer: Trager der Gegenreformation im 19. Jahrhundert* (Hamburg: Hanseatische, 1939), pp. 4–6.

69. Hans Frank, "Die Verwirklichung des Parteiprogramms," *Westdeutscher Beobachter* (Cologne), Feb. 11, 1936. Messerschmidt, Gustav, *Juden schänden deutsches Recht* (Berlin: Hammer, 1940).

70. "Berlin Worked Out Anti-Jewish Rules," and "German Constitutional Freedom Re-stored after Lapse," *New York Times*, Oct. 2, 1935. "Hitler's Speech to the Reichstag," *Times* (London), Sept. 12 and 16, 1935.

71. Carl Schmitt, "Die deutsche Rechtswissenschaft," *Deutsche Juristen-Zeitung* 41 (Oct. 15, 1936), cols. 1193–1200. George Schwab asserts that Schmitt, alarmed at the news that he was about to be denounced, endorsed the antisemitic purge in order to bolster his credit with powerful Nazis. Introduction to Carl Schmitt, *The Leviathan in the State Theory of*

Thomas Hobbes: Meaning and Failure of a Political Symbol (Westport, Conn.: Greenwood, 1996), pp. vii–xxxii.

72. Bernd Rüthers, *Carl Schmitt im Dritten Reich: Wissenschaft als Zeitgeist-Verstärkung?* (Munich: Beck, 1990), pp. 99–100: "This cannot be accomplished with a merely emotional antisemitism . . . It requires objective certainty." A few days later, on October 21, 1936, Hans Frank opened the exhibition "Das Recht" in Munich. Weinreich, *Hitler's Professors*, p. 39. *Das Judentum in der Rechswissenschaft*, ed. Reichsgruppe Hochschullehrer des National-sozialistischen Reichswahrerbundes (Berlin: Deutscher Rechts-Verlag, 1936). Friedländer, *Nazi Germany and the Jews*, vol. 1, pp. 192–193. Mark Lilla, "The Enemy of Liberalism," *New York Review of Books* 44 (May 15, 1997): 38–44. Ruth Groh, *Arbeit an der Heillosigkeit der Welt: Zur politisch-theologischen Mythologie und Anthropologie Carl Schmitts* (Frankfurt am Main: Suhrkamp, 1998), pp. 9–24, 87–102.

73. Of nine articles in *Das Judentum in der Rechtswissenschaft*, two concerned Jewish criminality and the rest analyzed the Jewish mentality (*Jüdischen Geist*).

74. Dieter Schiefelbein, *Das Institut zur Erforschung der Judenfrage, Frankfurt am Main: Vorgeschichte und Gründung, 1935–1939* (Frankfurt am Main: Stadt Frankfurt Dezernat für Kultur, 1993). Von Papen, "'Scholarly' Anti-Semitism," pp. 9, 70, 75.

75. Adam, *Judenpolitik*, p. 107. For a detailed account of the infighting between Frank, Grau, and their sponsors in the SS and Nazi Party, see Heiber, *Walter Frank*, pp. 938–1212; Von Papen, "'Scholarly' Anti-Semitism," pp. 63–186.

76. Theodor Pugel, with Robert Körper, Benno Imendörffer, and Erich Führer, *Anti-semitismus der Welt in Wort und Bild: Der Weltstreit um die Judenfrage* (Dresden: Groh, 1936), p. 306. See also Wilhelm Grau, *Die Judenfrage in der deutschen Geschichte*, 2nd ed. (Berlin: Teubner, 1937), pp. 6–7, 32.

77. Hans Diebow, *Der ewige Jude: 265 Bilddokumente* (Munich: Eher, 1937). Hans Diebow, *Die Juden in USA über hundert Bilddokumente* (Berlin: Eher, 1941). *Przeglad Kartolicki*, quoted in Henryk Grynberg, *Drohobycz, Drohbycz*, trans. A. Nitecki (New York: Penguin, 2002), p. 15.

78. Heiber, *Walter Frank*, pp. 627–630; Von Papen, "'Scholarly' Anti-Semitism," pp. 234–238. "Alfred Dreyfus—der ewige Jude," *Frankfurter Zeitung*, Jan. 14, 1939.

79. Herbert Obenaus, "The Germans: 'An Anti-Semitic People,'" in David Bankier, ed., *Probing the Depths of German Anti-Semitism: German Society and the Persecution of the Jews, 1933–1941* (New York: Berghahn, 2000), pp. 158–162. Armin Human, *Geschichte der Juden in Sachsen-Meiningen-Hildburghausen*, series Thüringer Untersuchungen zur Judenfrage, no. 2 (Weimar: Fink, 1939).

80. Obenaus, "The Germans," 162–165. Erwin Fleischauer, *Ein Jude gegen Jehova: Die internationale Lösung der Judenfrage*, series Welt-Dienst-Bücherei, no. 10 (Erfurt: Bodung-Verlag, 1939).

81. Susannah Heschel, "When Jesus Was an Aryan: The Protestant Church and Antisemitic Propaganda," in Robert P. Ericksen and Susannah Heschel, eds., *Betrayal: German Churches and the Holocaust* (Minneapolis, Minn.: Fortress, 1999), pp. 68–71. Kurt Emmerich, *Die Juden*, series Theologische Studien, vol. 7 (Zollikon: Evangelischen Buch-handlung, 1939). Wilhelm Stoffers, *Juden und Ghetto in der deutschen Literatur bis zum Ausgang des Weltkrieges* (Graz: Stiasnys Söhne, 1939).

82. Susannah Heschel, *Transforming Jesus from Jew to Aryan: Protestant Theologians in Nazi Germany* (Tucson: University of Arizona Press, 1995).

83. Walter Grundmann, preface to *Christentum und Judentum* (n.p.). Theodor Pauls, *Luther und die Juden*, 3 vols. (Bonn: Scheur, 1939). Hilfswerk für die Bekennende Kirche, ed., *Juden, Christen, Judenchristen: Ein Ruf an die Christenheit* (Zollikon: Verlag der Evangelischen Buchhandlung, 1939), p. 52.

84. Walter Grundmann, *Die Entjudung des religiosen Lebens als Aufgabe deutscher Theologie und Kirche* (Weimar: Deutsche Christen, 1939).

85. Heschel, "When Jesus Was an Aryan," in Heschel and Ericksen, *Betrayal*, pp. 71–82.

86. Weinreich, *Hitler's Professors*, pp. 64–66. Weinreich notes that opinion was divided within Nazi circles about supporting scholarship on Christianity. Susannah Heschel, *Abraham Geiger and the Jewish Jesus* (Chicago: University of Chicago Press, 1998), pp. 127–161, 231–142.

87. Institut zur Erforschung der Judentum, YIVO Archives, record group (RG) 222.

88. For example, George Lange, "Bevölkerungspolitik und Kultur," *VB* 48 (Aug. 3, 1935), "Der Jude als Verbrecher," *VB* 48 (Apr. 30, 1936), and Walter Gross, "Universität und Rassengedanke," *VB* 48 (May 12, 1936).

89. "If the products of their research work, even apart from their rude tone, strike us as unconvincing and hollow, this weakness is due not to inferior training but to the mendacity inherent in any scholarship that overlooks or openly repudiates all moral and spiritual values and, by standing order, knows exactly its ultimate conclusions well in advance." Weinreich, *Hitler's Professors*, p. 7.

90. Prof. C. Schmidt asserts, in "Nuremberg Laws . . . Make Constitutional Conception Entirely German," *New York Times*, Oct. 2, 1935; "Hitler's Assumption," Dec. 13, 1935, p. 24; "Racial Policy Explained," *New York Times*, Mar. 23, 1935 and Apr. 24, 1935; "V. Lutz Says Philosophy Plays Big Role," *New York Times*, Jan. 20, 1935; "Hails Hitler," *New York Times*, Aug. 28, 1935; "Frau Schirmacher-Oncken Declares Jews Caused Own Persecution," with a reply by E. Blumenthal, *New York Times*, Aug. 27, 1935. Several articles in monthly periodicals lamented the state of German research. Among the most significant are S. B. Fay, "German Learning in Decline," *Current History* 44 (Apr. 1936), pp. 87–88; C. G. Robertson, "Nazis and Scholarship," *New Republic* 86 (Apr. 1, 1936), p. 221. For a defense of German scholarship, see F. E. Hirsch, "With Honors Crowned," *Living Age* 350 (July 1936), pp. 393–399. In 1937, the *New York Times* reported without comment Frank and Grau's discovery: "Rothschild Linked to Marx by Nazis," *New York Times*, July 8, 1937.

91. For a survey of the components of Rosenberg's *hohe Schulen*, see Poliakov and Wulf, *Denker*, pp. 131–139. For an examination of the museums built from stolen objects, see Dirk Rupnow, *Täter, Gedächtnis, Opfer: Das "Jüdische Zentralmuseum" in Prag, 1942–1945* (Vienna: Picus, 2000), pp. 147–181.

92. Representative titles include Klaus Schickert, *Die Judenfrage in Ungarn: Jüdische Assimiliation und antisemitische Bewegung im 19. und 20. Jahrhundert* (Essen: Essener Verlagsanstalt, 1937), and *Bibliographie zur Nationalitätenfrage und zur Judenfrage der Republik Polen* (Stuttgart: Weltkriegsbücherei, 1941).

93. Apr. 24, 1939, *Kurze Inhaltsangabe der Schrift* "Rasse, Volk Staat und Raum," *Sprachregelung* (Linguistic guidelines), BAB/5001/1031/Bl. 1–2. Gerd Simon, *"Art, Auslese, Ausmerze . . .": Ein bisher unbekanntes Wörterbuchunternehmen* (Tübungen: Gesellschaft für Interdiziplinäre Forschung, 200).

94. REM, BAB/4901/521/Bl. 94. On October 1, 1935, a memo commented that the use of the term *geschützte Nichtarier* (in sense of April 25, 1933) was unclear and proposed *ungeschützter' Nichtarier*.

95. "Die amtliche Sortierung der Halbjuden," Oct. 5, 1935, BAB/R18/5513/Bl. 116, 79.

96. Karl Löwith, *My Life in Germany before and after 1933: A Report* (Champaign-Urbana: University of Illinois Press), pp. 60–61.

97. Tzvetan Todorov, *Mémoire du mal, tentation du bien: Enquête sur le siècle* (Paris: Lafont, 2001), pp. 26–34, 88–90.

98. Roger Uhle, "Neues Volk und reine Rasse: Walter Gross und das Rassenpolitische Amt der NSDAP" (Ph.D. diss., Rheinisch-Westfälische Technische Hochschule Aachen, 1999), p. 81.

99. Schmitt was denounced in 1936 in *Das Schwarze Korps* on the basis of a passing comment in a 1916 publication condemning racism, and Heidegger was dropped because longtime Nazi intellectuals did not trust ideas they could not understand.

100. By the autumn of 1942 Hitler had declared 339 "legal Jews" as *Mischlinge;* allowed 258 *Mischlinge* to serve in the military; and converted 394 first-degree *Mischlinge* into Aryans. Hermann Graml, *Antisemitism in the Third Reich,* trans. Tim Kirk (Cambridge, Mass.: Blackwell, 1992), p. 122. Lösener estimated that "thousands" of "mixed race" couples petitioned for exception status, but that only a few hundred were successful. Schleunes, *Legislating the Holocaust,* p. 64. H. A. Adler noted that Hitler became more rigid after 1940: *Der verwaltete Mensch: Studien zur Deportation der Juden aus Deutschland* (Tübingen: Mohr, 1974), p. 297.

101. Ludwik Fleck, *Genesis and Development of a Scientific Fact* (1934), introduction by Thomas S. Kuhn (Chicago: University of Chicago, 1979), pp. 4–6, 125–145.

102. Quoted by Martin Gilbert, foreword to Weinreich, *Hitler's Professors,* p. xi.

103. Heim and Aly, *Vordenker der Vernichtung,* pp. 188–206.

104. Klemperer, diary entry of July 12, 1938, *I Will Bear Witness,* vol. 1, p. 262. These political scholars cannot be written off as "pseudo-" researchers. Margit Szöllösi-Janze, "Wir Wissenschaftler bauen mit!" in Bernd Sösemann, ed., *Der Nationalsozialismus* (Stuttgart: Deutsche Verlags-Anstalt, 2002), pp. 157–167.

105. "Der Terror gegen die Juden," *Sopade,* Aug. 1935, p. 924.

106. Alice Baerwald, "My Life in Germany," Houghton, bMS Ger 91 (15).

107. Quoted in John Van Houten Dippel, *Bound upon a Wheel of Fire: Why So Many German Jews Made the Tragic Decision to Remain in Nazi Germany* (New York: Basic Books, 1996), p. 178.

108. *Sopade,* Jan. 1936, pp. 20–32.

109. David Bankier, *The Germans and the Final Solution,* pp. 73–74. Bankier examines the district led by virulent *Gauleiter* Grohe, and notes that while mass rallies and SA violence did little to popularize antisemitism, the shift to "legal" methods were successful. By the mid-1930s, "The fate of the Jews was not important enough to elicit criticism." Ian Kershaw, *Popular Opinion and Political Dissent in the Third Reich: Bavaria, 1933–1945* (New York: Oxford University Press, 1983), pp. 333–336.

110. Alison Owings, *Frauen: German Women Recall the Third Reich* (New Brunswick, N.J.: Rutgers, 1993), pp. 13–16. Jews will, like blacks, she insisted, be racially different with a distinctive mentality. Frank Stern, *The Whitewashing of the Yellow Badge,* trans. William Templer (Oxford, Eng.: Pergamon, 1992), pp. 1–11, 213–262.

111. Benno Müller-Hill, *Murderous Science: Elimination by Scientific Selection of Jews, Gypsies, and Others, Germany, 1933–1945* (New York: Oxford University Press, 1988), p. 108.

112. Klemperer, diary entry of Aug. 16, 1936, *I Will Bear Witness,* vol. 1, p. 184. This imagined retribution is hauntingly similar to Hitler's 1919 fantasy of how he would murder Jews in the Rathaus square in Munich. See also Lise Meitner to Otto Hahn, June 27, 1945, in Deichmann, *Biologists,* pp. 333–335.

9. RACIAL WARRIORS

1. Jason Epstein, "Always a Time to Kill," *New York Review of Books* 7 (Nov. 4, 1999): 57–64.

2. Among the "situationalists," four stand out: Hans Buchheim, Hans Mommsen, Richard Rhodes, and Christopher Browning. And among those who posit the existence of a uniquely German racism, Paul Rose, John Weiss, and Daniel J. Goldhagen have written most forcefully in recent years.

3. Herbert C. Kellerman and V. Lee Hamilton, *Crimes of Obedience: Toward a Social Psychology of Authority and Responsibility* (New Haven, Conn.: Yale University Press, 1989), pp. 46–48.

4. Daniel J. Goldhagen, *Hitler's Willing Executioners: Ordinary Germans and the Holocaust*

(New York: Knopf, 1996), p. 428. On the relation between this debate and broader historiographical trends, see Richard Bessel, "Functionalists vs. Intentionalists," *German Studies Review* 26 (Feb. 2003): 15–20.

5. Christopher R. Browning, *Ordinary Men: Reserve Police Battalion 101 and the Final Solution in Poland* (New York: Harper Perennial, 1998), p. 48. Of the seven reserve lieutenants, five belonged to the Nazi Party; of thirty-two noncommissioned officers, twenty-two belonged to the Nazi Party.

6. Peter Fritzsche, "May 1933," in *Germans into Nazis* (Cambridge: Harvard University Press, 1998), pp. 215–235. Bernd Stöver, *Volksgemeinschaft im Dritten Reich: Die Konsensbereitschaft der Deutschen aus der Sicht sozialistischer Exilberichte* (Düsseldorf: Droste, 1993), pp. 35–55, 115–220.

7. Canetti adds that in Old French, *meute* means both "rebellion or insurrection" and "the hunt." Elias Canetti, *Crowds and Power* [*Masse und Macht*, 1960], trans. Carol Stewart (New York: Farrar, Straus and Giroux, 1998), p. 97.

8. Canetti, *Crowds*, p. 99. Wehrmacht soldiers, as Klaus-Jürgen Müller notes, were indoctrinated to believe in Germany's right to military preparedness, the justice of revenge, the mission of *Lebensraum,* and the readiness to lay down their lives for *Volk* and Führer. Müller, *Das Heer und Hitler: Armee und nationalsozialistisches Regime, 1933–1940* (Stuttgart: Deutsche Verlags-Anstalt, 1969), doc. 2, pp. 591–593.

9. Hitler claimed, "History is made only by" all-male fighting groups, in "Warum die nationalsozialistische Bewegung dennoch siegen muß," speech at a National Socialist gathering at a beer hall, Eberhard Jäckel, ed., *Hitler: Sämtliche Aufzeichnungen, 1905–1924* (Stuttgart: Deutsche Verlags-Anstalt, 1980), p. 737. "What made men die (in World War I) was not concern for their daily bread, but love of the fatherland, faith in its greatness, a general feeling for the honor of the nation." *Mein Kampf,* trans. Ralph Mannheim (Boston: Houghton Mifflin, 1962), p. 437.

10. See the debates with Lyda Gottschweski in Alfred Bäumler, *Männerbund und Wissenschaft* (Berlin: Junker & Dünnhaupt, 1934). Harry Oosterhuis, "Medicine, Male Bonding and Homosexuality in Nazi Germany," *Journal of Contemporary History* 32 (Apr. 1997): 187–110. Joanna Bourke writes, "Love for one's comrades was widely regarded as the strongest incentive for murderous aggression against a foe identified as threatening that relationship. Hatred was less significant." *An Intimate History of Killing: Face-to-Face Killing in Twentieth-Century Warfare* (New York: Basic Books, 1999), pp. 129, 158. Geoffrey Giles, "Why Bother about Homosexuals? Homophobia and Sexual Politics in Nazi Germany," lecture at the U.S. Holocaust Memorial Museum, Washington, D.C., May 30, 2001.

11. Bäumler, *Männerbund,* pp. 14–37.

12. Canetti, *Crowds,* p. 94.

13. Wolfgang Sofsky, *The Order of Terror: The Concentration Camp,* trans. William Templer (Princeton, N.J.: Princeton University Press, 1999), pp. 234–236.

14. Hans Mommsen, "Die Realisierung des Utopischen: Die 'Endlösung der Judenfrage' im 'Dritten Reich,'" *Geschichte und Gesellschaft* 9 (1983): 381–420.

15. Bruce Campbell, *The SA Generals and the Rise of Nazism* (Lexington: University Press of Kentucky, 1998), p. 116.

16. Tom Segev, *Soldiers of Evil: The Commandants of the Nazi Concentration Camps* (New York: McGraw-Hill, 1987), pp. 58–60. Campbell, *The SA Generals,* pp. 118–153. Robert Koehl, *Black Corps: The Structure and Power Struggles of the Nazi SS* (Madison: University of Wisconsin, 1983), pp. 83–84. Jens Banach, *Heydrichs Elite: Das Führerkorps der Sicherheitspolizei und des SD, 1936–1945* (Paderborn: Schöningh, 1998), pp. 99–114.

17. Walther Darré, circular, Rasse und Siedlungs Haupt Amt, Munich, Mar. 1934, NA/T-611/91.

18. By December 1940, the Waffen SS increased to 150,000; and the SS VT (special forces) numbered between 8,000 and 9,000, while the concentration camp units, in the Death's Head division, included about 6,500. Bernd Wegner, *Hitlers Politische Soldaten: die Waffen-SS, 1933–1945—Studien zu Leitbild, Struktur und Funktion einer nationalsozialistischen Elite* (Paderborn: Schöningh, 1982), pp. 175–195. George C. Browder, *Foundations of the Nazi Police State: The Formation of Sipo and SD* (Lexington: University Press of Kentucky, 1990), pp. 221–230. Segev, *Soldiers of Evil*, pp. 94–122. Ursula Nienhaus, "Himmlers willige Komplizinnen—Weibliche Polizei im Nationalsozialismus, 1937 bis 1945," in Michael Grüttner, Rüdiger Hachtmann, and Heinz-Gerhard Haupt, eds., *Geschichte und Emanzipation* (Frankfurt am Main: Campus, 1999), pp. 517–539.

19. Heinrich Himmler, "Ansprache des Reichsführers-SS, am 11. Oktober 1934," quoted in Browder, *Foundations*, p. 158.

20. Joseph Wulf, *Presse und Funk im Dritten Reich: Eine Dokumentation* (Gütersloh: Mohn, 1964), p. 252.

21. "Ein Kampfblatt, das geliebt und gehaßt wird, wie kein zweites." Looking back after the war, a cabinet minister recalled that Streicher's "hold on Germany can only be compared with that of Goebbels' propaganda." *Trial of the Major War Criminals before the International Military Tribunal* (Washington, D.C.: Government Printing Office, 1948) (henceforth *IMT*), vol. 5, pp. 91–118, 547–549, *http://www.yale.edu/lawweb/avalon/imt*.

22. Lutz Graf Schwerin von Krosigk, "Rassenkampf der Minderwertigen," *Es Geschah in Deutschland: Menschenbilder unseres Jahrhunderts* (Tübingen: Wunderlich, 1952), pp. 265–268. Streicher was hanged for, among other acts, spreading the "virus of antisemitism" and calling repeatedly for the "extermination" of all Jews in the late 1930s. "Without the Streichers, the Kaltenbrunners, etc. would have had no one to do their orders." *IMT*, vol. 5, docs. 001M–045M, pp. 111–158. "Judgment," Streicher, Avalon Project at Yale Law School, consulted on March 30, 2003, *http://www.yale.edu/lawweb/avalon/imt*

23. Himmler quoted in *Der Stürmer* 14 (July 1937). The prosecution at the *IMT* identified more than fifty passages in which Streicher called for the extermination of Jewry. Nuremberg Trials, *IMT*, vol. 5, p. 118.

24. Randall L. Bytwerk, *Julius Streicher* (New York: Dorset, 1983), pp. 25, 148–149, 164–165.

25. Robert Gellately, *The Gestapo and German Society: Enforcing Racial Policy, 1933–1945* (Oxford, Eng.: Clarendon, 1990), pp. 132–143. Eric A. Johnson, *Nazi Terror: The Gestapo, Jews, and Ordinary Germans* (New York: Basic Books, 2000), pp. 364–375, and Gisela Diewald-Kerkmann, "Denunziantum," in Gerhard Paul and Klaus-Michael Mallmann, eds., *Die Gestapo: Mythos und Realität* (Darmstadt: Primus, 1996), pp. 288–305.

26. The verdict on Streicher quotes from *Der Stürmer* at length. *IMT*, vol. 22, pp. 547–549.

27. These allegations are from *Der Stürmer*: "Jüdische Trauung in Bielefeld," *Der Stürmer* 13, no. 47 (Nov. 1935); "Die Beerdigung: Wie die Jüdin Felsenthal zu Grabe geleitet wurde," *Der Stürmer* 14, no. 9 (Apr. 1936); "Ein unerhörter Fall jüdischer Gefühlsroheit," *Der Stürmer* 11, no. 31 (July 1933); Hildegard Staub "NSFS Tagung in Liegnitz i. Schl," *Der Stürmer* 12, no. 13 (Mar 1934); "Die jüdische Pest an der Saar," and "Salie Aronowsy: Der Zahnbehandler von Dietfurt," *Der Stürmer* 13, no. 1 (Jan. 1935); "Der Herr Pfarrer kauft heute noch sein Brot beim Jüdenbäcker," *Der Stürmer* 13, no. 4 (Feb. 1935); "Wann wird der deutsche Bauer gescheit?" *Der Stürmer* 13, no. 38 (Sept. 1935); "Der Jude als Viehhändler" *Der Stürmer* 13, no. 43; "Pfarrer Wolff," *Der Stürmer* 13, no. 47; "Wer beim Juden kauft," *Der Stürmer* 14, no. 29; "Juden sonnen sich in Deutschland," *Der Stürmer* 16, no. 45 (Nov. 1938); "Der Strandbad," *Der Stürmer* 1 no. 29 (July 1936).

28. "Diese Betriebe sind jüdisch," *Der Stürmer* 16, no. 42 (Oct. 1938): 4.

29. Gerta Pfeffer, "Ich hätte gern mitgetanzt," Margarete Limberg and Hubert Rübsaat,

eds., *"Sie durften nicht mehr Deutsche sein": Jüdischer Alltag in Selbstzeugnissen, 1933–1938* (Frankfurt am Main: Campus, 1990), pp. 140–143.

30. "Ein sonderbarer Frauenverein" (A most unusual women's league), *Der Stürmer* 15 no. 40 (Sept. 1937).

31. "Was Christus sagt," and "Hitlertreue," *Der Stürmer* 2, no. 12 (Aug. 1924).

32. "Unser Zeichner Fips bei der Marine," *Der Stürmer* 17, no. 42 (Oct. 1939).

33. A collection of twenty-four prints of Jewish men from various occupations by Fips, printed on high-quality paper with unnumbered pages, *Juden stellen sich vor* (Nuremberg: Stürmer Verlag, 1934).

34. "Tiere sehen dich an," *Der Stürmer* 11, no.47 (Nov. 1933). For a visual variation on this theme, see the Fips caricature of a caged ape and a Jewish male looking at one another. *Der Stürmer* 10, no. 10 (Mar. 1932), and "Das Tier im Juden," *Der Stürmer* 13, no. 31 (Aug. 1935).

35. "Protests against Serums," *New York Times*, Feb. 15, 1935; "Bars Wrestling Matches," *New York Times*, Mar. 11, 1935; "Appointed to Academy for German Law," *New York Times*, Sept. 7, 1935; "Streicher Dines 15 Reds," *New York Times*, Dec. 22, 1935.

36. "Das geschändete Kind: Viehjude vergeht sich an zweijährigem Mädchen," *Der Stürmer* 13, no. 4 (Jan. 1935); "Paul Rehfisch der Kinderschändler von Gelsenkirchen," *Der Stürmer* 12, no. 50 (Dec. 1934); "Jud L. Leopold: Der Kinderschändler in Weimar," *Der Stürmer* 13, no. 2 (Jan. 1935); "Die Viehjuden Hildesheimer," *Der Stürmer* 13, no. 4 (Feb. 1935).

37. "Jüdische Knabenverderber," *Der Stürmer* 14 (Mar. 1936).

38. Fred Hahn, *Lieber Stürmer! Leserbriefe an das NS-Kampfblatt, 1924 bis 1945* (Stuttgart: Seewald, 1978), p. 105.

39. On the basis of the putative Talmudic axiom, "The Jew is human and the non-Jew is an animal," non-Jews could repay Jews in kind without feeling guilty. "Gesinnungslosigkeit," *Der Stürmer* 14, no. 29 (July 1936). "So wirtschaftet der Jude!" *Der Stürmer* 13, no. 15 (Apr. 1935). The source is given as "Baba unezia 114 b." Max Weinreich, *Hitler's Professors: The Part of Scholarship in Germany's Crimes against the Jewish People* (New Haven, Conn.: Yale University Press, 1999), pp. 39–40, 51–55, discusses Streicher's intellectual pretensions.

40. One of several examples of the tendentious pseudo-erudition that appeared during the late Enlightenment was a book by two Jesuits, Carl Anton and Johann Eisenmenger, *Einleitung in die rabbinischen Rechte* (Braunschweig: Meyer, 1756). One of Hitler's earliest comrades, Hermann Esser, compiled putative lists of Jews wanted for crimes in the eighteenth century. *Die jüdische Weltpest: Kann ein Jude Staatsbürger sein?* (Munich: Eher, 1927).

41. Peter Deeg, *Hofjuden*, Julius Streicher, ed. (Nuremberg: Stürmer, 1939).

42. Richard Wilhelm Stock. *Die Judenfrage durch fünf Jahrhunderte* (Nuremberg: Stürmer, Verlag, 1936).

43. Rejoicing at the death of Jews was a constant theme. See "Der Tod des Juden Guckenheimer," *Der Stürmer* 9, no. 53 (Dec. 1931); "220 Volt Spannung," *Der Stürmer* 16, no. 1 (Jan. 1938); Ernst Hiemer, "Und wieder die Juden-Frage!" *Der Stürmer* 13, no. 32 (Aug. 1937).

44. *Was soll mit den Juden geschehen? Kritische Vorschläge von Julius Streicher und Adolf Hitler* (Paris: Carrefour, 1936), p. 52. "The Organization of Spontaneity," in *The Yellow Spot: The Outlawing of a Half a Million Human Beings—A Collection of Facts and Documents Relating to Three Years' Persecution of German Jews*, introduction by the bishop of Durham (London: Victor Gollancz, 1936), pp. 177–196, 209–384.

45. Streicher, lecture, Bernau, July 1935, NA/T-81/75, 86592–86599. "Herr Streicher and the Jews: Extirpation the Only Solution," *Times* (London), Sept. 16, 1936.

46. "Der Jude ist ungerufen in unser Land gekomme'. Also kann er wieder gehen." *Der Stürmer* 12, no. 25 (1934); Christa-Maria Rock, "Die Judenfrage," *Der Stürmer* 13, no. 47 (Dec. 1935). "Zurück zum Ghetto," *Der Stürmer* 13, no. 12 (Mar. 1935).

47. "Die Judenfrage ist eine Weltfrage," a discussion of the "Kampf gegen Alljuda," *Der Stürmer* 13, no. 48 (Nov. 1935).

48. "Ehrlichkeit und Lumperei," *Der Stürmer* 12, no. 9 (Feb. 1934). Reader's letter, "Madagaskar," *Der Stürmer* 12, no. 40 (Nov. 1934). Among other references to extrusion, see, "Die Lösung der Judenfrage," *Der Stürmer* 13, no. 46 (Nov. 1935), followed by "Das Ende: Madagaskar," *Der Stürmer* 16, no. 1 (Jan. 1938).

49. "Judentum ist organisiertes Verbrechertum . . .," *Der Stürmer* 12 (Feb. 1934).

50. In the original it reads, "bis sich diese selber vertilgt und aufgefressen haben." The phrase ends, "in so far as the absence of all sense of self-sacrifice, expressing itself in their cowardice, did not turn battle into comedy here too." Hitler, *Mein Kampf*, p. 302.

51. "Ein englisches Blatt empfiehlt Madagaskar für die Juden," *Der Stürmer* 13 (Apr. 1935). See also Peter Longerich, "Some time in the future we want to ship the Jews out to Madagascar," *The Unwritten Order: Hitler's Role in the Final Solution* (Charleston, S.C.: Tempus, 2001), pp. 55–56.

52. Special issue for the annual Nuremberg Rally, "Menschenmörder von Angfang an: Der jüdische Weltbolschewismus von Moses bis zur Komintern," special issue 3, *Der Stürmer* (Sept. 1935). "Hölle Sowjetrußland: Der Todesschrei eines Riesenvolkes—Mord und Hunger bringen das russische Volk zur Strecke," *Der Stürmer* 13 (Dec. 1935).

53. Fips, a portfolio of nine "solutions" to racial "problems," including a drawing of a lynch victim with the notation that in America no one worries when a Negro hangs. *Der Stürmer* 14, no. 21 (May 1936).

54. "So sagen sie! Das taten sie!" *Der Stürmer* 17 (Oct. 1939).

55. Otto Dov Kulka, "The German Population and the Jews," in David Bankier, ed., *Probing the Depths of German Anti-Semitism: German Society and the Persecution of the Jews, 1933–1941* (New York: Berghahn, 2000), pp. 272–273. Ian Kershaw, "The Persecution of the Jews and German Public Opinion," *Leo Baeck Institute Yearbook* 26 (1981): 261–289.

56. Otto Dov Kulka, "Die Nürnberger Rassengesetze und die deutsche Bevölkerung im Lichte geheimer NS-Lage- und Stimmungsberichte," *Vierteljahrshefte für Zeitgeschichte* 32 (1984): 582–600. "Nachrichtenerfassung" (News-gathering), Dec. 15, 1936, USHMM, RG-11-001M.01/183/roll 1, pp. 2–6, describes the Security Service network. For information on the SS campaign to make antisemitic actions tasteful, see Hess's circular of Jan. 29, 1936, USHMM, RG-11.001M.01/261/roll 4.

57. Memorandum, SD Office 4/2 to Heydrich, May 24, 1934, in Michael Wildt, ed., *Die Judenpolitik des SD, 1935 bis 1938: Eine Dokumentation* (Munich: Oldenbourg, 1995), doc. 1, p. 67. Emphasis in the original.

58. "Antisemitismus, der uns schadet," *SK* 1 (June 5, 1935).

59. Staatspolizeistelle, Bez. Wiesbaden in Frankfurt am Main. Feb. 6, 1935, USHMM, RG-11.001M.01, Reichssicherheitshauptamt, SD Berlin, 346, roll 5.

60. The cartoon (entitled "The Heroes" and signed Lazslo) originally appeared in *Time and Tide*, probably in 1937. USHMM, RG-11.001M.01/346/roll 5.

61. Walther Darré, in describing the *Schulungsaparat*, advised instructors to adapt their approach to trainees' intellectual background and to consult the "Rassefachberater." NA/T-611/91. SS "ideology," as reflected in *SK* and training manuals, bore little relation to Himmler's idiosyncratic notions.

62. Wegner, *Hitlers politische Soldaten*, pp. 106–111, 192–203.

63. "Wir Kriegsfreiwilligen von 1914/15 und der Nationalsozialismus," *SK* 1 (Mar. 6, 1935), p. 1. Several historians revise the conventional image of SS men as technocrats without ideology. Michael Thad Allen, *The Business of Genocide: The SS, Slave Labor, and the Concentration Camps* (Chapel Hill: University of North Carolina Press, 2002), pp. 1–29, 92–96. For a narrower examination of SS financial schemes, see Peter-Ferdinand Koch, *Die Geldgeschäft der SS* (Hamburg: Hoffmann & Campe, 2000). Jürgen Matthäus, "Ausbildungsziel Judenmord? Zum Stellenwert der 'weltanschaulichen Erziehung' von SS und Polizei im

Rahmen der 'Endlösung,'" *Zeitschrift für Geschichtswissenschaft* 47 no. 8 (1999): 677–699. Edward Westerman, *Himmler's Political Soldiers: The German Uniformed Police and the Prosecution of Racial War, 1933–1945* (Lawrence: University of Kansas Press, in press).

64. Werner Augustinovic and Martin Moll, "Gunter D'Alquen, Propagandist des SS-Staates," in Ronald Smelser and Enrico Syring, eds., *Die SS: Elite unter dem Totenkopf—30 Lebensläufe* (Paderborn: Schöningh, 2000), pp. 100–118.

65. George C. Browder, *Hitler's Enforcers: The Gestapo and the SS Security Service in the Nazi Revolution* (New York: Oxford Univrsity Press, 1996), pp. 136–138. On the prevalence of aristocrats among SS officers, see Heinz Höhne, *The Order of the Death's Head: The Story of Hitler's S.S.*, trans. Richard Barry (New York: Coward-McCann, 1970), pp. 132–160.

66. August Heißmeyer, twenty-one-page report on morale dated Sept. 4, 1936, BA/NS2/38

67. Banach, *Heydrichs Elite*, pp. 98–100.

68. "S.S. auf Vorposten an der Weichsel," *SK* 2 (Feb. 13, 1936).

69. "Weiße Juden in der Wissenschaft," *SK* 2 (July 15, 1937).

70. "Der Kampf gegen den Rassengedanken," *SK* 2 (June 4, 1936). This is the fourth in a series about critics of National Socialism.

71. Visual essay with examples of kitsch, *SK* 2 (Oct. 8, 1936).

72. "Frauen sind keine Männer!" *SK* 2 (Mar. 12, 1936); "Wir brauchen Frauen!" *SK* 4 (Jan. 27, 1938); "Mädchen in Uniform," *SK* 2 (May 28, 1936); and "Schluß mit der Frauenbewegung," *SK* 1 (July 24, 1935).

73. "Das Maß aller Dinge ist der Mensch," *SK* 4 (Mar. 17, 1938). Other examples of the female representing virtue include "Schönheit ist die Wahrheit selbst," *SK* 4 (Feb. 17, 1938), and "Was ist schamloser?" *SK* 4 (Jan. 20, 1938).

74. Banach, *Heydrichs Elite*, pp. 136–139.

75. Cited in Norbert Frei, *National Socialist Rule in Germany: The Führer State, 1933–1945* (Oxford, Eng.: Blackwell, 1993), p. 103.

76. "Berichte der SD-Oberabschnitte zum Stand der Judenreferate auf der Schulungstagung in Bernau," Mar. 13–14, 1936, Bernau, in Wildt, *Die Judenpolitik*, doc. 6, p. 81.

77. Robert Gellately, *The Gestapo and German Society: Enforcing Racial Policy, 1933–1945* (Oxford, Eng.: Clarendon, 1990), tables on pp. 162, 164.

78. "Der Internationale Jude," *SK* 2 (June 4, 1936).

79. *SS-Leitheft* 3 (Apr. 22, 1936): 7–14.

80. "Programm für die Schulungstagung der Judenreferenten der SD-Oberabschnitte und Abschnitte in Bernau," Mar. 9–14, 1936. Wildt, *Die Judenpolitik*, doc. 5, p. 80. Banach, *Heydrichs Elite*, pp. 114–121.

81. "Wird abgegessen," *SK* 2 (June 4, 1936); "Nathan der Waffenschmiede?" *SK* 3 (Jan. 20, 1938); "Jüdischer Lotterieschwindel," *SK* 2 (July 2, 1936); "Im Wein liegt Wahrheit nur allein," *SK* 2 (Sept. 17, 1936).

82. "Antisemitismus, der uns schadet," *SK* 1 (June 5, 1935); and "Parteibuch ist kein Versorgungsschein," *SK* 2 (May 7, 1936).

83. Readers were admonished not to resort to violence and to drive Jews ruthlessly out of Germany, perhaps to Palestine. "Zur Lösung der Judenfrage," *SK* 1 (Aug. 21, 1935): 1.

84. Memorandum des SD-Amtes, May 24, 1934, in Wildt, *Die Judenpolitik*, doc. 1, pp. 66–69, and "Wohin mit den Juden?" *SK* 4 (Feb. 10, 1938).

85. "Gleiche Methoden—Gleiches Ziel," *SK* 4 (Sept. 23, 1938): 8.

86. As late as May 1940, Himmler had rejected mass murder of the Jews "from inner conviction [seeing] the Bolshevist method of physical extermination of a people as un-Germanic and impossible." Quoted in Höhne, *The Order of the Death's Head*, p. 325.

87. "Juden unerwünscht!" *SK* 4 (Sept. 1, 1938).

88. "Memorandum des SD-Amtes," to Heydrich, May 24, 1935, in Wildt, *Die Judenpolitik*, doc. 1, p. 67. Typical intelligence reports made detailed lists of Jewish organizations

and their memberships. Dieter Schwarz, *Das Weltjudentum: Macht und Politik* (Berlin: Eher, 1939). On the contrast with SA methods, see Matthäus, "Erziehung," pp. 686–688.

89. Wislicensys, "Judenfrage," Apr. 7, 1937, and "Richtlinien" (Guidelines), in Wildt, *Die Judenpolitik*, docs. 11, 12, pp. 108–115. See also Westerman, "Himmler's Political Soldiers," in Alan Steinweis and Daniel Rogers, eds., *The Impact of Nazism: New Perspectives on the Third Reich and Its Legacy* (Lincoln: University of Nebraska Presss, 2003).

90. "Das Ghetto, in diesem Falle das geistige, ist die Lebensform der Juden seit 800 Jahren" and "Jüdische Schlußbilanz," *SK* 2 (Feb. 27, 1936). See also "Die Legende vom anständige Juden," *SK* 3 (Jan. 13, 1938).

91. Manfred Messserschmidt, *Die Wehrmacht im NS-Staat: Zeit der Indokrination* (Hamburg: Deckers Verlag, 1969), pp. 17–83.

92. "Material specifically designed to harden the policemen for the personal task of killing Jews is conspicuously absent from the surviving documentation." Browning, *Ordinary Men*, pp. 176–180. Data on SS men collected by social scientists immediately after 1945 confirms the absence of vulgar antisemitism among SS men. A psychological analysis of fifty-eight SS men who had been convicted of war crimes revealed that only 17 percent displayed an obsessive hatred for Jews, while 25 percent expressed a global "ethnocentric or undifferentiated generalized hate." Henry V. Dicks, *Licensed Mass Murder: A Socio-Psychological Study of Some SS killers* (London: Chatto-Heinemann, 1972), pp. 77–80. The authors err in assuming that incitements to commit genocide must be expressed in violent language.

93. "Nächstenliebe, Barmherzigkeit und Demut" to him were cardinal sins. Wegner, *Hitlers Politische Soldaten*, p. 51.

94. Quoted in Hans Witek and Hans Safrian, *Und keiner war dabei: Dokumente des alltäglichen Antisemitismus in Wien, 1938* (Vienna: Picus, 1988), pp. 79–80.

95. *Sopade*, Aug./Sept. 1935, pp. 922, 928, 1020. Three years later, people accepted anti-Jewish laws as just. *Sopade*, July 1938, p. 753. Bernd Stöver, ed., *Berichte über die Lage in Deutschland* (Bonn: Dietz, 1996), pp. 25–26. "It was not anti-Semitism as such, but its extent and degree, that aroused public criticism." David Bankier, *The Germans and the Final Solution: Public Opinion under Nazism* (Oxford, Eng.: Blackwell, 1992), p. 73.

96. Göring's speech is reprinted in Jeremy Noakes and Geoffrey Pridham, *Nazism: A History in Documents*, vol. 1 (New York: Schocken, 1984), doc. 427, pp. 558–559. His comments about corruption in the party are quoted in Hermann Graml, *Antisemitism in the Third Reich*, trans. Tim Kirk (Oxford, Eng.: Blackwell, 1992), pp. 9–12.

97. Orlow, *History*, vol. 2, pp. 246–249. Helmut Genschel, *Die Verdrängung der Juden aus der Wirtschaft im Dritten Reich* (Göttingen: Musterschmidt, 1966), p. 236. Höhne, *The Order of the Death's Head*, p. 316. BAB/R58/1096/110/Bl. 31–32.

98. "Aus der Reichshauptstadt," *Der Stürmer* 17, no. 47 (Nov. 1938); "Ist die Judenfrage erlöst?" *Der Stürmer* 17, no. 48 (Dec. 1938).

99. "Wer andern eine Grube grab" *SK 4* (Dec. 1, 1938). Attacks on liberal's hypocrisy were not new in the periodical. See "Winston Churchill und die Barbarei," *SK* 2 (Oct. 15, 1936).

100. "Eine kleine Auswahl," *SK 4* (Nov. 24, 1938): 5; "Zweite Auswahl," *SK 4* (Dec. 8, 1938).

101. "Juden, Was nun?" *SK 4* (Nov. 24, 1938), pp. 1–2.

102. With the approach of war, the number of policemen under SS command increased from 62,000 to 131,000; the Death's Head concentration camp guard units expanded to 6,500; the Waffen SS grew to 100,000; and the SS-VT combat troops grew to 9,000. Karin Orth, "The Concentration Camp SS as a Functional Elite," in Ulrich Herbert, ed., *National Socialist Extermination Policies: Contemporary German Perspectives and Controversies* (New York: Berghahn, 2000), pp. 306–336.

103. Unlike the *Wehrmacht* generals who objected when they witnessed or learned about the massacres of 7,000 Jews and 7,000 Poles during the early months of the Polish in-

vasion, the SS *Einsatzkommando* that received explicit orders to kill did its work without hesitation. Even so, when a very different unit found itself guarding an eastern Polish village and the situation made collaboration with local Jews and Poles reasonable, the unit also functioned well. The point here is that SS men so thoroughly absorbed racial values that they were adept at either obedience or innovation, depending on the context. Alexander B. Rossino, "Nazi Anti-Jewish Policy during the Polish Campaign: The Case of the Einsatzgruppe von Woyrsch," *German Studies Review* 24 (Feb. 2001): 35–54; Christopher R. Browning, *Nazi Policy, Jewish Workers, German Killers* (Cambridge, Eng.: Cambridge University Press, 2000), pp. 116–169.

10. RACIAL WAR AT HOME

1. The translation of this passage is from, "Herr Hitler's Forecast, 'Long Period of Peace'" *Times* (London), Jan. 31, 1939, p. 12. J. P. Stern, *Hitler and the People* (Berkeley: University of California Press, 1973), pp. 78–84.

2. Max Domarus, ed., *Hitler Speeches and Proclamations, 1932–45: The Chronicle of a Dictatorship*, vol. 3, trans. Mary Fran Gilbert (Wauconda, Ill.: Bolchazy-Carducci, 1990), pp. 1441–1449. In his September 1935 speech introducing the Race Laws, Hitler had remarked that if "tolerable relations" could not be established with "the Jewish *Volk*," he would reevaluate the situation. Domarus, *Hitler Speeches*, vol. 2, p. 706. Other significant conversations took place in January 1939 that make it clear Hitler was not speaking metaphorically. Klaus P. Fischer, *The History of an Obsession: German Judeophobia and the Holocaust* (New York: Continuum, 1998), pp. 283–288. Nazi language introduced *vernichten* into many discussions of enemy intentions, for example, "Deutschland soll vernichtet werden," *VB* 49 (Apr. 30/May 1, 1936).

3. Göring, who took careful notes, overlooked it. Goebbels said nothing in his diary. Victor Klemperer did not comment, although he noted several days later that Hitler had "once again turned all his enemies into Jews and threatened the annihilation of the Jews in Europe if they were to bring war about against Germany." Victor Klemperer, diary entry of Feb. 5, 1939, *I Will Bear Witness: A Diary of the Nazi Years, 1933–1941*, trans. Martin Chalmers (New York: Random House, 1998), vol. 1, p. 292.

4. "Herr Hitler's Forecast, 'Long Period of Peace,'" and "Herr Hitler's Speech," *Times* (London), Jan. 31, 1939, pp. 12, 14. "Hitler Demands Colonies," *New York Times*, Jan. 31, 1939, p. 1. *Der Völkische Beobachter*, however, carried headlines announcing Hitler's "epoch-making" threat to Jewry. "Prophetische Warnung an das Judentum," *VB* 52 (Feb. 1, 1939).

5. Max Domarus, ed., *Hitler: Reden und Proklamationen, 1932–1945*, vol. 2 (Munich: Suddeutscher, 1965), pp. 1047–1067. The English translation has been abridged. Domarus, *Hitler Speeches*, vol. 3, 1939–1940, pp. 1460–1465.

6. *Sopade*, July 1939, p. 921.

7. *Sopade*, Feb. 6, 1939, pp. 201–202.

8. Klemperer, diary entries of Dec. 15 and 23, 1938, *I Will Bear Witness*, vol. 1, pp. 280, 283.

9. Otto Dov Kulka, "The German Population and the Jews," in David Bankier, ed., *Probing the Depths of German Anti-Semitism: German Society and the Persecution of the Jews, 1933–1941* (New York: Berghahn, 2000), pp. 274–276.

10. Alexandre Koyre, "The Political Function of the Modern Lie," *Contemporary Jewish Record*, June 1945, pp. 294–296, 298.

11. Marlis G. Steinert, *Hitlers Krieg und die Deutschen: Stimmung und Haltung der deutschen Bevölkerung im Zweiten Weltkrieg* (Düsseldorf: Econ, 1970), pp. 78–79.

12. Monthly report, Ansbach, Steinert, *Hitlers Krieg*, p. 81.

13. Heinrich Hoffmann, *Ein Volk ehrt seinen Führer: Der 20. April 1939 im Bild* (Berlin: Andermann, 1939), unpaged.

14. Reports dated Nov. 10 and 13, 1939, in Heinz Boberach, ed., *Meldungen aus dem*

Reich, 1938–1945: Die geheimen Lageberichte des Sicherheitsdienstes der SS., 17 vols., vol. 3 (Herrsching, Germany: Pawlak, 1984), pp. 466–467.

15. Quoted in Ernest K. Bramsted, *Goebbels and National Socialist Propaganda, 1925– 1945* (n.p.: Cresset, 1965), p. 221.

16. Boberach, *Meldungen*, vol. 6, p. 1813; "Zur Aufnahme der Wochenschauen vom 25. bis 31. Januar und vom 1. bis 7. Februar 1941," ibid., vol. 7, p. 2005. "Man of Destiny," *Times* (London), Nov. 11, 1939, p. 5.

17. Heinrich Himmler, "Menschen Einsatz," Dec. 16, 1939, NA/T-81/52/55068–55070.

18. "Wissenschaft gegen Weltjudentum," *VB* 54 (South German edition, Mar. 25, 1941).

19. "So sieht Frankreich die schwarzen Franzosen," and "Weltkampf der Rassen," *NV* 8 (Oct. 1940), and *NV* 8 (Nov. 1940).

20. Patricia von Papen, "'Scholarly' Antisemitism during the Third Reich: The Reichs- institut's Research on the 'Jewish Question' (Ph.D. diss., Columbia University, 1999), pp. 241–265. Dirk Rupnow, *Täter, Gedächtnis, Opfer: Das "Jüdische Zentralmuseum" in Prag, 1942–1945* (Vienna: Picus, 2000), pp. 80–124.

21. Dr. Johann Pohl, *Jüdische Selbstzeugnisse*, series International Institut zur Aufklärung über die Judenfrage (Munich: Eher, 1943).

22. Richard Tetzlaff, *Die armen Juden*, vol. 25 in the series Völkisches Erwachen (Leipzig: Klein, 1939).

23. Eugen Fischer and Gerhard Kittel, *Das antike Weltjudentum* (Hamburg: Hanseatische, 1943).

24. Johann von Leers, *14 Jahre Judenrepublik: Die Geschichte eines Rassenkampfe* (Berlin: Verlag Deutsche Kultur-Wacht, 1942?); Franz Schattenfroh, *Wille und* Rasse (Berlin, Stubenrauch, 1943).

25. Hannah Arendt's portrait of Eichmann cast a very long shadow that began to be dis- credited only after important archival studies. Among the most important are Ulrich Her- bert, "Ideological Legitimization and the Political Practice of the Leadership of the National Socialist Secret Police," in Hans Mommsen, ed., *The Third Reich between Vision and Reality: New Perspectives on German History, 1918–1945* (New York: Berg, 2001), pp. 95–98. Michael Wildt, *Generation des Unbedingten: Das Führungskorps des Reichssicherheitshauptamtes* (Ham- burg: Hamburger Edition, 2002), pp. 23–24 examined a random sample of 221 men in the headquarters of the Reich Security Office, the *Reichssicherheitshauptamt*. Michael Thad Al- len, *The Business of Genocide* (Chapel Hill: University of North Carolina, 2002), pp. 14–29, 272–285. Yaacov Lozowick, *Hitler's Bureaucrats: The Nazi Security Police and the Banality of Evil*, trans. Haim Watzman (New York: Continuum, 2000), pp. 3–23 and 253–255.

26. Claude Lanzmann, *Shoah: The Complete Text of the Acclaimed Holocaust Film* (New York: Da Capo, 1995), pp. 129–134. Hilberg reminisced about this conversation and the role of Nazi transport in his research: Raul Hilberg, *The Politics of Memory: The Journey of a Holo- caust Historian* (Chicago: Ivan R. Dee, 1996), pp. 40–41 and 70–73.

27. Omer Bartov, *Hitler's Army: Soldiers, Nazis and War in the Third Reich* (New York: Ox- ford University Press, 1992), pp. 59–76.

28. Der Reichsführer SS, Schulungsamt, "Richtlinien," Nov. 16, 1942, BAB/NS31/155. A pamphlet designed to bolster Wehrmacht morale in 1944 devoted less than a dozen of 163 pages to specifically antisemitic topics. Dr. Karl Christoffel, *Volk—Bewegung—Reich* (Frank- furt am Main: Diesterweg, 1944). This booklet was part of the Unterrichtswerk für Heeres- schulen.

29. Hermann Erich Seifert, *Der Jude an der Ostgrenze*, vol. 3 of material published for Gruppe 7 der osten Europas (Munich: Eher, 1940).

30. Adolf Schmalix, *Sind die Roosevelts Juden?* (Weimar: Knabe, 1939), Wilhelm Matthiessen, *Israels Ritualmord an den Völkern* (Munich: Ludendorff, 1939), vol. 7 of Laufender Schriftenbezug. Walther Jantzen, *Die Juden* (Heidelberg: Vowinckel, 1940).

31. SS-Handblätter für den weltanschaulichen Unterricht [Pamphlets for Ideological

Instruction]; Nationalsozialistische Deutsche Arbeiter-Partei, SS-Hauptamt; Reichsführer-SS, Thema 17: "US-Amerika—Handlanger der jüdischen Weltmacht," and Thema 18: "Der Jude zerstört jede völkische Lebensordnung."

32. Major Trapp, quoted in Daniel J. Goldhagen, *Hitler's Willing Executioners: Ordinary Germans and the Holocaust* (New York: Knopf, 1996), p. 212.

33. Egon Leuschner, Reichsschulungsbeaufrager des Rassenpolitischen Amtes des NSDAP, *Nationalsozialistische Fremdvolk-Politik: Der deutsche Mensch und die Fremdvölkischen*—Nur für den Dienstgebrauch [for in-house use only], vol. 82 (1943).

34. Hans Hinkel, *Judenviertel Europas: Die Juden zwischen Ostsee und Schwarzen Meer* (Berlin: Volk und Reich Verlag, 1940).

35. Albert Dreezt and Dietmar Schmidt, *So seid Ihr wirklich: Kulturhetze und Kulturzerfall in England*, introduction by Hans Hinkel (Berlin: Becker, 1940). Heinz Ballensifen, *Juden in Frankreich* (Berlin: Nordland, 1939).

36. Max Hildebert Boehm, *Der befreite Osten: Eine volkspolitische und wirtschaftliche Darstellung mit zahlreichen Kartenskizzen und Diagrammen* (Berlin: Hofmeier, 1940).

37. "The subhuman has arisen to conquer the world. Woe unto all humans if you don't stand together. Europe, defend yourself!" Gottlob Berger, *Der Untermensch* (Berlin: Nordland, 1942), p. 1. After more than a dozen photographs of wretched people and corpses, a new section announced, "In contrast to these beings stand the fighters for everything honorable and good."

38. That the *Times* of London carried news of these events suggests that they were widely known in Germany as well: "Food Scarcity in Germany," Oct. 23, 1939, p. 10; "Germany's War Burdens," Jan. 9, 1940, p. 7; "Berlin under the Cold Spell," Jan. 30, 1940, p. 5; "Expulsion of Jews from Germany," Oct. 23, 1941, p. 3.

39. David Bankier, *The Germans and the Final Solution: Public Opinion under Nazism* (Oxford, Eng.: Blackwell, 1992), p. 135.

40. Klaus-Jürgen Müller, *Das Heer und Hitler: Armee und nationalsozialistisches Regime, 1933–1940* (Stuttgart: Deutsche Verlags-Anstalt, 1969), pp. 422–451. "Todesmarch von Lublin–Krakau," Mar. 28, 1940, YIVO, G-213. For a comprehensive account of mass murder in the Polish campaign, see Alexander B. Rossino, *Hitler Strikes Poland: Blitzkrieg, Ideology, Atrocity* (Lawrence: University of Kansas Press, 2003), pp. 80–83, 115–120.

41. Lothar Gruchmann, *Justiz im Dritten Reich, 1933–1940: Anpassung und Unterwerfung in der Ära Gürtner* (Munich: Oldenbourg, 1988), pp. 80–82.

42. Bernhard Lösener, "At the Desk," in Karl A. Schleunes, ed., *Legislating the Holocaust: The Bernhard Loesener Memoirs and Supporting Documents*, trans. Carol Scherer (Boulder, Colo.: Westview, 2001), pp. 100–104. Lösener tentatively began to help the Resistance before being arrested in November 1944 and expelled from the Nazi Party. Roland Freisler during these months became the notorious "hanging judge" who sentenced thousands to hang for treason.

43. Bronwyn Rebekah McFarland-Icke, *Nurses in Nazi Germany: Moral Choice in History* (Princeton, N.J.: Princeton University Press, 1999), pp. 210–256.

44. For a comparative perspective, see Yad Vashem's "Righteous of Nations" national list, which, as of 2003, included 342 German, 83 Austrian, 103 Czech, 5,632 Polish, and 2,171 French rescuers.

45. Klemperer, diary entry of June 4, 1943, *I Will Bear Witness*, vol. 2, p. 235.

46. Else R. Behrend-Rosenfeld, diary entry of Dec. 14, 1942, in *Ich stand nicht allein* (Frankfurt am Main: Europäische, 1949), pp. 195–196.

47. Issues of *Informationsdienst* can be found in The Hoover Institution, (issues, 112–151 [May 20, 1941 to Nov. 1944]), and (scattered) NA/T-81/9. RPO press releases are preserved in BAB/NS2/168.

48. Zygmunt Bauman has founded his interpretation of the Holocaust on philosophical assumptions that follow from decades of research based on the idea that perpetrators lost

their moral bearings when they donned their uniforms. Bauman, *Modernity and the Holocaust* (Ithaca, N.Y.: Cornell University Press, 1989), pp. 151–168, 190–193.

49. Walter Gross, "Die Lösung der Judenfrage," *NV* 8 (Mar. 1941); Gross, "Die rassenpolitischen Voraussetzungen zur Lösung der Judenfrage," typescript, Erzbischöfliches Archiv Freiburg, B2/28/12. The full text was circulated as a thirty-two-page pamphlet, *Die rassenpolitischen Voraussetzungen zur Lösung der Judenfrage*, no. 1 in the series Kleine Weltkampfbücherei (Munich: Hoheneichen, 1943), p. 29.

50. Walter Gross, "Rassenpolitik," in *Deutschlands Erneuerung* (Munich: Lehmanns, 1942).

51. Peter Weingart, *Doppel-Leben: Ludwig Ferdinand Clauss—Zwischen Rassenforschung und Widerstand* (Frankfurt am Main: Campus, 1995), p. 141. Ludwig Ferdinand Clauss, "Das Erlebnis der Arbeit: Seelische Reaktion der Rassen," *Das Reich* 1 (June 23, 1940): 5.

52. "Zum laufenden Filmprogramm," Nov. 28, 1940, in Boberach, *Meldungen*, vol. 1, pp. 2, 115.

53. "Zur Aufnahme des politischen Aufklärungsfilmes," Jan. 1941, in Boberach, *Meldungen*, vol. 6, pp. 1917–1918.

54. Robert Ley, *Pesthauch der Welt* (Dresden: Franz Müller, 1944).

55. Norbert Frei, *Journalismus im Dritten Reich* (Munich: Beck, 1989), pp. 108–135.

56. Hans H. Wilhelm, "The Holocaust in National Socialist Rhetoric," *Yad Vashem Studies* 16 (1984): 104–105.

57. Goebbels, quoted in Michael Balfour, *Propaganda in War, 1939–1944* (London: Routledge and Kegan Paul, 1975), pp. 114–115.

58. Henry Friedlander, *The Origins of Nazi Genocide: From Euthanasia to the Final Solution* (Chapel Hill: University of North Carolina Press, 1995), pp. 113–116. After this point, when between 70,000 and 100,000 Germans had been killed, the operations moved out of the Reich and continued without official authorization in the East. On the debates concerning the yellow star, see Lösener, "At the Desk," in Schleunes, *Legislating the Holocaust*, pp. 87–90.

59. Joseph Goebbels, diary entry of Aug. 26, 1941, in Elke Fröhlich, ed., *Die Tagebücher von Joseph Goebbels: Sämtliche Fragmente*, part 2, *Diktate, 1941–1945*, vol. 1 (Munich: Saur, 1996), p. 311.

60. Joseph Goebbels, "Die Juden sind schuld!" *Das Reich*, Nov. 16, 1941. Hans H. Wilhelm, "The Holocaust in Rhetoric," pp. 104–114.

61. Heidi Gerstenberger, "Acquiesence?" in Bankier, *Probing the Depths*, pp. 28–30. Robert Gellately, *Backing Hitler: Consent and Coercion in Nazi Germany* (New York: Oxford University Press, 2001), pp. 121–150.

62. "Jewish Sufferings," *Times* (London), Sept. 18, 1942, p. 8.

63. Klemperer, diary entry of May 29, 1943, *I Will Bear Witness*, vol. 2, p. 234.

64. Eugen Kogon, *Der S.S. Staat* (Stockholm: Bermann-Fischer Verlag, 1947). Kogon, an Austrian economist and journalist who was arrested in March 1938, survived five years in Buchenwald. David A. Hackett, *The Buchenwald Report* (Boulder, Colo.: Westview, 1995), p. 16. Hans Rothfels, "Zur Umsiedlung der Juden im Generalgouvernement," *Vierteljahrshefte für Zeitgeschichte* 7 (1959): 333–336.

65. Eric A. Johnson, *Nazi Terror: The Gestapo, Jews, and Ordinary Germans* (New York: Basic Books, 2000), pp. 442–450. Kaplan notes, however, that many Jews decided not to grasp the enormity of the news. Marion A. Kaplan, *Between Dignity and Despair: Jewish Life in Nazi Germany* (New York: Oxford University Press, 1999), p. 195.

66. Wolf Gruner, *Der geschlossene Arbeitseinsatz deutscher Juden: Zur Zwangsarbeit als Element der Verfolgung, 1938–1943* (Berlin: Metropol, 1997), pp. 167–168, 250–252.

67. Report from Southwest Germany, Feb. 6, 1939, *Sopade*, Feb. 1939, p. 219. This particular transport was turned back at the French border. On the numbers of trains, see Christopher R. Browning, *Ordinary Men* (New York: HarperCollins, 1998), p. 27.

68. Kaplan, *Dignity and Despair*, p. 197.

69. Heiner Lichtenstein, "Punctuality on the Ramp: The Horizon of a German Railroad Worker," in Jörg Wollenberg, ed., *The German Public and the Persecution of the Jews, 1933–1945,* trans. Rado Pribic (Atlantic Highlands, N.J.: Humanities Press, 1996), pp. 164–165.

70. Beate Meyer, "The Mixed Marriage: A Guarantee of Survival or a Reflection of German Society during the Nazi Regime?" in Bankier, *Probing the Depths,* pp. 36–53. Of the 164,000 Jews living in Germany in 1941, 123,000 perished in the camps.

71. Bankier, *The Germans and the Final Solution,* p. 102.

72. Uniformed police officer, Zhitomir, May 1942, quoted by Edward Westerman, "Shaping an Instrument for Annihilation: Creating the Police Soldier" Daniel E. Rogers and Allen Steinweis, eds., *The Impact of Nazism: New Perspectives on the Third Reich and Its Legacy* (Lincoln: University of Nebraska Press, 2003). Peter Lieb, "Täter aus Überzeugung? Oberst Carl von Andrian und die Judenmorde: Der 707 Infantriedivision, 1941/42," *Vierteljahrshefte für Zeitgeschichte* 4 (2002).

73. Yaacov Lozowick, *Hitler's Bureaucrats: The Nazi Security Police and the Banality of Evil,* trans. Haim Watzman (New York: Continuum, 2000), pp. 268–280.

74. Alain Badiou, *Ethics: An Essay on the Understanding of Evil,* trans. Peter Hallward (London: Verso, 2001), pp. 78–80, 85. Eric Michaud has explored the Nazis' appropriation of religious tropes in the production of this very real mirage in *Un art de l'eternité: L'image et le temps du national-socialisme* (Paris: Gallimard, 1996), pp. 15–48, 139–163.

75. Tzvetan Todorov, *Mémoire du mal, tentation du bien: Enquête sur le siècle* (Paris: Lafont, 2000), pp. 87–93, 331–338.

Acknowledgments

I have anticipated this moment for years. At last, the manuscript has taken its final form, and I have a chance to acknowledge the support of colleagues, family, and friends who have sustained me at every phase of its creation.

Before *The Nazi Conscience* was even a concept (much less a title), Charlotte Sheedy's enthusiasm inspired me to draft the proposal from which this book evolved. Thanks to her, I have benefited from working with the Harvard University Press team, especially Joyce Seltzer, editor par excellence. Over a longer period of time than either of us had imagined, Joyce offered unstinting support. By "support," I do not mean that Joyce offered constant praise. After I submitted each chapter to her in what I deemed was polished, press-ready form, it came back covered with densely penciled notes—cautions against jargon, warnings about digression, and challenges to glib generalizations. "Support" meant critical engagement —intellectual friendship at its best.

At every stage, I felt immense gratitude to colleagues I have never met—the historians who have created an immense body of scholarship on Nazi Germany and the avid readers who have made the publication of this work possible. Reading the early classics in the history of Nazi genocide by H. A. Adler, Max Weinreich, Léon Poliakov, Theodor Abel, Eugen Kogon, Raul Hilberg, and George Mosse, I felt a respect verging on awe for their persistence in delving into questions most of their contemporaries in the postwar years preferred to forget. As I approached every chapter of *The Nazi Conscience,* I have been grateful for the high quality and sheer quantity of recent monographs, articles, websites, and conference papers devoted to specialized issues, such as Nazi education, racial policy, the ethnic community *(Volksgemeinschaft),* health care professionals, intellectuals, surveillance networks, and murder battalions. Without this solid academic infrastructure, I could not have explored the shadow side of ethnic revival in so many facets of life in Nazi Germany.

Besides this anonymous connection with the international scholarly world, I had the immense good fortune to experience the thrill of close personal collaboration at the National Humanities Center. During my year there I had a chance to savor the kind of life I had imagined academics lived when I was in graduate school. Having arrived at the NHC with a book virtually complete, I took full advantage of the atmosphere (and the services) of the NHC and left with a very different book in its earliest stages.

Although archives provide indispensable support, it takes individuals to realize the potential of meters and meters of sources accessible only by call numbers and finding aids. I am particularly indebted to Torsten Zarwel, Herr Volker Lange, and

Herr Scharmann at the Bundesarchiv, to Mag. Dr. Maria Seissl at the University of Vienna Library, to Dr. Bachmann and Dr. Hermann Römshottel at the Staatsarchiv in Munich, to Carol Leadenham, Remy Squires, and Agnes Peterson at the Hoover Institution, and to Henry Mayer at the United States Holocaust Memorial Museum for their assistance.

Since arriving at Duke University in 1989, I have been fortunate to enjoy strong institutional support, in the form of funding and leaves, from the administration and the History Department. Thanks to Wayne Lee, Allen Creech, and the OIT, sophisticated software has lightened the burden of writing, scanning, and organizing materials. Graduate students Michael Meng and Andrew Sparling provided invaluable on-site help in retrieving materials from the Bundesarchiv. At Perkins Library, a host of enthusiastic and talented people has facilitated every aspect of on-campus research. Thanks to a dynamic acquisitions policy in the 1940s, Perkins Library is home to a major collection of Nazi materials. In the Duke Rare Book, Manuscripts, and Special Collections Library, Linda McCurdy and Elizabeth Dunn have imaginatively searched rare books and manuscripts related to Nazi culture that have enriched my research and teaching. Art Librarian Lee Sorenson has called my attention to dozens of acquisitions related to Nazi visual culture; Helene Baumann and Michael McFarlane have rescued valuable Nazi imprints from general circulation; Eleanor Mills and Jason Morningstar captured many of the images on which this book depends; Robbin Ernest's creative web sleuthing uncovered even the rarest books; and Rebecca Gomez, Faye Bennett, Sonya Hinsdale, and their staffs provided indispensable services in making rare and distant materials available.

Immersed in the grim environment of racist hatred, I welcomed the many opportunities to return to what we take for granted as "the real world" of family, friends, and colleagues. In scores of conversations over many years, Carol Gluck has insightfully commented on the larger intellectual terrain within which my investigation of Nazi public culture is situated and sharpened my prose style with admonitions to write boldly. Barbara Herrnstein-Smith has pointed out my unacknowledged assumptions and pushed me to identify the particular strategies by which Nazi persuaders made their contingent and, indeed, chaotic universe appear to be fixed. In one of several conversations with Alice Kaplan about fascist collaborators, I casually used the words "Nazi conscience." Thanks to Alice's response, this book acquired its title. Many colleagues from several disciplines at Duke have generously given me feedback on individual chapters. Stanley Hauerwas and Kathy Rudy guided my thinking about the ethical complexities of crimes of obedience. Miriam Cooke, Janet Ewald, Nancy Hewitt, Bruce Lawrence, Dirk Rupnow, Irene Silverblatt, Kristine Stiles, Susan Thorne, and Kären Wigen read chapters and provided crucial comments at important junctures.

Discussions with Gudrun Schwarz and Theresa Wobbe about the ways gender potentializes race have been inspiring. Françoise Basch has provided insights from her knowledge of the Nazi occupation in France. From colleagues in German history who read chapters of the manuscript—Susannah Heschel, Isabel Hull, Marion Kaplan, Robert Moeller, Mary Nolan, Karl Schleunes, and Edward Westerman—I received thoughtful criticism and encouragement. I am particularly grateful to Alan Steinweis, Robert Proctor, and two anonymous readers for their extraordinarily helpful feedback. I have benefited immensely from generous colleagues' reactions to this book; if errors remain, they are my responsibility.

I also thank my sisters, Robbie Kingston and Marcy Hodges, and my father, Oliver Koonz, for their forbearance. Having expressed my gratitude to so many individuals for their generosity in particular aspects of my research and writing, I close with a single and all-encompassing thank you to Jan Paris, who read multiple versions of each installment and conversed at great length about every permutation in my outlook. More even than this, she has sustained me with her wry good humor and steady confidence.

Illustration Credits

1 An early Nazi antisemitic postcard. Image provided by Wolfgang Haney, Berlin.

2 Six postcards of Hitler the orator. Reproduced in Eric Michaud, *Un Art de l'eternite: L'image et le temps du national-socialisme* (Paris: Gallimard, 1996), p. 73.

3 Crowds during Hitler's 1932 campaign by airplane. Heinrich Hoffmann and Josef Berchtold, *Hitler über Deutschland* (Munich: Fritz. Eher Nachf. Gmbh, 1932). RBMSCL, Duke University.

4 "Enough!" An election poster by Mjölnir. Item GE 895, Hoover Institution Archives, Stanford University. Image provided by Remy Squires.

5 "Our last hope." An election poster by Mjölnir. Item GE 792 Hoover Institution Archives, Stanford University. Image provided by Remy Squires.

6 Photograph of Hitler, master of the "soft sell." Heinrich Hoffmann, *Hitler wie ihn keiner kennt: 100 Bilddokumente aus dem Leben des Führers* (Berlin: Zeitgeschichte-Verlag, 1941). Special thanks to Annemarie Rasmussen for providing a copy of this book.

7 Cartoon, "The nit picker." *Die Brennessel* 4, no. 24 (June 12, 1934). RBMSCL, Duke University.

8 Martin Heidegger in 1933. Item 139364, AKG, London. Reproduced by permission.

9 "Hitler's hands." Heinrich Hoffmann, *Hitler wie ihn keiner kennt: 100 Bilddokumente aus dem Leben des Führers* (Berlin: Zeitgeschichte-Verlag, 1941). RBMSCL, Duke University.

10 Caricature of Austen Chamberlain expelling "troublesome" Jews. *Die Brennessel* 4, no. 2 (January 9, 1934). RMBSCL, Duke University.

11 Caricature of two Jews watching a balloon leave without them. *Die Brennessel* 5, no. 51 (December 19, 1933). RBMSCL, Duke University.

12 Formal portrait of the Führer. 12″ × 20″ commemorative book without a title or publication data.

13 Photograph of Hitler relaxing. Heinrich Hoffmann and Friedrich Wilhelm Brückner, *Hitler abseits vom Alltag: 100 Bilddokumente aus der Umgebung des Führers* (Berlin: "Zeitgeschichte," Verlag und Vertiebs-gesellschaft, 1934?). RBMSCL, Duke University.

14 Trading card publicizing the Winter Charity drive. Heinrich Hoffmann, *Der Staat der Arbeit und des Friedens* (Hamburg, Altona-Bahrenfeld: Cigaretten-Bilderdienst, 1934). RBMSCL, Duke University.

15 Hitler surrounded by young followers. 12″ × 20″ commemorative book without a title or publication data.

16 Trading card depicting Stormtroopers peeling potatoes. *Adolf Hitler: Bilder aus dem Leben des Führers*. Item 83.2.401. Image provided by The Mitchell Wolfson Jr. Collection, The Wolfsonian-Florida International University, Miami Beach, Florida.

17 Drawing of a Stormtrooper bringing coal to a poor family. *Die Brennessel* 3, no. 46 (November 14, 1933): 597. RBMSCL, Duke University.

18 Hitler portraits from 1914 to 1936. *Illustrierte Beobachter*, 1936, reproduced in Claudia Schmölders, *Hitlers Gesicht: Eine physiognomische Biographie* (Munich: C. H. Beck, 2000), pp. 148–149.

19 "The *Volk* listens to its Führer." *Berliner Illustrierte*, 1936.

20 "The new obelisk in Carolingian Square, Munich." Karl Arnold, "Let us Build Monuments," *Simplicissimus*, May 1932.

21 Ernst Ludwig Kirchner, "Self-portrait as soldier" (1915). The Allen Memorial Art Museum, Oberlin College. Reproduced by permission.

22 Adolf Ziegler, *"Die vier Elemente"* (The four elements), 1937. Bayerische Staatsgemäldesammlungen. Reproduced by permission.

23 Hitler gazes sternly into the eyes of a Stormtrooper. 12″ × 20″ commemorative book without publication data.

24 "Long live Germany!" Image provided by Randall Bytwerk, German Propaganda Archive, Calvin College, courtesy of Dr. Robert D. Brooks.

25 Photographs of four pioneering racial scientists. Charlotte Köhn-Beherns, *Was ist Rasse?* (Munich: Eher Verlag, 1934). RBMSCL, Duke University.

26 "The law to protect the genetic health of the German *Volk.*" Slide from the *Bildband, "Gesundes Leben,"* Hitler Youth Slide Program, produced in conjunction with the Office of Racial Politics. Image provided by Miriam Krant, National Center for Jewish Film, Brandeis University.

27 Photograph, "Only genetically healthy offspring guarantee the continuation of the *Volk.*" *Neues Volk* 4, no. 3 (March 1936): 37. RBMSCL, Duke University.

28 Photomontage, "Sterilization: not punishment." "Filme zur Volksaufklärung," *Neues Volk* 4, no. 2 (February 1936): 13. RBMSCL, Duke University.

29 "The genetically ill damage the community. The healthy preserve the *Volk.*" *Leithefte*. SS training manual. RBMSCL, Duke University.

30 Photomontage, "Jews persecuted in Germany?" *Neues Volk* 2, no. 12 (December 1934): 32–33. RBMSCL, Duke University.

31 Hitler and a member of the Hitler Youth. Heinrich Hoffmann, *Jugend um Hitler: 120 Bilddokumente aus der Umgebung des Führers* (Berlin: Zeitgeschichte, 1935).

32 "Youth serves the Führer!" Poster popularizing membership in the Hitler Youth. Image provided by Randall Bytwerk, German Propaganda Archive, Calvin College.

33 Illustration and poem, "Blood is holy and sacrosanct." Jakob Graf, *Biologie für höhere Schulen,* 2nd ed. vol. 3 for Class 5 (Munich: Lehmanns, 1943), plate 21, page 144.

34 Three images illustrating sources of racial danger. The components of this chart are in Jakob Graf, *Biologie für höhere Schulen* (Munich: Lehmanns, 1943), pp. 165, 166, 171. Jakob reproduced two images from Otto Helmut, *Volk in Gefahr: Die Geburtenrückgang und seine Folgen für Deutschlands Zukunft* (Munich: Lehmans, 1934), p. 35, and *Volk und Rasse* 8 (1933): 156.

35 A Nazi children's prayer to Hitler. *Ich will Dir was erzählen. Erstes Lesebuch für die Kinder des Hessenlandes, Braunschweig* (Marburg: Westermann, 1936), p. 64. Image from Friedrich Dickmann and Hanne Schmitt, *Kirche und Schule im nationalsozialistischen Marburg* (Marburg: Magistrat der Stadt Marburg, 1985), p. 197.

36 "Behind his glasses, two criminal eyes peer out." *Der Giftpilz: ein Stürmerbuch für Jung u. Alt.* (Nuremberg: Verlag Der Stürmer, 1938). Image provided by Randall Bytwerk, German Propaganda Archive, Calvin College.

37 A school class visits the Führer. Heinrich Hoffmann, *Jugend um Hitler: 120 Bilddokumente aus der Umgebung des Führers* (Berlin: Zeitgeschichte, 1935). RBMSCL, Duke University.

38 Photograph, "The teacher uses a racial chart." "Rassenkunde in der Voksschule," *Neues Volk* 2, no. 7 (July 1934): 9. RBMSCL, Duke University.

39 Slide, "A crippled idiot. Bound forever to his bed." *Bildband, "Gesundes Leben,"* Hitler Youth Slide Program, produced in conjunction with the Office of Racial Politics. Image provided by Miriam Krant, National Center for Jewish Film, Brandeis University.

40 Postcard warning against "Racial treason." Originally published in *Der Stürmer* 13, no. 37 (September 1935). Image provided by Wolfgang Haney, Berlin.

41 Sketch, "Encounter in Vienna." *Die Brennessel* 5, no. 32 (August 13, 1935), p. 512. RBMSCL, Duke University.

42 "The Nuremberg Laws summarized in tables." Reichsführer SS, SS-Hauptamt, ed., *SS-Mann und Blutsfrage: Die biologischen Grundlagen und ihre sinngemässe Anwendung für die Erhaltung und Mehrung des nordischen Blutes* (Berlin: NSDAP, 1936?). RBMSCL, Duke University.

43 "The number of Jews living in Berlin" from 1774 to 1930.

44 An illustrated graph warning about "racial treason." *Volk und Rasse* 12 (1937): 390. Thanks to Robert Proctor for identifying this illustration.

45 Max Liebermann, watercolor of woman mourning. Reichsbund Jüdischer Frontsoldaten, ed., *Kriegsbriefe Gefallener deutscher Juden* (Berlin: Vortrupp Verlag, 1935). RBMSCL, Duke University.

46 "The Jews' intellectual invasion." Exhibit catalogue, Bavarian Staatsarchiv/Gesundheitsämter/498. Bavarian Staatsarchiv, Munich.

47 "The eternal Jew." Image provided by Randall Bytwerk, German Propaganda Archive, Calvin College.
48 "The front soldier: your spirit restores my honor!" *Die Brennessel.* RBMSCL, Duke University.
49 SS man and his baby. *Neues Volk* calendar.
50 Fips caricature of a "ruined" woman. *Der Stürmer* 15, no. 34 (October 1933).
51 Fips caricature warning about "racial treason." "Das Ende. Vom Juden noch im Tode betrogen," *Der Stürmer* 15, no. 37 (September 1935).
52 "The execution of the court Jew Lippold in Berlin." Peter Deeg, *Hofjuden,* ed. J. Streicher (Nuremberg, 1939). RBMSCL, Duke University.
53 Cartoon by Fips, "Two kinds of children; two kinds of human beings." *Der Stürmer* 11, no. 34 (August 1933).
54 Stormtroopers ridiculed in a British cartoon. USHMM/RG-11.001M.01, 436, Roll 5.
55 Caricature of Stalin and "The Jew" who commands him. *Das Schwarze Korps* 2, no. 41 (October 8, 1936).
56 Portrait of Hitler illustrating an article on the "Jewish problem." "Wohin mit den Juden," *Das Schwarze Korps* 4, no. 6 (February 10, 1938).
57 A collage criticizing President Roosevelt. *Das Schwarze Korps* 4, no. 48 (December 1, 1938): 10.
58 Mug shots of purported Jewish criminals. "Eine kleine Auswahl," *Das Schwarze Korps* 4, no. 47 (November 24, 1938): 8.
59 Photograph of emaciated children in the Soviet Union. Reichsführer SS, ed., *Der Untermensch* (Berlin: Nordland, 1942). Reproduced from a photocopy of this rare book in Widener Library, Harvard University.
60 Scene from the Lublin ghetto, sketched by a German soldier. Item GD1.7391.stehr.Ghetto Lublin, U.S. Army Art Collection, U.S. Army Center of Military History. Reproduced by permission.
61 A map of concentration camps at home inside the Reich. Reproduced by permission of the U.S. Holocaust Memorial Museum.
62 A yellow star and a warning, "When you see this badge." Reproduced from a copy of this rare booklet in the YIVO research center, New York, New York.

Index

Abel, Theodore, 27–28

Academics, Jewish, 9, 11, 178

Academics, Nazi: antisemitic research of, 193–220; collaboration by, 191, 197; credibility of, 214; denials by, 219–20; on ethnic solidarity, 67; on Final Solution, 259; freedom of, 216; *Gleichshaltung* of, 196–97; role in genocide, 213; support for Hitler, 48, 55, 68; support for cold pogrom, 194, 220; on universal humanism, 216; and *Volk,* 11, 196. *See also* Intellectuals

Academy for German Law, 170

Adenauer, Conrad, 189

African Americans, 119; lynching of, 8, 237, 249

African-Germans, 127

American Jewish Congress, 39

Der Angriff (periodical), 128, 180

Anschluß, of Austria, 224, 246

Anthropology, antisemitic, 199–200, 214, 215; academic collaboration in, 197

Antimiscegenation laws, 171, 176

Antisemitism: of academics, 191, 193–220; in anthropology, 197, 199–200, 214, 215; denial of, 219–20; downplaying of, 160, 230, 245, 253, 267; in educational retreats, 157; "emotional," 174, 185, 208, 259; ethics of, 1; European, 7; in film, 12, 125–26, 266; in German political culture, 221–22; German public opinion on, 11, 70–71, 127–28, 164–65, 218; Heidegger's, 50–52, 68; Hindenburg on, 43; history of, 235; of intellectuals, 48, 68; in journalism, 212; Kittel's, 64–67, 68; Kittel's types of, 62; linguistic problems in, 179–80, 216; in *Mein Kampf,* 6, 28, 100, 102, 200, 236, 245, 253; in Nazi education, 141, 144–52; in Nazi print media, 9, 165, 180, 192, 209–10; polite, 124, 166, *167,* 245; popularization of, 1, 68; postwar recollections of, 219–20; propaganda, 12–13, 40–42; of Protestant leaders, 212–13; public opinion campaigns on, 40–41, 42, 127–28; "rational," 185, 193, 217; research

supporting, 191, 193–220; resistance to, 178; Schmitt's, 59, 68; in *Das Schwarze Korps,* 242–48, 250–52; selective compliance with, 12; as self-defense, 209, 236, 259, 265; situational factors affecting, 221; in SS training, 238; in *Der Stürmer,* 228–38; in teaching materials, 141, 144–46, 210, 214; think tanks on, 202–3, 218; in United States, 43; vulgar, 62, 164–65, 188, 220, 224, 237; of white-collar workers, 38. *See also* Violence, antisemitic

April Laws, 43–44; enforcement of, 168; racial quotas in, 163. *See also* Racial laws

Arendt, Hannah, 12, 164

Armenians, extermination of, 8, 255

Art: degenerate, 152; National Socialist Realist, 98

Artificial insemination, 128

Artists, under Nazis, 71

Aryans: defective, 9; definition of, 15, 170; depiction in print, 119, *120,* 121, *138;* Hitler on, 215; honorary, 187; moral maxims of, 1; photographic exhibitions on, 122–23; proof of ancestry, 177; scientists, 202–3; sexual relations with Jews, 25, 171–74, 180, 184, 188–89, 232, 247. *See also* Germans, ethnic; *Volk*

Aufklärung (enlightenment), in racial education, 110

Augstein, Rudolf, 266

Authenticity: Heidegger on, 48, 55; *versus* rationality, 68; Schmitt on, 60

Baeck, Leo, 41

Baeumler, Alfred, 214, 223, 226

Baker, Josephine, 119, 210

Barbusse, Henri, 56–57

Bartels, Adolf, *109*

Bartov, Omer, 10

Bauer, Fritz, 107

Baum, L. Frank, 7–8

BBC, reports on extermination, 269

Beer Hall Putsch: Hitler's trial following, 19, 21–22, 24, 31–32, 38; Stormtroopers in, 21